Powell and Pressburger's War

Powell and Pressburger's War

The Art of Propaganda, 1939–1946

*Greg M. Colón Semenza and
Garrett A. Sullivan, Jr.*

BLOOMSBURY ACADEMIC
NEW YORK • LONDON • OXFORD • NEW DELHI • SYDNEY

BLOOMSBURY ACADEMIC
Bloomsbury Publishing Inc
1385 Broadway, New York, NY 10018, USA
50 Bedford Square, London, WC1B 3DP, UK
29 Earlsfort Terrace, Dublin 2, Ireland

BLOOMSBURY, BLOOMSBURY ACADEMIC and the Diana logo are trademarks of
Bloomsbury Publishing Plc

First published in the United States of America 2023
Paperback edition published 2024

Copyright © Greg M. Colón Semenza and Garrett A. Sullivan, Jr., 2023, 2024

For legal purposes the Acknowledgments on p. viii constitute an extension of this copyright page.

Cover design: Eleanor Rose
Cover image: David Niven in *A Matter of Life and Death*, 1946, directed by Michael Powell and Emeric Pressburger © Pictorial Press Ltd / Alamy

All rights reserved. No part of this publication may be reproduced or transmitted in any form or by any means, electronic or mechanical, including photocopying, recording, or any information storage or retrieval system, without prior permission in writing from the publishers.

Bloomsbury Publishing Inc does not have any control over, or responsibility for, any third-party websites referred to in this book. All internet addresses given in this book were correct at the time of going to press. The author and publisher regret any inconvenience caused if addresses have changed or sites have ceased to exist, but can accept no responsibility for any such changes.

A catalog record for this book is available from the Library of Congress.

ISBN: HB: 979-8-7651-0573-3
PB: 979-8-7651-0577-1
ePDF: 979-8-7651-0575-7
eBook: 979-8-7651-0574-0

Typeset by Deanta Global Publishing Services, Chennai, India

To find out more about our authors and books visit www.bloomsbury.com and sign up for our newsletters.

CONTENTS

List of Figures vii
Acknowledgments viii

Introduction 1

PART ONE 31

1   "You Are English. I Am German. We Are Enemies": Anticipating Propaganda in *The Spy in Black* 33

2   "Taking the War Against Hitler": Blockade and Blackout in *Contraband* 56

PART TWO 81

3   *49th Parallel* and the Dangerous Interpretability of Wartime Propaganda 83

4   From "We Can Take It" to "V for Victory": Agency, Gender, and Propaganda in *One of Our Aircraft Is Missing* 111

5   "England Isn't as Bad as All That": Propaganda and Censorship in *The Life and Death of Colonel Blimp* 142

PART THREE 177

6   "The Values That We Are Fighting For": Reconciling Tradition and Modernity in *A Canterbury Tale* 179

7   Building Up a New Britain: Scotland and Postwar
    Reconstruction in *I Know Where I'm Going!* 204

8   "Conservative by Nature, Labour by Experience": The
    Propaganda of Futurity in *A Matter of Life and Death* 227

Coda 258

Index 263

FIGURES

1.1 Conrad Veidt, man's man and ladies' man, in *The Spy in Black* (1939) 42
1.2 Censored German newspaper in *The Spy in Black* (1939) 44
1.3 Captain Hardt and Fraulein Tiel in *The Spy in Black* (1939) 47
2.1 Captain Anderson among the Patriotic Plaster Products (*Contraband*, 1940) 78
3.1 The Canadian vessel through the eyes of U-boat officers in *49th Parallel* (1941) 100
3.2 The U-boat Kommandant from below in *49th Parallel* (1941) 100
3.3 Hirth pushing Hitler's propaganda in *49th Parallel* (1941) 103
3.4 The first shot of Winnipeg in *49th Parallel* (1941) 105
4.1 The Archers' famous logo, with its undeniable likeness to the RAF roundel. From *A Canterbury Tale* (1944) 120
4.2 Michael Powell himself as the dispatching officer in *One Of Our Aircraft Is Missing* (1942) 126
4.3 The similarly framed dispatching officer of *Target for Tonight* (1941) 127
5.1 Clive being given the bad news by the BBC director in *The Life and Death of Colonel Blimp* (1943) 143
5.2 Betteridge's seeming disinterest in Clive's stories about German propaganda in *The Life and Death of Colonel Blimp* (1943) 153
6.1 Another kind of pilgrim walks the way (*A Canterbury Tale*, 1944) 184
6.2 Colpeper shut out of the happy ending in *A Canterbury Tale* (1944) 198
6.3 Canterbury Cathedral among the ruins in *A Canterbury Tale* (1944) 203
7.1 Joan's dream of Scotland in *I Know Where I'm Going!* (1945) 212
7.2 Joan enters Erraig House in *I Know Where I'm Going!* (1945) 218
8.1 The majestic—and also bureaucratic—Other World of *A Matter of Life and Death* (1946) 250
8.2 The diverse American jury of *A Matter of Life and Death* (1946) 255

ACKNOWLEDGMENTS

As Michael Powell's autobiography makes clear, the films he made with Emeric Pressburger testify not only to their close working relationship over many years but also to the deep friendship they shared. Just as the movies they produced together brought the filmmakers a great deal of joy, so has this book been a source of intellectual satisfaction and pleasure for its authors. It is the expression of a long-standing friendship built over time spent in archives and movie theaters, at conferences and on trips (we're looking at you, Isle of Mull), over Zoom and in craft breweries (and you, Hill Farmstead). Among our many reasons for being grateful to the Archers, near the top of the list is the simple fact that their work, and our shared love for it, has provided us with the occasion to collaborate on this book.

Conducting research in the Michael Powell and Emeric Pressburger collections at the British Film Institute has been a particular source of delight. We would like to thank everyone at Special Collections at the BFI Reuben Library, especially Jonny Davies, Victoria Bennett, and Storm Patterson. We are also extremely grateful to the Michael Powell estate for granting us permission to examine his papers. The staff members of several other institutions and libraries have helped to make this book possible: the British Library, London's Imperial War Museum, the George Eastman House, the U.S. Library of Congress, and, nearer to home, Penn State's Pattee and Paterno Libraries, and UConn's Homer Babbidge Library. Thanks to Cambridge University Press for granting us permission to reprint in modified form a few paragraphs of Garrett's book on *Shakespeare and British World War Two Film* (2022). We have repeatedly turned to the invaluable website on Powell and Pressburger (https://powell-pressburger.org) run by Steve Crook and have benefited from his enthusiasm for and knowledge of the Archers. Thanks also to Alan Robson for ably shepherding us from Craignure to Carsaig and points in between.

Our editor at Bloomsbury, Katie Gallof, has been supportive of this project from its inception; she has not only tolerated our frequent questions with grace but has also demonstrated her expertise and professionalism through her answers. We would also like to thank Bloomsbury production team members Stephanie Grace-Petinos and Alyssa Jordan, as well as our project manager Akshaya Ravi Pemmasani, for their hard work and assistance. Additionally, we are indebted to the press's anonymous readers, who provided thoughtful feedback on our project as well as a much appreciated vote of confidence in it. Special thanks to Alexander Mika, who generated the index. We have both had the great pleasure of teaching Alex, and with this book we have benefited from his intelligence, equanimity, and attention to detail.

We would like to thank many mutual friends and colleagues who have provided feedback and/or support along the way: Mark Thornton Burnett, Patrick Cheney, Bob Hasenfratz, Liz Jenkins, Philip Jenkins, Brendan Kane, Courtney Lehmann, David Loewenstein, Niamh O'Leary, Paul Stevens, Christopher Vials, and Simon Yarrow. Andrew Moor, whose work on Powell and Pressburger has served as an inspiration, offered us valuable encouragement. We're especially grateful to Brendan and Patrick for their companionship and forbearance on our annual treks to the Northeast Kingdom (we know where we're going!).

Greg dedicates this book to "The Young Cinephiles," a small group of recent/current undergraduate students whose dedication to film and film history motivates him every day: Sarah Bradshaw, Catherine Casey, Emily Graham, Alexander Grant, Dan Milovic, Phil Michel, and Liam Thomas. To the following friends and family members, who've either allowed him to bend their ears about Second World War film or given him a break from thinking about it altogether: Tim Baeder, Keith Champagne, Ty and Erin Christopher, Bob and Terri Colón, Victoria Ford-Smith, Sean Grass, Danna and Justin Jacobs, Clare King'oo, Eric Lorentzen, Charles Mahoney, Aaron Proudfoot, Karen Renner, Iris Rivero, Geri and Greg Semenza, Sr., Marti Semenza, Matt and CJ Semenza, Jennifer van Frank, Reggie Wilburn, and, finally, the members of the MMM (Mark Ballou, Frank Gifford, John Hodgson, Ken Johnson, Mark Roberts, and Simon Wells). Greg is most grateful to Cristina, Alexander, and Benjamin, of course, who always endure his films—and his unreasonably strong thoughts about them—with patience, love, and a certain, appropriate amount of moxie.

Garrett would like to thank the following friends, colleagues, students, and family members who have aided, inspired, or sustained him during the period he has been working on this book: Dan Beaver, Kevin Bell, Taylor Bielecki, Tim Donovan, Bob Edwards, Jim Egan, Mike Gadaleto, Ryan Hackenbracht, Morgan Hamill, Peter Hegarty, Florence Hojnacki, Coppélia Kahn, Tracy Kirk, John Marsh, David McInnis, Mark Morrisson, Andrew Penman, Brice Peterson, Amy Prince, Marcelo Prince, Ben Rowles, Julie Sanders, Jim Schultz, Karen Schultz, Alan Stewart, Garry Sullivan, Lorry Sullivan, Peirce Sullivan, Sheila Sullivan, Matt Tierney, and Paul Zajac. Most of all, Garrett is thankful for the love and companionship of Marie, with whom he happily watched *The Red Shoes* at the Film Forum many years ago (and whose delighted response when first seeing *Kind Hearts and Coronets* at the NFT can still make him smile).

INTRODUCTION

This book focuses on the feature films produced by Michael Powell and Emeric Pressburger before, during, and just after the Second World War. Among the most heralded of all British filmmakers, Powell and Pressburger—often referred to as The Archers, after the production company they formed in 1941—made at this time works of art that were also pieces of cinematic propaganda.[1] The first Powell and Pressburger feature was screened as the conflict commenced; the final film that we discuss post-dates the war but was conceived of and put into production toward the end of it. All the movies we consider here are "war films" not merely because of the historical moment at which they were generated. They also concern themselves with life during wartime on the home front or abroad, if not both; and (with the exception of *The Spy in Black* [1939], which predates the conflict) they were made in explicit service of the war effort, and usually in concert with the government: more specifically, the Films Division of the Ministry of Information (MOI).[2] While at different points we take up three propaganda films made by one or both of The Archers—*The Lion Has Wings* (1939), *An Airman's Letter to His Mother* (1941), and *The Volunteer* (1944)—as well as one produced by them—*The Silver Fleet* (1943)—we do not devote chapters to these works because they are not commercial features and/or were not made by both Powell and Pressburger.[3]

---

[1]Kevin Macdonald, *Emeric Pressburger: The Life and Death of a Screenwriter* (London: Faber and Faber, 1994), 188. Macdonald states that The Archers were incorporated in 1941 but introduced in the trade press in 1942.
[2]We omit from this analysis three films by The Archers that, while set during the conflict, otherwise do not match our definition of the war film: *The Small Back Room* (1949), *The Battle of the River Plate* (1956), and *Ill Met by Moonlight* (1957).
[3]The first propaganda film of the war, *Lion* has Powell as one of its directors, but Pressburger is not involved. As for *The Volunteer* and *An Airman's Letter*, the former was a 45-minute recruitment film for the Fleet Air Arm, while the latter, a 5-minute short, features John Gielgud reading from the titular letter of a pilot killed in action; and while Archers' regulars like production designer Alfred Junge and cinematographer Erwin Hillier were involved in the making of *The Silver Fleet*, its credits identify it as having been written and directed by Vernon Sewell and Gordon Wellesley.

The films at the heart of our analysis are ones which conform with The Archers' credo as Powell articulated it to Wendy Hiller in the hope of casting her in *The Life and Death of Colonel Blimp* (1943): "[W]e owe allegiance to nobody except the financial interests which provide our money; and, to them, the sole responsibility of ensuring them a profit, not a loss"; and "every single foot of our films is our own responsibility and nobody else's. We refuse to be guided or coerced by any influence but our own judgement."[4] Perhaps surprisingly, they did not see their artistic independence as incompatible with the production of films made in the service of the war effort. Indeed, while acknowledging the importance of turning a profit for their backers, these statements also offer us a glimpse of the filmmakers' felt sense that there was no necessary contradiction between their commitment to their art and to the propaganda imperatives animating their wartime films.

In the rest of this chapter, we will first tell the story of the beginnings of the Powell and Pressburger partnership, as well as introduce their relationship with the MOI Films Division. Next, we will turn to period conceptions of propaganda, with attention paid to perceived differences between British and German versions of it; by doing so, we highlight the degree to which definitions of and ideas about propaganda are contested and historically contingent. We then examine both the MOI Films Division's propaganda program and the significantly different one that The Archers develop through their films. Finally, after providing a brief overview of the book's contents, we will conclude with a discussion of how this study seeks to change the critical story we tell about Powell and Pressburger's wartime cinematic production.

Powell, Pressburger, and the Ministry of Information

The partnership between Powell and Pressburger began with *The Spy in Black*, which was released less than a month before Britain declared war against Germany.[5] The careers of the two men—one the son of a Kentish hop farmer born in 1905, the other a Hungarian Jew and exile from Hitler's Germany who was nearly three years his senior—had taken divergent paths

---

[4]Quoted in Michael Powell and Emeric Pressburger, *The Life and Death of Colonel Blimp*, ed. Ian Christie (London: Faber and Faber, 1994), 16. Hiller did not appear in *Blimp* because of her pregnancy, but she later starred in *I Know Where I'm Going!*

[5]The first three paragraphs of this section contain material from Garrett A. Sullivan, Jr., *Shakespeare and British World War Two Film* (Cambridge: Cambridge University Press, 2022), 138–42.

up until the time of their first meeting in 1938. Powell had worked in the British film industry for several years before then, mainly as the director of numerous so-called "quota quickies." These films were produced in the wake of the Cinematograph Films Act of 1927, also known as the Quota Act, which was a piece of protectionist legislation designed to address the significant problem of Hollywood's domination of the British box office. According to Steve Chibnall, in 1926 British-produced films made up less than 5 percent of the total screenings in UK cinemas.[6] The Act responded to this dire situation in the following manner:

> There was to be a quota of British films—films made by a British subject, or a company based in the British Empire, with all studio scenes shot within the Empire—for both exhibitors and distributors, the latter being a higher percentage than the former so that exhibitors would be guaranteed choice in their selection of films. This quota was to rise incrementally over the next ten years from 5-20 per cent for exhibitors, and 7.5-20 per cent for distributors.[7]

While critics have disagreed about the general quality of the films produced under the Act, there is no doubt that, first, "quota quickies" were often derided at the time; and, second, that they represented a significant increase in the number of films made in Britain, even though many were made for production units owned by American studios.[8] Crucially, quality was not the primary objective when it came to making these quota films. Some of them were cheap, sloppy affairs produced for the express purpose of meeting the quota; these were sometimes even rented by exhibitors who had no intention of ever screening them.[9] The involvement of American studios in the making of these films, then, was often in the service of working around obstacles put in place by the Quota Act; Hollywood underwrote inexpensive, quickly made, and often bad movies in order to maintain their dominance of the British market, which was necessary for the profitability of the American studios. Even those "quota quickies" that made it into the nation's cinemas,

---

[6] Steve Chibnall, *Quota Quickies: The Birth of the British 'B' Film* (London: British Film Institute Publishing, 2007), 1. According to Rachael Low, there were around 4,000 cinemas in the country by 1929 (*Film Making in 1930s Britain* [London: George Allen and Unwin, in assoc. w/ the British Film Institute, 1985], 17).
[7] Chibnall, *Quota Quickies*, 2.
[8] On critical differences of opinion about the quota films, see Chibnall, *Quota Quickies*, 14–15, note 9; on American-owned production units, see Jeffrey Richards, *The Age of the Dream Palace: Cinema and Society in 1930s Britain*, 2nd ed. (London: I. B. Tauris, 2010), 39; and Low, *Film Making*, 34.
[9] Low, *Film Making*, 34.

commonly as "B" pictures on a double bill, were usually produced as hastily and inexpensively as possible.[10]

For the purposes of this study, the most important thing about the Quota Act is that it provided Powell with the opportunity to cut his teeth as a director. Between 1931 and 1936, Powell directed a remarkable twenty-three films.[11] His big break came, however, with a more ambitious project entitled *The Edge of the World* (1937). A lyrical and affecting movie set on a remote Scottish island, *The Edge of the World* caught the attention of arguably the most important figure in 1930s British film, Alexander Korda. This great Hungarian-born director, producer, and impresario was responsible for *The Private Life of Henry VIII* (1933), a lavish, high-budget production that became an international hit and led some to conclude that the British movie industry might be able to compete with Hollywood. Over the next two decades-plus, Korda directed and/or produced some of the most important films of the period, in both Britain and the United States, including *The Thief of Bagdad* (1940, which Powell co-directed), *That Hamilton Woman* (1941), and *The Third Man* (1949). Korda put Powell under contract at London Films, and it was through him that Powell met his longtime cinematic collaborator, Emeric Pressburger.

Pressburger's path to London Films was more fraught than Powell's. He started working as a screenwriter for the legendary German studio UFA at the beginning of the 1930s. With the ascendance of Hitler to the German chancellorship in 1933, Pressburger's position became untenable; in March of that year, UFA's board moved to fire all of its Jewish employees.[12] Acting upon a warning that the Gestapo was about to pick him up, Pressburger fled Berlin in May.[13] After spending a couple of years in Paris, he relocated to London, where he struggled to find his footing until, in 1938, he was hired by Korda as a screenwriter. While laborious and uncertain, Pressburger's journey to the British film industry was not a novel one. As Tobias Hochscherf has shown, "almost all major British production companies from the mid-1920s to the early postwar years ... employed personnel who

---

[10]See H. Mark Glancy, "Hollywood and Britain: MGM and the British 'Quota' Legislation," *The Unknown 1930s: An Alternative History of the British Cinema, 1929–1939*, ed. Jeffrey Richards (London and New York: I. B. Tauris, 1998), 57–72, 60.

[11]For more information on Powell's "quota quickies," see James Howard, *"I Live Cinema": The Life and Films of Michael Powell* (UK: CreateSpace Independent Publishing Platform, 2013), 41–83; and the filmography in the first volume of Powell's autobiography, *A Life in Movies* (1986; London: Faber and Faber, 2000).

[12]Macdonald, *Emeric Pressburger*, 94. On the "Aryanization" of the German film industry, see also Thomas Doherty, *Hollywood and Hitler, 1933–1939* (New York: Columbia University Press, 2013), 21–4.

[13]Macdonald, *Emeric Pressburger*, 99–100.

had previously worked in the Weimar Republic or Austria."[14] We will have more to say about émigré filmmakers in Britain in the first two chapters of this book. For now, it is enough to note that, by the time the war came, the presence of these film practitioners, many of them luminaries in their professions, engendered a fascinating cultural paradox. On the one hand, the war marked the moment at which, according to numerous critics, "a national cinema was born, encouraged by the need to stress unity and in recognition of the importance of film as propaganda."[15] On the other hand, this national cinema was produced with the significant participation of continental émigrés and exiles, sometimes to the dismay of British-born film professionals (as we will discuss in Chapter 2). The Archers offer a case in point. Both during and after the war, they made a range of films that are high watermarks for British cinema, including *The Life and Death of Colonel Blimp*, *A Canterbury Tale* (1944), *I Know Where I'm Going!* (or *IKWIG*, 1945), *A Matter of Life and Death* (or *AMOLAD*, 1946), *Black Narcissus* (1947), and *The Red Shoes* (1948).[16] They did so, moreover, with the essential participation not only of the screenwriter Pressburger but also of numerous other continental émigrés.

Whereas auteur theory conventionally centers upon the distinctive imprint made by the director on his films, and while Powell himself has been identified as an auteur,[17] we agree with Sarah Street that "the desire to herald Powell as an auteur . . . under-appreciat[es] the complexity of his collaborations with Pressburger, cinematographer Jack Cardiff, set designer Alfred Junge, costume designer Hein Heckroth and the many striking screen performers with whom he worked."[18] This desire, both critical and popular, also neglects the simple fact that most of Powell's major works—credited as "Written, Produced and Directed by Michael Powell and Emeric Pressburger"—announce themselves as productions of The Archers. At the very least, then, we should view Powell and Pressburger's wartime films as making the case for the two of them as co-auteurs.[19] However, we go

---

[14]Tobias Hochscherf, *The Continental Connection: German-speaking Émigrés and British Cinema, 1927–1945* (Manchester: Manchester University Press, 2011), 1–2.
[15]Sarah Street, *British National Cinema*, 2nd ed. (London and New York: Routledge, 2009), 60. See also Andrew Higson, *Waving the Flag: Constructing a National Cinema in Britain* (Oxford: Clarendon Press, 1995); and, for a slightly revised version of that book's argument, Higson, "The Instability of the National," *British Cinema, Past and Present*, ed. Justine Ashby and Andrew Higson (London and New York: Routledge, 2000), 35–47.
[16]For a discussion of The Archers and English national identity, see Maroula Joannou, "Powell, Pressburger, and Englishness," *European Journal of English Studies* 8 (2004): 189–203.
[17]Julian Petley, "The Lost Continent," *All Our Yesterdays: 90 Years of British Cinema*, ed. Charles Barr (London: BFI, 1986), 98–119, 106.
[18]Sarah Street, "Introduction," *Michael Powell Centenary Issue*, spec. issue of *Screen* 46 (2005): 1–4, 1.
[19]Ian Christie, *A Matter of Life and Death* (London: BFI, 2000), 64–5.

further. Building on Powell's own insistence on "movies [as] the greatest of collaborative arts," we contend that The Archers' wartime films exemplify what we term *distributed auteurism*: a conception of filmmaking that understands the objectives and vision of the director—or, in this case, of the director and screenwriter—as being not merely articulated but also clarified, modified, enhanced, and/or complicated by the actions of those working on the film.[20] Thus, while we talk throughout this book about the cinematic efforts of Powell and Pressburger, we take it as given that those efforts could not have been realized as they were if not for, in Powell's terms, the "perhaps two hundred clever men and women who are intimately involved in the texture of each film."[21] For primarily practical reasons, our own analysis takes up the contributions of only a small handful of those "clever men and women" who helped to shape as well as actualize The Archers' cinematic ideas and ambitions. Among those collaborative agents upon whom we do focus is a somewhat surprising one: the MOI Films Division.

Starting with *Contraband* (1940), The Archers began to coordinate with the Films Division on producing propaganda.[22] Like the MOI more broadly, the Films Division initially experienced a rapid turnover in leadership; consequently, it proved slow to generate a coherent policy for the making of cinematic propaganda.[23] However, it eventually established good relationships with both commercial and documentary film producers, to the extent that, as Anthony Aldgate and Jeffrey Richards observe, "The story of the British cinema in the Second World War is inextricably linked with that of the [MOI]."[24] Moreover, few feature filmmakers' efforts were more linked with the operations of the Films Division than were those of Powell and Pressburger. In fact, we think it important to expand the widely accepted view of The Archers as the collaborative film unit *par excellence* by acknowledging the British government's involvement in their work.[25] True collaborators, the filmmaking duo and the MOI served one another symbiotically, with Powell and Pressburger helping to shape the MOI film

---

[20]Michael Powell, *Million Dollar Movie* (1992; New York: Random House, 1995), 418. See also Garrett A. Sullivan, Jr., "'More Than Cool Reason Ever Comprehends': Shakespeare, Imagination and Distributed Auteurism in *A Matter of Life and Death*," *Shakespeare Bulletin* 34 (2016): 373–89.
[21]Powell, *A Life*, 48.
[22]Macdonald, *Emeric Pressburger*, 160.
[23]See James Chapman, *The British at War: Cinema, State and Propaganda, 1939–1945* (London: I. B. Tauris, 1998), esp. 41–57.
[24]Anthony Aldgate and Jeffrey Richards, *Britain Can Take It: British Cinema in the Second World War*, 2nd ed. (London and New York: I.B. Tauris, 2007), 4.
[25]As will be noted throughout, this cooperation with the government included working directly with the leadership of the various branches of the armed forces as well as the MOI. For Powell's description of how The Archers liaised with the Lords of the Admiralty, for example, see *A Life*, 420.

and the MOI helping to shape the Powell and Pressburger film. This does not mean that things always went smoothly or that the relationship was not tense at times; to a certain degree, tension was a crucial factor contributing to the complexity, nuance, and perhaps even the stylistic originality of the films. Ultimately, though, Powell and Pressburger's productive, push-and-pull relationship with the MOI—defined by competing drives toward cooperation and complicity, on the one hand, and autonomy and independence, on the other—worked to confirm and challenge commonly held assumptions about art and propaganda, the individual and the state, the auteur and the collaborative filmmaker.

As we've suggested, the early days of the MOI were marked by confusion and controversy. However, by the time of Brendan Bracken's appointment as (the Ministry's *fourth*) Director in July 1941, it had begun to discover its role, to quell the mockery of its numerous critics, and to begin functioning effectively.[26] Until that time, much of the Ministry's stumbling, and much of the bad press it invited, related specifically to the perceived attitude of its officials toward the people. To the degree that the MOI could be called condescending, distrustful, or secretive, it could easily be equated, whether seriously or jokingly, with the Reich Ministry of Enlightenment and Propaganda.[27] To the degree that it could be said to trust in the people and value honesty and transparency, it could allay legitimate concerns about the proper relationship of a democratic government to its citizens, especially in wartime.

---

[26] One positive assessment came from Michael Powell himself: "The Ministry of Information was a great success, and its Films Division was one of its triumphs" (*A Life*, 383). James Chapman notes that Powell's praise made him unusual among his contemporaries, even well after the early years of the War: "Although the MOI was to function quite efficiently later in the war, . . . it never completely shook off the negative impression that it had made at the beginning and was stuck thereafter with a reputation for blundering and incompetence" (*The British at War*, 14).

[27] Two famous examples of such perceived condescension were the MOI's "YOUR COURAGE" poster campaign, and what would come to be known as the "Cooper's Snoopers" affair. In the former case, upon the outbreak of the war, an MOI publicity artist/designer named A. P. Waterfield sought to motivate the people by ensuring them that "YOUR COURAGE, YOUR CHEERFULNESS, YOUR RESOLUTION WILL BRING US VICTORY." *The Times* blasted "the insipid and patronising invocations": "There may be no intrinsic harm in their faint, academic piety, but the implication that the public morale needs this kind of support, or, if it did, that this is the kind of support it would need, is calculated to provoke a response which is neither academic nor pious" (qtd. in Ian McLaine, *Ministry of Morale: Home Front Morale and the Ministry of Information in World War II* [London, Boston, and Sydney: George Allen & Unwin, 1979], 31). In the latter case, then-Minister of Information Duff Cooper's wartime public survey team was accused by a large swath of the British press of prying too much into citizens' private lives. Though Cooper eventually managed to defend his survey of public morale to the satisfaction of most government officials, the MOI learned important lessons about transparency and respect for the people from this controversial affair (see especially McLaine, *Ministry of Morale*, 84–8).

Ian McLaine helpfully summarizes the lessons the Ministry learned in the first years of the war regarding its relationship with the people:

> Through stern practical experience the Ministry came to realise the cardinal importance of full and honest news as a factor in civilian morale. The sheer doggedness with which the department fought the service ministries and even Churchill himself over news and censorship was a measure of the strength of this conviction and, indeed, of a determination that, in fighting totalitarianism, Britain should not borrow one of its chief weapons. With the constant and thorough analyses of the Home Intelligence Division as a sure guide, the Ministry also came to regard the British people as sensible and tough, and therefore entitled to be taken into the government's confidence. Possessed of this belief, the erstwhile propagandists became the evangelists of a novel attitude towards the people, furnishing them and the government with the means for a more cohesive national war effort.[28]

McLaine is speaking here about the news division, specifically, but his account of the MOI's transformation—from "erstwhile propagandists" (the latter term is defined here in purely negative terms) to liberal "evangelists"—certainly applied to the other divisions as well, including the Films Division. As we shall see again and again, Powell and Pressburger always positioned the "people" as capable, intelligent, dedicated contributors to the war effort and the democratic nation, even as the filmmakers' ideas about propaganda continued to undergo subtle changes.

Interwar Conceptions of Propaganda

Something like a consensus exists among historians that the meaning of the word "propaganda" changed most dramatically during and just after the First World War, when the largely neutral term describing the propagation of ideas began to accrue the negative connotations we associate with it today.[29] Mark Crispin Miller argues that the change was attributable mainly to Allied attempts to characterize the Germans during the Great War, a "paradoxical result of the [primarily British and American] war propagandists' winning enterprise: for the propagandists had themselves besmirched the word by

---

[28]McLaine, *Ministry of Morale*, 11.
[29]The *Oxford English Dictionary* reveals how the term "propaganda" first came into use around 1622 to describe the missionary messaging and activities of the Roman Catholic Church.

using it always and only in dark reference to *the enemy*."[30] Powell and Pressburger inherited this much-transformed, often-negative concept of propaganda, but their efforts were also informed, directly or indirectly, by an unusual number of propaganda theories published in the interwar years—including several that did not regard propaganda entirely negatively. Ultimately, they would draw on a combination of contemporary ideas about propaganda to generate their own vision of the ideal propaganda film.

Debates raged during the interwar period in both the United States and the United Kingdom about the power and proper uses of propaganda, and they influenced one another in direct and profound ways. In the United States, the debate centered on the appropriate role of propaganda in a democratic society. According to Brett Gary,

> In the aftermath of the Great War, "propaganda consciousness" contributed significantly to the chastened democratic faith of an entire generation of U.S. liberal intellectuals. Indeed, liberal faith in democratic theory would never recover from what one writer calls the American "discovery of propaganda," a discovery marked by an outpouring of popular and scholarly literature by political and social critics, historians, journalists, novelists, philosophers, and others aghast . . . by this technologically enhanced capacity of nation-states, revolutionaries, and interest groups to direct attention and emotion by bombarding apparently susceptible "mass" audiences with persuasive images and ideas.[31]

According to data gathered by Harold D. Lasswell in the 1930s and 1940s, the years between 1919 and 1945 saw the publication worldwide of over three thousand articles and books on the topic of propaganda.[32] The year 1928 alone saw the publication of British writer Arthur Ponsonby's *Falsehood in Wartime* and the American author Edward Bernays's classic *Propaganda*;[33] both books appeared shortly after the publication of

---

[30]Mark Crispin Miller, "Introduction," *Propaganda*, by Edward Bernays (1928; New York: IG Publishing, 2005), 14. Bernays quotes a contemporary complaint in *The Scientific American*: "There is no word in the English language whose meaning has been so sadly distorted as the word 'propaganda.' The change took place mainly during the late war when the term took on a decidedly sinister complexion" (49). He goes on to label this postwar conception of the term "the new propaganda" (55).
[31]Brett Gary, *The Nervous Liberals: Propaganda Anxieties from World War I to the Cold War* (New York: Columbia University Press, 1999), 2.
[32]Ibid.
[33]According to Ponsonby, "Falsehood is a recognized and extremely useful weapon in warfare, and every country uses it quite deliberately to deceive its own people, to attract neutrals, and to mislead the enemy. The ignorant and innocent masses in each country are unaware at the time that they are being misled, and when it is all over only here and there are the falsehoods discovered and exposed" (*Falsehood in Wartime, Containing an Assortment of Lies Circulated Throughout the Nations During the Great War* [London: Garland, 1928], 13). According

Lasswell's important 1927 social study of *Propaganda Technique in the World War* and a series of lectures about propaganda that same year by John Dewey.[34]

Among all the variety of ideas about propaganda that emerged in America in the interwar years, there were two dominant—and largely opposed— strands of thought. The first, best represented by Dewey, said that propaganda is intrinsically damaging to democracy and necessitates a strong public education program to counteract its poisonous influence on the citizenry. The second, best represented by Walter Lippmann, sought to place intellectuals and experts—an elite class of technocrats—in charge of a governmental propaganda machine that could limit the damaging impact of propaganda upon democracy and its citizenry, which Lippmann deemed benighted and incompetent. Whereas Dewey would articulate an idealist conception of democracy, convincing his followers that propaganda's insidious power could be blunted through the educational and social reformation of each citizen, Lippman influenced the so-called "democratic realists," a group which gradually gained more traction prior to the Second World War. This group believed that most people were fundamentally irrational, and that democracy would function best if popular participation in the political process was minimized and top-down governance increased.[35] Influenced especially by the British social psychologist Graham Wallas (who argued, most importantly, for more rigorously empirical approaches to social science), Lippmann's "withering attack on the irrationality of the public was a powerful culmination in the U.S. sphere of a several-decade-long trend among European and American intellectuals warning about the dangers of 'crowd psychology'[,] . . . the rising tide of 'barbarism' attendant to mass democracy, the 'fallacy' of human intellectualism, and the 'instincts of the herd.'"[36] In post–First World War America, then, propaganda's undeniable influence and utility were constantly weighed against its potentially deleterious effects on democracy.

In Britain, interwar conversations about propaganda took on many of these same dimensions,[37] but as war gradually approached in the mid-1930s, hitherto theoretical debates gained a practical urgency lacking

---

to Gary, "One of the most important components of Ponsoby's [sic] work was its detailed refutation of wartime atrocity stories, showing many of them to be propagandists' concoctions" (*The Nervous Liberals*, 23–4).

[34]Gary sums up Lasswell's approach to propaganda thus: "propaganda was at least a value-neutral tool, one that potentially had highly ethical social uses, especially when used for the purposes of avoiding violence and reducing conflict" (*The Nervous Liberals*, 65).

[35]Lippmann's key work was the seminal 1922 book *Public Opinion* (New York: Harcourt, Brace), which analyzes the gap between individual perception and reality in relation to the malfunctioning of democratic societies.

[36]Gary, *The Nervous Liberals*, 3.

[37]See especially Mariel Grant, *Propaganda and the Role of the State in Inter-War Britain* (Oxford: Clarendon, 1994).

in the earlier American ones. Britons were also profoundly influenced by the emergence in their backyards, so to speak, of Joseph Goebbels's formidable propaganda machine, the clearest example ever devised of how totalitarian propaganda could be used and eventually weaponized (we will say more about Nazi propaganda in what follows). The stark visibility and effectiveness of Goebbels's efforts had the somewhat paradoxical effect of forcing British government officials and theorists to work to define the positive functions of propaganda for a free people. As Mariel Grant rightly concludes, the perceived "evil or goodness" of propaganda would come to depend entirely "on who controlled it and their motives"; the necessity of propaganda, however, would hardly be questioned in serious corners.[38] From about 1935, then, when the government created a so-called "shadow" MOI to begin preparing for the war, British governmental debates about propaganda were focused on entirely practical questions about how to "present the national case to the public at home and abroad in time of war. To achieve this end," officials acknowledged, "it is not only necessary to provide for the preparation and issue of National Propaganda, but also for the issue of 'news' and for such control of information issued to the public."[39] The objectives were now clear, and the necessity of a British "National Propaganda" was largely taken as a given.[40] What was less clear was precisely what form it should take.

Wartime Conceptions of Propaganda

In contemporary discussions of propaganda, British commentators regularly claimed that the British variety, unlike its German counterpart, was simply a form of truth-telling. Thus, a *New Statesman* writer could confidently claim in September of 1939 that "It is strictly true that Britain to-day has no need of propaganda. The Ministry of Information can be a Ministry of Information and not a Ministry of Lies, Dr Goebbels has made truth Britain's greatest asset."[41] A useful binary suggested itself: whereas

---

[38] Grant, *Propaganda and the Role*, 17.
[39] The "Report of a Sub-Committee on Plans for the Establishment of a Ministry of Information" was issued on July 27, 1936, and is quoted in McLaine, *Ministry of Morale*, 12.
[40] The situation was quite different in America where, especially early in the war, governmental suspicion of propaganda appeared to be much stronger. As Christopher Vials notes, for example, "Like much of the American public, . . . Franklin Roosevelt was deeply averse to war propaganda because of his memory of (and participation in) the hysteria of World War I" ("*Why We Fight*: Contending Narratives of World War II," *American Literature in Transition: 1940–1950*, ed. Christopher Vials [Cambridge: Cambridge University Press, 2017], 13–28, 16).
[41] Quoted in Siân Nicholas, *The Echo of War: Home Front Propaganda and the Wartime BBC, 1939–45* (Manchester: Manchester University Press, 1996), 2.

German propaganda was complacent toward authority, manipulative, and generative of falsehoods, British propaganda was transparent, truthful, and merely informational and/or factual.[42] Both generalizations are, of course, misleading and self-serving. We will have ample opportunity to focus on the latter claim, about British propaganda, throughout later sections of this book. The former one is worth lingering on here, however, leaning as it does on blinkered and monolithic near-parodies of Nazi propaganda as nothing more than the bluntest of instruments. The two most important (inextricably linked) elements of this distortion held that, first, Nazi propaganda was little more than a program of outright lies; and, second, that these lies were propagated primarily through a method of ceaseless repetition. On the first point, the war criminal Goebbels perhaps deserves to be remembered for that most famous line, "Repeat a lie often enough and it becomes the truth." However, it is also undeniable that he saw the utility of the truth and understood that lies alone would not suffice to sell the Nazi party to the German people.[43] On the second point, regarding the Nazi *method* of propaganda, Thomas Doherty usefully refers to the "hypodermic needle" theory of mass communications propounded by Joseph Goebbels: inject the message into mass consciousness through repetition, simplicity, and raw emotion.[44] As we shall see, especially in the chapter on *49th Parallel* (1941),

---

[42]It almost goes without saying that the MOI was regularly critiqued for not living up to the ideals it espoused. In 1940, John Hargrave published an angry critique of the MOI aimed at improving the democratic (vs. totalitarian) use of propaganda. He specified the need for a "propaganda of truth," in spite of the risks: "Truth is no respecter of persons, nor of ideologies, nor of idealistic catch-phrases" (*Words Win Wars: Propaganda, the Mightiest Weapon of All* [London: Wells Gardner, Darton & Co., 1940], 180). As noted earlier, Ponsonby's more famous book of 1928 uncovered many of the major lies and untruths of the Great War, admitting that "Falsehood is a recognized and extremely useful weapon in warfare, and every country uses it quite deliberately" (Ponsonby, *Falsehood*, 13). The binary also had impressive applicability beyond specific cases of propaganda since it could easily be extended to encompass all totalitarian states on the one hand, and all democratic states on the other.
[43]According to Leonard W. Doob, "Goebbels' moral position in the diary was straightforward: he told the truth, his enemies told lies. Actually the question for him was one of expediency and not morality. Truth, he thought, should be used as frequently as possible; otherwise the enemy or the facts themselves might expose falsehood, and the credibility of his own output would suffer. Germans, he also stated, had grown more sophisticated since 1914: they could 'read between the lines' and hence could not be easily deceived" ("Goebbels' Principles of Propaganda," *The Public Opinion Quarterly* 14 (1950): 419–22, 428). Jay Baird explains in one of the definitive studies of Nazi propaganda that "The peculiar genius of Hitler and Goebbels was to merge the themes of traditional German patriotism with Nazi ideological motifs, a course pursued from the days of the earliest Munich rallies in 1919 to 1945" (*Nazi War Propaganda* [London: Oxford University Press, 1974], 4). In other words, the construction of a Nazi mythology was at least as important to Goebbels as the perpetuation of outright lies, however thin the line often was between these two practices. Certainly, the construction of just such a mythology was both the goal and the result of Leni Riefenstahl's major propaganda films, *Triumph of the Will* (1935) and *Olympia* (1938).
[44]Doherty, *Hollywood and Hitler, 1933–39* (New York: Columbia University Press, 2013), 106.

Powell and Pressburger portray Nazi propaganda as defined by relentless, mindless repetition, but this accusation—like so many others—needs to be understood as a tool serving the British attempt to dichotomize British and Nazi propaganda rather than as an entirely accurate characterization of their differences.

To put it slightly differently, the actual forms of propaganda deployed by the two nations did not always conform to the distinctions implicit in the binary rhetoric we've been examining—and this fact could apply to Britain's own self-mythologization during the war. As Jo Fox demonstrates in her comparative analysis of British and German Second World War propaganda, "the propaganda outputs conformed far less to the official rhetoric emanating from the RMVP [Reichsministerium für Volksaufklärung und Propaganda] and the MoI regarding their 'information policies' than might be expected, thus blurring the distinction between democratic and authoritarian propaganda whilst at the same time not forgetting that the state mechanisms were not the same or largely similar."[45] Philip Taylor also zooms in on both the logical effectiveness of the official binate rhetorical line, and the lie undergirding it:

> Propaganda has never been an activity with which the British have felt comfortable; it is felt to be the sort of thing which foreigners go in for. . . . [However] the British have proved that they have a peculiar talent for propaganda, particularly in wartime. . . . The very fact that most people in Britain do not believe that the British normally go in for that sort of thing is, in itself, good propaganda.[46]

To sum up Taylor's point, Britons' belief in transparent, honest, or respectful propaganda is something of a contradiction in terms—not to mention a useful propaganda concept that blinds them to how homegrown propaganda impacts them. Only the most successful propaganda can convince its intended audience that it is reflective of the unvarnished truth rather than being self-interestedly manipulative.

Part of the challenge of working through the contradiction Taylor introduces involves sorting out contemporary definitions of "propaganda" itself. As Siân Nicholas rightly notes, "one finds the word 'propaganda' used throughout this [war] period to refer both to the straightforward dissemination of information, and to more covert attempts to influence

---

[45]Fox, *Film Propaganda in Britain and Nazi Germany* (Oxford and New York: Berg, 2007), 12.
[46]Philip Taylor, *Britain and the Cinema in the Second World War* (London: Palgrave Macmillan, 1988), 3. John Mackenzie takes on the myth that British audiences are impervious to propaganda in *Propaganda and Empire: The Manipulation of British Public Opinion 1880–1960* (Manchester and New York: Manchester University Press, 1986), 2–3.

hearts and minds. Only the specific context determined the appropriate meaning" of the word.[47] One might observe, moreover, how easily the "straightforward dissemination of information" could be associated with so-called democratic propaganda practices, on the one hand, and how "covert" manipulation could just as easily be associated with so-called totalitarian propaganda practices, on the other hand. The large range of meanings the word "propaganda" denoted at this time served contemporary efforts to differentiate the putatively benign information campaigns of Britain and its democratic Allies from the insidious brainwashing campaigns of the Nazis and their fascist brethren. Far from being a source of embarrassment, then, British propaganda efforts were understood to perform a valuable, ethically defensible role in protecting democracy.

This historical context helps us to understand why Powell and Pressburger were largely untroubled by their status as producers of propaganda; it was their wartime work, and they were proud to undertake it, especially insofar as it did not impede them or impact negatively the quality of their films. Further, The Archers' roles as propagandists, far from compromising their art, actually served it in numerous ways. This idea, unexamined, can seem almost heretical: How can the activity of producing propaganda be regarded as anything other than shameful, at best? As we shall see, Powell and Pressburger were not uninterested in this question; in fact, their awareness of how dangerous propaganda could be—indeed, their willingness to explore this dangerousness in the films themselves—is precisely what allowed their art to thrive during the war years. Rather than approaching propaganda as a necessary burden, as necessarily negative, they followed the lead of the MOI itself in seeking to make a positive case for both its practicality, its ethicality, and its compatibility with their artistic vision.

The Ministry of Film Propaganda

Both British and German governmental authorities recognized the utility of film as a propaganda tool. The aforementioned "shadow MOI" (1935–8), operating years before war was declared, was preoccupied with the cinema's potential utility in reaching the masses. That organization's Director General, Stephen Tallents, had built his reputation as a titanic figure in the field of British public relations—and he had also greatly influenced the course of British cinema. Having sponsored the creation of John Grierson's documentary film group as Secretary of the Empire Marketing Board (EMB), Tallents eventually transferred the struggling EMB film unit to the General

---

[47]Nicholas, *The Echo of War*, 2–3.

Post Office as a condition for agreeing to serve as its head between 1933 and 1935. Once there, the GPO Film Unit went on to produce such immensely successful documentaries as Basil Wright and Harry Watt's *Night Mail* (1936), which sought specifically to transform and modernize the traditional image of Britain. Even before that, in 1932, Tallents had authored an influential pamphlet entitled *The Projection of England*, in which he'd argued that film was "the greatest agent of international communication at the moment" and therefore the most powerful propaganda medium available for arguing Britain's case as a key player in "the new world order."[48] Thus, it seems safe to say that the importance of cinema was never in doubt as the modern, official MOI began to take shape—even if the fledgling Ministry needed time to figure out how best to use British film and filmmakers. Certainly, the first months of the war would provide ample opportunity for testing the waters.

Perhaps the crucial moment in the Ministry's formation of a coherent film propaganda policy came with the circulation in early 1940—by the MOI's second Films Division Director, Kenneth Clark—of a memorandum entitled the "Programme for Film Propaganda." Its first sentence announces that the Films Division "assumes the importance of films as a medium of propaganda" and is committed to applying to film production the three major themes of British propaganda outlined by the first Minister of Information, Hugh Macmillan.[49] These themes are as follows: "What Britain is fighting for"; "How Britain fights"; and "The need for sacrifices if the fight is to be won."[50] Under the first category, the Programme suggests that the "main objects of feature films" should be "*British life and character*"; "*British ideas and institutions*"; and "*German ideals and institutions in recent history.*"[51] Documentaries and animated cartoons are also treated. Under the second category, "How Britain fights," the emphasis is on how various departments (the fighting services, Agriculture, Education, etc.) are contributing to the war effort. Interestingly, both *The Lion Has Wings* and *Contraband*, which was then in production, are referenced as examples of feature propaganda films focused on how Britain fights; whereas the former spotlights the putatively awesome power of the Royal Air Force, the second highlights the operations of Contraband Control during the "Phoney War."

---

[48]Scott Anthony, *Public Relations and the Making of Modern Britain: Stephen Tallents and the Birth of a Progressive Media Profession* (Manchester and New York: Manchester University Press, 2012), 221, 213.
[49]Clark, "Programme," *Powell Pressburger and Others*, ed. Ian Christie (London: BFI, 1978), 121.
[50]Ibid.
[51]Ibid., 121–2.

The third and final category stresses that films must show the equal sacrifices of "all classes of workers."[52]

Beyond outlining these major themes of propaganda, the Programme recommends three additional production principles we feel it important to record here. The first is that propaganda intended for British citizens will not necessarily be appropriate for continental or American allies, or members of the British Dominions or Empire. This fact authorizes making cuts and providing alternative endings to films depending on the specific audiences they are addressing. This principle would have a direct bearing on decisions made when it came to the overseas exhibition of such Powell and Pressburger films as *Blimp*. The second principle is that any film "must be good entertainment if it is to be good propaganda."[53] As we shall see, Powell and Pressburger prided themselves on their ability to make great films that contributed to the war effort, and their films were often recognized to be effective as both entertainment and propaganda by contemporary reviewers.[54] Finally, the Programme emphasizes a point we will spend much more time analyzing later, the idea that "film propaganda will be most effective when it is least recognisable as such."[55] The government's own role in facilitating film production should be disguised or minimized, the Programme suggests, both to convince wary, domestic audiences that they can expect to escape into a dark cinema for ninety minutes or so, and to reassure American distributors that the British respect their political neutrality.

So how systematically—and with how much self-consciousness—did Powell and Pressburger deploy propaganda strategies or techniques derived from the Films Division's Programme? In what ways did they complicate and innovate upon previously established propaganda strategies, especially those specifically relevant to film storytelling and form? We certainly would acknowledge the ease with which Powell and Pressburger's films can be said to have conformed to the MOI Programme. Indeed, our book is concerned in part with showing the degree to which they were influenced and informed by the Films Division throughout the war period. As mentioned earlier, though, we also are struck by the extent to which the filmmakers' collaboration with the government served as a spur toward artistic autonomy and independence. Clearly, Powell and Pressburger felt the equal, occasionally competing, desires to assist in the war effort by embracing their designated role as propagandists, and to use the opportunity that role provided them to build their reputations as artists. In short, Powell and Pressburger were driven to construct *their own program* for film propaganda, and this

---

[52]Ibid., 123.
[53]Ibid., 124.
[54]In *A Life in Movies*, Powell suggests that a lesson of *49th Parallel*'s success was that "propaganda that people paid to see was the only propaganda worth talking about" (387).
[55]Clark, "Programme," 124.

program challenged and expanded the definition of British film propaganda even as it sought to honor the basic goals and priorities of the MOI. To be clear, they did not formalize this program; instead, it can be gleaned from the ways in which their wartime films serve both as *acts of* and *meditations upon* cinematic propaganda. What we would identify as the "Powell and Pressburger Program for Film Propaganda"—which is also an *aesthetic* program because the filmmakers do not take art and propaganda to be antithetical—consists of six recurrent themes or qualities of the films that they made between 1939 and 1946.[56]

1. Self-Reflexivity. One thing is true of nearly all of Powell and Pressburger's wartime films: they present propaganda *as a subject of the films*, and they permit, sometimes even plead with, their audiences to think about how that subject works. Very often, it is introduced directly through the presentation of physical objects or paraphernalia related to Allied or enemy propaganda: in *Contraband*, for example, the German spies occupy a building wherein are housed hundreds of manufactured plaster busts of Neville Chamberlain, perhaps a jab at the Prime Minister's failed attempts to "appease" the Nazi war machine; in *49th Parallel*, we witness a debate about the veracity and value of Hitler's *Mein Kampf*, a copy of which is in the possession of a German soldier. Sometimes, the impact of propaganda is registered through symbols and signs generated by characters intent either upon signaling their alliances or facilitating their allies; in *One of Our Aircraft Is Missing* (1942), for example, "V for Victory" graffiti—associated with the successful 1941 propaganda campaign initiated by Victor de Laveleye, former Belgian Minister of Justice—is visible on the walls of numerous Dutch buildings, suggesting the seriousness of the resistance against the Nazi occupation of The Netherlands. In yet other cases, Powell and Pressburger show the state and institutional processes according to which propaganda is actually generated, as in *Blimp*'s extended treatment of BBC and War Office operations. And in several of the most mature of The Archers' wartime films, propaganda is specifically allied to the cinema so that Powell and Pressburger's efforts as propagandists come under direct scrutiny. Perhaps the most obvious case of such self-reflexivity is in *The Volunteer*, where we witness a film-within-the-film projected aboard an RAF aircraft carrier. More often in Powell and Pressburger, the cinema—and indirectly, the cinema of propaganda—is referenced through analogues to film itself, as in the lantern slide lecture in *A Canterbury Tale* or the camera obscura scene early in *AMOLAD*. In these and many other remarkable instances of self-reflexivity, Powell and Pressburger appear to be marking their films as examples of a *specifically*

---

[56]For clarity's sake, we will continue to refer to the Clark MOI document as the Programme, and to the Powell and Pressburger propaganda approach as the Program.

democratic art of wartime propaganda. By promoting a type of distantiation effect, à la Brecht, Powell and Pressburger simultaneously advance the propaganda aims of the MOI and manage to differentiate their work from propaganda films designed to manipulate their audiences outright. For Powell and Pressburger, propaganda need not be approached as antithetical to critical thought; their films' characteristic self-reflexivity allows them to self-represent as specifically democratic propagandists invested in openness and honest dealings with their audiences.

In order to get a sense of the kind of works that The Archers sought to differentiate their own films from, we need look no further than the first British propaganda movie made during the war—a film co-directed by Powell: *The Lion Has Wings*. Hastily constructed in about a month by London Film Productions and Alexander Korda Film Productions, and featuring sections directed by Powell, Brian Desmond Hurst, Adrian Brunel, and Korda himself—as well as a great deal of stock footage—*The Lion Has Wings* aimed to reassure the British people of the nation's readiness for war, thanks especially to its exaggerated view of the cutting-edge modernity and power of the Royal Air Force (RAF), which it practically mythologized. The film is divided into three chapters. Its first chapter contrasts the British and German ways of life, using footage from Leni Riefenstahl's *The Triumph of the Will* (1935) to establish the rigidity and militarization of German culture; the second chapter reconstructs the RAF bombing of German warships in the Kiel Canal in December of 1939; and the final chapter imagines a successful RAF defense of an attack on England, thanks to the help of barrage balloons. These sections are loosely tied together through a focus on the family of one RAF officer played by Ralph Richardson.

The film's misrepresentations and exaggerations of British military strength were necessary to raise the morale of a nation that was not yet fully defensible. Many reviewers at the time saw the need for such a film, even if they understood that they were being manipulated or spoken down to by its producers,[57] which is probably why it did so well at the box office in 1939—and is certainly why many contemporary reviewers were forgiving of its many flaws. The left-wing press was not so forgiving, however, especially regarding the film's lack of realism and subtlety.[58] With the passing of time, scholars have tended to agree more with the film's fiercer critics, and

---

[57]According to S. P. Mackenzie, for example, at least one respondent to the Mass Observation survey of filmgoers noted that "a claim made by the RAF commander, played by Ralph Richardson, early in *The Lion Has Wings*—'We've never been better prepared'—provoked audible derision among members of one audience" (*Battle of Britain on Screen: The "Few" in British Film and Television Drama* [Edinburgh: Edinburgh University Press, 2007], 18).
[58]Chapman quotes at length the reviewers of the *Documentary News Letter*, who claimed that the film exhibited a "poor understanding of the psychology of film propaganda" (Chapman, *The British at War*, 64).

rightly so. Without question, *The Lion Has Wings* is quite primitive, both ideologically and formally. As Clive Coultass explains, the film "was meant to be a justification, in crude propaganda terms, of Britain's intervention in Europe, and it was expressed through a text clearly conditioned by traditional concepts of Tory Paternalism."[59] James Chapman concurs, noting the film's patronizing tone, and he adds: "Most commentators . . . now agree that the film is propaganda of an old-fashioned, overtly patriotic sort."[60] We would add here only that Powell's contributions do very little to rescue the film from such a negative view.

Though generally regarded as the best of the film's three sections, Powell's scenes of RAF bomber raids misrepresent the truth about the nation's technological and strategic preparedness for the war. Chapman singles out Powell's reconstruction of the Kiel Canal raid as being "as much fiction as . . . documentary: the success of the Kiel raid was greatly exaggerated."[61] Indeed, Powell himself would later describe the film as "an outrageous piece of propaganda, full of half-truths and half-lies, with some stagy episodes which were rather embarrassing and with actual facts which were highly distorted."[62] In short, *The Lion Has Wings* might be said to have represented precisely the sort of manipulative, non-self-reflective propaganda film that was difficult to distinguish from the Nazi variety associated with Riefenstahl's myth-making documentaries. Moreover, it was propaganda of the sort that Powell and Pressburger would deliberately work against in their future filmmaking efforts.

In its embrace of self-reflexiveness and even skepticism about more overtly patriotic and manipulative wartime cinema, Powell and Pressburger's propaganda strategy appears to go well beyond—and on occasion even to contradict—the recommendations of the MOI. According to the Clark Programme, "film propaganda will be most effective when it is least recognizable as such."[63] This conclusion follows logically from an earlier claim that good propaganda "must be good entertainment," but its import is nonetheless clear: good film propaganda, like good ideology, functions best when it's invisible. One of the hallmarks of The Archers' wartime films, however, is their brazen flaunting of propaganda's *visibility*. Especially through their characteristic self-reflexivity and ideological ambiguity, the films go so far as to invite audiences to ruminate upon their status as propaganda, and not in uncritical ways.

---

[59]Coultass, *Images for Battle: British Film and the Second World War, 1939–1945* (Newark, DE: University of Delaware Press, 1989), 21.
[60]Chapman, *The British at War*, 60.
[61]Ibid., 59.
[62]Powell, *A Life*, 335.
[63]Clark, "Programme," 124.

While unusual for wartime propaganda, The Archers' self-reflexivity does not spring from nowhere. Instead, it should be considered in relation to contemporary and early-twentieth-century debates about "critical thinking" as a relevant item of concern for propagandists. Central to these debates were questions about the nature and capacities of consumers of propaganda: How capable are the people of thinking analytically about the propaganda they are encountering? How easily manipulated might they be by outright lies? Almost always in such discussions, propaganda figures as being antithetical to critical thinking. According to Steve Neale, for instance, the "liberal humanist position on propaganda" posits that ideology is to the propaganda film as critical thinking is to its non-propagandistic counterpart.[64] In other words, the propaganda film imposes ideological positions onto an audience prefigured as passive and helpless, whereas the non-propaganda film caters to an audience construed as capable of sorting out complex, potentially contradictory ideas.[65] As a way of differentiating between these two types of films and their audiences, Neale contrasts Pudovkin and Eisenstein's faith in the totalitarian potential of montage and Bazin's hopes for a "democratic cinema" whose emblematic film "inscribes spaces for reflection and discussion, for counter-proposition and counter-argument, even if, necessarily, it sets the terms for this."[66] Defying such standard ways of construing the connections between propaganda, democracy, and critical thinking, Powell and Pressburger methodically and counterintuitively position themselves as democratic propagandists by crafting wartime films that deliberately stimulate audience reflection, discussion, and even counterargument. This maneuver sometimes puts pressure on their relationship with the government, even as they work on its behalf.

At times, the MOI seemed open to the idea that propaganda need not be hostile to critical thinking. In moments of crisis, however, when giving direction to the people seemed to be necessary, the MOI showed a willingness to appropriate ideas such as those of E. H. Henderson, who said that "the aim of the propagandist is to inculcate certain attitudes by means which prevent critical thinking."[67] This would occur especially in cases when "the

---

[64] Neale, "Propaganda," *Screen* 18 (1977): 9–40, 10.

[65] Similarly, Francois Chevassu contends that "the propaganda film aims to impose a political or 'ideological' point of view and to force its spectators to adopt this point of view without thought or consideration; and this with the aim of serving a determinate cause" (qtd. in Neale, "Propaganda," 10).

[66] Ibid., 33.

[67] Qtd. in Mclaine, *Ministry of Morale*, 137–8. That Powell and Pressburger's contemporaries understood the nondogmatic propaganda approach of *49th Parallel* is best captured by a *Sunday Dispatch* review from October 12, 1941: "Of course the inevitable question is—what is the propaganda value of this Government-sponsored film? Frankly, I don't know. Even more frankly, I don't care. Democracy v. Hitlerism. . . . Praise for the British character . . . . Anglo-Canadian amity. . . . Whatever the propaganda angle, this is an excellent film" (2).

propagandists did select facts to serve ends and they did offer . . . truth statements which at best could be described as convenient assumptions."⁶⁸ In other words, the Ministry, while falling short of lying outright, did at times perpetuate ideas whose persuasiveness hinged on their packaging as truths straightforward enough to discourage critical scrutiny. McLaine holds up such practices as evidence that Orwell was right when he argued that "All propaganda is lies, even when one is telling the truth."⁶⁹

Furthermore, the MOI was not always forthcoming, or even capable of being so, when it came to the dissemination of news and information:

> [T]he newly founded Ministry of Information was initially badly organized, and while its News Division aspired to tell "the truth, nothing but the truth, and near as possible the whole truth", it had no access to the whole truth. The pre-war assumption that "news would flow to Broadcasting House from the Ministry through a pipe line with a tap which they could regulate at will" lost all its force as the Armed Services acted independently of the Ministry and of each other.⁷⁰

Nonetheless, as we've seen, the basic trajectory of the wartime MOI was from greater opaqueness to greater transparency, from a more condescending to a more respectful attitude toward the "people" and their capacity for critical thought. These developments in the MOI chimed with, but were obviously not identical to, The Archers' deliberate attempt to promote critical thinking about, and through, propaganda, rather than to simplify audience thinking about the British and their allies, the Germans, or the nature of the war more generally. Of course, this fact alone should not be taken to mean that we think their films are always progressive or somehow enlightened. In our chapter on *Blimp*, for example, we focus much of our attention on the film's ethically confusing, and potentially fraught, arguments and sympathies.

2. *Ideological Ambiguity.* A government official charged with the task of reviewing The Archers' treatment for *Blimp* raised the following concern: "[W]e must be very careful not to appear to stand behind and support a film which can be taken in the wrong way by a fair proportion of people."⁷¹ As we shall see, similar concerns were also raised about a number of the duo's other films, not only by government officials but also by film critics and moviegoers. Time and again, the films were interpreted in diametrically opposed ways, as either effective propaganda or as erosive of the war effort. To

---

⁶⁸McLaine, *Ministry of Morale*, 137.
⁶⁹Ibid.
⁷⁰Asa Briggs, *The BBC: The First Fifty Years* (Oxford: Oxford University Press, 1985), 178.
⁷¹Qtd. in Ian Christie, ed. *The Life and Death of Colonel Blimp*, by Michael Powell and Emeric Pressburger (London: Faber and Faber, 1994), 31.

a degree, the ideological ambiguity of Powell and Pressburger seems a direct byproduct of their commitment to a self-reflexive wartime propaganda art. A more directly manipulative or fascist type of propaganda would strive to eliminate uncertainty in an audience or minimize the equivocality of crucial scenes in a film. The greatness of so much of Powell and Pressburger's work hinges on its ambiguity, especially at moments when propaganda seems to be a subject of the film.

This ambiguity may also reflect, and shed light upon, the distinctive political beliefs of Powell and Pressburger—as both a collaborative team and as individual artists. Though a majority of their wartime films can be characterized as intensely political, The Archers are not ideologues. While they are traditionalists in many ways, their films record—and not unsympathetically—the powerful social and cultural changes wrought by the war. In many ways, their idiosyncratic politics (which may be the key to their famously idiosyncratic style) is epitomized by *AMOLAD* protagonist Peter Carter's (David Niven) identification of his personal belief system as "Conservative by nature, Labour by experience." Though the words are spoken by a fictional character, and though they apply only in the context of the late war years, they nonetheless capture, certainly better than other labels that have been placed on Powell and Pressburger (such as High Tory or traditionalist or even fascist!),[72] something of the filmmakers' contradictory impulses and hard-earned pragmatism. This phrase also acknowledges how the experience of the Second World War caused many Britons to scrutinize and reevaluate their most basic political tendencies and beliefs.

There is another point that should be made about the ideological complexity of The Archers' films, which is that it is as much an expression of Powell and Pressburger's aesthetic and narrative commitments as it is of their political ones. Like many great artists, The Archers produce works that are marked by ambiguity, and that respect their audience's ability to draw their own conclusions about complex issues unfolding in difficult circumstances. Is *AMOLAD*'s Other World a vision of the postwar welfare state, or, as their most virulent critics, the Robsons, would have it, a fascist dystopia? Is *A Canterbury Tale*'s Thomas Colpeper a spokesperson for enduring cultural values or a misogynist crackpot? And how are we to view the implied actions of the Boer interrogator in *Blimp*: as morally unjustifiable acts of torture, or as a necessary antidote to the Blimpish gentlemanly ethic? That questions such as these are provoked by Powell and Pressburger's films arguably speaks

---

[72]In *A Mirror for England: British Movies from Austerity to Affluence*, Raymond Durgnat explores the "High Tory" politics of Powell and Pressburger (2nd ed. [London: Palgrave Macmillan, 2011], e.g. 66). On the other side of the spectrum, the Robsons infamously detect Powell and Pressburger's "naked German-Nazi-Fascist philosophy," especially as it is expressed in *AMOLAD* (E. W. and M. M. Robson, *The World is My Cinema* [London: Sidneyan Society, 1947], 68).

less to the moviemakers' political convictions than to their aesthetic ones, and to the richness and sophistication of their filmmaking and storytelling.

3. *Pluralism*. The most obvious case for Powell and Pressburger's systematic endorsement of pluralism is made by *49th Parallel*, which highlights how democracy celebrates and protects the diversity of those various, distinct communities that, together, constitute the democratic nation. Arguments can be made, however, for The Archers' prioritization of pluralism in most of the wartime films, most obviously *A Canterbury Tale*, *IKWIG*, and *AMOLAD*. As we've seen, the MOI Programme recommended that filmmakers emphasize the equal sacrifices of "all classes of workers," and we could certainly view such a recommendation as informing Powell and Pressburger's commitment to representing the regional and class-based diversity of British society and culture. Nothing in the Programme prepares us, though, for the films' thorough embrace of such diversity, their opening up of the category beyond class to embrace issues of ethnicity, gender, national identity, and even race. Pressburger's own immigrant status is an obvious point of relevance to which we will return, as is the geographically diverse backgrounds of The Archers' creative team more generally. The films are profoundly informed by an awareness of what it means to be regarded as both an insider and outsider in British society, an awareness that even the Kent-born Powell sought to cultivate; as he liked to boast about *Colonel Blimp*, "this is a 100% British film but it's photographed by a Frenchman, it's written by a Hungarian, the musical score is by a German Jew, the director was English, the man who did the costumes was Czech; in other words, it was the kind of film that I've always worked on with a mixed crew of every nationality, no frontiers of any kind."[73] Powell's pride in this "mixed crew" leads us to the next aspect of The Archers' program.

4. *Cosmopolitanism*. Martha Nussbaum famously defines the cosmopolitan as a person "whose primary allegiance is to the community of human beings in the entire world."[74] In doing so, she clarifies how cosmopolitanism centers

---

[73]Qtd. in *Michael Powell Interviews*, ed. David Lazar (Jackson, MS: University Press of Mississippi, 2003), 107. Further study is needed of what Powell means when he talks about "British" film and "Britain." Though this book will deal with the ways in which individual films engaged or reflected attitudes toward such concepts as British heritage, British sensibility, et cetera, and with how Powell and Pressburger represented non-English Britain (for example, their view of the Dominions in *49th Parallel*, of Empire in *Blimp*, or of Scotland in *IKWIG*), it offers no overarching claim about their broad perspectives on Britain, Great Britain, or the British Empire (they have relatively little to say, it would seem, about either Northern Ireland or Wales, though Scotland looms large especially in Powell's imagination).

[74]Nussbaum, "Patriotism and Cosmopolitanism," *Boston Review*, October 1, 1994, https://www.bostonreview.net/articles/martha-nussbaum-patriotism-and-cosmopolitanism/ (accessed January 10, 2023).

not on the autonomy and distinctiveness of local cultures within the nation state, as in pluralism, but on the notion that all human beings belong to a single global community. Though pluralism's relationship with cosmopolitanism is not straightforward, in Powell and Pressburger's propaganda films, pluralist and cosmopolitan principles mix quite naturally: respect for local cultures implies respect for the individual humanity of those occupying them, and respect for individuals makes possible the cohesiveness of the much larger spaces—national, international, global—within which different individuals and their cultures mix. While the later wartime films show a special preoccupation with international and even global relationships (again, *A Canterbury Tale* and *AMOLAD* stand out), even the earliest Powell and Pressburger collaborations explore such relationships (*Contraband*'s London prominently features Danish émigrés living alongside the English natives; *49th Parallel*'s capacious vision of Canada represents the Dominion as a land shared by indigenous peoples, by refugees such as those at the Hutterite camp, and by the French- and English-speaking citizens of the major cities, many of whom mix even in remote locations like Hudson Bay).

5. *Germanic Individualism.* One logical outcome of Powell and Pressburger's advocacy of cosmopolitanism is that Germans, as members of the human race, are understood to contain the potential to be good men and women. The MOI Programme urged filmmakers to stress the sinister rather than the sadistic aspect of the Gestapo's activities, presumably to discourage cartoonish portraits no one could take seriously; another section of the Programme says that the Gestapo has broken up families and taken away liberties. Beyond these general statements, no recommendations are made regarding how filmmakers should depict Germans. Although propaganda focusing on the "good German" flourished immediately after the war,[75] many of Powell and Pressburger's wartime films—especially *49th Parallel* and *Blimp*—anticipate this trend by highlighting German characters whose cosmopolitanism or basic morality distances them from the majority of sinister Nazis.

---

[75]See Pól Ó Dochartaigh and Christiane Schönfeld, *Representing the "Good German" in Literature and Culture After 1945: Altruism and Moral Ambiguity* (Rochester, NY: Camden House, 2013); and Wendy Webster, "'Europe against the Germans': The British Resistance Narrative, 1940–1950," *Journal of British Studies* 48 (2009): 958–82. Tobias Hochscherf argues that "the contribution by many German-speaking immigrants to British wartime cinema can help to explain the nuanced depictions of Germans and foreigners in British films" including *49th Parallel* and *Blimp* ("'You Call Us "Germans," You Call Us "Brothers"—But We Are Not Your Brothers!': British Anti-Nazi Films and German-speaking Emigrés," *Destination London: German-speaking Emigrés and British Cinema, 1925–1950*, ed. Tim Bergfelder and Christian Cargnelli [New York and Oxford: Berghahn Books, 2008], 181–94, 182).

6. *Romantic Sensibility.* In their influential study of the "classical Hollywood cinema," David Bordwell, Janet Staiger, and Kristin Thompson argue that one of the lines of action linking a film's major characters almost always "involves heterosexual romantic love."[76] The vast majority of Hollywood films, in other words, regardless of genre and subject matter, prioritize romantic lines of action. Perhaps because Powell and Pressburger (like most British commercial filmmakers) came to internalize a causal link between romance and the sort of "entertaining" film the MOI Programme solicited and associated with America, five of their eight wartime films focus heavily on heterosexual romantic love; as for the remaining three, even they offer faint intimations of possible amorous alliances.

To suggest that romance was merely a convenient tool for entertaining audiences, however, would be to mistake its conceptual and ideological importance. That importance, moreover, emerges out of the ways in which romance is used to advance other aspects of their propaganda program.[77] In *AMOLAD*, for example, the alliance between Britain and America—an alliance grounded in a respect for pluralism—is symbolically secured through the love affair of an English airman and an air traffic controller from Boston, while in *Blimp*, a "good" German officer's marriage to an English governess is integral to the development of that film's cosmopolitan ethos.

Intriguingly, amatory relations loom largest in the earliest and latest of the films we cover in this study. In *The Spy in Black* and *Contraband*, Powell and Pressburger seek to reframe the romance plots of spy movies like Hitchcock's *The 39 Steps* (1935) to the demands of the new wartime reality. In *IKWIG* and *AMOLAD,* the filmmakers' hopes for the postwar future are expressed by means of amorous alliances; these two works tether social renewal to heterosexual love in a fashion that is a familiar part of the legacy of Shakespearean comedy. In contrast, the comparative devaluation of romance in *49th Parallel, Aircraft,* and *A Canterbury Tale* is of a piece with those films' emphasis on the collective rather than on the individual.

The Structure of This Book

Powell and Pressburger's War is organized into three main parts. In Part One, we take up two films: *The Spy in Black* and *Contraband*. While the making

---

[76] Bordwell, Staiger, and Thompson, *The Classical Hollywood Cinema: Film Style & Mode of Production to 1960* (New York: Columbia University Press, 1985), 16.

[77] In making this point, we are referring exclusively to erotic relations and not gesturing toward the elements of neo-romanticism that critics have located in Powell and Pressburger's work. See Stella Hockenhull, *Neo-Romantic Landscapes: An Aesthetic Approach to the Films of Powell and Pressburger* (Newcastle upon Tyne: Cambridge Scholars Publishing, 2008).

of *Spy* precedes the war, it shows The Archers both anticipating the conflict and beginning to engage with the subject of propaganda. With *Contraband*, the filmmakers achieve a somewhat awkward, if entertaining, synthesis of the Hitchcockian thriller and the documentary-style propaganda feature. These are transitional works, as The Archers strive to reconcile the narrative logic of the 1930s spy film, and of the romance plot attendant upon that genre, with the (anticipated or actual) demands of the war. In the case of *Contraband*, the film was in production as the MOI was in the process of clarifying for itself its own conception of cinematic propaganda. As we have suggested, Powell and Pressburger both build upon that conception and develop it in distinctive ways.

Part Two centers on films in which The Archers hit their stride as both propagandists and artists. It begins with *49th Parallel*, which Powell referred to as "the start of wartime films, the proper start,"[78] and which was the first (and last) commercial feature to receive significant financial backing from the MOI.[79] With *49th Parallel*, *One of Our Aircraft Is Missing*, and *The Life and Death of Colonel Blimp*, The Archers make direct contributions to the war effort while meditating upon their roles as both artists and propagandists. Each of these films is reflexive about its nature and objectives, with *49th Parallel* musing over the differences between German and British propaganda; *Aircraft* taking up the "V for Victory" campaign; and *Blimp* engaging with the dubious legacy of British imperial propaganda.

In each of the films in Part Two, Powell and Pressburger are responding directly to the events and exigencies of the war. With the movies we analyze in Part Three, however, we see the filmmakers not only reacting to wartime issues and events but also turning their attention to the postwar future. *A Canterbury Tale* and *AMOLAD* each owe their existence to MOI concerns about Anglo-American relations in the latter stages of the conflict; the former film shares with *IKWIG* an anti-materialist ethos associated with the traditional culture of rural Britain. These films do not merely celebrate the past and the values associated with it, they also attend to reforms that must be made in order to create a better future both within Britain and in its relationship to the United States. In considering these issues, moreover, all three films chime with that portion of the MOI's propaganda program that stresses "the spiritual values and traditions" that Powell and Pressburger see themselves as fighting for.

---

[78] David Badder, "Powell and Pressburger: The War Years," *Sight and Sound* 48.1 (Winter 1978): 8–12, 10.
[79] Chapman, *The British at War*, 70–2.

Conclusion

Over the last few decades, a particular critical story has consistently been told about Powell and Pressburger's relationship to British cinema. The central elements of this story are succinctly captured by Andrew Moor: "Powell and Pressburger have been seen as rogue outsiders because of the fantasy elements in their work and the European profile of their collaborative team. They do not fit into the understated 'quality realist' cinema which has been taken to represent our authentic national cinematic style."[80] The "quality realist" tradition referenced by Moor is born in the 1930s, with the documentary films of John Grierson, but it becomes fully entrenched in the 1940s and especially during the war years, when realism becomes nearly synonymous with responsible, and ethical, filmmaking. Moreover, according to John Ellis, "It was during the war that the successful fusion [of the documentary and the commercial feature] took place, to the benefit of each form"; this fusion was hailed by many critics as the natural evolution of a British "quality" cinema.[81] Crucially, and as Moor suggests, The Archers do not appear to play an obvious role within this evolution. Instead, they have been taken to represent a counter-tradition—one that sees them sometimes aligned with Gainsborough costume melodramas and Hammer horror films—marked by "the Gothic, the fantastic, the melodramatic."[82]

No recent scholar has explored The Archers' place in British cinema history more directly, or effectively, than Moor, who argues from the beginning of his influential monograph that "Powell and Pressburger's cinema betrays their oblique relationship to accepted, national models of 'British Cinema,'" especially the "narrow realist concerns which would become more central to British cinema by the 1940s."[83] In Moor's characterization of what he calls The Archers' "cinema of magic spaces," "topographical space is abandoned in favour of a more controlled studio-based aesthetic, the inner terrain of the unconscious is presented, or pure, sustained fantasy worlds unfurl. Reality is banished. They escape the empirical to lodge in the sequestered territory

---

[80] Andrew Moor, "No Place Like Home: Powell, Pressburger Utopia," *The British Cinema Book*, 3rd ed., ed. Robert Murphy (Basingstoke: Palgrave Macmillan for the BFI, 2009), 240–6, 240.
[81] Ellis, "The Quality Film Adventure: British Critics and the Cinema 1942–1948," *Dissolving Views: Key Writings on British Cinema*, ed. Andrew Higson (London: Cassell, 1996), 66–93, 85.
[82] Andrew Higson, "'Britain's Outstanding Contribution to the Film': The Documentary-Realist Tradition," *All Our Yesterdays*, 72–97, esp. 73. Higson does not explicitly link this tradition to Powell and Pressburger in this essay, but the connection is frequently made. See, for example, Petley, "Lost Continent," 106: "Powell explores a very different dimension of 'Englishness' that is almost diametrically opposed to the cold, hard empiricism which lies at the cultural root of the realist aesthetic: Powell's ancestors are not Mill, Locke and Hume but Romanticism and the Gothic."
[83] Moor, *Powell & Pressburger: A Cinema of Magic Spaces*, 2nd ed. (London and New York: I.B. Tauris, 2012), 3, 2.

of the artistic imagination."[84] In Moor's work, the anti-realist reputation of The Archers looms large. This was a reputation first established in the mid- to-late 1940s, when critical insistence on documentary realism was at its height: "Powell and Pressburger's company, The Archers, is the source of the most [critically] reviled films of the period, moving increasingly further 'away from the essential realism and true business of the British movie.'"[85] It is a reputation that finds confirmation in postwar Powell and Pressburger films such as *Black Narcissus*, *The Red Shoes*, and *The Tales of Hoffmann* (1951). And, we contend, it is a reputation that is distortive of The Archers' wartime movies. To put it another way, we would argue that critics have tended to read the more fully developed anti-realist elements of some of the postwar films back into the filmmakers' wartime output. If we focus solely on their wartime movies, then the picture of Powell and Pressburger that emerges for us is significantly different from the one that has dominated recent criticism.

The wartime films of The Archers—especially earlier ones such as *Contraband*, *49th Parallel*, and *Aircraft*—contain many of the documentary elements associated with realist cinema; more generally, they were produced in a largely realist register and were closely attuned to the specific historical contexts in which they were created. Not only did they respond directly to the MOI's shifting needs and imperatives regarding a useful propaganda cinema but they also constantly showed the filmmakers' willingness to engage in political occasions and events. These topicalities ranged from the general—the conditions of the blackout (*Contraband*); the problem of American isolationism (*49th Parallel*); and the realities of women's wartime labor (*A Canterbury Tale*)—to the specific—the emergence of J. B. Priestley as the voice of the people following the battle of Dunkirk (*Blimp*);

---

[84]Ibid., 3. Raymond Durgnat also references escape: "[Powell's] central problem, as an artist, is another permutation of Lean's, his tendency to escape from realism, yet only play with romanticism" (*A Mirror*, 254), while David Thomson calls Michael Powell "the ardent antirealist" with a reputation as an "eccentric decorator of fantasies." Thomson continues, "Against persistent British attempts to dignify realism, Powell must have seemed gaudy, distasteful, and effete" (*The New Biographical Dictionary of Film* [New York: Knopf, 2002], 693).

[85]Ellis, "Quality Film Adventure," 72. The interpolated quotation is from Richard Winnington in 1946 who, like so many of his contemporaries, saw *A Canterbury Tale* as most emblematic of the problem. Interestingly, other reviewers throughout the 1940s felt inclined to praise other of the Archers' films specifically for their realism: for example, *Aircraft* was singled out as "an admirable example of the new kind of English film, actual, thrilling, taking its tune from events" (*Spectator*, April 5, 1946, qtd. in Ellis, "Quality Film Adventure," 69–70). Similarly, by defining realism as having to do with atmospheric authenticity, specifically, one could argue that thanks to "the flurries, flounces, turmoils and sweat of that esoteric life behind the curtains of the ballet" in *The Red Shoes*, "Messrs Powell and Pressburger touch better cinematography and better realism than in any other of their films" (Richard Winnington in the *News Chronicle* on July 26, 1948, qtd. in Ellis, "Quality Film Adventure," 82–3).

the 1941 inauguration of the pan-European "V for Victory" propaganda campaign (*Aircraft*); and a US Senate committee's release in 1944 of an inflammatory report on the merits of the Anglo-American lend-lease policy (*AMOLAD*). Additionally, the filmmakers were painstakingly intent on creating a realistic wartime *mise-en-scène*, often engaging through the MOI Films Division the various military branches for access to equipment, uniforms, facilities, and locations so as to best recreate the most appropriate settings for the stories they sought to tell. Powell and Pressburger also were not loath to directly appropriate techniques associated with the Griersonian documentary. These included voice-over narration (e.g., *Canterbury Tale* and *AMOLAD*); explanatory, fact-based title cards and captions (e.g., *49th Parallel*); strategically unscored soundtracks (as in the remarkable opening sequence of *Aircraft*); and even the inclusion of documentaries-within-a-film (as in the blockade plot of *Contraband* or the alternative opening of *Canterbury Tale*, in which a voice-over narrator relates the meaning of various graphs and statistics to the behavior and practices of American GIs stationed in Britain[86]). Nor should the use of any of these realist documentary techniques seem particularly surprising, appearing as they did in the works of filmmakers who produced literal documentaries and docufictions during these years, from *The Lion Has Wings* to *The Volunteer* and beyond. Although the feature films were marked by complex and multifaceted stories, experimental and variable cinematographic styles, bold and multilayered editing processes, innovative uses of color and effects, and, of course, those occasional flights of fancy that contributed to the popular and critical struggle to categorize them, the wartime Archers were hardly thoroughgoing anti-realists.

In stressing the presence of realist and documentary elements in Powell and Pressburger, we don't mean to deny that their wartime films contain evidence of the fantastic: consider the crewless Wellington bomber at the beginning of *Aircraft*; the metaphorical and mythical resonances of the Corryvreckan whirlpool in *IKWIG*; the peculiar actions of the Glue Man in *A Canterbury Tale*; or the blurring of fantasy and reality in *AMOLAD*. Instead, we are suggesting that, having been conditioned by the movies Powell and Pressburger would make after the war (and here we would include *AMOLAD*, the most fantastic of the films taken up in this book), critics have not attended as closely as they might to the realist dimensions of their wartime corpus. And if those dimensions have been given short shrift, so has the status of these works as propaganda. Certainly, critics have recognized the propagandistic impetus behind and content of films such as

---

[86] For a more detailed description of this alternate American opening, see Greg M. Colón Semenza and Bob Hasenfratz, *The History of British Literature on Film, 1895–2015* (New York and London: Bloomsbury, 2015), 215–19.

49th Parallel, *Blimp*, *A Canterbury Tale*, or *AMOLAD*. What they have not examined, however, is The Archers' sustained and profound engagement with the topic of propaganda itself. As we have suggested, Powell and Pressburger did not merely produce propaganda but they also meditated upon its nature and reflected upon their role in its promulgation; they also understood its making to be of a piece with their commercial and aesthetic ambitions.

At the beginning of this Introduction, we allude to The Archers' credo as articulated by Powell: "[W]e owe allegiance to nobody except the financial interests which provide our money; and, to them, the sole responsibility of ensuring them a profit, not a loss"; "every single foot of our films is our own responsibility and nobody else's. We refuse to be guided or coerced by any influence but our own judgement." What is remarkable is that, for most of the war, Powell and Pressburger lived up to this credo. (As we will discuss in the book's coda, the cessation of conflict brought with it doubts and complexities and, a couple of years later, a loss of autonomy.) Even more remarkable, though, is the richness and sophistication of the films The Archers produced during this period. At a time when film was still denigrated by many as cheap entertainment, The Archers assumed that they were making art. As Powell puts it in the opening paragraphs of his autobiography's first volume, "*All art is one, and there is no difference in the mystery of the craft, only in the hand and eye of the craftsman. . . . Is filmmaking art? Well, if telling a story is not art I don't know what is.*"[87] Neither do we. Significantly, for the first years of their partnership, The Archers' art was enabled rather than impeded by the exigencies of wartime propaganda. We hope that the readers of this book will come away from it with an increased appreciation for the extraordinary films Powell and Pressburger generated as the central part of their war work.

---

[87]Powell, *A Life*, 4 (emphasis in original).

PART ONE

1

"You Are English. I Am German. We Are Enemies"

Anticipating Propaganda in *The Spy in Black*

In September 1941, a subcommittee of the US Senate's Committee on Interstate Commerce began hearings on whether the movie industry was engaging in a propaganda campaign designed "to influence public sentiment in the direction of [US] participation . . . in the present European war."[1] The subcommittee acted in pursuance of a resolution proposed by Senators Gerald P. Nye (Republican, North Dakota) and Bennett Champ Clark (Democrat, Missouri). Early in the hearings, Nye and Clark each spoke forcefully, and in tacitly antisemitic terms, against what he perceived to be the monopolistic nature of a movie industry dominated by a small cabal of warmongering executives, a number of whom were born elsewhere (as Nye puts it, "They came to our land and took citizenship here entertaining violent animosities toward certain causes abroad"—namely, Nazism).[2] Both men also decried the propagandistic nature of the films produced by this cabal. In Clark's words, "dozens of pictures, great features costing—

---

[1] *Propaganda in Motion Pictures: Hearings on Senate Resolution 152, September 9–26, 1941* (Washington: United States Government Printing Office, 1942), 1. For a lively discussion of these hearings, see Mark Harris, *Five Came Back: A Story of Hollywood and the Second World War* (New York: Penguin Books, 2014), 89–98.
[2] While Nye strenuously rejects the claim that he is motivated by antisemitism, he observes that, were he to identify "those primarily responsible for propaganda in the moving-picture field," each of them would be Jewish and all but one of them a foreigner (*Propaganda in Motion Pictures*, 11).

some of them hundreds of thousands of dollars, some of them millions of dollars—are used to infect the minds of their audiences with hatred, to inflame them, to arouse their emotions, and to make them clamor for war. And not one word on the side of the argument against war is heard."[3] Nye develops the same theme, arguing that these movies "have served to drive some Americans under their very beds for fear of Hitler and his minions. They have served, these propaganda pictures, to change if not warp, a lot of clear thinking in American minds."[4] For both senators, movies such as Frank Borzage's *The Mortal Storm* (1940) or Anatole Litvak's *Confessions of a Nazi Spy* (1939) engender a strong affective response and, in doing so, "destroy straight thinking, honest thinking, American thinking."[5] As we shall see, certain British movies, including *The Spy in Black* (1939), were also singled out as producing such an effect.

The spokesperson for the movie industry during these hearings was Wendell Wilkie, the unsuccessful Republican candidate in the previous year's presidential election. Whereas Nye and Clark see the films under discussion as disabling thought through an overwhelming appeal to emotions, Wilkie sees them as truthful representations of the world with a very different relationship to "straight" and "honest thinking": "The pictures portraying England and Germany do not purport to tell the American people what they should do about nazi-ism [sic], save as the knowledge of the true facts may, as it always has, influence the judgment of right-thinking men and women."[6] For Wilkie, films focused on the war provide moviegoers with the raw materials for making up their own minds about not only the conflict itself but also, by extension, the issue of future American involvement in it. For Clark and Nye, these films circumvent rational deliberation by inspiring hatred for the Nazis; they also downplay the full horror of war itself in order to remove any potential barriers to US entry into the conflict.

On Thursday, September 11, 1941—the same day that the isolationist aviation hero Charles Lindbergh decried Jewish influence over the movie industry in a radio address at an America First rally in Des Moines, Iowa—the subcommittee called John T. Flynn, chairman of the America First Committee for New York City. Flynn appeared at the hearing not, he claimed, as a representative of the AFC but "as a complainant, if you wish to put it that way, against what I believe to be the propaganda abuses of the moving-picture industry."[7] Like Clark and Nye, Flynn links these abuses to the monopolistic nature of Hollywood, which has led to both the promulgation of a pro-British viewpoint across a range of films and

---

[3] Ibid., 73.
[4] Ibid., 36.
[5] Ibid., 38.
[6] Ibid., 20.
[7] Ibid., 92.

the censoring of projects seen to challenge that viewpoint. More generally, Flynn accuses the movie industry of "using the motion-picture instrument in their hands for propaganda to raise a war spirit in America."[8] While echoing Nye and Clark in emphasizing the emotional impact of film propaganda, especially when it comes to promoting anti-Nazi hatred, Flynn also stressed that "propaganda technique in our modern society consists in planting root ideas in men's or women's minds"—ideas such as "We are next on Hitler's list" and "You cannot make peace with dictators."[9]

In the service of developing his argument, Flynn presents the subcommittee with a list of films, not all of which are American in origin, that he urges them to examine. Among the British films mentioned by Flynn are Roy Boulting's *Pastor Hall* (1940), Carol Reed's *Night Train to Munich* (1940),[10] and, unsurprisingly, *The Lion Has Wings* (1939), which Powell co-directed and which we discussed in the Introduction. While acknowledging that "all these pictures are not poisonous pictures," and, indeed, that some of them are "very fine," Flynn claims: "The object of these pictures [when taken altogether] ... is to keep pounding at you like the man haranguing the mob in the streets, to get your hatreds in control of your reason and turn you loose on war." However, definitively discerning the "object" of these films requires more than just screening the finished project (which he, of course, urges the subcommittee to do):

> Ask the moving-picture people to give you the whole process of producing these pictures. Get the original story. Get the report from the Hays Producers Association, what they said you could not put in, what they said you could put in. Get the report of the cutout. In other words, see every process in the production of those films—the things that were put in and the things that were taken out, the things that were put in to increase emphasis and the things that were taken out for the purpose of soft-pedaling emphasis.[11]

If the subcommittee performs this series of tasks, Flynn confidently asserts, they will "see what kind of propaganda [they] are getting."[12]

The final Senate subcommittee hearing took place on September 26, 1941. Plans for further action were definitively shelved in the wake of Pearl Harbor and America's entrance into the war in December of that year. So nothing substantive came of the subcommittee's deliberations. Why, then, have we devoted this much space to them, especially given that they

---

[8]Ibid., 106.
[9]Ibid., 109, 110.
[10]This film is referred to as *Night Train* by Flynn.
[11]Ibid., 115.
[12]Ibid.

took place in the United States? There are three main reasons. First, Nye, Clark, and Flynn develop a theory of film propaganda as that which rouses strong emotions and disables "straight thinking." This theory contrasts starkly not only with Wilkie's depiction of Hollywood films but also with the propaganda programs of both the Ministry of Information (MOI) and Powell and Pressburger themselves, both of which are explored in the Introduction. In noting these differences, we are offered a salutary reminder of the wide range of meanings that the term "propaganda" could hold at this time.[13] Second, Flynn's exhortation to the senators that they examine "the whole process of producing these pictures" loosely approximates our own method for considering *The Spy in Black* as well as The Archers' other wartime films. And finally, we take up these hearings because, as suggested earlier, *Spy* is among those films identified as "get[ting audience members'] hatreds in control of [their] reason and turn[ing them] loose on war"—this despite the fact that it was made before the war began.[14] Should it, then, be considered a propaganda film?[15]

Thought of from the perspective of production rather than reception, and notwithstanding the US Senate subcommittee's findings, *The Spy in Black* is hard to describe as a cinematic work of propaganda. And yet, the film occasionally engages with that topic, as if in anticipation of the fact that, once hostilities commenced, its narrative of Anglo-German hostilities during the First World War would inevitably resonate with the current moment. In short, *The Spy in Black* is a prewar spy thriller that offers intimations of Powell and Pressburger's more profound engagement with films as works of propaganda. Of necessity, then, our discussion of the film will not consistently focus on propaganda, although that topic will intermittently come to the fore.

In the remainder of this chapter, we will first discuss the making of *Spy*, paying particular attention to the German actor Conrad Veidt's significance to the project. From there we will consider how the film's opening locates in Captain Ernest Hardt (played by Veidt) a model of martial masculinity that is jeopardized by his stint as a spy as well as his relationship with Fraulein Tiel (Valerie Hobson). The dissolution of that relationship coincides with his resumption of his military identity, and it is accompanied by his—and

---

[13]The main differences between these conceptions of propaganda can be explained by a divergence in objectives, actual or imputed. Both Hollywood and British filmmakers, according to Clark and Nye, are trying to frighten a reluctant America into joining a foreign conflict; the MOI and The Archers, on the other hand, are at this time working primarily to maintain the commitment of the British people to the war effort.

[14]*Contraband* is also included on this list. Flynn identifies *Spy* and *Contraband* (1940) by their American titles, *U-Boat 29* and *Blackout*.

[15]Jo Fox notes that "the analysis of reception forms an essential part of the film and propaganda scholars' work" (*Film Propaganda in Britain and Nazi Germany: World War II Cinema* [Oxford and New York: Berg, 2007], 10).

the film's—starkest articulation of the terms of national animosity. More generally, we will argue that there is an unresolved contradiction in *Spy*. On the one hand, it intermittently emphasizes national difference in a fashion that is commensurate with a propaganda film, and it even makes a pointed joke about German propaganda efforts. On the other hand, the film is constructed so as to foster our identification with a central German character who strives, in collaboration with his love interest, to destroy two squadrons of British cruisers. (In this regard, Captain Hardt represents the first example, albeit a somewhat equivocal one, of the "good German" in the Powell and Pressburger canon.[16]) Indeed, the film is primarily concerned with the issue of that character's transition from naval commander to spy and back again.

Korda, Veidt, and the Making of *The Spy in Black*

The Spy in Black centers on the secret mission of U-boat Captain Hardt during the First World War. Under cover of darkness, Hardt disembarks from his submarine on the Isle of Hoy. He travels by motorbike to a remote schoolhouse, where he meets Fraulein Tiel, a German spy who, having taken the place of the new schoolmistress, goes by the name of Anne Burnett. The schoolhouse is located near Scapa Flow, in sight of the British Grand Fleet. Tiel has cultivated a source within the British navy, a disgraced, alcoholic officer called Lieutenant Ashington (Sebastian Shaw), who has access to information about the Fleet's maneuvers; he promises to inform Hardt and Tiel when two cruiser squadrons will travel to Sandwick Bay, thereby making it possible for German U-boats to inflict catastrophic damage on a significant portion of the Fleet. Even though the conspirators' efforts are interrupted by the arrival of the real Anne Burnett's fiancé, whom they subdue and tie up, and the meddling of a local minister and his wife, Hardt is able to convey Ashington's information to the crew of his U-boat. On the eve of what promises to be a great victory for the German spies, Hardt acts upon his ardor for Tiel, who, while recognizably attracted to him, rebuffs his advances. Hardt pretends to retire to his room, the door to which Tiel subsequently locks. When she sneaks out of the house, Hardt follows her and witnesses her meeting with Ashington. We then learn that "Tiel" and "Ashington" are actually a married couple, Jill and David Blacklock, the former of whom at the last minute substituted herself for the German agent assigned to rendezvous with Hardt. Much to his horror, Hardt overhears the couple discussing how the U-boats they have lured

---

[16]See the Introduction for a discussion of this figure.

to Sandwick Bay are to be sunk by British destroyers. Shortly thereafter, Hardt escapes onto the *St. Magnus* in the guise of Anne Burnett's captive fiancé—the same ferry on which Jill Blacklock is traveling in advance of what she believes will be the arrest of Hardt at the schoolhouse. After freeing some German prisoners being transported on the *St. Magnus*, Hardt doffs his disguise and takes over the vessel with the intention of warning the U-boats. In a concluding irony, the ferry is shelled by Hardt's own submarine, which is subsequently sunk by a destroyer. Hardt goes down with the *St. Magnus*, while Jill Blacklock, the other passengers, and the ferry crew all escape in lifeboats.

The Spy in Black is an adaptation of J. Storer Clouston's 1917 novel of the same title. Alexander Korda had rights to the book, and he enlisted Powell and Pressburger to turn it into a vehicle for Veidt, who had been languishing under contract with Korda's London Films. Korda had already commissioned a script for *Spy*, but he was dissatisfied with it; his first assignment for Pressburger was to see if he could do better. In *A Life in Movies*, Powell memorably describes the way in which the "small Hungarian wizard" Pressburger, at a meeting which also included Korda, producer Irving Asher, and the original screenwriter, Roland Pertwee, "completely restructured the film."[17] At the end of this meeting, Korda sent Pressburger and Powell off to find Veidt and Valerie Hobson, with whom they would continue working on the script—much to the annoyance of Pertwee and Asher, the latter having originally been assigned the task of shepherding the project to completion.[18]

As we noted in the Introduction, Korda was a titanic figure in British movie production during the 1930s. *The Private Life of Henry VIII* (1933), which Korda directed as well as produced, was an international sensation, and it spurred his efforts to compete with Hollywood film studios. It also indirectly helped engender a crisis within the British movie industry, as Rachael Low explains:

> The great success of *Henry VIII* seems to have misled financial institutions in the City, especially when European film makers were involved. Although it was well known that even established British film companies found it difficult to survive, finance was made easily available on a film-by-film basis to many companies with hardly any capital of their own. There was a great air of prosperity, with companies running out of money before a

---

[17] Michael Powell, *A Life in Movies: An Autobiography* (1986; London: Faber and Faber, 2000), 302. Powell does not identify Pertwee by name, but Kevin Macdonald does (*Emeric Pressburger: The Life and Death of a Screenwriter* [1994; London: Faber and Faber, 1996], 144). Moreover, Pertwee received screen credit for the scenario.
[18] Powell, *A Life*, 303.

film was finished and borrowing again, or using money already raised for another project.[19]

There was, in other words, a film bubble, and the inevitable collapse of the industry, which occurred when lenders anxiously began calling in loans, came in early 1937. While Korda weathered the storm better than most, in part because London Films had reassured investors by turning a profit in the months before the crash, the nature of his involvement in the film business underwent a change.[20] He became "almost exclusively an executive producer, a film impresario, and a business manipulator. Between the outbreak of industry crisis in January 1937 and the outbreak of war in September 1939, Korda carried on in a supervisory capacity at Denham [Studios], but he directed no films."[21] More generally, the post-crash period was marked for Korda by what Charles Drazin has called "an intellectual retrenchment. Unpredictable box-office risks like *Things to Come* [1936] or even *Rembrandt* [1936] were put aside in favour of projects that had clear popular appeal."[22] *The Spy in Black* was one of those projects.

Korda's greatest successes were prestige films over which he exerted close control even when he wasn't directing them. *The Spy in Black* is a very different kind of creature. For one thing, the film was made on a medium-sized budget at Denham Studios in co-production with Columbia Pictures;[23] Powell has referred to it as "an expanded quota-quickie except for the exceptional talent on the acting side, and the quality of the thinking and of the dialogue."[24] For another, Korda did not attempt to micromanage the production of *Spy*, partly because of the distance between this film and the kind of movies about which he was most enthusiastic. As mentioned earlier, Korda's primary objective was to find a role worthy of Conrad Veidt, and Powell and Pressburger were happy to oblige. As Powell notes in his autobiography, Veidt was "a legendary figure. For us, he *was* the great German cinema."[25] The star of classic silent films such as *The Cabinet of Dr. Caligari* (1920), *The Student of Prague* (1926), and *Waxworks* (1924), Veidt

---

[19]Rachael Low, *Film Making in 1930s Britain* (London: George Allen and Unwin, in assoc. w/ the British Film Institute, 1985), 199–200.
[20]Karol Kulik, *Alexander Korda: The Man Who Could Work Miracles* (London: W.H. Allen, 1975), 172.
[21]Ibid., 179.
[22]Charles Drazin, *Korda: Britain's Only Movie Mogul* (London: Sidgwick & Jackson, 2002), 195.
[23]Macdonald, *Emeric Pressburger*, 144.
[24]Powell, *A Life*, 315. Charles Drazin notes that *Spy* was a "treble quota" film, meaning that it benefited from the 1938 Cinematograph Films Act rewarding more expensive productions than did its 1927 predecessor ("The Distribution of Powell and Pressburger's Films in the United States, 1939-1949," *Historical Journal of Film, Radio and Television* 33 [2013]: 55–76, 56).
[25]Powell, *A Life*, 305.

had emigrated to Britain in 1933, becoming a British citizen in 1939. He had a Jewish wife and was fervently anti-Nazi, which did not prevent Goebbels from attempting to enlist him for his cinematic propaganda efforts.[26] By the time Powell and Pressburger met under Korda's auspices, Veidt was approaching the end of his contract with London Films without having completed a movie. *The Spy in Black* was designed to address that problem.

Based on the plot summary offered earlier, one can see how *The Spy in Black* could be received as an anti-Nazi propaganda film. It represents not only a victory for the British navy but also the triumph of a resourceful British couple over a devious German spy. In this regard, the movie would seem perfectly suited to the country's new wartime footing. Complicating this view, however, is the fact that Captain Hardt is the primary locus of attention within the film, in a way that is commensurate with Veidt's status as a major international movie star.[27] (Here, as in other ways, Pressburger radically revises Clouston's novel, which does not invite the reader to identify with Hardt's counterpart, Conrad von Belke.) In developing Hardt's character, Pressburger drew extensively on the screen personae Veidt developed in the sound era. While many of his silent film roles were of exotic or even demonic characters—"somnambulant murderers, misshapen clowns, sinister magicians, intriguing statesmen, maniacal Hindus," as a *New York Times* reporter put it in 1940[28]—by the time of *Spy* he had become known for "portraying men who were torn apart by their duty."[29] Veidt had also come to embody continental sophistication, often of a sinister or menacing form. And yet, Veidt was widely admired for his ability to play both heroes and villains—so much so that in May 1940, around the time of *Contraband*'s release, one British fan magazine invited readers to offer ideas as to which type of part he should next take up.[30] (The results of this poll were inconclusive, as participants offered "views . . . as varied as the

---

[26] Jerry C. Allen, *Conrad Veidt: From Caligari to Casablanca*, 2nd ed. (Pacific Grove, CA: The Boxwood Press, 1993), 207.

[27] Moreover, he was a star during an era in British cinema in which "the star was a major determinant in [an audience member's] choice of film" (Sue Harper, "'Thinking Forward and Up': The British Films of Conrad Veidt," *The Unknown 1930s: An Alternative History of the British Cinema 1929–1939*, ed. Jeffrey Richards [London: I. B. Tauris, 1998], 121–37, 121). John Sedgwick shows that Veidt was the fourth most popular movie star appearing in British films between 1932 and 1937 ("Cinema-going Preferences in Britain in the 1930s," *The Unknown 1930s*, 1–35, 18).

[28] Theodore Strauss, "The Return of the Somnambulist," *New York Times* May 12, 1940: 135 (X3). Andrew Moor alludes to *The Spy in Black* as exploiting Veidt's "exotic, erotic and yet threatening potential" (*Powell and Pressburger: A Cinema of Magic Spaces* [London: I.B. Tauris, 2005], 37).

[29] Harper, "Thinking Forward," 135; "by" is italicized in the original. See also Pt. 2 (of 3) of Pat Wilks Battle's article on Veidt ("Conrad Veidt," *Films in Review* 44 5/6 [May/June 1993], 155–64).

[30] See Hubert Cole, "Conrad Veidt: Hero or Villain?" *Picturegoer* 9.467 (May 4, 1940): 19.

roles that Veidt has played in the past, and ... often expressed with great vehemence."[31]) Moreover, Veidt was widely recognized for his considerable sexual allure. A full-page advertisement in the February 27, 1935, issue of *Variety* asserts: "Women Fight for Conrad Veidt ... The Man's Man ... The Perfect Ladies' Man." Amusingly, Veidt's name is presented in large caps while the Gaumont-British film project that the ad is putatively touting appears only, and in much smaller letters, as "(Title Later)."[32] As the advertisement suggests, the precise nature of the project is less important than the identity of the famous actor who will star in it.

The centrality of Veidt to Pressburger's original conception of the film is apparent in the "skeleton treatment" of *Spy* that is housed in the British Film Institute's Special Collections.[33] This treatment was completed between October and December 1938. Veidt is identified by name rather than character, and he is the only actor explicitly referenced in the document. Moreover, the very plot of the film plays upon the combination of allure and menace that is central to Veidt's star persona: on the one hand, he is a German enemy out to disable the British Grand Fleet; on the other, he is charismatic and attractive, both "man's man" and "ladies' man." This is made most obvious in the treatment's handling of the scene between Hardt and Tiel on the night before the fatal rendezvous of the U-boats and British cruisers: "His gaiety and charm are irresistible. It is difficult to tell how she feels towards him. Certainly she must feel something, but she has herself under control, that is as much under control as it is possible for a young lady to be, who is alone with Conrad Veidt at midnight."[34] Even a British spy masquerading as a German one must feel the sexual pull of Veidt's enemy agent. Moreover, in describing Veidt's effect on Fraulein Tiel/Jill Blacklock, Pressburger also indirectly alludes to the impact the German star is expected to produce on moviegoers who identify with Hobson's character (Figure 1.1).

In its interweaving of espionage and romance, *The Spy in Black* not only takes full advantage of Veidt's star persona but also reveals a debt (that it shares with *Contraband*) to Alfred Hitchcock's great thrillers of the 1930s, perhaps most notably *The 39 Steps* (1935).[35] While Andrew Moor and others have perceptively written about the nature of that debt, one fundamental aspect of it has gone unexamined. Robin Wood has noted of

---

[31]Hubert Cole, "Conrad Veidt Replies," *Picturegoer* 9.469 (May 18, 1940): 11.
[32]*Variety* 117.11 (February 27, 1935), 14. The untitled film does not seem to have been made. It was widely thought that Veidt was underutilized during his years with Gaumont-British, a charge that then-studio head Michael Balcon vigorously contested ("What We Did With Conrad Veidt," *Film Weekly* 18.449 [May 22, 1937]: 11).
[33]All quotations are derived from Emeric Pressburger, *The Spy in Black*, Treatment #2, ITM-18465 (Item S-24, Box 1 of the Michael Powell Collection).
[34]Ibid., Scene 22.
[35]See Moor, *Powell and Pressburger*, 30; Scott Salwolke, *The Films of Michael Powell and the Archers* (Lanham, MD and London: The Scarecrow Press, 1997), 57.

FIGURE 1.1 *Conrad Veidt, man's man and ladies' man, in* The Spy in Black *(1939)*.

Hitchcock's "double chase" films, of which *The 39 Steps* is the foundational example, that the espionage plot typically is "a cover for the film's real concerns with gender relations and sexuality."[36] In applying Wood's point about Hitchcockian narrative norms to Powell and Pressburger's film, we would modify it slightly and suggest that *Spy* interweaves the espionage and romance plots in a way that makes neither of them completely coherent without the other.[37] This is because, as we suggested earlier, the foundational difference in the film's narrative is not primarily *national* in nature—Germany versus England—but *occupational* or *vocational*—sailor versus spy.[38] As Moor nicely articulates it, Hardt is "dispatched into a spy genre" in which his military identity, predicated upon precision, duty, and self-regulation,

---

[36]Robin Wood, *Hitchcock's Films Revisited* (1989; New York: Columbia University Press, 2002), 275–87, 275.
[37]It should be pointed out that the narrative norm Wood identifies with Hitchcock is close kindred to a key element of the classical Hollywood film: "The classical film has at least two lines of action, both causally linking the same group of characters. Almost invariably, one of these lines of action involves heterosexual romantic love" (David Bordwell, "The Classical Hollywood Style, 1917–1960," *The Classical Hollywood Cinema: Film Style and Mode of Production to 1960*, ed. Bordwell, Janet Staiger and Kristin Thompson [New York: Columbia University Press, 1985], 1–84, 16). On Hitchcock's British films and classical cinema, see Tom Ryall, *Alfred Hitchcock and the British Cinema* (1986; London: Athlone Press, 1996), 141–67.
[38]It is interesting to note that one appreciative contemporary description of Veidt's performance and Hardt's character ignores entirely the latter's stint as unwilling spy: "He is throughout a tragic if slightly sinister figure, and wins respect and sympathy as a patriot with the qualities most admirable and admired in soldier, sailor, or airman of any nationality—loyalty, courage, obedience, and steadfast endurance" (E.P., Review of *The Spy in Black*, *Monthly Film Bulletin* 6.61 [March, 1939]: 41).

is jeopardized.[39] More specifically, the narrative of *Spy* can be broken into three parts, each of which can be coordinated to changes in the nature of Commander Hardt's identity. In the first part, we are introduced to Hardt the accomplished U-boat commander. The second part presents us with Hardt the reluctant spy, tugged back and forth between his military identity and what he ironically but tellingly calls the "comfortable profession" of espionage. The comforts promised by spying are both gustatory and sexual, and his desire for Fraulein Tiel is a catalyst for Hardt's oscillations. As for the film's final part, it is marked by Hardt's discovery that he has been duped, his escape disguised as a minister, and his resumption of naval command, albeit of the *St. Magnus* rather than U-boat 29; most importantly, his return to maritime authority coincides with the kind of articulation of national difference conventionally associated with wartime propaganda.

Hardt the Accomplished U-boat Commander

In a perceptive close reading of the first four minutes of *Spy*, Charles Barr has argued that the film "sets up its own series of 'founding lacks'"[40]— most importantly, the food, sex, and tobacco that are denied to Hardt and Lieutenant Felix Schuster (Marius Goring). Food is first referenced by way of a newspaper headline proclaiming that "England [Is] Starving." A German officer at the lobby desk of the Hotel Kieler Hof whistles at the headline, then picks up the newspaper for a closer review. A second officer looks over his shoulder, then asks, "Well, is it true?," at which point the first man hands the paper to him. We can easily make out the large subheadline "Immediate Success of 'Sink On Sight' Policy," as well as a portion of the article's first line, which the second man reads aloud: "We learn from a reliable source that following on the success of our glorious U-boats, it has been decided . . ." As to what exactly has been decided, that remains a mystery: a significant portion of the article is blacked out, with the word "censored" emblazoned across it. The first man then wryly comments, "So now we know, sir," to the amusement of his superior officer (Figure 1.2).

Beyond introducing the subject of German U-boats sinking food supply ships, this moment in the film emphasizes two things: first, the question of the veracity of what is printed in the Kiel newspaper; and second, government censorship of the press, to which the officers respond with ironic familiarity. Neither seems terribly surprised that what "has been decided" by those in

---

[39]Moor, *Powell and Pressburger*, 33. Moor's emphasis is on the Gothic dimensions of the film.
[40]Charles Barr, "The First Four Minutes," *The Cinema of Michael Powell: International Perspectives on an English Film-Maker*, ed. Ian Christie and Andrew Moor (London: BFI Publishing, 2005), 20–35, 22.

FIGURE 1.2 *Censored German newspaper in* The Spy in Black *(1939)*.

authority has not been shared with the German people, while the superior officer inquires about the truth of the headline. The propaganda point is two-pronged, suggesting both that newspapers don't necessarily print the truth and that the government restricts the dissemination of news.[41] Moreover, the episode's emphasis on a famished England resonates ironically with scenes later in the film in which we learn that Britain, or at least the portion of it represented by the Orkneys, is far from starving.

Later in this scene, we discover that putative British scarcity finds its match in the restaurant of the Kieler Hof Hotel. What is abundant in the hotel is the promise of sexual activity: a couple of self-identified newlyweds eagerly request, and are granted, a room before the husband is to ship out the next day; a German officer asks the front desk clerk to send a woman named Lottie to his room for "another manicure," which request a listening sailor greets with a knowing expression; and a young woman grabs Schuster ("Felix, darling!") as he and Hardt are ushered to their restaurant table. However, Hardt insists to his junior officer that sex should take a back seat to supper; like cigar smoking, Hardt suggests, romance should come "*after* dinner." (The progression from food to sex and tobacco will be playfully but significantly reworked later in the film.) While the sailors postpone sex for food, they are soon discouraged to learn that their culinary options are far from appetizing. Having subsisted on tinned rations on their most

---

[41] On the British Second World War home front, the veracity of news services like that of the BBC was a point of pride, although the need for some degree of censorship was widely understood.

recent sixteen-day mission, Hardt and Schuster eagerly anticipate a feast, only to discover that the hotel restaurant's offerings are both limited and unappealing. The irony here is not lost on the two sailors, whose U-boat, we learned moments earlier, was responsible for the sinking of four British food ships. As Hardt bitterly puts it, "we pave the sea with the finest food the world produces, and when we return to port, they give us boiled fish and carrots." Moreover, Hardt and Schuster's desires for sex and food are to be further postponed. A messenger catches up with Hardt and tells him that he and his junior officer are both wanted for another U-boat mission.

This opening scene has two primary functions. The first, as Barr notes, is to establish narrative "lacks" to be at least partially fulfilled later in the film. If Hardt is denied food here, British agriculture ironically comes to the rescue later when Fraulein Tiel presents him with a feast that gives the lie to German propaganda. Moreover, and as we shall discuss further, the satiation of hunger in that scene exists in close conceptual relation to the promise of sexual satiety. The second and more important function is to construct a particular model of martial masculinity that is predicated upon both a hierarchy of needs—sustenance before not only sex but also tobacco and sleep—and, more significantly, the subordination of even those needs, as well as one's desire, to duty. While this is clear enough in the film, it is made even more apparent in Pressburger's skeleton treatment. In the completed film, an amorous woman approaches Schuster in the restaurant. In the treatment, however, Hardt (or Veidt) is the object of attraction:

> The table next to them contains a cocotte, who has just finished dinner, and is amused by the two men and attracted by Veidt. She goes out ahead of him, and they enter the lift together. He notices her and wakes up. She has an appointment with another officer, but she leaves him and goes with Veidt. As they enter his room the messenger from headquarters is waiting for him, with orders to report immediately.[42]

Whereas here the "cocotte" and Veidt take the lift together, only to meet the messenger in Veidt's room, in the film Hardt enters the lift alone and is identified there by the messenger. The treatment offers clear evidence of Pressburger's intention to capitalize on Veidt's sexual allure (while the "cocotte" is presumably a prostitute, the fact that she opts for Hardt over "another officer" attests to the former's magnetism). However, somewhere between the treatment and the film's completion the decision was made to make Commander Hardt so thoroughly a man of duty that indications of his sexual desire needed to be relocated onto Schuster. The effect is to

---

[42]Pressburger, "Treatment #2," Scene 2.

make Hardt's infatuation with Fraulein Tiel seem a stark deviation from his previous behavior.

Hardt the Reluctant Spy

Much as sex and duty are opposed in the film's first part, so are espionage and military service in its second one. Hardt's insistence upon wearing his naval uniform attests to his tenacity in clinging to his military identity. Clouston's novel provides a practical reason for this: Conrad von Belke, the book's analogue to Hardt, thinks that were he to be caught in uniform, he would be taken prisoner rather than shot as a spy.[43] In the film, Hardt gives a different reason, asserting that, if he is to be shot, it will be "as an officer, not as a spy." (Hardt's reservations about espionage are registered on more than one occasion.) However, one can also read his dangerous insistence on remaining in uniform as an extension of the logic developed in the film's opening scene: in clinging to his military identity, Hardt also performs the subordination of his appetites to both his duty and his mission.[44]

Now, this reading may seem odd insofar as Hardt's desire for Fraulein Tiel is not incommensurate with the terms of that mission. After all, Tiel is not attempting to distract Hardt from his objectives; she is, instead, his superior, as well as the orchestrator of the plot that he is helping to carry out. Moreover, the film does not suggest that the erotic tension between Tiel and Hardt comes at the expense of his mission. Indeed, unlike in the Hotel Kieler Hof, Hardt's satiety is not antithetical to his duty. This is made plain in a key sequence in the Scottish schoolhouse. After first meeting Tiel, with whom he speaks in German, Hardt enters the schoolhouse and, to the accompaniment of suspenseful music, proceeds to investigate it. Upon returning to the main room, his eyes widen, and the music quickens. The viewer's impression is that Hardt has identified a danger that, as a cut to Tiel's puzzled face suggests, has eluded his companion. The music climaxes just as he lifts to his nose a glass bowl; closing his eyes, he contentedly sighs, "Butter." The promise of gustatory satisfaction, represented by the block of butter, is tied to its sexual counterpart only seconds later when Hardt, who focuses on Tiel for the first time, looks her up and down appreciatively. Perhaps coincidentally, his scrutiny comes at the same time they start speaking in English. Shortly thereafter, Hardt digs into the meal Tiel has prepared for them. "A whole ham, white bread, and butter," he declaims while excitedly rubbing his hands;

---

[43] J. Storer Clouston, *The Spy in Black* (New York: George H. Doran, 1918), 15.
[44] "The theme of clothing and identity is returned to in the film's concluding section. Hardt is dressed as the Reverend Harris when he seizes control of the *St. Magnus*. When he identifies himself to the ship's captain as a German naval officer, the captain replies, "In those clothes?"

he also offers a comment on British abundance that casts an ironic light on his own U-boat's past activities: "These English are a long time feeling the pinch."

The next short sequence is worth attending to closely. Hardt gleefully cuts into the ham while Tiel looks on. We then get a close-up of Hardt's hands as he slices off a large piece of butter, then another of them again carving the ham, which is now noticeably smaller. This elliptical representation of the couple consuming their meal concludes with a close-up of Hardt and Tiel in profile. In this shot, the two lean in towards one another as Hardt lights Tiel's cigarette with the tip of his own. This is followed by a medium shot in which both, now in the living room, lie back contentedly, and synchronously, into their respective chairs. "I had no idea that secret agents were such a comfortable profession," Hardt ungrammatically says. When he states this, Hardt is in his uniform, having shortly before made his declaration about being shot "as an officer, not as a spy." He might be referring to this "comfortable profession" as Tiel's alone. And yet, he has just embarked upon a life of espionage—and just partaken of some of its comforts—so his comment serves to acknowledge the potential benefits to him of his new position. Hardt's statement is at least partly a joke, but it advances the vocational theme introduced earlier and scrambles the relationship between duty, need, and pleasure articulated at the film's outset. In the Hotel Kieler Hof, Hardt the U-boat commander is called upon to put duty before both needs and pleasures; here, at the outset of his brief career as a spy, Hardt's mission—his duty—coincides with his indulgence in both food and tobacco (Figure 1.3).

Sex shadows the scene we have just discussed in a somewhat contradictory fashion. If earlier in the film tobacco and sex are figured as postprandial activities, both of which are to be subordinated to duty, here, upon completion

FIGURE 1.3 *Captain Hardt and Fraulein Tiel in* The Spy in Black *(1939)*.

of their meal, the two spies turn to tobacco. The close-up of Hardt lighting Tiel's cigarette is highly eroticized. Both on its own terms and in light of the logic developed in the Kieler Hof Hotel scene—food, tobacco, then romance—this shot is suffused with the promise of sex. The next moment, however, evokes the postcoital when Hardt and Tiel contentedly recline in their chairs.[45] Obviously, Powell and Pressburger are having some fun here playing with cinematic codes. What is important about such play, however, is the way in which it constructs espionage as the arena in which the film's "founding lacks" can be addressed. For Hardt, the female spy he meets in Scotland would seem to fulfill needs and desires that have heretofore been either antithetical to his duty or (in the case of food) unattainable within Germany. On the one hand, the shot of postcoital satisfaction is a *joke*: the satiety provided by food and tobacco is a stand-in for that provided by sex; on the other, it is a *promise*, as sex is what espionage seemingly has to offer Hardt, alongside and as part of his reconfigured sense of duty.[46] Indeed, much of the film is given over to his intertwined pursuit, first, of a victory over the British Navy and, second, of Fraulein Tiel herself.

It should also be noted that Hardt's twin pursuits are bound up in the fact that he is Tiel's subordinate. The eating scene is followed by a brief power struggle: Hardt asks to know the plan and, when Tiel states that he will be told of it the next day, he turns his request into a demand. Tiel rebuffs that demand by making Hardt rehearse his orders, which require that he be completely obedient to her. "Exactly," she replies. "Now pick up your motorbike and go to bed." Hardt's reply—"Do I take it to bed with me?"—suggests he was hoping for a different companion, and Tiel's locking him in his room, ostensibly because of a housekeeper's arrival the following morning, further advances the sexual theme. Her command over Hardt extends to the regulation of his sexual desires. At the same time, Powell and Pressburger intimate that Hardt's subordination to Tiel, while antithetical to his commanding presence heretofore in the film, increases his ardor for her. Being a spy under Tiel's authority both threatens his military identity and intensifies Hardt's desire for her. To put it another way, the U-boat commander finds pleasure in being commanded.

If Tiel's authority over Hardt extends to the simultaneous curtailing and provoking of his erotic ambitions, it's worth noticing that Tiel's sexual desirability plays a larger role in the film. Critics have neglected an

---

[45]This is one of several moments early in the film in which the blocking and framing of Veidt and Hobson work to suggest a romantic connection between them even before Hardt first declares his attraction to Tiel. Another such moment occurs when Hardt and Tiel sit together on a window seat, with legs almost touching, to examine the British fleet.
[46]This promise is intimated again moments later when Hardt gazes longingly at Tiel's silk-stockinged legs. Britain is associated not only with food but also with consumer goods like those stockings, which Hardt tells us are unavailable in Germany.

important element of the representation of both Tiel and "Anne Burnett": she is an independent, unchaperoned single woman living by herself in a remote schoolhouse. The Reverend Hector Matthews recognizes the significance of this when he tries to convince "Anne Burnett" that "It would be highly improper for so young a girl" to live alone at the schoolhouse. While Matthews's motives seem partly mercenary—he wants to convince "Burnett" to be a paying lodger at his house—they are also clearly animated by a sense of sexual propriety. Similarly, Matthews's outrage at "Burnett" and her fiancé, the Reverend John Harris, putatively skipping the dinner to which Matthews had invited them is fueled by both parsimony and concern about what the unwed couple is getting up to alone in the schoolhouse. A scene from Pressburger's treatment that does not make it into the film develops this point further. In that scene, Tiel is away from the schoolhouse, awaiting, along with Ashington, Hardt's return from the U-boat. "The Reverend Matthews, whose mind is now full of monstrous suspicions about the pretty school-mistress and the foolish young clergyman, arrives with the firm intention of dealing with the situation."[47] Upon entering the schoolhouse, he hears noises emanating from an upstairs room. These are the sounds of Burnett's fiancé struggling to free himself from his bonds, but Matthews takes them to be aural evidence of lovemaking. So, while "Matthews has [in fact] discovered nothing, . . . the reputations of the school-mistress and her fiancé will evidently be down the drain."[48] In both Powell and Pressburger's film and Pressburger's treatment, the Reverend Matthews is recognizably a prig, which means his puritanical attitude toward sex is not to be taken as authoritative. Nevertheless, Matthews draws our attention to something of central significance to *The Spy in Black*, which is that the site of espionage in the film is one that is presided over by a single woman who, over the course of the film, has multiple male visitors.[49]

If the central romantic business of the film is Hardt's pursuit of Tiel, that pursuit is mirrored in the actions of two other characters, Lieutenant Ashington and Reverend Harris. In the case of Harris, the pursuit reads

---

[47]Pressburger, "Treatment #2," Scene 21.
[48]Ibid., Scene 22. In the film, Matthews is troubled by the notion that Harris, whom "Burnett" says has taken ill and has gone to bed, is alone with her, and he tries to convince "Burnett" that his wife should stay the night with the unwed couple. Importantly, an unnamed British naval officer dresses down Matthews near the end of the film for meddling with the Blacklocks' counterespionage efforts. His chastisement does the narrative work of transforming the potentially scandalous narrative of the unchaperoned single woman into a story of heroic daring and self-sacrifice.
[49]In Clouston's novel, the scandal of an unmarried woman entertaining multiple men plays out differently. Tiel is a man who, while harboring Belke, is visited by his putative sister, Eileen Burnett. Belke falls in love with Burnett and, unconvinced that she is really Tiel's sister, jealously references "her defiance of all conventionalities in living alone here with two men" (Clouston, *The Spy in Black*, 230).

as largely comic in nature because he comes to the remote Scottish village to see Anne Burnett, not "Anne Burnett." It is worth noting that while the real Anne Burnett has supposedly been murdered, the shadow of that fact doesn't darken these scenes, partly because of Harris's slightly bumbling nature but also because of the fundamentally comic scenario created by his arrival. When Harris appears at the schoolhouse, awkwardly hauling a gramophone, he is greeted not only by "Burnett"/Tiel but also by her two male visitors. There is a faint whiff of the sex farce in all this: the goodly reverend arrives to discover his fiancée entertaining two unfamiliar men—and one in a German uniform! The difference, of course, is that Harris does not recognize his fiancée in "Anne Burnett." Instead, he encounters his betrothed's sinister double without realizing it—a double who, insofar as she is not the real Anne Burnett, may not be betraying him but is apparently betraying Britain.

The connections between sexual and national betrayal are more explicit and significant in the relationship between Ashington and Tiel. The bibulous Ashington's main reason for conveying British naval secrets to the Germans is bitterness about his demotion after a drunken incident in which he jeopardized a destroyer under his command. However, Tiel also intimates that she has been sleeping with Ashington in order to secure his cooperation—an action she justifies in nationalist terms (the high price for Ashington's cooperation has been paid by Germany, she says, "and me"). When both Hardt and the audience first see Ashington and Tiel together, they are holding hands. If espionage offers Hardt the promise of satisfaction, it also requires that he negotiate the fact of Tiel's other liaisons. More immediately, Hardt and Ashington are established not only as natural enemies—members of warring navies—but as rivals for Tiel's affections. This rivalry lies at the heart of the film's twinned romance and espionage plots. However, whereas Tiel acknowledges an affair with Ashington, an enemy of her country, it is her relationship with Hardt that the film emphasizes. Moreover, their attraction to one another is commensurate with their shared loyalty to Germany. This all changes, of course, when the eavesdropping Hardt learns that the Blacklocks are masquerading as Fraulein Tiel and Lieutenant Ashington; husband and wife are both British spies, albeit of an amateur variety. Tiel's dubious affair with Ashington is thus recast as the marriage of the Blacklocks, whereas it is Jill Blacklock's relationship with Hardt that she developed for the good of her country. The devastating effect of this revelation on Hardt is brilliantly conveyed through Veidt's anguished facial expressions as he overhears the exchange between the Blacklocks.[50] Certainly, his anguish can be primarily attributed to the fact that he has

---

[50] To be more precise, Hardt does not discover that the Blacklocks are married until Jill informs him of this on the *St. Magnus*.

unwittingly put his and some other U-boats in what will prove to be fatal danger, but it is also motivated by the revelation that it is he, not Ashington, whose romantic feelings have been exploited by "Fraulein Tiel."

In suggesting that Hardt's desire for Tiel has undermined his martial identity, we might seem to be suggesting that Tiel plays the role of *femme fatale* to that of Hardt's ensnared victim. However, such a view does not do justice to the complexity of this scenario. As we have seen, part of Tiel's allure for Hardt seems to reside in the fact that she functions as his superior in the German espionage scheme. For example, on the early morning of the encounter between the U-boats and destroyers, Hardt tells Tiel, "I've served under many commanders, but none that I admire more than you." He says this shortly after fantasizing about the two of them celebrating their victory together in Germany. Moor has written persuasively about the anxiety attendant upon Hardt's "masquerade" as a spy, but he does not account for the possibilities for satisfaction created by the sailor's role-playing as a spy.[51]

If Hardt finds pleasure in his subordination to Tiel, she and Jill Blacklock are both attracted to the German commander. While Tiel's attraction to Hardt is compatible with their shared mission, Jill's is obviously not; it comes in spite of Hardt's status as her nation's enemy, not to mention her own marital status. Thus, when Pressburger writes in his treatment about the way in which (the as-yet-to-be-named) Jill Blacklock keeps herself under control—or at least "as much under control as it is possible for a young lady to be, who is alone with Conrad Veidt at midnight"—he references the intertwined issues of sexual desire and both national and matrimonial loyalty. Were she to lose control entirely, she would betray both her husband and her country. Needless to say, Jill does not do this, although she does share a passionate kiss with the German officer.[52] Moreover, the film registers the fact that her loyalty is at odds with her desire for Hardt when she hastily departs the island in order to avoid witnessing his arrest.[53]

Hardt's Return to Command

That the second part of *The Spy in Black* traffics in adopted identities, doubles, and triangulated erotic relationships tells us that the film comes close to the terrain not only of Gothic, as Andrew Moor has argued, but also of

---

[51] Moor, *Powell and Pressburger*, 33.
[52] Macdonald rightly observes that Hobson's character "is caught between admiration for her magnetic and charming enemy and the rather limited appeal of her impotent-sounding husband Ashington" (*Emeric Pressburger*, 149).
[53] She also "feel[s] rather sick" at the thought of the U-boats being reduced to, in her husband's words, "just a few spots of grease."

romantic comedy. However, there is a decisive shift away from comedy that begins when Hardt learns the truth about both the Ashingtons and the threat to the U-boats that he has unwittingly helped to engender. The culminating moment occurs on the *St. Magnus* when Hardt sheds his disguise as the Reverend Harris. In engaging in an act of what we might call national cross-dressing by taking on the identity of a British reverend, Hardt also mimics Jill Blacklock's performance as a German spy. It is this act of mimicry, as well as the characters' shedding of their disguises, that we need to keep in mind if we want to understand their resonant exchange below decks on the *St. Magnus*.

After seizing control of the ship with the aid of eight German prisoners whom he liberates while still in the guise of the Reverend Harris, Hardt commandeers the captain's cabin of the *St Magnus*, in which Jill Blacklock had been temporarily ensconced. While their conversation is focused on the war, the two spar in the manner of recently estranged lovers. When Jill expresses alarm at his plan to race to Sandwick Bay to warn the U-boats—an endeavor that would take them through a minefield and endanger the civilians on board—Hardt sardonically observes, "I am no longer under your orders." The most important part of their exchange, though, centers upon clarifying the terms of national difference:

> Hardt: "We are at war. Perhaps you forget that, as I did for a while. You are English. I am German. We are enemies."
> J. Blacklock: "I like that better."
> Hardt: "And I. It simplifies everything."

Andrew Moor argues that this exchange "mark[s] a shift in the text back to a clearly demarcated conflict-based drama and away from a plot which has been so complicated that points of identification have begun to crumble."[54] In suggesting that he forgot for a time that he was at war, Hardt intimates that his stint as a spy, as well as his infatuation with Fraulein Tiel, constituted an abdication of his military responsibilities. He then proceeds to assert a clear nation-based antagonism between himself and Jill, one that she claims to "like better." One assumes she expresses here a preference for honest antagonism over the dishonest alliance with Hardt that she cultivated in the guise of Fraulein Tiel. Hardt concurs that such honesty "simplifies everything."

Of course, it is reductive to suggest that Hardt and Jill Blacklock are no more than enemies; their attraction to one another belies that point. Moreover, this scene does not state the preexisting animosity of natural foes as much as it performs it. What Moor has described as Hardt's "masquerade" as a spy here comes to an end, just as Jill Blacklock's recently has; Hardt

---

[54] Moor, *Powell and Pressburger*, 41.

doffs the ministerial garb of the Reverend Harris and reveals the naval uniform underneath at the very moment that this exchange occurs. For Hardt, reasserting his Germanness and remembering the war require that he both resume his military identity and renounce the satisfactions associated with both Britain and Fraulein Tiel.

The complexity of this scene is worth keeping in mind as one considers the place of propaganda in *The Spy in Black*. As we mentioned earlier, there are elements of the film that are well suited to wartime propaganda—we see this most obviously in the victory of the Royal Navy over the U-boats, and in the pluck and resourcefulness of those accidental spies, the Blacklocks. Moreover, the aforementioned exchange between Hardt and Jill affirms the primacy of national difference in a way that seems admirably suited to Britain's wartime footing: "You are English. I am German. We are enemies." Additionally, this exchange immediately follows a discussion of Hardt's willingness to endanger the civilians on the *St. Magnus* in order to rescue the U-boats in Sandwick Bay. In this instant, Hardt comes closest to the ruthless German familiar from British First World War propaganda.[55] To put it another way, after declaring his Germanness, we see Hardt become more stereotypically German than ever before, and less like the figure of the "good German" we will encounter in Powell and Pressburger's later films.[56]

All that being said, when taken as a whole *The Spy in Black* undermines a simplistic view of national difference, most obviously by grounding the statement of animosity between Hardt and Jill Blacklock in a narrative of romantic betrayal in which the characters have adopted identities other than their own. Additionally, even after the battle lines have been so clearly drawn, we see evidence of their smudging. In the final shots of the film, Jill Blacklock watches the sinking of the *St Magnus* from a lifeboat with a stricken expression on her face; her sorrow at Hardt's death registers far more powerfully than does her relief at spotting her husband aboard the rescue ship that has come for her and her fellow passengers.

It is not only through its romantic narrative that *The Spy in Black* belies the simplicity of Hardt and Jill's exchange in the captain's cabin of the *St. Magnus*. As we have seen, Powell and Pressburger's film was written as a vehicle for its German-born star. This is just one of the ways in which the making of this British movie depended upon collaboration with German and German-speaking film personnel—a topic about which we will have more to say in the next chapter.[57] Indeed, in creating a heroic role for Conrad Veidt

---

[55] On the legacy of First World War British propaganda in the Second World War, see the introduction to Fox, *Film Propaganda*.
[56] There are limits to what he is willing to do, however; he spares an infant from a general order that any of the captured passengers who make noise will be shot.
[57] For a recent, thorough treatment of this topic, see Tobias Hochscherf, *The Continental Connection: German-speaking Émigrés and British Cinema, 1927–1945* (Manchester:

that brings his character to Scotland, the Hungarian-born, UFA-trained Pressburger must have been reminded of his own complex assimilation into Britain and its film industry. "You are English. I am German. We are enemies." These are lines that, when it came to himself or countless other continental émigrés working in British film, Pressburger would not subscribe to. Indeed, the sentiment they articulate is one that Powell and Pressburger would later contest in *The Life and Death of Colonel Blimp* (1943).[58]

If in its final act *The Spy in Black* comes closest to anticipating the fervent nationalism one might expect from wartime propaganda, it is important to show how the film frames and contextualizes such expressions of nationalism: as an English woman's and German man's angry denial of the affinity between them. To put it another way, this moment is marked by the refusal of the cosmopolitan values that, as we stated in the Introduction, would come to be a part of The Archers' propaganda program. In this regard, Pressburger could be seen in his screenplay as trying to set the tone for their cinematic propaganda to come. In anticipation of future Manichean articulations of national difference, and in repudiation of First World War propaganda efforts, the émigré Pressburger humanizes and valorizes the German as well as the Englishwoman. As if to emblematize this fact, the film concludes with an image that manifests its broader confounding of national difference: that of Captain Hardt standing at attention on the deck of the sinking *St. Magnus*. The nature of Hardt's demise makes narrative sense insofar as he has taken command of the ship, claiming it as a German vessel. In doing so, however, he is misrecognized by his own crewmen as a British officer. What's important here is not merely that Hardt is killed by his own men; it is also that he mimics the role of the heroic British captain going down with his ship. For all of the moment's ironies, the key point is that the film presents the audience with an iconic image of naval leadership in extremis, with the wrinkle being that it is the noble German officer who dies a heroic death.

"What Had Never Been Intended as Propaganda Suddenly Took on That Role"

In the first volume of his autobiography, Powell comments upon the way in which *The Spy in Black* was both at odds with Britain's new wartime footing

---

Manchester University Press, 2011). For a focus on Veidt, see Harper, "Thinking Forward"; and Gerd Gemünden, "Allegories of Displacement: Conrad Veidt's British Films," *Destination London: German-speaking Emigrés and British Cinema, 1925–1950*, ed. Tim Bergfelder and Christian Cargnelli (New York and Oxford: Berghahn Books, 2008), 142–54.

[58]In that film, of course, the German soldier and the English governess marry.

and able to benefit from it: "It didn't matter that [the film represented] the 1914-18 war. It didn't matter that the hero was a heroic German.... It was a war picture, all about submarines and spies, full of action and suspense, looking authentic. The British Navy triumphs in the end and it was all lovely!"[59] Pressburger's biographer Kevin Macdonald makes a similar point about his grandfather's first collaboration with Powell: "What had never been intended as propaganda suddenly took on that role."[60] While *The Spy in Black* cannot comfortably be considered a propaganda film, it would be naïve to think that Powell and Pressburger weren't contemplating impending war with Germany as they made it. Moreover, we have seen that at certain points *Spy* wanders, however fleetingly, onto the terrain of propaganda. It is interesting to note that Pressburger's treatment for the film went a good deal further in this vein by entertaining a question of great importance to the British in both world wars: When would the United States enter the fray? Whereas Veidt's yet-to-be-named character boldly proclaims that America will never fight, his female counterpart is not so sure. "She asks him if he has ever been to America and he says no. She says: 'I have. What they set themselves to do they do with all the strength and enthusiasm of a young people.'"[61] It is hard to imagine that Pressburger wasn't considering the future as well as the past when he penned these lines. As for the US Senate subcommittee chaired by Nye and Clark, this scene, had it appeared in the film, would doubtlessly have confirmed its worst fears about movies engineered to "turn [American audiences] loose on war." However, even if the scene had been included, *The Spy in Black* would fail to answer to Clark's somewhat hysterical vision of propaganda pictures designed to "infect the minds of their audiences with hatred, to inflame them, to arouse their emotions, and to make them clamor for war." (The same is true, of course, for The Archers' subsequent wartime films.) For our purposes, the central point is that *The Spy in Black* is *not* a propaganda film by design. And yet for all that, the film's intermittent engagement with the theme of propaganda offers faint intimations of the complex part that Powell and Pressburger's later work would play in the British war effort.

---

[59]Powell, *A Life*, 335–6. Interestingly, evidence derived from Mass Observation suggests that most film exhibitors failed to capitalize on the sudden timeliness of the film; see *Mass-Observation at the Movies*, ed. Jeffrey Richards and Dorothy Sheridan (London and New York: Routledge and Kegan Paul, 1987), 147.
[60]Macdonald, *Emeric Pressburger*, 158. An unidentified contemporary reviewer notes: "This picture has acquired topical interest since it was suggested by the ruthless U-boat campaign of 1917, which has a special application to the submarine campaign being waged in the present war" (*Picturegoer & Film Weekly*, October 14, 1939; quoted from *The Powell and Pressburger Pages*, https://powell-pressburger.org/Reviews/39_SiB/index.html [accessed February 8, 2023]).
[61]Pressburger, "Treatment #2," Scene 22.

2

"Taking the War Against Hitler"

Blockade and Blackout in *Contraband*

Whereas *The Spy in Black* (1939) is a thriller that tentatively engages the theme of propaganda, *Contraband* (1940) was produced in consultation with the Ministry of Information in its early days of dubious efficacy.[1] What is most striking about *Contraband* in comparison with subsequent Powell and Pressburger features such as *49th Parallel* (1941) or *One of Our Aircraft Is Missing* (1942) is the imperfect fit between the film as a work of entertainment and as a piece of propaganda. Indeed, one can distinguish in it two distinct plots. The first, which is preeminent early in the film, centers on the operations of contraband patrols in British ports. Much of this plot would be at home in a Crown Film Unit documentary, and it also accords well with the MOI Films Division's interest in features that demonstrate "How Britain fights."[2] The second plot is a Hitchcockian romantic spy thriller that transpires not, like *Spy*, on Britain's periphery, but in the blacked-out metropole of London. For ease of reference, we will identify these, respectively, as the "blockade" and the "blackout" plots. While it would be fair to say that *Contraband*'s propaganda function is largely performed by way of the blockade plot, and that the blackout plot is

---

[1] Kevin Macdonald, *Emeric Pressburger: The Life and Death of a Screenwriter* (1994; London: Faber and Faber, 1996), 160. The Admiralty, Ministry of Economic Warfare, and the MOI are all thanked in the film's opening credits.

[2] The Programme, which we discuss in the Introduction, mentions *Contraband*, then still in production, as an example of a feature film that shows this. See "Programme for Film Propaganda," *Powell Pressburger and Others*, ed. Ian Christie (London: BFI Publishing, 1978), 121–4, 122.

dominated by romance and espionage, it would be simplistic to draw sharp, absolute distinctions between them. Most notably, the German spy network we encounter in the latter plot serves as the doppelganger to the smoothly functioning British naval authorities we encounter in the former one. The broader point to make, though, is that *Contraband* is best approached as Powell and Pressburger's fledgling effort at crafting an artistically and commercially successful work of cinematic propaganda.

Both *Contraband*'s blockade plot and the film as a whole begin with harbor footage of (the fictional town of) Eastgate-on-Sea in November 1939. A message, conveyed via Morse code, appears on the screen: the Danish freighter *Helvig* is to be detained and examined. Aboard the *Helvig*, we witness a clash of wills between Captain Hans Anderson (Conrad Veidt) and Mrs. Sorenson (Valerie Hobson), who has refused to obey the Captain's order to wear a life jacket. At the moment that Anderson is about to force the issue, he is interrupted by the appearance of a British patrol boat. The *Helvig* is boarded and inspected for contraband, and we learn that the ship is bearing badly needed medical supplies for neutral Denmark. As part of this general inspection, passport officers interview the passengers. By this means, we are introduced to Mr. Pidgeon (Esmond Knight), a talent scout for variety acts, and we learn that Mrs. Sorenson, who lives in America, is traveling to see her daughter. Anderson and his First Officer Axel Skold (Hay Petrie) agree to dine that night with the British officers and are given travel passes for that purpose. They later realize that Pidgeon and Sorenson have stolen the passes and intend to journey to London by train. The two sailors sneak off the ship and row their way to port without being detected. While Skold joins the British officers, claiming his captain is sick, Anderson catches up with Sorenson; she tries to shake him, but he stays with her, intent on taking her back to the *Helvig* on a subsequent train. Thus commences the film's blackout plot, with the two characters navigating a city plunged into darkness by the war.

Anderson and Sorenson eventually make their way to The Three Vikings, a Danish restaurant run by Axel's brother, Erik (also played by Hay Petrie). After a meal, they go to visit her aunt, Mrs. Clayton, only to discover German agents are occupying her house. The agents take them to their underground headquarters, which the captives deduce is beneath a cinema and near a nightclub. It is there that Anderson learns that Mrs. Sorenson (also known as Margaret Clayton) is actually a British spy. The German spy master Van Dyne (Raymond Lovell) discovers that Sorenson and Pidgeon have identified German ships masquerading as neutral; they had journeyed to London in the hope of conveying that information to the Admiralty Office. Instead, with our heroes tied up in spy headquarters, Van Dyne sets off to feed the Admiralty false information. Anderson subsequently escapes and travels back to the Three Vikings, where he enlists the aid of the Danish restaurant staff in locating the German headquarters. With their help, Anderson rescues Sorenson and defeats Van Dyne. The transition back to the blockade plot begins with Anderson, Pidgeon, and Sorenson reuniting on the train after she has returned from the Admiralty Office, having supplied it with the correct information about the German ships. The film concludes with a reprise of Anderson and Sorenson's initial conflict over the life jacket, only this time the two embrace rather than spar with one another.

In what follows, we will first discuss the role of continental émigrés, including Pressburger, in the British movie industry and in the making of the film. As part of our analysis of *Contraband*'s two plots, we will consider both the importance of the military blockade during the so-called "phoney war" period and the social and cultural impact of the blackout. If the blockade plot resembles that of a documentary about the success of the Ministry of Economic Warfare's contraband control operations, the blackout plot moves us onto the terrain of expressionism; it presents not only the defeat of the German spy network but also the way in which a Danish ship captain, with the aid of some of his countrymen, learns to navigate both the darkened city of London and his own feelings of inadequacy as a lover and a would-be spy. It is through the blackout plot, moreover, that Powell and Pressburger begin to develop some of the key themes of their propaganda program: cosmopolitanism, pluralism, and self-reflexivity.

Pressburger and Other Movie-making Exiles

The period leading up to the war found Emeric Pressburger searching for a way to aid his adopted country. Around the time of the Munich crisis, he wrote to the Ministry of Labour volunteering his services. When Britain finally entered the war, Pressburger learned that he was "to be put on the secret Central Register of Aliens with Special Skills and told to await notification of duties."[3] Eventually, of course, the determination was made that his contribution to the war effort would take the form of producing cinematic propaganda.

Pressburger's fierce desire to help Britain fight Germany, the country from which he fled in 1933, did not insulate him from the suspicious treatment extended to many exiles from Nazi rule. As Kevin Macdonald notes, "The week war was declared Emeric was asked to report to the Central Registry of Aliens, where his camera and wireless were confiscated and he was told to observe the aliens' curfew—home before twelve and report to the police once a week."[4] Even after Powell and Pressburger had established themselves as major filmmakers with a strong working relationship with

---

[3] Macdonald, *Emeric Pressburger*, 158.
[4] Ibid., 159.

the MOI, Pressburger faced constraints: for example, he was not allowed to travel to Kent for the shooting of *A Canterbury Tale* (1944).[5] And yet, he fared better than many of his fellow émigrés. Alfred Junge, the brilliant set designer and art director on several Powell and Pressburger films, had worked in Britain since the mid-1920s but nevertheless spent some of the war in an internment camp as an "enemy alien."[6]

Pressburger and Junge were not the only émigrés who relocated to Britain and found employment in its film industry. (They both worked on *Contraband*, along with their fellow exile Conrad Veidt.) Tobias Hochscherf has identified 400 German-speaking émigrés working in the British film industry during the period 1927–1945. This list includes, among other types of film personnel, directors (Berthold Viertel, E. A. Dupont), actors (Lilli Palmer, Anton Walbrook), producers (Alexander Korda, Erich Pommer), scriptwriters (Lajos Biró, Pressburger), art directors (Hein Heckroth, Junge), and cinematographers (Karl Freund, Günther Krampf). Moreover, the influence of these émigrés has led Hochscherf to assert that "many of the achievements of British cinema are to a great extent based upon the contributions of continental talent, which introduced pioneering camera techniques, rationalised production processes and increased the importance of mise-en-scène."[7] Hochscherf also notes that to enter into the British film industry was effectively to relocate to London, which "underwent a significant cultural transformation. Within less than a decade from the late 1920s to the late 1930s, its relatively small film business changed into a multi-cultural industry which not only made films for international consumption but also attracted many foreign staff."[8] There is little doubt that the influx of continental talent had a powerful positive impact on the quality of work produced by a film industry that, before its wartime golden age, was widely felt to be second-rate.[9]

---

[5] Michael Powell, *A Life in Movies* (1986; London: Faber & Faber, 2000), 443–4. See also Powell's discussion of Pressburger's arrest on returning from Canada for the shooting of *49th Parallel* (376).

[6] Tobias Hochscherf, *The Continental Connection: German-speaking Émigrés and British Cinema, 1927–1945* (Manchester: Manchester University Press, 2011), 172. For more on Junge, see also Sarah Street, "Extending Frames and Exploring Spaces: Alfred Junge, Set Design and Genre in British Cinema," *Destination London: German-speaking Emigres and British Cinema, 1925–1950*, ed. Tim Bergfelder and Christian Cargnelli (New York and Oxford: Berghahn Books, 2008), 100–10.

[7] Hochscherf, *The Continental Connection*, 2, 1. Kevin Gough-Yates puts it bluntly: "European exiles dominated British film production in the 1930s" ("Exiles and British Cinema," *The British Cinema Book*, 3rd ed., ed. Robert Murphy [London: Palgrave Macmillan for the BFI, 2009], 125–32, 125).

[8] Hochscherf, *The Continental Connection*, 2–3.

[9] On the negative valuation of the British film industry, see Charles Barr, "Introduction: Amnesia and Schizophrenia," *All Our Yesterdays: 90 Years of British Cinema*, ed. Barr (London: BFI Publishing, 1986), 1–29.

The fact that foreign-born personnel were abundant in the British film industry was not always greeted warmly. As Rachael Low has shown, throughout the 1930s the Association of Cine-Technicians (ACT), which became a trade union in 1934, consistently resisted the efforts of British studios to hire more foreign-born film professionals.[10] In an infamously xenophobic review of *The Marriage of Corbal* (1936), Graham Greene touches on the kind of labor-based argument advanced by the ACT, but Greene is most concerned by what he sees as a process of cultural contamination. Greene writes about "an English film unit . . . completely staffed by technicians of foreign blood"; and a "dark alien executive tipping his cigar ash behind the glass partition in Wardour Street."[11] Greene's anti-foreign (and perhaps, in its reference to an "alien executive" pulling the commercial strings, also antisemitic) depiction of a film industry infiltrated by "dark alien[s]" expresses an anxiety about the putative adulteration of English cultural products, as Greene makes apparent earlier in his review:

> But an English film? Is that a fair description of a picture derived from a novel by Rafael Sabatini, directed by Karl Grune and F. Brunn, photographed by Otto Kanturek, and edited by E. Stokvis, with a cast which includes Nils Asther, Ernst Deutsch and the American Noah Berry?[12]

It's striking that Greene does not identify the nationality of anyone except the American actor who, on the basis of his name, might be misrecognized by his British readers as "one of their own"; he lets the names of the other film personnel stand unadorned as emblems of their alterity, and of all that is antithetical to a *truly "English"* film.

Despite its hysterical nature, Greene's reaction to a "film unit . . . of foreign blood"— the very kind of "mixed crew of every nationality" that Powell boasted about working with[13]—making English movies anticipates a seeming contradiction of wartime cinematic production that we referenced in the Introduction. On the one hand, this is the historical moment at which, as various critics have argued, "a national cinema was born, encouraged by the need to stress unity and in recognition of the importance of film

---

[10]Rachael Low, *Film Making in 1930s Britain* (London: George Allen and Unwin, in assoc. w/ the British Film Institute, 1985), 27.
[11]Graham Greene, *The Graham Greene Film Reader: Reviews, Essays, Interviews and Film Stories*, ed. David Parkinson (New York: Applause Books, 1995), 107–9, 108, 109. The review was originally published in *The Spectator* on June 5, 1936.
[12]Ibid., 107.
[13]*Michael Powell Interviews*, ed. David Lazar (Jackson, MS: University Press of Mississippi, 2003), 107.

as propaganda."[14] On the other hand, that national cinema was enabled by continental émigrés and exiles, a phenomenon that was understood by some as a threat to the integrity of the nation. As Andrew Higson notes of Greene's review, "This extreme anxiety about 'cultural invasion' is typical of certain strands within 1930s British film culture. Asserting a very restricted understanding of English culture, it fails completely to recognise the potential benefits of such transnational influences, which clearly enrich British cinema's cultural repertoire."[15] Higson's point chimes with Hamid Naficy's influential postulation of an "accented" style of classical cinema that is marked by the participation of exiled film professionals in its making:

> [Accented films] are created with awareness of the vast histories of the prevailing cinematic modes.... From the cinematic traditions they acquire one set of voices, and from the exilic ... traditions they acquire a second. This double consciousness constitutes the accented style that not only signifies upon exile and other cinemas but also signifies the condition of exile itself.[16]

Especially through the depiction of the Danish émigré community in its blackout plot, *Contraband* is a film that "signifies the condition of exile" while also serving, however imperfectly, as a piece of British propaganda.[17]

The Blockade Plot and the "Phoney War"

As Michael Powell tells the story of *Contraband*'s making, the film's genesis was prompted by a combination of opportunism and the desire to contribute to the war effort. In the wake of *The Spy in Black*'s success and during the lull in film production that accompanied the beginning of the war, Powell told Pressburger: "We ought to follow [*Spy*] up.... With no films being made we ought to get Connie Veidt and Valerie Hobson for another picture

---

[14]Sarah Street, *British National Cinema*, 2nd ed. (London and New York: Routledge, 2009), 60.
[15]Andrew Higson, "The Instability of the National," *British Cinema, Past and Present*, ed. Justine Ashby and Andrew Higson (London and New York: Routledge, 2000), 35–47, 43.
[16]Hamid Naficy, *An Accented Cinema: Exilic and Diasporic Filmmaking* (Princeton, NJ: Princeton University Press, 2001), 22. Naficy differentiates between three types of accented films: exilic, diasporic, and ethnic. For purposes of clarity, we have omitted from this passage Naficy's reference to diasporic films.
[17]Gough-Yates discusses the Powell and Pressburger partnership as illustrating the influence of exiles on British film during the war ("Exiles and British Cinema," 128–30). It is interesting to note that, while Pressburger had promised the score to the Hungarian-born Miklós Rózsa, Powell wanted more English contributors on *Contraband* and forced his partner to accept Richard Addinsell as music composer (Powell, *A Life*, 341).

for peanuts."[18] Powell promptly took a vacation to the Isle of Skye and returned to discover that Pressburger, who was supposed to be mulling over the prospect of a follow-up, had "half written" the story for *Contraband*.[19] Whereas Alexander Korda had brought Powell, Pressburger, Hobson, and Veidt together for *The Spy in Black*, he played no role in *Contraband's* making. Instead, John Corfield of British National Films produced the film. British National was formed in 1934 by Corfield, Lady Annie Henrietta Yule, and J. Arthur Rank, a figure who would loom large in the histories of Powell and Pressburger and of British cinema more generally.[20] In his autobiography, Powell emphasizes that he recognized not only that the film provided "stunning" parts for Veidt and Hobson, but also that it had great propaganda potential: "[The film] explained how the Contraband Control was being operated against neutrals . . . I thrilled to my Kentish toes at the prospect of showing how my country . . . was already taking the war against Hitler . . . . We both saw a chance to prove once more that films can be a weapon of war."[21] What Powell does not mention is that Pressburger, according to Macdonald, wrote the story while "[l]iasing with the newly founded and still thoroughly disorganized Ministry of Information."[22] To the contrary, Powell's autobiography suggests The Archers' involvement with the MOI commences in the wake of *Contraband*.

While Powell revels in the idea that *Contraband* could serve as a weapon of war, Macdonald notes the apparently offbeat nature of the film as a propaganda vehicle:

> *Contraband* was concerned with the activities of the contraband patrols which operated in all British ports, stopping and searching neutral vessels to ensure they were not carrying cargo destined for the enemy. It seems an oddly marginal choice for the first real propaganda feature of the war—an unexpected sabre to rattle. Perhaps the Ministry of Information saw it as a trial run.[23]

Indeed, it does seem hard to believe that Powell was "thrilled to [his] Kentish toes" by depicting the operations of the Contraband Control. Instead, the film's topic seems well suited to the so-called "phoney war" period in which

---

[18]Ibid., 336.
[19]Ibid., 338.
[20]By the time of *Contraband*, Rank had left British National. Powell says in his autobiography that he insisted the film be made at Denham Studios, over Corfield's desire that he use Elstree Studios (Ibid., 340). On Rank, see Geoffrey Macnab, *J. Arthur Rank and the British Film Industry* (Abingdon: Routledge, 1993).
[21]Powell, *A Life*, 338.
[22]Macdonald, *Emeric Pressburger*, 160.
[23]Ibid.

it was made. Put simply, the term "phoney" or "bore" war is applied to the historical span from Germany's invasion of Poland at the beginning of September 1939 to the fall of France and the Low Countries in May 1940. From the British perspective, it is the period between the nation's official entrance into the war and its inauguration of significant combat operations. It is also a period that would not seem to hold much promise for the cinematic propagandist intent on making crowd-pleasing feature films.

All that being said, the "phoney war" designation is misleading. While the term certainly captures the nervous anticipation of a populace awaiting the beginning of violent military engagement, it fails to account for the ways in which Britain *had* entered the broader conflict against Germany.[24] One of the most significant of those ways was by means of a maritime blockade, with the seizure of contraband representing a key element of that blockade.[25] The blockade was initiated by the newly reformed Ministry of Economic Warfare and implemented by the Royal Navy. Its objective was to minimize the traffic of essential goods to Germany by means of neutral shipping, with the aim of "produc[ing in that country] starvation and economic ruin [to] win the war."[26] A royal proclamation released in September 1939 itemized different types of "absolute" and "conditional" contraband. Absolute contraband was broken down into four basic categories: arms and ammunition; fuel and forms of transport; any devices (of communication, navigation, etc.) that would help Germany wage war; and currency. As for conditional contraband, it is defined in the proclamation as "[f]ood, foodstuffs, and clothing."[27] Hopes that the blockade would disable Germany were wishful, to say the least. Nevertheless, there is no doubt that, during the winter of 1939–40, the blockade served as "Britain's chief offensive weapon";[28] it was the primary means by which the war was being fought. Given this, Powell and Pressburger's choice of subject, while perhaps not of obvious dramatic interest, is not really a marginal one.

In order to enforce the blockade, the Ministry of Economic Warfare established six Contraband Control stations: two in England (Weymouth

---

[24]On public attitudes toward the war in its opening months, see *War Begins at Home, By Mass Observation*, ed. Tom Harrisson and Charles Madge (London: Chatto and Windus, 1940). It is worth keeping in mind that many believed and feared that the Germans would start bombing Britain immediately after it entered the war.

[25]Whereas contraband operations and economic blockade are sometimes treated synonymously, the former represents a specific iteration of the latter. See Philip Drew, *The Law of Maritime Blockade: Past, Present, and Future* (Oxford: Oxford University Press, 2017), 6–7. The key point is that not all blockades are centered upon intercepting goods destined for the enemy.

[26]Tom Shachtman, *The Phony War 1939–1940* (New York: Harper and Row, 1982), 116.

[27]W. N. Medlicott, *The Economic Blockade*, vol. 1 (of 2) (London: His Majesty's Stationery Office and Longmans, Green and Co., 1952), 70.

[28]Ibid., 43. Medlicott notes that "During the first phase of the war, from September 1939 to June 1940, the story of economic warfare was one of great expectations" (43).

and Ramsgate), one in Scotland (Kirkwall), and one each in Gibraltar, Haifa, and Aden.[29] Moreover, the British blockade was met by its German equivalent, which, operating by way of U-boats and mine fields, was both far more deadly and, in the early months of the war, quite effective at preventing Britain access to food and trade.[30] In a speech to the House of Commons on September 21, 1939, Neville Chamberlain draws a distinction between the British and German blockades, noting that no one had been killed "by the exercise of British sea power, and no neutral property has been unlawfully detained. Germany's method of submarine warfare and the laying of mines on the high seas has already resulted in the death of many innocent victims, regardless of nationality, and in the unwarranted destruction of neutral property."[31] Of course, this argument has an obvious propaganda value and was undoubtedly appealed to by Contraband Control agents who sought to assuage the angry feelings of neutral ship captains. Indeed, a British naval officer advances this very line of argument in Powell and Pressburger's film.

Overconfidence in the efficacy of the blockade is on display in a discussion of Contraband Control that appeared in *Life Magazine* in January 1940. Frederic Sondern, Jr., combines a largely accurate account of the basic cargo inspection efforts of the Contraband Control with references to the seemingly near-miraculous efficiency of those efforts: "But the British net is hard to get through. Most neutral shipmasters now stop voluntarily at one of the three Contraband Control Stations on the British coast before braving European coastal waters. . . . 'Those Britishers seem to have second sight,' an irate Swedish master said bitterly to the writer."[32] Sondern stresses that the efficacy of Contraband Control emerges out of the coordinated activity of a "remarkable intelligence organization" at the center of which stood the Ministry of Economic Warfare:

> In Rome, New York, Rio de Janeiro, Tokyo, all over the world, British trade contacts function as an information system. A British banker in Rio hears from a friend that Germany is buying hides to be shipped via Holland. He reports it to his consul. The consul, through his agent at the docks, finds out what ship they are going on. A flash goes to the Ministry of Economic Warfare in London. And when the Dutch captain steams into Weymouth for inspection, he is surprised to find that the contraband officer knows exactly where to look for the hides.[33]

---

[29]Ibid., 70–85.
[30]Shachtman, *The Phony War*, 116.
[31]Quoted in "If It's Contraband It Won't Get to Germany," *The War Illustrated* 1.7 (October 28, 1939): 202.
[32]Frederic Sondern, Jr., "Contraband Control: England's Ministry of Economic Warfare Seeks a Death Grip on Germany's Trade," *Life Magazine*, January 15, 1940: 44–50, 47.
[33]Ibid., 47–8.

Sondern exaggerates the capabilities of the Ministry, which by the spring of 1940 was mocked by some as the "Ministry of Wishful Thinking."[34] However, he does accurately capture the Ministry's method of exploiting international trade networks for information, not to mention its reliance upon detailed prewar studies of the economic resources and production of Germany, its allies, and the neutral countries with which it traded.[35]

Significantly, Sondern's sanguine account of the Ministry and Contraband Control's operations chimes with a brief depiction of the British authorities in *Contraband*. Powell and Pressburger use the scene in which Axel Skold meets up with his dinner companions as an opportunity to offer a snapshot of those authorities in action. The moving camera precedes Skold as he passes through the Lord Nelson Hotel, which is a beehive of official activity. The short, largely comic sequence culminates in the office of the Chief Boarding Officer, where he has an exchange with a naval officer who has just returned from a ship inspection. The CBO asks his subordinate if he has found anything, and the latter's reply is "Lots of stuff that wasn't manifested.... Looks like parts of an aeroplane." The CBO responds, "I thought so. Get me MEW on the direct line." Significant here is not the discovery of contraband as much as it is the fact that the discovery confirms the CBO's information about illicit cargo on the ship. The result, in other words, is to suggest something akin to the "second sight" of these particular Britishers. Also on display is Contraband Control's close coordination with the Ministry of Economic Warfare, which the CBO calls on "the direct line." Although this sequence is not guilty of the wishful thinking we encounter in Sondern's article, it depicts through a kind of cinematic shorthand the British authorities as diligent, capable, and possessed of a highly formidable intelligence network.

Espionage, Romance, and the Blackout Plot

While the blockade plot of *Contraband* resembles that of a documentary focused on Naval Contraband Control, the blackout plot presents us with a romantic spy thriller in the vein of *The 39 Steps* (1935) or *The Lady Vanishes* (1938). Certainly, the blackout plot dovetails thematically with the blockade one, which dominates the first act. However, there is a disconnect between the film's documentary function—its representation of how (in Powell's words) "my country ... was already taking the war against Hitler" into the seas— and its more fanciful narrative of a shadowy German spy ring operating in blacked-out central London, the defeat of which is intertwined with the

---

[34]Medlicott, *The Economic Blockade*, vol. 1, 46.
[35]Ibid., 47.

emergence of an amorous relationship between Anderson and Sorenson. Interestingly, Pressburger's treatment, which is housed in the British Film Institute's Michael Powell Collection, suggests the filmmakers' awareness of this disconnect, as it works to stitch the two plots more tightly together. Whereas in general the treatment and film closely resemble one another, the treatment commences with six scenes that do not appear in the movie. The first is set in the Houses of Parliament, where a member of the opposition is making a speech to an Under Secretary of State. The member mentions both German ships sailing under neutral flags and the existence of a spy ring with an international reach: "[I]t is safe to presume, that the enemy must know exactly where a neutral ship is lying if it wants to use its name. This would need a world-wide organization, with agents all over the world: in Singapore, in New York, in Naples, Murmansk, Yokohama and London."[36] In this way, the treatment seeks to situate the activities of Contraband Control within an espionage narrative. The treatment's subsequent unfilmed scenes continue to develop the cloak-and-dagger theme: a character named Vaughan retrieves a secret message left for him in his gas mask;[37] later, he finds a note in his car warning him, "You might be followed";[38] and, as we come to learn from the Naval Intelligence agent who has been tracking him, Vaughan has been stealing information about international shipping from his employer, Lloyd's of London.[39] In sum, the treatment suggests that Powell and Pressburger at one point intended to embed the blockade-centered portion of their film—the portion with the clearest propaganda value—within a narrative that from the film's beginning more clearly telegraphed its status as a spy thriller.

It is unclear why Powell and Pressburger decided not to include the first six scenes described in the treatment. Certainly, the movie survives their excision. Whatever the filmmakers' motives, the cuts sharpen the distinction between the documentary-style blockade plot and the Hitchcockian espionage narrative. Of course, the blackout seems an optimal environment for the latter. However, its significance for Powell and Pressburger extends beyond atmospherics. The blackout plot comprises three overlapping and interwoven subplots: one centers upon the thwarting of the German spy ring; a second explores and resolves the triangulated relationship between Anderson, Sorenson, and Pidgeon; and a third focuses on the place of the (Danish) émigré in wartime London.

If *Contraband*'s blackout plot bears the influence of Hitchcock's British thrillers, it also shares with those films a debt to German expressionist

---

[36]Emeric Pressburger, *Black-Out*, Michael Powell Collection S-31, British Film Institute, Scene 1.
[37]The treatment has fun with the ubiquity of the gas mask during the "phoney war." In the climactic nightclub fight, during which Anderson rescues Sorenson, combatants wield their gas masks as weapons (Ibid., Scene 29).
[38]Ibid., Scene 5.
[39]Ibid., Scene 6.

cinema.[40] Ian Christie asserts that *Contraband* "is a virtual anthology of motifs from German thrillers, notably [Fritz] Lang's *Mabuse* [1922] and *Spione* [*Spies*, 1928], which are used to create unease and a sense of constant hidden menace."[41] We would add that Lang's *M* (1931) is also a relevant intertext: just as that film famously mirrors the operations and structure of the criminal underworld and the police, *Contraband* creates a symmetrical relationship between the spy network and the naval authorities we saw in action in the blockade plot. This relationship is suggested most clearly in the first scene in spy headquarters, which is located in a subterranean office.[42] The aptly named Miss Lang (Phoebe Kershaw) types at a desk with a chart of nautical flags hanging above it. In response to a request from Van Dyne, Lieman (Dennis Arundell) removes a card from a filing cabinet that contains information about an American ship ("7,000 tons. Oil-burning. Cargo: machinery consigned for Lisbon"). Lieman resembles an office clerk, to the degree that he even wears an eyeshade. Insofar as the German agents both track and are aware of the movements of various international vessels, the spy headquarters is the institutional doppelganger of the Ministry of Economic Warfare as depicted in Sondern's article for *Life*: "a world-wide organization, with agents all over the world."

The saga of Anderson's pocket watch invites further comparison between the German spy network and the British authorities. Both film and treatment feature Anderson losing a beloved watch while escaping from Van Dyne and his crew. The watch is found by the British police and, at the conclusion of the film, it is returned to Anderson in a manner that suggests their full awareness of his unauthorized and furtive journey to London. The implications of this awareness are spelled out in the treatment: "[W]e realise that the watch must have passed from Policeman to Police Station, from Police Station to Scotland Yard, from Scotland Yard to the Admiralty Intelligence, from Admiralty Intelligence to the Control Port and from the Control Port back to his pocket."[43] Most obviously, this sentence suggests the efficient and effective integration of different forms of civil and military authority as together they track the passage of a Danish neutral through the metropolis. In this regard, the story of the watch serves the film's propaganda aims. At the same time, the saga of the watch performs

---

[40]For a discussion of connections between *Contraband* and Hitchcock's British thrillers of the 1930s, see Macdonald, *Emeric Pressburger*, 161–2; and Andrew Moor, *Powell and Pressburger: A Cinema of Magic Spaces* (London: I.B. Tauris, 2005), 45.
[41]Ian Christie, *Arrows of Desire: The Films of Michael Powell and Emeric Pressburger* (1985; London: Faber and Faber, 1994), 34.
[42]The treatment describes the space in this way: "[T]he greater part of the room is taken up with a very elaborate office and filing cabinet. The walls are covered with maps and Admiralty charts. The files all relate to Shipping Information" (Pressburger, *Black-Out*, Scene 22).
[43]Ibid., Scene 33.

an important symbolic and narrative purpose, offering a reassuring vision of British organization as the antidote to (as well as the mirror image of) the menacing efficiency of the German spy network; it also tropes the Ministry of Economic Warfare's capacity to monitor the passage of goods from their point of embarkation. Additionally, the filmmakers repeatedly pair the two organizations because doing so provides them with a way of representing the conflict against Germany during the putatively "phoney" war; the organizations function as two surrogate armies pitted against one another on the British home front. Powell and Pressburger's narrative suggests that, despite the absence of military action, there is still a war going on, with the blackout as the milieu within which it is being fought.

If in *Contraband* the British authorities and the spy network can be analogized as opposing armies, the film also compares two groups of aliens whose differences from one another need to be clarified: the German enemies and the Danish neutrals, the latter of whom are represented most significantly by Captain Anderson. The very premise of the film depends upon there being no certain distinction between the two groups: Contraband Control's operations draw our attention to the fact that commanders of seemingly neutral vessels could actually be agents of the enemy. Moreover, the initial actions of Captain Anderson raise questions about his neutrality. When a British patrol boat orders the *Helvig* to "heave to" for inspection, Anderson says, "Let them come and get me"; after the *Helvig* is taken to a control port, Anderson's behavior is prickly and suspicious when asked to produce the ship's manifest.[44] Lieutenant Commander Ellis (Harold Warrender) makes plain that the raw materials for medical supplies the *Helvig* is carrying are not only extremely valuable, they would also greatly benefit the enemy.[45] Shortly thereafter, relations between the Danish captain and the British officers grow warmer. The latter's suspicions about Anderson are allayed through both their inspection of the ship's contents and Anderson's earnest desire to rush the supplies to his countrymen. The crucial point, though, is that neither the film nor the British naval officers take Anderson's neutrality as given. Indeed, one of the major narrative functions of the early scenes aboard the *Helvig* is to stage the process by which his neutrality is confirmed, under close scrutiny from the naval authorities. (The fact of that scrutiny, of course, serves the film's propaganda objectives; it telegraphs the vigilance and thoroughness of the naval officers who board the *Helvig*.)

---

[44] Anderson's stated reason for wanting to evade the British authorities is that he "did not want to lose time with your Contraband Control."

[45] Interestingly, medical supplies do not appear on official lists of absolute or conditional contraband items.

As we shall see, the film's romance plot converts Anderson's neutrality into active resistance to the German spies operating on British soil.[46]

If Anderson comes to betray his neutrality, so does Mrs. Sorenson. More accurately, she is eventually revealed to be not a Danish neutral living in New York, but a British spy who, along with Mr. Pidgeon, is tasked with discovering the false names and nationalities under which German sailing vessels travel as neutral. What Moor terms the "masquerade of national identity" operates at the levels of both persons and ships.[47] It is significant, moreover, that after Ellis and his compatriots confirm Anderson's neutrality aboard the *Helvig*, the Danish captain embarks on a task that will not only bring Sorenson and Pidgeon back to the ship, but will also end Sorenson's "masquerade." Anderson's motives for performing this task are threefold, the first two of which are verbalized. First, as Anderson states early in the film, his mission is to transport everyone on his ship to the port to which they are ticketed, a mission threatened by the stealthy departure of Pidgeon and Sorenson from the *Helvig*. Second, Lt. Cmdr. Ellis informs Anderson that, until he receives his clearance papers on the following morning, he will be held responsible for the ship "and everyone on her." These overlapping motives hinge upon Anderson's sense of responsibility to his ship and his passengers. It is Anderson's third, unarticulated motive that serves as the engine that drives the narrative in the next portion of the film.

The nature of this motive is revealed slowly. In the wake of Captain Anderson and First Officer Skold's discovery that their travel passes have been stolen, the two search the ship to determine who is missing. When Anderson enters Mrs. Sorenson's empty cabin, the music swells. He lingers over the smell of her perfume, and his examination of her silk stockings leads to a romantic reverie that is interrupted by the sight of a cigar in her ashtray. When he learns from Skold that Pidgeon is also missing, Anderson is galvanized, angered, and puzzled. He asks Skold, "Mrs. Sorenson and Mr. Pidgeon: does it make sense to you?" As the Captain and First Officer travel to shore in a row boat (the runaway couple having decamped with the ship's motor boat along with the travel passes), Anderson twice mutters in disbelief, "Mrs. Sorenson and Mr. Pidgeon."

Anderson's reaction to the flight of Sorenson and Pidgeon requires both contextualizing and unpacking. In the opening minutes of the film, Anderson says of Mrs. Sorenson, "When I saw her come abroad, I knew we were in for trouble," following that statement up by observing, "Not that I don't like them that way." In their initial squabble over her not wearing a

---

[46]Van Dyne makes this explicit when he says to Anderson, "I have no quarrel with any neutral, Captain—so long as he remains neutral. Since you got yourself mixed up in this affair, I must treat you as an enemy."
[47]Moor, *Powell and Pressburger*, 44.

life jacket, Sorenson responds to Anderson's question, "Have you ever been put in irons?," with a wry, suggestive expression. Sorenson's later interview with the passport officers reveals that she is estranged from her husband, and, somewhat shockingly, that he has custody of their daughter. Moreover, when Mrs. Sorenson notes that she is "*allowed to* visit her [daughter] at frequent intervals" (our emphasis), there is a further intimation of a morally dubious background. In other words, the film associates Mrs. Sorenson with sexual license well before we learn that she has run off with Mr. Pidgeon— and thus it invites us to see their unsanctioned disembarkment as an erotic escapade. This association informs both Anderson's attraction to her, which is registered in the way he examines her cabin, and his fit of pique at her having slipped off the ship with another man. Most obviously, it frames his subsequent actions in terms of sexual desire, jealousy, and the triangulated relationship between himself and the two absconders.

While Captain Anderson catches up with the couple on the train, Mr. Pidgeon soon eludes him, and he finds himself traversing the blacked-out city with only Mrs. Sorenson. As we shall discuss, the theme of navigating the blackout is central to this film. For now, what matters is the way in which Mr. Pidgeon is invoked after the two come in contact with the German spies. In the wake of being knocked unconscious, Anderson slowly comes to in the spies' headquarters. This is represented in a highly expressionist fashion. Anderson's face appears in extreme close-up. In a manner that evokes the rousing of the somnambulist Cesare in 1920's *The Cabinet of Dr. Caligari* (a role also played by Veidt), Anderson's eyes suddenly open, while an image of his pocket watch in motion is superimposed over his features, a juxtaposition that suggests hypnosis (another nod in the direction of *Caligari*). The watch is then replaced by other superimposed images: Miss Lang, in partial darkness but framed by the light of an open doorway, looks down upon the camera, which adopts Anderson's point of view; then we see, again from the imagined perspective of Anderson, the canted, menacing visages of the three Germans dubbed the Brothers Grimm. What is oddest about this sequence is that first Lang, and then the Grimm brothers, repeatedly intone the phrase, "Not Mr. Pidgeon." At this point, the focus shifts from a depiction of Anderson's experience of regaining consciousness to a shot of his prone body as he struggles to rouse himself, during which time he twice mutters the same phrase. Off-screen, we hear a man, whom we will soon learn is the spymaster Van Dyne, authoritatively observe, "No, he's certainly not Mr. Pidgeon."

At the level of plot, the references to Mr. Pidgeon are easily explained. In the scene in which Mrs. Sorenson and Captain Anderson first encounter Miss Lang and the Brothers Grimm, Lang sarcastically says to the seafarer, "And you, I suppose, are not Mr. Pidgeon?" It is the last three words of her question that reverberate in Anderson's mind as he slowly rouses himself. However, the phrase has greater significance. In deploying the formal strategies of expressionist cinema, Powell and Pressburger direct our attention to Anderson's subjective experience. His return to consciousness is bound up with his growing recognition that Mr. Pidgeon and Mrs. Sorenson are far from what he imagined them to be. As the Germans recognize, Pidgeon is Mrs. Sorenson's able partner in espionage, and one who has come to her aid in the past ("She doesn't have Mr. Pidgeon to help her this time," notes Van Dyne). Along with this recognition comes a new concern. What might appear as simply a question of identification—who is this man accompanying Mrs. Sorenson?—also articulates Anderson's anxiety that he falls far short both of his apparent rival ("No, he's *certainly not* Mr. Pidgeon") and of the woman he so badly misjudged. Van Dyne's interrogation of the British spy provides Anderson with a glimpse of her previous exploits, as well as an introduction to her true character. "It's in your nature to ask for trouble," Van Dyne observes of her; he also states that adventure is "in [her] blood." The broader point is that, in registering his potential inferiority to Mr. Pidgeon, Anderson also begins to reckon with the distance between his initial conception of Mrs. Sorenson and the woman she is revealed to be in this scene. Here romance and espionage are tightly intertwined, as Anderson's fears of inadequacy encompass his status as both a would-be lover and an accidental spy. Much of the rest of the film is devoted to demonstrating his worthiness in both endeavors.

If Mrs. Sorenson proves to be different than Captain Anderson believed her to be, she is also revealed not to be Mrs. Sorenson at all. After Miss Lang first addresses her in her aunt's house as Mrs. Sorenson, she claims her name is Margaret Clayton, much to the surprise of Anderson. Lang and the German spies don't believe her, and they persist in referring to her as Mrs. Sorenson. And yet, we are invited to think that Margaret Clayton is the character's "real" name (that she shares a surname with her aunt suggests as much). The irony, then, is that the spies take the false for the real—indeed, they insist upon doing so. And yet, in terms of the film's narrative logic, they are not wrong to do so. Rather than thinking in terms of "true" and "false" identities, we should see the two names as serving different functions and representing different stages in the narrative. As the film unfolds, "Mrs. Sorenson" is first associated with illicit sexuality and then with espionage (in both instances, she is aligned with Mr. Pidgeon); she is attractive and attracted to Captain Anderson, but her seemingly dubious character is not suited to a romantic denouement. However, shed of her alter ego's vexed marital and sexual history while retaining her capacity for adventure, "Miss Clayton" is free to pair off with the captain. While *Contraband* centers upon Captain Anderson and Mrs. Sorenson, the latter character is replaced by Miss Clayton at the film's end.[48]

---

[48]This is why we continue to refer to "Mrs. Sorenson" even after her "true identity" is revealed to be that of "Miss Clayton."

Before embarking upon a romance with Miss Clayton, however, Captain Anderson must prove himself worthy of Mrs. Sorenson. After freeing himself from spy headquarters, Anderson returns and rescues both Mrs. Sorenson and Mr. Pidgeon, the latter having in the interim been abducted by the German agents. In conducting this rescue, Anderson thoroughly takes charge—he even single-handedly subdues Van Dyne—and Mr. Pidgeon mutely obeys his orders. Near the end of the film, as the two men await Mrs. Sorenson's return from the Admiralty Office, Pidgeon observes that she is going to miss the train. Anderson playfully rebukes him: "Pidgeon, you don't know that girl at all." Whereas Anderson once misconstrued Sorenson's motives and actions, she is now transparent to him and opaque to her longtime fellow spy. After Mrs. Sorenson settles in next to Anderson in the train carriage, she takes his hand, which elicits from Pidgeon both an amused look and some cheerful humming. This scene demonstrates not only that Anderson has outstripped Pidgeon in matters of love and espionage, but also that Pidgeon was not his romantic rival in the first place. The scene thus also thoroughly recasts Mrs. Sorenson's dubious sexual history as a part of her cover as a spy, thereby paving the way for a romantic finale featuring Miss Clayton and Captain Anderson.

The distance between Anderson's original conception of Sorenson and her revealed character is never greater than in the scene in the Three Vikings. Much to the female spy's amusement, Anderson indulges over dinner in some self-satisfied, sexist condescension: "The smaller the ship, the bigger the adventure," he opines. "But you wouldn't understand that." After referencing his retirement from the Danish navy, he notes that he "wanted to sail everywhere a ship can sail." And then, once again, "But you wouldn't understand that." As Van Dyne's later observations about Mrs. Sorenson make plain, the joke is on Captain Anderson. At issue in this scene is not only the good captain's misapprehension of his companion's character, however; it is also the model of adventure to which he subscribes. Mrs. Sorenson asks, "Did you ever try being married? That can be quite a big adventure." Anderson scoffs at this notion; it is clear that, for him, marriage and adventure are antithetical categories. A secondary function of the subsequent conflict with the German spies is to reveal to him that romance and adventure are, instead, compatible. The film's conclusion depends upon Captain Anderson's acceptance of the possibility, which he previously spurned, of adventure *within* marriage.

Navigating the Blackout

The enlightenment of Captain Anderson is part of the film's development of the broader theme of navigation, a theme that encompasses the actions not only of the two romantic leads but, as we shall soon discuss, also those of the Danish émigré community in London (and, by imaginative extension, of Pressburger and his fellow exiles in the film industry). This theme is both introduced in and necessitated by the blackout. Shortly after their train arrives in London, Captain Anderson rebuffs a vendor of electric torches, insisting that he does not need one, while Mrs. Sorenson replies, "Everybody needs a torch in the blackout." Anderson prides himself on his ability to maneuver his way through any environment, boasting that he knows precisely where he is in the middle of the Atlantic by way of the stars. That boast is undercut immediately, when he walks blindly into a policeman. At the same time, Anderson marvels at Mrs. Sorenson's knowledge of exactly where she is in London at that moment. This scene telegraphs what is at issue in his first foray into the blacked-out metropolis: he is at sea now that he is not on the water. His disorientation is not just spatial; it includes, and arguably emblematizes, his misrecognition of Mrs. Sorenson's character.

Anderson's navigational boast notwithstanding, traversing the city is for Powell and Pressburger not only a matter of getting one's geographic bearings. Instead, they approach the blackout with an eye to its impact on social behavior. As Powell notes in his autobiography, "we made the conditions of London . . . so interesting and so fascinating that they called the film *Blackout* when it was released in America, and I wish we had too."[49] (What Powell seems to have forgotten is that the filmmakers originally considered using that title: the treatment of the film held at the BFI identifies it as *Black-Out*.[50] If the film's British title short-changes the blackout plot, then its American one downplays that portion of the movie most closely associated with "How Britain fights.") Powell's captivation with the blackout is understandable when we consider how dramatic a change from past experience it represented, especially in urban settings. The blackout was designed to deny German aircraft a clear view of both navigational landmarks and potential targets; to achieve this end, all artificial light sources had to be extinguished or obscured. As a result, familiar nocturnal landscapes were dramatically transformed, while in urban areas the night sky became newly visible. The blackout rendered both city and country alien to themselves.[51]

---

[49] Powell, *A Life*, 339.
[50] Additionally, Mass Observation File Report 24, entitled "The Cinema in the First Three Months of the War," gives the title of this film "to be produced between the end of November and June" as "Black-Out" (8). This and other MO File Reports are available on the Mass Observation Online database: http://www.massobservation.amdigital.co.uk (accessed August 18, 2019).
[51] "The physical landscape of London began to change in the early weeks of war to reflect London's military importance as the nerve center of an Allied war effort, as well as its vulnerability. The city was transformed by air raid shelters, the removal of street signs, and the imposition of darkness under a blackout order" (Amy Bell, "Landscapes of Fear: Wartime London, 1939–1945," *Journal of British Studies* 48.1 [January 2009]: 153–75, 157).

It is worth pointing out that Powell's almost gleeful depiction of the blackout deviates from most of the popular reactions to it. In *War Begins at Home*, a 1940 Mass Observation account of the opening months of the conflict, Tom Harrisson and Charles Madge note that "resentment against the war fastened on one aspect far above all others—the black-out."[52] Drawing on reports submitted by Mass Observers throughout the country, Harrisson and Madge show that the reasons for such resentment were manifold, and also varied by gender. The daily grind of blacking out the house, most often by way of heavy curtains, irked many, as did the curtailment of their regular nighttime activities.[53] The Mass Observers' findings suggest both men and women decreased the number of visits they made to friends, cut down on nocturnal walks, and took fewer trips to the cinema, theater, and dance halls, among other things.[54] (On the other hand, the BBC's radio audience grew over the course of the war "since the blackout kept people indoors."[55]) And, of course, numerous people injured themselves, or came close to doing so: a female pub manager hurt her leg after colliding with a pile of sandbags, while a railway porter reports that he "fell off the platform the other night. Clean over the edge I fell."[56] Significantly, women reported being more adversely affected by the blackout for a variety of reasons; while fear of sexual assault is not one of the stated reasons, one assumes that it played a role in some women's reactions to the blackout.[57] (It should be noted, moreover, that Powell and Pressburger would take up the topic of blackout-enabled assaults on women in *A Canterbury Tale*.) Harrisson and Madge observe that "the whole structure of British leisure is being changed by the black-out."[58]

If the blackout was widely felt to be a nuisance if not a danger—and, during the period of *Contraband*'s making, one that was perceived by some as unnecessary—it also served as the perfect emblem of a country at ("phoney") war. Antonia Lant puts it well: "Living through the wartime dark was experienced by everyone, regardless of class, age, sex, race, or regional abode. Universal in nature, the image of the blackout became a synecdoche for war in cultural life." Lant also observes that the blackout came to function as "a cornerstone of cinematic vocabulary. . . . [It] serves as a demarcating device in all British films made and set in wartime, and has been deployed ever since, perhaps more frequently than any other code, to

---

[52]Harrisson and Madge, *War Begins at Home*, 184.
[53]Ibid., 192–3.
[54]Ibid., 193.
[55]Angus Calder, *The People's War: Britain 1939–1945* (New York: Pantheon Books, 1969), 358.
[56]Harrisson and Madge, *War Begins at Home*, 190, 191.
[57]Ibid., 193.
[58]Ibid., 194.

recall World War II on the screen."[59] In this regard, Powell and Pressburger anticipated, or even helped set, the trend: *Contraband* is the first wartime feature to put the British blackout on screen.

The blackout signifies somewhat differently in the first half of *Contraband* than it does in the second, thanks to the revelation of the German spy network. In the scenes leading up to Sorenson and Anderson's first encounter with Miss Lang and the Brothers Grimm, the film approaches the blackout in a fashion that is part comedy and part sociology. We have seen Anderson's pride in his navigational skills being undercut when he blunders into a policeman. A later scene in which Anderson and Sorenson compete to attract a taxi evokes a similar, famous contest in Frank Capra's *It Happened One Night* (1934), while the couple's conversation over and across an irritated fellow bus rider registers as a comic bit of business out of Hitchcock.[60] At the same time, Powell and Pressburger's inclusion of a vendor of torches and gas masks hawking his wares outside of a sandbagged Victoria Station answers to the filmmakers' desire to record for their audience some of the distinctive details of life in the blackout. Interestingly, the film combines the disorientation of the blackout with a degree of geographic precision: shortly after leaving the station, Mrs. Sorenson notes, to Anderson's amazement, that the couple are on Buckingham Palace Road. Shortly thereafter, we see them board the Oxford St. bus; they get off that bus near Hyde Park Corner, from where they take a taxi to the Three Vikings restaurant.[61] Part of the pleasure of these scenes, in other words, comes from the way in which they first disorient the viewer (by means of blackout) only to reorient her (by way of these place markers).[62] Moreover, the scenes imbue Mrs. Sorenson with a geographic authority that Captain Anderson lacks, and which he will acquire later in the film with the help of the Danish émigrés who work in the Three Vikings.

In the movie's second half, the filmmakers' depiction of the blackout retains elements of the comical and sociological. For instance, we witness a brief argument between two zealous Air Raid Precautions (ARP) wardens and an unnamed citizen (played by Bernard Miles) who expresses his irritation at being told that lighting his pipe in the street contravenes

---

[59]Antonia Lant, *Blackout: Reinventing Women for Wartime British Cinema* (Princeton, NJ: Princeton University Press, 1991), 114.
[60]The comedy of the former incident is darkened by the two predatory young men in a car who materialize at the sound of Mrs. Sorenson's voice, one of whom asks "Can we give you a lift, or something?"
[61]The cabbie mentions the name of the street that the restaurant is on, but it is difficult to make out.
[62]This process of reorientation can involve varying degrees of precision. While seasoned Londoners might envision exactly where our heroes are, those unfamiliar with the city would at least recognize the names of Hyde Park Corner or Buckingham Palace.

blackout regulations.⁶³ (Here we catch a glimpse of the dominant cultural theme identified by Harrisson and Madge: the blackout as a source of annoyance, one that, Miles's character seems to imply, isn't even necessary at this point in the war.) Humorous in itself, this exchange occurs in front of a darkened multistory building the lights of which are suddenly turned on by Anderson in his effort to escape from spy headquarters. This episode gently pokes fun at the ARP, overly concerned with the light of a match but initially oblivious to an illuminated building. That being said, having been introduced to the German spies, our sense of the blackout is colored by their adumbral activities. If the joke is on the ARP, it is the pipe smoker who is in the wrong; in his disdain for wartime regulations, he treats the war as "phoney" when (as both the blockade and the enemy espionage activity suggest) it is not.

Anderson's earlier inability to locate himself in the blackout becomes significant when it comes time to rescue Mrs. Sorenson. With the aid of a map and information gleaned from the stars—visible only because of the blackout—Anderson and the Danes in the Three Vikings plot a course that, after some trial and error, takes them to the German hideout, located beneath a cinema and adjacent to a nightclub. To do so, the Danish émigrés draw on their extensive knowledge of the city, identifying within the region designated by Anderson a number of cinemas that abut nightclubs. The scene suggests both that Anderson is less at sea in the city than he initially was, and that his compatriots are very much at home there, having developed a keen mastery of its geography. In other words, the Danes reveal themselves also to be Londoners. Moreover, they are anything but neutral, eagerly joining Anderson's fight against the Germans. It is hard not to see these Danish Londoners as evoking Pressburger and his fellow émigrés in the British film industry. Indeed, the climactic fight scene that enables Anderson to free the two British spies should be understood as thematizing the battle that Pressburger sees himself as having entered into, one in which he fights not with his fists but by way of film. In this regard, *Contraband* is a piece of wartime propaganda that is also "accented" by the involvement of Pressburger and other exiled filmmakers who worked on it.

In championing the actions of the Danish Londoners, *Contraband* offers evidence of three elements of Powell and Pressburger's propaganda program: cosmopolitanism, pluralism, and (insofar as the Danes stand in for Pressburger and other exiles working in British film) self-reflexivity. It is worth noting, however, that *Contraband* also hints at a more Greeneian

---

⁶³In Evelyn Waugh's *Put Out More Flags* (1942; New York: Back Bay Books, 2012), the narrator's sketch of British life in late September, 1939, alludes to "air-raid wardens roam[ing] the remote hamlets of the kingdom, persecuting yokels who walked home from the inn with glowing pipes" (56).

understanding of émigré involvement in British film. Lieman is not only a clerk for the German spies; he also works in the cinema directly above their headquarters. Lieman leaves spy headquarters as the cinema is shutting down, and, just as he enters the theater itself, the Union Jack is visible on the screen while "God Save the King" is broadcast to the standing cinemagoers.[64] Viewed through the lens of exilic involvement in the film industry, this brief, metacinematic scene might be understood to allegorize the presence of malevolent alien forces, represented by Lieman and the other spies, within that industry.[65] From this perspective, such alien forces are undermining Britain's "national cinema," emblematized here by the Union Jack, as they seem to be contributing to it. Given that this reading is entirely at odds with both Pressburger's biography and the film's ethos, it does not seem defensible. However, the inclusion of this scene makes sense once we recognize that it advances a viewpoint that the movie as a whole works to disavow. More specifically, the scene develops further the pattern of doubling discussed earlier in this chapter. Just as the German spies shadow the British naval authorities that finally outdo them, so does this toxic vision of émigré involvement in the British film industry mirror the more positive one that finally wins out over it. Like the spies themselves, this toxic vision appears in the film in order to be defeated. After all, *Contraband* is itself both an accented film and an example of an emergent national cinema; it demonstrates that Pressburger and other émigré filmmakers, like the film's Danish characters, can and will fight for Britain, with cinematic propaganda their weapon of choice.

Patriotic Plaster Propaganda

In concluding, and with The Archers' reflexivity in mind, we would like to talk briefly not about *Contraband* as a propaganda weapon, but about a propaganda weapon that appears in *Contraband*. In a climactic scene, Anderson subdues Van Dyne by hitting him over the head with a bust of Neville Chamberlain. This bust and dozens like it take up most of the darkened top floor of the building that houses the German spy headquarters. They are merchandise produced by a company called Patriotic Plaster Products—a company that serves as a front for the Germans. As in the cinema scene, the enemy hides beneath a patriotic mask. Anderson comments upon the bust with which he knocks Van Dyne cold: "They always said he was tough." Andrew Moor notes that, in the period between the film's trade screening in March 1940 and its mid-May general UK release, Chamberlain had resigned

---

[64]This scene is a clear homage to Hitchcock's *Sabotage* (1936).
[65]See Moor, *Powell and Pressburger*, 45–6.

FIGURE 2.1 *Captain Anderson among the Patriotic Plaster Products (*Contraband, 1940*)*.

as prime minister, but long before that date, the question of Chamberlain's toughness was a debatable one;[66] today, of course, he is strongly associated with appeasement and capitulation to Hitler by means of the Munich Agreement of September 1938. At the time of the film's release, then, this moment would likely be construed as jesting at Chamberlain's expense. And yet, as Anderson's tone is not obviously comic, there is some uncertainty as to whether that joke was originally designed as such (Figure 2.1).

Regardless of whether or not Chamberlain is the intended butt of this joke, there is another comic element to this scene, although the humor is more sardonic in nature. For Powell and Pressburger, the patriotic plaster bust symbolizes a model of propaganda that, in *Contraband* but especially in their subsequent features, they seek to distance themselves from. The scenario is practically cartoonish: the German spy is defeated when he is hit over the head with a bust of the British prime minister. Add to this the additional irony that the jingoistic weapon of choice is distributed, if not manufactured, by enemy agents as part of their cover.[67] In including this scene, then, Powell and Pressburger state their preference for a model of propaganda that is far more sophisticated than the one that they mock. And yet, *Contraband*, with its imperfectly integrated blockade and blackout plots, does not offer us a coherent picture of what that model might look

---

[66]Ibid., 46.
[67]One could read the choice of Chamberlain as suggesting that the German agents benefitted from his ill-advised policy of appeasement.

like; such a picture will start to emerge only with *49th Parallel*. In other words, this scene suggests that Powell and Pressburger know what they want to do, which is to make propaganda films that, unlike Chamberlain's plaster bust, are not cheap patriotic hokum. However, *Contraband*, as entertaining as it is, tells us that they haven't yet determined how best to do that.

Finally, it's worth noting that Patriotic Plaster Products, a company manufacturing "British" products that is actually run by dangerous foreign concerns, evokes Greene's xenophobic depiction of the film industry. In including this dubious purveyor of jingoism in their film, Powell and Pressburger present us with another example of the doubling that proliferates in *Contraband*. We have seen that while the operations of the German spies may mirror those of the British authorities, the latter are more than a match for the former; Patriotic Plaster Products serves as the evil twin to a vision of the film industry in which émigrés are integral to the production of a national cinema. Moreover, *Contraband* itself stands as evidence of such a cinema, accented as it is by the invaluable participation of Pressburger, Veidt, and Junge and focused on the heroics of Danes as well as Brits. In a city rendered foreign to itself by the blackout, the foreigners prove to be as indispensable as the natives—and, in the case of the Danes of the Three Vikings, they also prove themselves to be Londoners able to navigate the physical and cultural geography of the city. In this regard, they serve as stand-ins for Pressburger. More importantly, they express the filmmaker's desire that he and his fellow émigrés be recognized not as "enemy aliens," but as wholehearted defenders of their adopted country. *Contraband* suggests that if the blackout renders London a city foreign to itself—that is, if it turns the city into its own uncanny double, familiar and strange all at once—no one is better able to come to its aid than the foreigner who calls it home.

PART TWO

PART TWO

3

49th Parallel and the Dangerous Interpretability of Wartime Propaganda

On October 27, 1941, the *Eastern Evening News*—a local paper serving Norfolk County in East Anglia—published a telling exchange between two viewers of *49th Parallel*. In a negative assessment of the film, a subscriber called Percival Moreton argued not only that it was belated ("two years too late") but also illustrative of "the weakness of British propaganda."[1] Acknowledging *49th Parallel*'s refusal to caricature its Nazi protagonists, Moreton declaimed that

> The intention was, as I see it[,] to present a case for democracy and, in contrast, a case against Nazism. The latter obviously is more important.... [But] the story is wrongly constructed.... After two years of war we are given a film which, first, provides excellent entertainment, second, presents a case for democracy (as though it were not already proven), and third, provides opportunities for sympathising with the hated enemy!

This paying customer identified precisely the feature of *49th Parallel* that preoccupied professional film reviewers: its treatment of German soldiers as complex, individual human beings, and thus as potential loci for audience sympathy. Whereas many critics regarded this aspect of the film as one of its strengths, Moreton expressed a common enough fear of the age about what might happen if anything other than German depravity was thoroughly on display in British wartime films.

---

[1] "Reader Critic of *49th Parallel*," *Eastern Evening News*, October 27, 1941. n.p.

In response, the paper assigned a critic called "Stargazer" to correct what they viewed as Moreton's shortsighted perspective. Beginning with the criticism that Moreton had missed the film's subtler elements, Stargazer continued,

> We do admire the U-boat men at times—for their admirable qualities—but we are constantly reminded forcibly of their vile ones. Their cruelty for instance is brought out against the background of kindness in the Hutterite camp, and the tortuousness of the Nazi mind is contrasted with the sweet simplicity of the girl Anna. Propaganda which reminds us of the value of the things we strive to preserve may be more effective than always reminding us of the evil things we are fighting.[2]

Stargazer thus concludes an exchange that reveals two important, inextricably related points about early wartime propaganda films: first, that filmgoers, like government officials and film producers, struggled actively to define just what constituted effective film propaganda; second, and more important for our purposes, the mere fact that a film served an explicit propaganda function in no way determined that its message would be construed in the same way by different audience members. In each reviewer's comments about *49th Parallel* we detect genuine trepidation about the British propaganda film's dangerous interpretability.

To put it another way, given that *49th Parallel*—which concerns the efforts of a U-boat crew to escape Canada to the United States—depicts the Nazi characters as humans rather than monsters, and it makes their actions the focus of the film, it is not surprising that the film has been taken up by some as "sympathizing with the hated enemy." We would go a step further and suggest that, in its self-reflexive meditation upon its own status as a propaganda film, *49th Parallel* demonstrates a startling awareness of the fact that the very events it chronicles could, were the plot to take a different turn at the end, form the basis for a German propaganda film. Moreover, this narrative affinity between Powell and Pressburger's film and its would-be German counterpart—the affinity that lies at the core of the film's dangerous interpretability—becomes the basis not for collapsing into one another Nazi and British propaganda efforts but for differentiating between them.[3]

What we wish to demonstrate in this chapter is that Powell and Pressburger made the dangerous interpretability of propaganda the very subject of *49th Parallel*, in turn provoking the type of debate we've just

---

[2]Ibid.
[3]The fact that *49th Parallel* was "the top British box-office success of 1941" seems like a rejoinder to those who thought of it as pro-Nazi (*Mass-Observation at the Movies*, ed. Jeffrey Richards and Dorothy Sheridan [London and New York: Routledge and Kegan Paul, 1987], 12–13).

witnessed. Such a self-reflexive propaganda strategy served precisely to differentiate British and German forms of propaganda by constructing the former as uniquely transparent, open to interpretation, even reluctant to perform its stated function. German propaganda, in contrast, is shown in the film to be deliberately opaque about its objectives, unequivocal in its messaging, and shamelessly unreflective. These distinctions would remain crucial to Powell and Pressburger throughout their wartime collaboration, and even undergo further development in films such as *The Life and Death of Colonel Blimp* (1943).

As we suggested in the Introduction, Powell and Pressburger's propaganda program built upon but also went beyond that of the MOI.[4] In fact, careful examination of the film's elaborate propaganda strategy suggests the limitations of Anthony Aldgate and Jeffrey Richards's now paradigmatic claim that "The film of *49th Parallel* . . . was nothing if not a thoroughly schematic and heavily programmed attempt to fulfil all the criteria of excellence for film propaganda laid down by the Films Division of the MoI."[5] Repeated in some form in nearly every subsequent scholarly commentary on the film, the argument fails to capture the inventiveness and complexity of *49th Parallel*'s own program for British film propaganda— its clear rejection of certain aspects of the MOI document and its positive development of concepts entirely absent from that document. The release of the Programme to filmmakers in early 1940, as well as the fact that *49th Parallel* was the only British wartime feature film extensively bankrolled by the MOI, has understandably led scholars to conclude that the film was more reactive than active, more deferential toward the government than independent, more derivative than creative.

In the first part of what follows, however, we'll see how *49th Parallel* seizes on the impressionistic, even underdeveloped, nature of the MOI Programme as providing an opportunity for building an exceptionally robust concept of British wartime propaganda. What we've called the Powell and Pressburger Program takes on its basic form in this production, especially through the film's emphases on pluralism, cosmopolitanism, and Germanic individualism—as well as its high degree of self-reflexivity. Through its reflexivity, *49th Parallel* shows itself to be a propaganda film concerned about the power and dangers of propaganda films. In the chapter's second part, we will explore the film's dangerous interpretability, which emerges directly out of the Powell and Pressburger Program's strong, self-reflexive juxtapositions of democratic and totalitarian propaganda techniques.

---

[4]The Clark "Programme for Film Propaganda" is reprinted as an Appendix in *Powell Pressburger and Others*, ed. Ian Christie (London: BFI, 1978), 121–4.
[5]Anthony Aldgate and Jeffrey Richards, *Britain Can Take It: The British Cinema in the Second World War* (Oxford and New York: Basil Blackwell, 1986), 37.

Somewhat riskily, the film takes up directly the relationship between propaganda and viewers' perceptions—or *interpretations*—of contestable wartime realities. By this means, Powell and Pressburger indirectly prompt viewers to question their own film's methods of truth-telling, aligning what they perceive to be the moral rightness of their messaging with propaganda techniques that prioritize audience freedom over directorial control.

Under the Auspices of the MOI

As Powell noted on many occasions, the plot of *49th Parallel* appropriates the "And then there were none" narrative structure.[6] It traces the gradual disintegration of a stranded, six-man U-boat party as it makes its way across Canada in the hopes of escaping into the neutral United States. The pursued Nazis are led by the humorless and brutal Lieutenant Hirth (Eric Portman). They travel from the wilds of Hudson Bay, where their U-boat is destroyed, to the rural lands of a Hutterite farming community, to the urban lights and liveliness of Winnipeg, to the idyllic big skies of Banff and the Rocky Mountains, to a final showdown at the US-Canadian Niagara Falls crossing. Along the way, the sailors encounter people, events, and aspects of Canadian life that lead some of them to question their faith in the Nazi way, and thus disrupt the group's cohesion. One particular sailor called Vogel (Niall MacGinnis), who experiences the greatest personal crisis while encamped at the Hutterite farm, emerges as precisely the sort of sympathetic or "good" German that seems to have troubled so many contemporary viewers. When Vogel decides to reject Nazism and join the Hutterites, Hirth immediately executes him for desertion and treachery—an act that dramatizes the gulf between Nazism and some conceptions of Germanness. Eventually, Hirth is the sole remaining fugitive, and he comes frighteningly close to crossing the US border. He is stopped at the last moment, thanks to the courage and conviction of a Canadian soldier (Raymond Massey) who discovers Hirth's plan, and to the willingness of two US border guards who concoct a way to bar his entry into the country. In the film's final scene, Brock pulls up his shirtsleeves and prepares to rough up a terrified Hirth, who will soon be turned over to the Canadian authorities. As we shall see when we delve more deeply into the details of the plot, the film suggests that the arrest of Hirth is as important for propaganda purposes as it is for national security ones: had the Nazi Lieutenant managed to cross the US border, he would have returned to Germany a national hero—the crafty evader of Canadian law and justice, and the exploiter of America's morally flawed policy of

---

[6]See Powell, *A Life in Movies* (1986; London: Faber and Faber, 2000), 350, 354–5.

neutrality. As things turn out, Hirth and his crew members are defeated by the unity and superior gamesmanship of two democratic nations, and the Nazi propaganda threat is eliminated by his capture.

Production of *49th Parallel* began in the final months of Neville Chamberlain's prime-ministership and the Phoney War and continued through the rise of Churchill, the disaster at Dunkirk, and the entire duration of the Blitz. Within two months of its London debut in October of 1941, the Japanese bombed the US naval base at Pearl Harbor. By the time of its New York premiere in March 1942, the United States had been at war with Germany for nearly three months. Had Powell and Pressburger begun *49th Parallel* much later than those early months of 1940, the film probably would not have been made; certainly, it would not have received the formal backing and relatively generous financial support of the MOI.

A sign of how intertwined the film's propaganda objectives were with those of the wartime British government, the film's central conceit—that the Germans, if not stopped, will soon invade America—has been attributed to both Michael Powell and the MOI itself.[7] Though in January 1940 the MOI recommended a "first-class feature film developing as an exciting story the history of the growth of freedom, referring to the American parallel,"[8] Powell was said to have conjured the idea while reading a Canadian newspaper in late 1939, and he discussed it with Pressburger shortly after. Kenneth Clark, head of the Films Division, responded positively to Powell's pitch for a film located in the dominion of Canada and aimed at bringing the United States into the war. In the end, the MOI would agree to finance about half of the film's production costs (the other half would be covered by J. Arthur Rank). Receiving almost £60,000, *49th Parallel* is famously the only British commercial feature film financed by the MOI (numerous documentaries were, of course, backed by the agency). By April 13, Powell and Pressburger were touring Canada on a government expense account, searching out shooting locations, reaching out to stars who might be willing to work for less money than usual, and meeting with various Canadian officials about how they should ideally represent their vast nation.[9]

As noted in the Introduction, the fact of the MOI's financial backing has influenced the notion that *49th Parallel* strictly adhered to the agency's propaganda guidelines. Clark's MOI Programme for British film propaganda recommended that films address three major themes: "What Britain is fighting for"; "How Britain fights"; and "The need for sacrifices if the fight

---

[7] See especially James Chapman, *The British at War: Cinema, State and Propaganda, 1939–1945* (London and New York: I.B. Tauris), 70–1.
[8] Qtd. In Chapman, *The British at War*, 70.
[9] The story of the pair's travels is recounted in Powell, *A Life*, 347–53; and in Kevin Macdonald, *Emeric Pressburger: The Life and Death of a Screenwriter* (London and Boston: Faber and Faber, 1994), 166–71.

is to be won." In the sense that *49th Parallel* engages these themes at least generally, Aldgate and Richards are correct in observing that it fulfilled most of the Programme's criteria of excellence (though we might reasonably point out that a majority of films about the war almost *inevitably* did the same[10]). Perhaps more to the point of their argument is the extent to which the film meditated on the Programme's recommended "main objects of feature films," which are included under the theme of "What Britain is fighting for." The first "object" is "*British life and character*, showing our independence, toughness of fibre, sympathy with the under-dog, etc."[11] The second is "*British ideas and institutions*. Ideals such as freedom, and institutions such as parliamentary government can be made the main subject of a drama or treated historically."[12] In contrast to the first two objects, the third is to display "*German ideals and institutions in recent history*," especially since Bismarck. Films should stress "the sinister rather than the sadistic aspect" of the Gestapo (which is "more easily credible"), and "Germans should also be shown as making absurd errors of judgement."[13] As we shall see, *49th Parallel* goes further than most British wartime films in presenting developed ideas about each of these "objects."

Nonetheless, the success and influence of *49th Parallel* have much to do with the ways the film exceeded the MOI Programme and created more precisely defined propaganda points about how British character and institutions (as well as those of their Allies) might be differentiated from German ones.[14] Specifically, the film can be characterized by, and helps to shape, four of those core characteristics of the Powell and Pressburger

---

[10]Kim Newman has gone so far as to conclude that "Strictly speaking, every film published in Britain during World War 2 was a propaganda movie." See "*49th Parallel:* That's for Thomas Mann.... That's for Matisse.... That's for Picasso.... And ... that's for me!" In Jay Slater, ed. *Under Fire: A Century of War Movies* (Surrey: Ian Allan Publishing, 2009), 33–42, esp. 34.
[11]Clark, "Programme", 121.
[12]Ibid.
[13]Ibid., 122. The Programme's short section on representing Germans does little to clarify whether Moreton's expectations for *49th Parallel* were in line with, or in conflict with, Ministry guidelines.
[14]Though she does not discuss *49th Parallel* in these terms, Jo Fox has argued that in general, the degree of compliance of Second World War propagandists with their respective state agencies has been overstated in many cases: "[This book] argues that each state possessed an intricate and complex relationship with its respective peoples and suggests that at times the propaganda outputs conformed far less to the official rhetoric emanating from the RMVP and the MoI regarding their 'information policies' than might be expected, thus blurring the distinction between democratic and authoritarian propaganda whilst at the same time not forgetting that the state mechanisms were not the same or largely similar" (*Film Propaganda in Britain and Nazi Germany* [Oxford and New York: Berg, 2007], 12). We don't disagree with James Chapman's claim that "*49th Parallel* was the foremost example of direct collaboration between the MOI and the film industry during the war" (*The British at War*, 72); we would simply emphasize that collaboration does not imply conformity or passivity, nor does it prevent innovation.

propaganda film that we discussed in our Introduction. First, The Archers reveal a commitment to democratic principles that involves celebrating and protecting the diversity of those various, distinct communities that, together, constitute the nation. In *49th Parallel*, numerous diegetic and non-diegetic maps display the vastness of Canada. These maps, along with distinct sequences set in, or at least referencing, various locations (Hudson Bay; a rural farm community in Manitoba; the whole of French Canada; cities such as Winnipeg and Vancouver; national parks such as Banff; etc.) serve to highlight the topological and climatological diversity not only of Canada, but also of the different cultures associated with the country: Inuit, Hutterites, Québécois, eastern "Indians," urbanites, and so forth. In such a way, the film celebrates racial, religious, and ethnic diversity and freedoms— and it views such freedoms as the most basic gift of democracy. Powell and Pressburger certainly emphasized the correlation between democracy and pluralism as part of their appeal to an unusually diverse nation, the United States of America; they might also have intended the correlation to serve as an analogue to the diversity of the British Empire.

Second, *49th Parallel* stresses the intrinsic links between cosmopolitanism and democratic values, and offers up their connection as part of an unambiguous rebuke of Nazi eugenics. In the Hudson Bay sequence early in the film, a German soldier bludgeons an Inuk with his rifle butt, leaving the man to die on the floor. Lieutenant Hirth defends the attack by declaring that "The Eskimos are racially as low as negroes. They are semi-apes, only one degree above the Jews." Citing *Mein Kampf*, he boasts proudly that these "are the Fuhrer's own words." Hitler's brutal ideology of racial differentiation and hierarchy is eventually contrasted with the Hutterite-leader Peter's (Anton Walbrook) moving speech against Nazism, in which he declares that Germans such as the Hutterites need not see their fellow countrymen as "brothers" simply because they share a common ancestry. In this and other scenes in *49th Parallel*, Powell and Pressburger repeatedly assert the idea that *all* human beings derive from a common ancestor—and that national borders such as the forty-ninth parallel are no more than arbitrary lines of division. Civility, tolerance, and empathy are human virtues that can—if anything can—*purify* the human race of the hateful Nazis who are, as Peter describes them to Hirth, like the "microbes of some filthy disease filled with the longing to multiply yourselves until you destroy everything healthy in the world." Only a Canada united, a British Empire united, a world united, can stop the Nazi disease of hatefulness from corrupting *all* cultures.

Once we step back from Peter's rousing words and the film's relatively progressive ideas, we must note that cosmopolitanism serves Britain's pro-democratic propaganda in much the same way that racism served German propaganda and isolationism served US propaganda. The overt goal of *49th Parallel* was, of course, to suggest to Americans why they should join the

British and the Canadians in their fight against Germany. Much of Powell and Pressburger's argument for the necessity of the United States doing so naturally hinges on downplaying the relevance of national borders and stressing the importance of universal human values. The film is therefore eager to show respect for North America's unique cultures and to stress how the current threat to Britain is also a threat to the United States.

Nothing in the MOI Programme, which focuses exclusively on the differences between British and German characters, institutions, and principles, prepares us for Powell and Pressburger's systematic case for ideal *human* characters, institutions, and principles.[15] Pluralism and cosmopolitanism will remain a crucial part of Powell and Pressburger's mature wartime propaganda films, many of which will expand upon *49th Parallel*'s relative de-emphasizing of class as an important part of their Program.

Third, the film highlights and defends the idea of Germanic individualism. We argued in the Introduction that Powell and Pressburger's strategic advocacy of cosmopolitanism logically demands that Germans, as members of the human race, always contain the potential to be good men and women. Certainly, their wartime films highlight and sometimes even construct their plots around German characters whose basic morality distances them from the majority of sinister Nazis. Even in the prewar feature film *The Spy in Black* (1939), which presents the charismatic and relatively sympathetic U-boat Commander Ernst Hardt, the filmmakers seem intent on exploring the narrative, characterological, and philosophical benefits of shunning cartoonish portraits of Germans.

This feature of their films would have been slightly less subversive in 1941 than it would seem several years later. This is because, as Ian McLaine has shown, by the time of Dunkirk, official policy of the MOI had shifted dramatically away from Chamberlain's position of constantly working to differentiate the German people from their leaders in the hopes of a peaceful resolution:

[T]he impulse to relieve the German people from blame lasted only as long as the German armies confined their attentions to Eastern Europe. When the war moved closer to home and it was realised the fight was on in earnest, the tone of the propaganda underwent an abrupt change, a process greatly hastened by Churchill's accession to the premiership on 10 May.[16]

---

[15]It does focus on changes that may need to be made to films in order to render British ideals and institutions more palatable to audiences on the continent or in the United States.

[16]Ian McLaine, *Ministry of Morale: Home Front Morale and the Ministry of Information in World War II* (London, Boston, and Sydney: George Allen & Unwin, 1979), 142. Siân Nicholas concurs, arguing that "With the Phoney War at an end . . . MOI policy veered towards a

Only weeks after Dunkirk, the MOI launched its famous "Anger Campaign" in order to increase "the intensity of personal anger felt by the individual British citizen against the German people and Germany."[17] According to Jo Fox, the British people never entirely stopped separating the German people and the Nazi leadership, showing throughout the war period a rather dynamic range of feelings toward Germans and Germany.[18]

Nonetheless, *49th Parallel*'s production straddles the two separate periods with their diametrically opposed approaches to propagandizing Germans—a fact that explains why, upon the film's release, its depiction of Germans seemed inappropriate to a number of critics and to audience members such as Percival Moreton. However, as the later films of The Archers would prove, Powell and Pressburger's emphasis on the good German cannot be said to have been dictated by the MOI. As we shall demonstrate, the basic principle informing their nuanced depiction of German characters remains consistent through the war years, in spite of shifting MOI policies and pronouncements.

In *49th Parallel*, the German soldier Vogel grows increasingly disgusted with the barbarism of his comrades. Early in the film, his actions suggest how his Christian beliefs supersede his Nazi ones. Before departing the Hudson Bay Company trading post, he fulfills Johnnie's (Laurence Olivier) dying request by secretly fetching him his rosary; then, in a fit of self-loathing, he violently carves a swastika into one of the trading post walls before storming out into the cold. Over time, however, Vogel's inner conflict leads him to reject his crew, especially after encountering the peaceful community of Hutterites, which reminds him of his life in Germany before Hitler's rise. "Being with you," he says to Peter, "has made me feel like it used to be, at home. I'd almost forgotten what it was like . . . before everything changed. The life I've been living seems to have no sense in it now." A moment later, the two men speculate about how a "simple good human being" like Vogel could wind

---

wholesale identification of the German nation, not simply their Nazi leaders, as the enemy, in a conscious mirroring of the First World War theme 'Once a Hun, always a Hun'" (*The Echo of War: Home Front Propaganda and the Wartime BBC, 1939–45* [Manchester: Manchester University Press, 1996], 154). See also Mark Wollaeger, *Modernism, Media, and Propaganda: British Narrative from 1900 to 1945* (Princeton, NJ: Princeton University Press, 2008), 41.

[17] TNA PRO INF 1/849, HPC "Anger Campaign" June 17, 1940. Qtd. in Fox, *Film Propaganda*, 137.

[18] Jo Fox, *Film Propaganda*, 139. Interestingly, something similar happened in Germany regarding the British, according to Gerwin Strobl: "Even in 1940, the evidence of a nation united in its contempt for, or hatred of, Britain is not wholly persuasive. In May 1940 the Princess Vassiltchikov, an objective and often shrewd observer, noted in her diary: 'Many Germans have still a lurking admiration for the English.' Some six months later, she was astonished to come across a vast building site where the Third Reich was constructing a new British embassy for use after the war. The fact that such a building was envisaged at all in Hitler's gigantic new capital is surely revealing" (*The Germanic Isle: Nazi Perceptions of Britain* [Cambridge: Cambridge University Press, 2000], 130).

up serving the Nazi party; Vogel lists coercion, propaganda, destitution, and fear as factors that influence young and old alike. The following day, after openly defying Hirth, his commanding officer, and revealing his intention to renounce Nazism and join the religious community, he is summarily executed by his Lieutenant's makeshift firing squad. Vogel's is perhaps the most tragic death in the film.

49th Parallel's measured treatment of the Germans proved controversial; as we suggested at the outset of this chapter, it served for some commentators as the foundation of the film's realism and excellence and, for others, as evidence of its naiveté and ineffectiveness as propaganda. While reviewers of all sorts interpreted the film's degree of sympathy with the German people in dramatically different ways, Powell and Pressburger did, in fact, deliberately set out to avoid caricaturing Germans, including Nazis. Even Powell's pitch to Duff Cooper, Minister of Information, stressed the point: "'This is a propaganda picture in which the only good Nazi is a dead Nazi,' I began. 'But as that kind of propaganda can be self-defeating, we have started out by making them human beings. There are all kinds of Nazis, as there are all kinds of human beings.'"[19] Those closest to Powell and Pressburger seem to have understood this strategy perfectly well. In April of 1942, for example, Pressburger received a letter from his friend Reinhold Schunzel, who claimed that "this is one of the finest pieces of writing I have ever seen . . . this is the first picture of this kind which faces the issue and does not try to ridicule the enemy."[20]

At the same time, in a purely technical sense, Powell and Pressburger must have understood that a balanced treatment of Germans would be more effective than any caricature in showing just how horrific the Nazi regime had become. According to Kevin MacDonald,

> On one significant point Emeric disagreed with the Ministry of Information memo. What was needed, in his opinion, was not the nostalgia and cosiness of *Goodbye Mr Chips*, but a film which realistically portrayed the brutality, sadism and proto-religious zeal of the Nazis. Gagged and bound by appeasement, the British public still had very little idea what it was they were really fighting against. As someone who had experienced Nazism first hand, Emeric thought it was his duty to tell it how it was.[21]

The quotation suggests the ways in which Powell and Pressburger's early war films committed to a form of propaganda that both respected realism over distortion and truth over lies, and depicted in clear-eyed fashion *Nazi*, and

---

[19] Powell, *A Life*, 354.
[20] The letter is in the Pressburger papers held by the British Film Institute (1/19/13 EPR).
[21] Macdonald, *Emeric Pressburger*, 166.

not *German*, villainy. They could not control, however, how others would understand or respond to their decision about how to depict Germans, especially after the war had entered a different phase and attitudes toward the enemy shifted.

Whereas more incisive observers could see the film's treatment of Germans as a strength of the script itself—indeed, of strong film-writing more generally[22]—others expressed feelings of discomfort, even guilt, over their reactions to the Nazi characters. The reviewer for the *Daily Express* acknowledged that "because they [the Nazis] are on the run, some people may feel a sneaking sympathy for them."[23] The *Liverpool Post* was yet more detailed in explaining the origins of that feeling:

> Stories of escape more or less demand that one's sympathies should be with the escapers, but the escapers here are murderers of the unarmed and hitters below the belt. . . . Towards the end, human nature being what it is, we can hardly help feeling a sneaking regard for Hirth, the officer and only survivor of the landing party; and indeed the extraordinary grasp with which Eric Portman handles this most difficult part does more than anything to hold the film together.[24]

In the *Weston Super Mare Gazette*, the reviewer respected that the film's "propaganda is incidental to the plot,"[25] but also noted that "the argument tries too hard to explain the Nazi creed [so] that one critic thought it was too kind to the Germans."[26] The reviewer for the *Sunday Express* agreed with that view, declaring more decisively that "The faults of the picture are that the Nazis are made too heroic."[27]

In perhaps the most well-known attack on the film, which prompted a debate stretching over multiple issues of the Scottish newspaper *Dumfries and Galloway Standard*, Mary Major Robson began an attack on Powell and Pressburger that would continue in different forms well beyond the war years. This right-wing assault would reach its apex in a 1944 pamphlet she coauthored with her husband Emmanuel, entitled *The Shame and Disgrace of Colonel Blimp*. In 1942, however, Robson's argument about *49th Parallel*, a "monumental example of filmic folly," was that it failed precisely because

---

[22] It should perhaps be mentioned that Pressburger won the 1942 Academy Award for Best Story.
[23] *Daily Express*, October 9, 1941.
[24] *Liverpool Post*, October 10, 1941.
[25] The comment is slightly cryptic, but the reviewer is espousing a common-enough view that a film's propaganda should serve its plot, not replace or compete with it.
[26] *Weston Super Mare Gazette*, November 1, 1941.
[27] *Sunday Express*, October 12, 1941.

it did not caricature the Nazis as bloodthirsty villains.[28] According to both of the Robsons, this same fault marred all of The Archers' films made during and just after the war. Speaking of the 1946 film *A Matter of Life and Death*, for instance, the authors would claim that The Archers' "blackhearted bitterness against Britain, which was implicit in their wartime output, 'The Spy in Black,' 'One of Our Aircraft is Missing,' '49th Parallel,' 'A Canterbury Tale,' and 'Blimp,' is now explicit, openly and sneeringly anti-British . . . now that the war is over."[29] In spite of the Robsons' harsh criticism of both their patriotism and their artistry, Powell and Pressburger continued to reject caricature as an acceptable, or effective, method for depicting Germans, choosing, instead, to characterize even some Nazi party members as ordinary men and women, misled by their leaders and guilty of the morally disastrous decision to follow them.

In addition to celebrating pluralism, cosmopolitanism, and Germanic individualism, *49th Parallel* is unusually self-reflective about its own status as a propaganda film. We have already seen in the first two chapters how Powell and Pressburger's earliest collaborations feature moments of clever self-reflexivity about their own functions as propagandists (consider the Chamberlain busts in *Contraband* [1940]). *49th Parallel* is their first feature to meditate extensively upon its own status as propaganda; it engages in the kind of self-interrogation that is arguably the most distinguishing characteristic of The Archers' wartime work. In this film, they challenge two common assumptions about propaganda: first, that effective propaganda must hide what it is; and second, that it must disable the critical faculties of those who consume it. *49th Parallel*, we should make clear, was perceived unequivocally as wartime propaganda by the British government, by its creators, and by a large percentage of its audience members alike. But rather than attempting to increase its so-called "entertainment value" by *disguising* its propaganda function, the film openly reflects upon its status as propaganda, and sees its reflexivity as one crucial source of its entertainment value. The film forces audiences to consider the very questions that Powell and Pressburger themselves must have pondered at the beginning of each wartime collaboration: What particular formal and thematic features

---

[28]*Dumfries and Galloway Standard*, April 8, 1942 (5). About this and other pieces by the Robsons, see John Russell Taylor, "Michael Powell, Myths and Supermen," *Sight and Sound* 47 (1978): 226–9. After eviscerating the ignorance of the Robsons, Taylor tries to understand what in the films might have led them to such a profound misunderstanding of their meaning and politics; he settles on "certain things in the Powell-Pressburger films that seemed . . . not totally anti-German," and then seeks to compare Powell to other artists (one is D. H. Lawrence; another, Martin Scorsese) whose works also possess such a "strong irritant quality": "Perhaps the easiest, because most provocative, way of encapsulating [that irritant quality] is to say that the most immediate comparison which springs to mind in the cinema is with the films of Leni Riefenstahl" (226).

[29]E. W. and M. M. Robson, *The World is My Cinema* (London: Drydens, 1947), 65.

define a propaganda film? How might we account for a particular film's effectiveness or failures as propaganda? Ethically speaking, how can we justify the creation and distribution of propaganda? Is it possible to differentiate propaganda that serves fascism from propaganda that serves democratic or representative forms of governance? Again, whereas most propagandists will very naturally attempt to prevent their audiences from thinking too directly about such questions—in part by disavowing their propaganda intentions—Powell and Pressburger invite their wartime audiences to brood over them.

Such a strategy is also, finally, the source of the film's dangerous interpretability, for in laying bare the practical difficulties of easily differentiating totalitarian and democratic propaganda, their film comes within a hair's breadth of being a German propaganda film. Had Hirth made it to the United States, after all, *49th Parallel* might have become a Nazi propaganda film rather than a British one—and this point bizarrely underscores how the film's most skeptical audiences and reviewers came close to being right about it. In the section that follows, we turn to the specific content of *49th Parallel*, elaborating on how Powell and Pressburger both made propaganda and reflected on the process of doing so—not merely as a mode of wartime filmmaking, but as the proper subject of filmmaking for the Second World War.

Showing Goebbels "a Thing or Two"

That *49th Parallel* works so well on the level of entertainment seems slightly miraculous when one considers the immense pressure Powell and Pressburger imposed on themselves to conjure a meaningful propaganda film. As Pressburger explains, "When a war breaks out, it is only natural that everybody to do with films is racking his brains: what sort of films to make during the war.... We agreed (Powell and I) that films were eminently suitable for one vital task: to enlighten American public opinion."[30] Rather than dreaming up a story in a fit of poetic inspiration, Powell and Pressburger "racked their brains" to address what they saw as one of the key problems of the moment: the stubborn isolationism of the United States in a war that required that country's intervention.[31] We would argue that their being forced to work in such a practical way, from the outside in, led to a self-conscious filmmaking process. More specifically, the necessity of having to think about what constituted effective and non-effective propaganda

---

[30] EPR/1/19/16 BFI Document 1, "Loose Diary of a Scriptwriter."
[31] As we saw in Chapter 1's discussion of the treatment for *The Spy in Black*, Pressburger was thinking about the possibility of US involvement in the war even before it had commenced.

resulted in a film about the difficulty and importance of that intellectual process itself.

Powell and Pressburger didn't craft *49th Parallel* out of an intuitive sense of what might raise morale or satisfy the MOI. Having made films such as *The Lion Has Wings* (1939) and *Contraband* that tested out what a propaganda film could and should be, Powell and Pressburger were in *49th Parallel* actually beginning to *theorize* propaganda. In preparing a speech in the late 1970s, Pressburger articulated the conclusions he and Powell drew from this process of theorization. His notes are archived in the BFI, and we quote them here at some length:

> With the war came the Ministry of Information and with it the question of Propaganda. Hitler and his Propaganda Ministry knew something about Publicity and Propaganda. . . . Hitler's propaganda chief, Göbbels [sic], knew the value of "repetition", but failed to recognize that it was wrong to expect the same results in a free country as he got on the home market. In a free country, if people had enough of propaganda, they switched over to another wave-length. In Germany there was little else to listen to. In a free country the media had to produce higher standards, too. Propaganda was—and is!—to persuade others to do something they would rather not do. For us, here, the richest prize to achieve with propaganda was to make the United States of America an active ally. But how to do it? The pitfalls seemed too dangerous. You made just one mistake and you did so much more harm that you wished you had never started with your propaganda. The riddle was that to be really effective we had to bring nazi [sic] doctrines face to face with the common people of the United States.[32]

Here, Pressburger acknowledges that Goebbels's propaganda machine emerged out of totalitarian ideals and thinking, and he professes faith in the idea that totalitarian and democratic propaganda methods are fundamentally distinct. He offers a slightly different version of this distinction in another draft of this speech:

> The Nazis made a mistake to confuse propaganda with publicity. Such a mistake is easily made in a totalitarian state. Publicity is based on repetition. Propaganda should be much more subtle. In a free country, repetition is boring, you change the wavelength. Only a totalitarian state can use repetition since there is nothing different available.[33]

---

[32] EPR/1/19/14 (Formerly 6/20).
[33] Ibid.

The straightforward definition of propaganda contained in the first passage—"to persuade others to do something they would rather not do"—is clarifying in that it seems to describe what for Pressburger is propaganda's ultimate purpose. Further, the passage's critical characterization of totalitarian propaganda as mere "repetition" becomes a hallmark of the Powell and Pressburger approach.[34] They may have appropriated the idea from F. C. Bartlett's influential 1940 study of propaganda, in which he lists as "one of the most constant" of all "methods of [totalitarian] Political Propaganda" "a tremendously strong belief in the virtues of sheer repetition."[35] The belief comes directly from Hitler, Bartlett argues, quoting the Fuhrer's critique of the stupidity of the masses: "Since the masses are slow to comprehend, they must be told the same thing a thousand times."[36] We will return to the bogeyman of "repetition" momentarily, as we delve deeper into *49th Parallel* itself.

Further into Pressburger's notes, we hear again of the problematic US policy of neutrality. Pressburger describes how he decided to address that policy as follows:

> Like many other foreigners who found refuge in this country, now at war, I too, wished to do something useful. I was staring for hours, for days, at the map of the United States for an inspiration. The longer I stared the more interested I got in a long, gently curving dotted line indicating the common border between the United States and Canada: the 49th Parallel. I had it! We didn't have to make any part of the film in the States. We'll make it in Canada. As part of the British Commonwealth, the Dominion of Canada was already at war with Germany. Canadians could say what they pleased. Their sympathies for the British cause could be expressed as strongly as they wished to express them. And still, everything that happened north of the 49th Parallel, had a bearing on what happened south of it.[37]

Canada: like the solution to some nagging mathematical equation, it finally emerges for Pressburger as the only answer to the American neutrality problem. Powell loved this idea and, not long after, he was able to convince

---

[34]We discussed the Nazi reliance on repetition in the Introduction. David Welch describes the method of repetition as a specific hallmark of totalitarian propaganda—though one that the Allies were willing to use when it suited them. See *Persuading the People: British Propaganda in World War II* (London: The British Library, 2016), 13. McLaine discusses the sense of dedication within the MOI to the principle that the basic tools of totalitarianism must be shunned. Of course, practice was a more difficult matter. See *Ministry of Morale*, esp. 11.
[35]F. C. Bartlett, *Political Propaganda* (Cambridge: Cambridge University Press, 1940), 67.
[36]Ibid.
[37]Ibid.

the MOI to grant them the money they needed for a reconnaissance tour of the Dominion. Soon a production was underway whose propaganda function was overt and systematically developed. "Goebbels considered himself an expert on propaganda," Pressburger has famously remarked, "but I thought I'd show him a thing or two."[38]

"All That We Have Learnt about Nazism and Democracy"

As we have noted, *49th Parallel* focuses on a stranded group of six Nazi sailors whose U-boat is bombed by the RCAF in the Hudson Bay. Generally speaking, the film is divided into five major sequences set in locations intended to display the richness and diversity of the Canadian landscape: a Hudson Bay trading post, a Hutterite commune in the Manitoba prairies, the bustling city of Winnipeg, a campsite in the Rockies near Banff National Park, and the US/Canadian border at Niagara Falls. Each of these locations appeals to a different US demographic, and each sequence contributes, we would argue, to the film's overall interest in the importance of constructing—and learning to deconstruct—propaganda.

The film opens in mimicry of a standard contemporary wartime documentary, establishing an immediate connection between itself as a fictional feature and what Bill Nichols calls the "discourses of sobriety"—"Science, economics, politics, foreign policy, education, religion, welfare" and other discourses that "assume . . . they can and should alter the world itself."[39] Following the opening credits, which are presented over a breathtaking aerial tracking shot of the Canadian Rockies, the camera zooms in on a map of North America until the 49th parallel dividing Canada

---

[38]Qtd. in Macdonald, *Emeric Pressburger*, 166.
[39]Bill Nichols, *Representing Reality: Issues and Concepts in Documentary* (Bloomington, IN: Indiana University Press, 1991), 3–4. We believe the film's deliberate use of documentary techniques has been under-studied, though Robert Murphy has correctly identified the film's realism in relation to British documentary films of the period: "Critics were uneasy about a return to the jingoistic film propaganda of the First World War, not only because it negated all the advances made in the use of films for educational and informational purposes by the British documentary movement but because it would not be acceptable abroad—particularly in the United States. Films like *49th Parallel* and *Convoy* were welcomed as harbingers of a new style of cinema" (*British Cinema and the Second World War* [New York: Continuum, 2000], 28). Even as early as the 1940s, critics understood the influence of documentary on the British feature film golden age; Dilys Powell was one of the first observers to note "a new movement towards concentration on the native subject, the movement towards documentary truth in the entertainment film. The war both encouraged a new seriousness of approach by British producers and directors, and drove them to look nearer home than before in their themes" (*Films Since 1939* [London: Longmans, Green and Co, 1947], 22).

and the United States becomes the focus. A classical documentary voice-over (supplied by Canadian Vincent Massey)—upper-class, male, with British rather than American pronunciation—explains that we are looking at "the only undefended frontier in the world." A montage of tracking shots then flaunts the beauty of the various Canadian sites we will visit, like a video postcard celebrating the wonders of this vast land: there's Banff, and a rural farming community, and Winnipeg from above, and the great eastern coastal and inland waters. The accompanying score, written by Ralph Vaughan Williams, shifts from whimsical and celebratory to ominous as a German U-boat smashes through the surface of the serene Gulf of St. Lawrence. The story proper begins here, and even this first scene highlights the centrality of propaganda in *49th Parallel*. U-boat 37 fires on and sinks a Canadian vessel containing oil and gasoline. The Canadian shipmen spill into the cold waters, or they pile into lifeboats, desperately struggling to evade fires and flotsam until they are face to face with the enemy. The confusion and shock of these men is marked by a notable silence in this unscored section of soundtrack, which soon is broken by Kommandant Bernsdorff's (Richard George) booming voice as he shouts at one of his subordinates: "What in the devil's name are you doing? Where's your camera?"

In many ways, Bernsdorff's question reveals the representational logic that will govern each sequence's distinctive treatment of propaganda. According to this logic—learned perhaps most profoundly after Dunkirk, but hardly novel—controlling the perception of wartime events impacts the nature of the truths that the public might derive from them. Bernsdorff is outraged by the possibility that his destruction of the Canadian vessel might go unseen, undocumented—what would be the value in sinking this ship if it couldn't be shown to both his superiors and the German people? It should also be noted that the particular line of thought implicit in Bernsdorff's question is, of course, established here as a *Nazi logic* specifically. As we shall see later in this scene, the film will associate propaganda that distorts reality with Germans, and propaganda that reveals reality with the Allies—upholding the basic totalitarian/democratic propaganda binary that contemporary theorists propagated (see Introduction).

Committed to a formal as well as thematic self-reflexivity, Powell and editor David Lean emphasize throughout the film the crucial importance of subjective perceptions in framing any reality. They will often highlight cutaways to objects and scenery that are framed through binocular PoV shots—so that the seeing subject is as perceivable as the seen object. At the moment when an angry Bernsdorff bemoans the missing camera, for example, he is isolated through an incredible deep focus shot taken from inside the U-boat and through the open hatch, which frames the Kommandant's head and upper torso like some heavenly cherub in a painting by Raphael. The effect is to suggest what the German superior officer appears like from an admiring subordinate's position. Here, as elsewhere in *49th Parallel*, the filmmakers reinforce ideas about the importance of individual perception and the meaningfulness of images and symbols through powerful, yet mainly subtle, compositions and edits (Figures 3.1 and 3.2).

The scene continues as Hirth interrogates the Canadian ship's second officer (its captain and first officer are dead) about its load and destination.

FIGURE 3.1 *The Canadian vessel through the eyes of U-boat officers in* 49th Parallel *(1941).*

FIGURE 3.2 *The U-boat Kommandant from below in* 49th Parallel *(1941).*

At this point, Lieutenant Kuhnecke (Raymond Lovell) appears between the two men with the camera that Bernsdorff ordered on to the deck. Hirth's objective is not to obtain information about the ship's load and destination, however; it is to perform getting that information, and to force a Canadian to acquiesce to German superiority for the benefit of the camera. Sensing the threat posed by the camera, the Canadian officer swats it into the gulf waters, prompting Kuhnecke to knock him overboard. With the camera gone, no point remains for continuing the interrogation, so Bernsdorff orders the U-boat immediately to dive, leaving the wreckage of the Canadian ship and her survivors behind. Then, in the first cut away from the exterior gulf shots into the submerged U-boat itself, we see a photograph of Hitler shaking the hand of a small blonde German boy and patting him on the cheek.[40] The photo underscores what was at stake in the fight for the camera just moments earlier. Whereas the Hitler image represents a successful instance of mythologizing the Fuhrer's beneficent domestic rule, the drowned camera of the previous scene represents a failed opportunity for the Nazis. The film's bridging of these two distinctive propaganda cases reveals a major theme of the entire film, which is that the war will be fought always with an eye towards the importance of propaganda. Although the film captures a successful Nazi military operation, it lingers on the war-within-the-war, highlighting how the Nazis' lost opportunity to use a demolished Canadian vessel as proof of their power and superiority marks a paradoxical victory for the Allied cause.

The Hudson Bay sequence proper begins when the U-boat is bombed by RCAF planes, and the Nazi survivors find themselves stranded near the Bay Company's famous trading post. Here we meet Albert, the Factor (Finlay Currie), who manages a provincial extreme-outpost that seems, in ways, more like a center of international affairs; a microcosmic portrait of the diverse, internationally engaged Canada that Powell and Pressburger wish to capture, the Hudson's Bay trading post is near an Inuit village and occupied by the Inuk, "Eskimo Nick"; Johnnie, the Franco-Canadian trapper (Laurence Olivier); and also, through a nightly two-way radio chess game, a Michigan friend and colleague named Russell and his wife Maude.

Throughout the film, both American and German characters learn from experience that skill at interpreting propaganda is as important as the ability to control and disseminate it. Often, the former skill involves the individual's gradual deprogramming of the propaganda by which he has already unwittingly been influenced. In the Hudson Bay sequence, Johnnie especially

---

[40]Such photographs of Hitler were common enough in the era, being propaganda attempts to portray the Fuhrer as a protector of German youth. To view several such images, see Maryse Godden, "Rare Adolf Hitler Propaganda Pictures Posing with Kids," which ran in the *The Sun* on March 31, 2017 (https://www.thesun.co.uk/news/3222051/rare-adolf-hitler-propaganda-pictures-posing-with-kids/ accessed July 7, 2021).

must come to terms with the murky line between true information and false propaganda. Having been in the wilderness for many months, cut off from news of any kind and unaware that the war has begun, Johnnie speaks to Albert about "war rumours," repeating his father's hunch that "this Hitler is only bluffing." When Albert explains that the war has begun, including the detail that the Germans have gunned down Polish women and children, Johnnie shakes his head in disbelief: "The Germans are ordinary men, same as you and me. I wouldn't do a thing like that, would you? Well, you can't tell me they do. That's all newspaper talk to try to bring us in." He is then shocked when Albert explains to him that Canada, even French Canada, has already joined the war effort. Johnnie responds suspiciously to these developments due to his belief that ulterior motives drive the news cycle, and that governments are "all the same." He and Albert comfort themselves in the knowledge that "We needn't worry about it out here." In doing so, they are, of course, offering a variation of American isolationist thought. Albert speaks these words only moments before the Nazis burst in the trading post door, brutalize Nick with the butt of a rifle, and take Johnnie and Albert hostage.

As Hirth and the other Germans converse with the Canadians, the full extent of their indoctrination into Nazism is made evident through their exchange with Johnnie, which we introduced earlier. When Johnnie criticizes the Nazis' barbaric treatment of Nick, who lies bleeding to death on the floor, Hirth responds,

"The Eskimos are racially as low as Negroes."
Albert: "What's the matter with Negroes?"
Hirth: "They are semi-apes, only one degree above the Jews."
Albert: "Is that so?"
Hirth: "Those are the Fuhrer's own words. From *Mein Kampf*."

To this, Johnnie explains that he makes his living trapping, but that if "I was meet half-ape, I wouldn't kick him in the stomach as you did that husky in there." Experience tells Johnnie that these are no ordinary men; disposition and decency show that the real "animals" are the Nazis. Nazi propaganda, in the form of "the Fuhrer's own words," has utterly dehumanized the German U-boat crew.

Johnnie revels in mocking the younger Nazis, those men who seem most like automatons, lacking many memories of a time prior to Hitler. At one point he asks Lohrmann (John Chandos), "Do you really march around in Berlin doing this?" mimicking the stiff marching position and hand salute to Hitler that Riefenstahl's *Triumph of the Will* (1935) introduced to much of the world. When Lohrmann replies simply, "yes," Johnnie asks him "Why?" Lohrmann's puzzled look gives away an internal grappling, however momentary. Subsequent dialogue between Johnnie and Hirth continues to emphasize how reality and German propaganda do not match:

Hirth: "You must know that after the war, the Fuhrer intends to liberate your people from the British tyranny."
Johnnie: "*Comment?* How?"
Hirth: "French Canada will be free. *You* will be free."
Johnnie: "I *am* free! Or I was plenty free till you guys got in."
Hirth: "I mean the freedom of your people, an oppressed minority. The freedom to speak their own language, to have their own schools and churches, to govern their own affairs. Here you will find it written in the Fuhrer's own words. (Hirth takes *Mein Kampf* from his pocket and presents it to Johnnie.) Perhaps you've read it. . . . This is the Bible. You must get a copy. It will explain everything to you as it has to me."

. . . .

Johnnie: "Maybe, uh, your Fuhrer ain't so smart as he think. Don't he know that we French Canadians have always our own school? And church? And the right to speak as we want? And run our own affair, by golly. . . . . Let me ask you one question . . . . How 'bout them, uh, Poles? How 'bout the French? Do you let them run their own affair?" (Figure 3.3)

When Hirth protests "that is different," Johnnie simply laughs. Accurate information, real experience, fortifies him against German propaganda. The reality of how Canada works butts up against how Hitler and propaganda say it works—and this fact causes the Nazis more and more consternation throughout the film. In this context, it is significant that what eventually

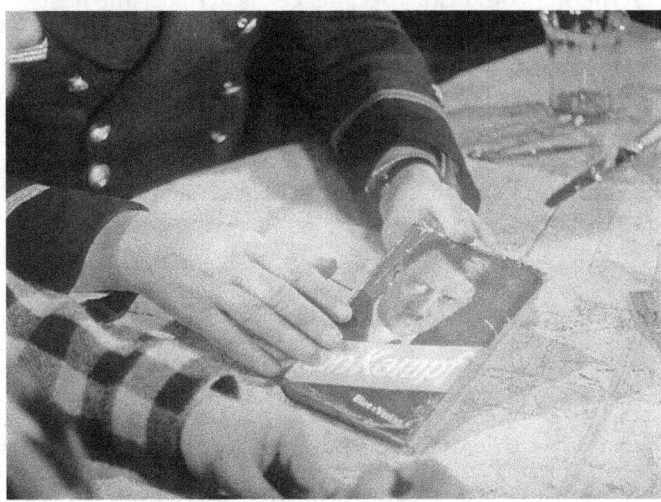

FIGURE 3.3 *Hirth pushing Hitler's propaganda in* 49th Parallel *(1941).*

forces a showdown in the trading post is Russell's relaying of accurate newspaper headlines about a downed U-boat nearby.

Later, in the relatively brief Winnipeg sequence, Powell and Pressburger play out the process of deprogramming—or at least represent the cognitive dissonance of the Nazis—in almost comically symbolic fashion. That nighttime sequence begins with an overhead shot of bustling crowds in the rainy streets checking the news feeds from the "Winnipeg Free Press," a direct callback to the earlier conversation between Hirth and Johnnie about free Canadian people. The liveliness in Winnipeg is signaled through shots of street scenes and well-lighted signs displaying the variety and wealth of the modern capitalist city. Into this city stumble the three surviving Nazis—cold, hungry, and dumbstruck by it all. Most striking to them, of course, are the bright advertisements for food products ranging from fresh fruits to succulent meats to Chinese food to Coca Cola and beer.[41] The three men eventually succumb to Canada's temptations, and, by hocking some field glasses for cash, they choose hot dogs as their particular poison—trading away that officially issued military tool of "the Fatherland," as they put it, for that iconic sausage imported from Germany but made famous in America. Without any irony, Hirth congratulates Lohrmann: "No field glass has ever had a better end." Lohrmann, in agreement, holds the last bite of hot dog up to his eyes and jokes, "We shall view the future better through these." The entire sequence never mentions propaganda outright, but somehow exposes fully the lies of German propaganda regarding the unfree peoples of North America. In the lights and splendor of the modern North American city, even as the Germans dig in their heels yet further, they see truths which contradict the lies they've been told by Hitler and Goebbels; they see, that is, that what Germany would call "decadence" is actually the nearly-unlimited freedom to choose.[42] The film stops short of telling us whether the Germans become aware of the gap between Nazi rhetoric and their experiences in Winnipeg, but we know from Vogel's example how cognitive dissonance can lead to real change (Figure 3.4).

At this point, Vogel is dead, and it was he, of all the Germans, who suffered the most pressing moral doubts about Nazi propaganda. Toward

---

[41]We view the scene as a self-conscious callback to the moment in *The Spy in Black* when Captain Ernst Hardt (Conrad Veidt) encounters British abundance after it is suggested at the outset of the film—via a German newspaper headline—that the Brits were starving.

[42]Pamela E. Swett has shown how, from at least the mid-1930s on, especially as the lifestyles of average Americans were improving and becoming more visible through film and other popular culture outlets, "German consumers were encouraged [by the Nazi Party] to dream of an abundance that, while not yet available to the vast majority of citizens, was promised to be just over the horizon" ("Individual Consumers and Consumption in Nazi Germany," *A Companion to Nazi Germany*, ed. Shelley Baranowski, Armin Nolzen, and Claus-Christian W. Szejnmann [New York: Wiley-Blackwell, 2018], 299–313; 301). The war severely hindered the Nazi party's ability to deliver on such promises, of course.

FIGURE 3.4 *The first shot of Winnipeg in* 49th Parallel *(1941)*.

the end of the Hudson Bay sequence, he reveals not only his closeted Catholicism but also the torment that the clash of ideologies and moral systems is causing within him. Vogel's struggle is developed most fully in the Hutterite sequence in which he is reminded of his life as a boy, prior to the Nazis' rise to power. For Vogel, seeing other Germans living simply, as he did all those years ago, operates like a mirror that gradually reveals to him who he really is.

It is also in the Hutterite sequence that Hirth begins to fantasize about the propaganda value of the crew's story—*his* story—if they should manage to escape from Canada. "Well, Vogel," he muses as the two men lie in bed, "Who knows? In a few years time, it may be the basis of compulsory lectures to the Hitler youth." This line returns us to one of the key themes of the film, which is its self-consciousness about the way in which events can be shaped so as to make them usable for propaganda purposes. The exchange clarifies the stakes of the Nazis' escape plan. Should Hirth and his cronies make it back to Germany, the propagandists could easily use their triumph to tout German ingenuity and toughness at the expense of Canadian carelessness and military inferiority. It is no mistake that, just as this idea is made most explicit, Vogel begins to interrogate his country's propaganda openly. Having just learned from the Hutterite girl Anna (Glynis

Johns) that her mother was drowned in her attempt to flee Germany—most likely by U-boat torpedoes—he replies, "The ships we sank, with women and children aboard . . . the lifeboats we shelled, mmmm, we were good at that. What we did to the Eskimos at the post, the unarmed men we shot in the back. . . ." Not believing his ears, Hirth reminds him that they are at war, asking "Did you never read what Bismarck said? Leave them only their eyes to weep with." Vogel repeats the line and asks whether Bismarck really could have spoken such abhorrent words. When Hirth assures him that he spoke those words in the War of 1870 and implores Vogel to study Bismarck because "He was a *great* German," Vogel repeats the claim sarcastically, "A *good* German." This response marks the moment when Vogel moves from questioning fascist propaganda to denying it outright. In the film's most rousing speech a few scenes later, the Hutterite leader, Peter, does the same, repudiating Hirth's absurdly patriotic call for the Hutterites to join the Nazi cause. Whereas Peter's rejection of Nazi propaganda confirms his morality and firm identification with the new Canadian homeland, Vogel's similar act of rejection gets him killed.

If the film up to this point has tended to focus mostly on the Germans' inner struggle to reconcile reality and propaganda, the prolonged sequence in the Rocky Mountain wilderness centers on a character who, like Johnnie and most Americans below the forty-ninth parallel, would like to believe the war does not concern him. The two surviving Germans, Hirth and Lohrmann, wander into the camp of the wealthy and witty author, Philip Armstrong Scott (Leslie Howard), who is writing *Red Men of the Rockies*, a history of local indigenous peoples. Upon first meeting the Nazis, Scott reveals how much he is like Johnnie and Albert, despite their significantly different class and national backgrounds: "Up here in the Rockies, the war seems so remote one can't take it so seriously. Of course one knows one half of humanity is trying to wipe out the other half, but up here among the mountains and spruce forests, one sees it in perspective so that it seems almost unimportant." A stereotypical embodiment of the decadent aristocratic artist-intellectual, Scott is so blind that he fails even to see that the enemies of all civilization stand only a few inches away from him.

Blindness does not equate necessarily with ignorance. Whereas Johnnie was simply impervious to the realities of the war in his corner of Canadian wilderness, Scott seems to believe that understanding the way Nazis work— as well as treating them historically—will be enough. At one point he reads to Hirth and Lohrmann from his book, drawing out a wonderful comparison of Blackfoot Indians and Nazis:

> From the earliest age, their small boys were trained in the arts of war, which they considered to be the only pursuit worthy of a man. But they preferred to attack by night rather than by day, and wherever possible, to shoot the enemy in the back. Their smaller neighbors lived in constant

danger from them. They also believed in first terrorizing their opponent by covering themselves in war paint and beating loudly on their tribal drums.

When Scott asks the men if the Indians remind them of a "certain modern European tribe," Hirth has to suppress his mounting fury. Scott then answers his own question with another: "What price Goebbels, eh?" He spins this analogy out further by explaining how the Blackfoot leaders managed to control their people: "When a tribal leader really desired to drive a point home, he used that most terrible of all public speakers' weapons: repetition. Constant and unutterably wearisome repetition." Anticipating aspects of Pressburger's lectures about totalitarian propaganda, Scott emphasizes repetition through repetition of his own, beating his fist in mockery of Hitler as he speaks the final few lines, and then—as if the point were not clear enough—he references "Old man Hitler himself." Scott is not inaccurate in defining Nazi propaganda's overreliance on repetition, of course, but he makes a crucial mistake in assuming the wisdom of his own position. He also assumes too much about his book's ability to change people's minds about such matters by educating them—as if his ability to draw an academic comparison between the propaganda techniques of Blackfoot Indians and Nazis might lead to actual change. Scott emerges as something like a caricature of a Deweyan idealist, investing too much in the idea that education and knowledge would transform the masses into vigilant beings capable of rejecting the monsters hiding in plain sight. His own blindness, in spite of his education, hammers the point home.

Powell and Pressburger, operating here in a decidedly pragmatist mode, reveal that their position is much closer to Walter Lippmann's democratic realism than Dewey's idealism (see Introduction), especially when they suggest that even historians, artists, and intellectuals will need to take up actual arms in this fight. There's no anti-intellectualism to their position, it's important to note. When Hirth and Lohrmann destroy Scott's Picasso and Matisse paintings, and when they burn his Thomas Mann novels—reenacting the Nazi book burnings begun by the Main Office for Press and Propaganda of the German Student Union in the 1930s—they expose their outright rejection of all human knowledge, civilization, and progress. They exercise the sword and demolish the pen. Through Philip Armstrong Scott, Powell and Pressburger ask us to consider the ability of the great minds of their generation to use their pens as swords when necessary.[43] In the

---

[43]Pressburger explained his choices in a long letter to Powell, dated September 5, 1940: "Regarding Howard's character, I kept the character of a rich man. I kept it because we think here that it represents not only millionaires in Canada, but generally people who still do not get the idea that to win the War one needs action and that nice words and philosophy about 'peace

end, Scott manages both to chase the desperate Hirth away and to face Lohrmann's gunfire, even taking a bullet in the leg, just to enjoy the pleasure of knocking him out a moment later. Prior to charging Lohrmann, one of Scott's men warns him that "the papers say these men are killers." Scott's reply suggests how his physical confrontation of Lohrmann represents a litmus test for differentiating how democratic and totalitarian newspapers negotiate the dangerous interpretability of events: "Yes, the Canadian papers. The Nazi papers call them heroes.... One armed Superman against one unarmed decadent democrat. I wonder how Dr. Goebbels will explain that."

In one of the more meaningful edits in the film, David Lean sutures Scott's discussion of Goebbels to the final Niagara Falls sequence through a brief montage in which democratic and Nazi radio announcers take turns attempting to control the news cycle. First, a German radio announcer is seen within his soundproof booth, putatively attempting to connect directly with Hirth but, more importantly, sending a message to the vast radio audience about German superiority:

> Wherever you may be on the North American continent, I hail you as the paladin of the Third Reich, and the upholder of the honor of the great German people. By express order of the Fuhrer himself, you have today been invested with the Iron Cross, first class. Heil Hitler.

A moment later, we see a Canadian CBC radio announcer simply reporting where Hirth has been spotted and indirectly encouraging vigilance from citizen observers. This is followed by a cut to a different German announcer, again speaking directly to Hirth, but this time rendering more explicit the motives of the Nazi propagandists: "One man versus eleven million. They know that even now the odds are not too heavy when the one man represents the might of the Third Reich, and the eleven million [of Canada] a collapsing democracy." A final cut shows an NBC announcer simply reiterating that Hirth is now the only Nazi at large, but also acknowledging that "The whole world's eyes are on southern Ontario." The scene serves to highlight Germany's rigorous propaganda machine, its attempt to control people's perception of events even 5,000 miles away by narrativizing those events according to a mythology of national superiority. In contrast, the democratic radio announcements focus only on providing information. This rather remarkable montage reestablishes just prior to the film's climax the crucial importance of Hirth's fate, not because any serious military operation

---

and war' and 'Nazi menace' and 'keeping the culture for better days' are not enough. Mr. Smith is the man who has to be woken up. And he is the man also who has, as so many have, the guts to do as much as the most active people can do after his eyes are opened" (EPR 1/19/6 BFI).

hinges on his escape or capture but because of the story's propaganda potential. Insofar as the narrative pits Germany against North America, Hirth's escape could further disincentivize US involvement in the war.

The final sequence at Niagara Falls shows the United States unofficially participating in the war effort when two of its customs officers send the stowaway Hirth back across the Whirlpool Rapids Bridge into Canada, where he will be apprehended. It also serves as the powerful culmination of the film's explicit commentary on propaganda. Every previous reference to that topic in the film, every open discussion of it, and every depiction of its essential tools and machinery, has led us to this point. Hirth deploys Nazi rhetoric until the end, gloating to Canadian soldier and fellow stowaway Andy Brock that "Field Marshall Göring has said, 'It doesn't matter even if we have only one plane and one man left, so long as victory is ours.'" In this brutal, Bismarckian logic, individual lives are worth nothing so long as the nation triumphs. Brock looks on incredulously as Hirth describes his seemingly inevitable escape to the United States as proof of German propaganda's accuracy:

> We've beaten these dirty democracies, these weaklings. I tell you there's something inside us, something beyond the dim, muddy minds of you in the democracies. What do you know of the glorious, mystical ties of blood and race that unite me with every German Aryan? When I step on American soil, I shall not be alone. Adolph Hitler and all the great German people will be with me. It's not the Canadian people we're against. It's your filthy government. The whole democratic system.

In this train car on a bridge between Canada and the United States, the words "democracies" and "democratic system" resonate in especially important ways. Indeed, Powell himself notes that the boxcar scene "sums up all that we have learnt about Nazism and democracy."[44] The objective of the film, to convince the United States to join the war effort, suddenly is made more explicit than at any other point, and so the focus shifts from Germany versus Canada to totalitarianism versus democracy more generally. Brock answers by explaining to Hirth, whom he calls a "spoon-fed louse," that he is incapable even of understanding what democracy is about: "We own the right to be fed up with anything we damn please, and to say so out loud when we feel like it." Brock's democratic propaganda, which stresses individual freedoms, registers as antithetical to the values espoused by Hirth and Göring, for both of whom blind compliance is a central virtue and a victorious state can be comprised of a single surviving citizen.

---

[44]Powell, *A Life*, 375.

Once across the bridge, the two US customs officers discover Hirth, and they claim to understand that "the whole German nation is waiting to see if he gets away with it" because, as they say, they read the papers. Still, they feel they have no choice but to take Hirth to the German consul in spite of a feeling that "sometimes I think we got too many laws." Brock seizes the opportunity, however, to point out that, if technicalities and laws are binding, the men might use this fact to their advantage by recognizing that only freight registered on the manifest can be taken into the country. Hirth, as a stowaway, is not registered and so he can be sent back to Canada. In a clever reversal, the customs officers determine that Hirth's arrest is important enough to warrant creative reinterpretation of the law. These two "neutrals"—precisely the sort whom Powell and Pressburger would love to persuade to join the war effort—effectively thwart the making of a Nazi propaganda film about Hirth's heroic escape.

49th Parallel concludes, then, by explicitly juxtaposing the value systems of democracy and totalitarianism. To put it another way, it ends as it begins, with an emphasis on propaganda. In this way, Powell and Pressburger once again consider their own roles as cinematic propagandists. What is most remarkable about *49th Parallel*, though, is how this cinematic paean to democracy stages events in such a way that Hirth and his cohort come perilously close to appearing heroic. Powell and Pressburger take some risks in making the complexities of propaganda an explicit subject of their film, knowing that their audiences could interpret *49th Parallel* as being insufficiently critical of the Nazi regime or overly kind to German individuals. As we saw at the beginning of this chapter, in fact, certain contemporary audience members such as Percival Moreton felt the film is "wrongly constructed," in part because it "provides opportunities for sympathising with the hated enemy!" This chapter has suggested not merely that Powell and Pressburger anticipated such interpretations of their film's politics, but that they consciously determined that a truly democratic propaganda film must be able to accommodate a wider range of different, even opposed, audience interpretations. Brock emerges as a key figure here, as his disgruntled comments about the Canadian army model the kinds of interpretive freedoms that Powell and Pressburger's film argues for. A totalitarian propaganda film would, by contrast, severely limit the possible ways in which an audience could interpret its intended messages. In *49th Parallel*, Powell and Pressburger go well beyond MOI guidelines to both announce and develop the terms of their own specifically democratic propaganda Program, which by necessity must (in Pressburger's words) "persuade others to do something they would rather not do," rather than force or trick them into doing it.

4

From "We Can Take It" to "V for Victory"

Agency, Gender, and Propaganda in *One of Our Aircraft Is Missing*

Near the finale of *One of Our Aircraft Is Missing* (1942), Jo de Vries (Googie Withers)—a Dutch resistance leader shepherding six downed British airmen out of occupied Holland—raises her glass in a good luck toast to their escape and, more importantly, their eventual return to active duty in the Royal Air Force: "It has been our motto ever since the House of Orange drove out the Spaniards 300 years ago! *Je Main-Tiendrai*!" When prompted to translate the phrase for the non-Dutch speakers, Jo answers, "We can take it!" A stunned front gunner, Geoff Hickman (Bernard Miles), exclaims, "Well, I never. 300 years ago! We don't seem to have progressed much, do we?" Geoff's unconscious shift to first-person plural reflects more than spiritual solidarity between the British and Dutch people; it marks his sudden awareness of how fiercely intertwined are their destinies as free peoples facing the threat of Nazi victory. The phrase "we can take it," Geoff indirectly acknowledges, is precisely the same motto, or propaganda line, that was pervasive throughout Britain early in the war, having been popularized by Humphrey Jennings's short film *London Can Take It!* (1940), and a slightly repackaged version of it entitled *Britain Can Take It!* [1]

---

[1] *London Can Take It!* was made with a US audience in mind; *Britain Can Take It!*, which is a minute shorter and has "amended commentary," was created for UK distribution and retitled because the former was seen to be too London-centric.

Jennings's Crown Film Unit production highlights the stoicism and dignity of Londoners as they endure a day of terror and destruction during the Blitz. Narrated by US war correspondent Quentin Reynolds, the film was intended, like *49th Parallel* (1941), to inspire US entry into the war. Also like *49th Parallel*, it achieved great success in America, reaching a wide audience and earning a nomination for an Academy Award. Powell and Pressburger's direct allusion to *London Can Take It!* is part of their characteristic reflexivity regarding their own films' propaganda functions. It serves here to establish a dialogic connectedness between government-sponsored documentaries and fiction films designed similarly to aid in the war effort. *Aircraft* works like the duo's other mature wartime films, in other words, as a form of propaganda that practically theorizes contemporary propaganda forms.

In referencing the worldview articulated in the title of Jennings's film, Powell and Pressburger are also gesturing toward a sentiment associated with an earlier stage in the war. By the middle of 1941, the "Britain Can Take It" motto was already wearing thin with numerous Britons who were "now more concerned about 'giving it.'"[2] According to Jo Fox, many within the MOI desired to shift to a propaganda campaign more focused on Britain's offensive wartime strategies.[3] Crucially, just a month before production began on *Aircraft* in August 1941, Churchill heartily endorsed the V for Victory campaign, which announced the strategic shift of focus for which exhausted and frustrated Britons had been clamoring.[4] Like the earlier "Britain Can Take It" campaign, the immensely successful V campaign comes to play a critical, explicit part in *Aircraft*, figuring centrally in the film's internal commentary on the diverse roles performed by different members of the Allied resistance to Nazism—both at home and abroad. As this chapter will show, *Aircraft* ponders the intricacies of, and power dynamics at play in, the numerous unfamiliar relationships born out of German assaults on European national autonomy and identity—relationships among Britons themselves, of course, but also between them and citizens of those recently occupied countries they were being asked to liberate. As part of this larger exploration, we argue, Powell and Pressburger expressed special concern for the vital role propaganda could play in defining how such relationships should ideally function.

---

[2] Qtd. in Jo Fox, *Film Propaganda in Britain and Nazi Germany: World War II Cinema* (Oxford and New York: Berg, 2007), 126.
[3] Ibid.
[4] According to Wendy Webster, "Although the V campaign was initiated by [Belgian exile] Victor de Laveleye, leadership was quickly taken over by the British. A BBC European Intelligence Report urged the need for 'radio leadership' in order 'to gain and keep the power of commanding action from disarmed and hungry peoples and to use that power exactly as and when it can most help the High Command'" ("'Europe Against the Germans': The British Resistance Narrative, 1940–1950," *The Journal of British Studies* 48 [2009]: 958–82, 971).

At this point in their wartime work, Powell and Pressburger were well beyond needing to test out ways of doing propaganda (as they did with *The Lion Has Wings* [1939] and *Contraband* [1940]) and had emerged—largely due to *49th Parallel*'s success—as major contributors to the MOI's film propaganda efforts. This chapter on *Aircraft* features three sections designed to clarify the increasingly confident role Powell and Pressburger were playing as artists in the fight against Hitler. In the first section, we discuss the film's general propaganda aims as it attempts to renegotiate Britain's shifting relationship to a devastated continental Europe, more and more of which was coming under Nazi occupation. In the second section, we examine the film's style by tracing The Archers' ever-ambivalent attitude and creative approach to the realist-documentary mode adopted by most of their contemporaries. Following in a tradition initiated by such films as *The Lion Has Wings* and *Target for Tonight* (1941), *Aircraft* comes closer than any of their other feature films to embracing documentary, yet it also constitutes an important statement about their unwillingness to go beyond producing what they referred to around that time—in reference to their short *The Volunteer* (1944)—as "semi-documentary." The third and final section delves deeper into the film's explicit embrace of the V for Victory campaign's messaging; it showcases Powell and Pressburger's provocative ideas about how the resistance movement provides opportunities for greater female action during the war, and redefines Britain's importance as the world's defender of freedom and democracy.

Aircraft: Propaganda Written, Produced, and Directed by The Archers

Nearly every commentator on *Aircraft*—contemporary critics, film scholars, and even Powell and Pressburger themselves[5]—has noted that its plot essentially reverses that of *49th Parallel*; whereas the former film features shipwrecked Nazis seeking passage out of Canada, now it's a stranded British crew that must escape Nazi-occupied foreign territory. The film begins with a memorable title sequence depicting an abandoned RAF Wellington Bomber smashing into a pylon and exploding. A caption explains that "B. for Bertie crashed on Sunday morning, 04.31, but our story starts some fifteen hours earlier." The film then methodically introduces us to B. for Berties's crewmembers, who include the Skipper John Glyn Haggard (Hugh Burden); Second Pilot Tom Earnshaw (Eric Portman); Observer Frank Shelley (Hugh Williams); Wireless Operator Bob Ashley (Emrys Jones);

---

[5]Kevin Macdonald, *Emeric Pressburger: The Life and Death of a Screenwriter* (London and Boston, MA: Faber and Faber, 1994), 191.

Front Gunner Geoff Hickman; and the senior member of the group, Rear Gunner Sir George Corbett (Godfrey Tearle). Soon they are at work. B. for Bertie successfully bombs a Mercedes-Benz-operated oil-storage facility on a night raid over Stuttgart, but one of the plane's engines is blown out by retaliatory flak. John decides that the crew will attempt to coast home on a single engine, and they manage to cross over into occupied Holland. When the port engine begins to splutter out moments later, they make the decision to abandon the aircraft, and soon the six men are parachuting into darkness. The audience now knows the circumstances behind the crash of the Wellington in the film's opening scene.

The following morning, the men are able to account for all but one of their crewmembers (Bob Ashley is missing), and a chance meeting with roaming Dutch children leads them to a local farm community whose leader is Els Meertens (Pamela Brown), a young schoolteacher with a command of English. Under Els's guidance, the disguised crew manages to traverse the Dutch countryside, reuniting with Bob along the way, to the heavily guarded North Sea coast. There they meet Jo de Vries, a leader of the Dutch resistance, who organizes their dangerous route home via row-boat into the open sea. Once away from shore, the men climb aboard a German rescue buoy where they wait nervously until being picked up by Royal Navy scouts a few hours later. In a brief epilogue, the men are seen preparing for the next bombing mission; this time, Berlin will be their target.

Aircraft is up-front about its multiple propaganda intentions and communicates the role the state played in its making. By this time, and in spite of *49th Parallel*'s success, Jack Beddington's MOI had expressed its unwillingness to provide financial assistance to feature filmmakers (*Aircraft* was funded entirely by British National Films); however, the Ministry did allow Pressburger "unlimited access to restricted military information about occupied Holland" and also helped organize visits to numerous airbases; it also authorized Powell's use of a British "lobster pot" to stand in for the German buoy.[6] The film's opening captions reassure audiences that *Aircraft* is "Produced with the full cooperation of the Royal Air Force and the Air Ministry and, above all, of the Royal Netherlands Government, London." The Dutch government in exile provided Powell and Pressburger with an advisor who assisted them in creating an authentic Dutch atmosphere in the film's primary shooting location in and around the Fens, East Anglia.

Aircraft's first, and perhaps most obvious, propaganda objective is to celebrate active resistance by the Dutch, which is especially fitting for a film

---

[6]Macdonald, *Emeric Pressburger*, 191; and Michael Powell, *A Life in Movies* (1986; London: Faber and Faber, 2000), 390. The Navy used the nickname "lobster pots" to characterize the floating steel rescue platforms (mainly for downed airmen) anchored in the North Sea by both the British and Germans alike.

released in the summer of 1942. British anxiety about the German threat increased dramatically with the Nazi invasions in 1940 of Western European countries "closer to home." Those invasions also prompted Churchill, in July of that year, to create the Special Operations Executive (SOE) under the auspices of the Ministry of Economic Warfare. The main function of the SOE, ministered by Hugh Dalton, was to foment underground resistance in the occupied countries. As Robert Murphy notes, "The idea that Europe was on the verge of revolt was as important to British morale as that of the German economy being gradually extinguished by the RAF's bombs and the Royal Navy's blockade."[7] In other words, Churchill believed that cultivating the idea of a vigorous underground resistance in occupied Europe had become a major propaganda priority. Given that SOE operations had already begun by the end of 1941, it is perhaps no surprise that the earliest films touting European resistance started being released a few months later. Murphy covers the dozens of resistance films made around this time, noting how nearly every occupied country was represented in at least one film, and how certain countries including Belgium, France, and Holland appeared in more than one.[8] The key resistance films about Holland were *Aircraft, The Silver Fleet* (dir. Vernon Sewell and Gordon Wellesley, 1943; also produced by The Archers), and *The Night Invader* (dir. Herbert Mason, 1943). This comparatively large number of films happens to correspond with the government prioritization of the Netherlands as a key target of SOE strategy.

In his history of the SOE, David Stafford shows that the majority of actual operations in Holland, always carried out with the cooperation of the Dutch government-in-exile, occurred during the period 1942–3.[9] Although reports as early as 1940 suggested a Dutch readiness to fight back against the Nazis,[10] historians disagree about how active and organized the Dutch resistance was. Joris A. C. van Esch, for example, argues that "the number of people in the Dutch resistance was still minimal [as late as 1943] in comparison with countries like France, Belgium and Denmark."[11] He cites Chris Van der Heijden's claim that the Dutch responded to the German

---

[7]Robert Murphy, *British Cinema and the Second World War* (London and New York: Continuum, 2000), 83.
[8]Ibid., esp. 90–102.
[9]David Stafford, *Britain and European Resistance, 1940–1945: A Survey of the Special Operations Executive, with Documents* (Toronto and Buffalo: University of Toronto Press, 1983), 159–60.
[10]In a 1940 report prepared for the "Chiefs of Staff Review of Future Strategy," the section on Holland reads, "The Dutch are already, according to reports, beginning to revive, and obstruction is beginning to grow. There is, therefore, a possibility of creating a 'freedom party' in this area" (qtd. in Stafford, *Britain and European Resistance*, 217).
[11]Joris A. C. van Esch, "Restrained Policy and Careless Execution: Allied Strategic Bombing on The Netherlands in the Second World War" (monograph, School of Advanced Military Studies, Fort Leavenworth, KS, 2011), 26.

occupation with a certain equanimity, which can be explained by "a lack of war experience, obedience to the government, and a culture of moderation."[12] In *Holland at War Against Hitler*, Michael Richard Daniell Foot's history of Anglo-Dutch relations during the war, a similar picture emerges of a country that faced numerous obstacles in organizing the strong resistance that sizable numbers of Dutch people clearly desired. His book is a useful account of such partially successful movements as the one organized by the Geuzen (a resistance group especially active in Vlaardingen, Maassluis, and Rotterdam), as well as the brutal acts of retaliation the Nazis took against members of such groups.[13] Without question, one objective of *Aircraft* is to paint a picture of an organized Dutch resistance that, while grounded in reality, was largely aspirational at the time the film was in production.

A second major objective of the film was to justify "the British bombing of the occupied countries," as James Chapman correctly says.[14] It should be noted, however, that *Aircraft* focuses on the RAF's use of occupied-nation airspace in order to bomb not those countries but Germany itself. In any case, and regardless of specific target locations, the very practice of strategic bombing required some justification early in the war.[15] Officials were, of course, well aware of how inaccurate bombing raids tended to be, and they had real concerns about civilian casualties.[16] Estimates suggest that at least 8,000 to 10,000 citizens were killed by Allied bombers in Holland alone.[17] Van Esch discusses "A well-known British government report in 1941 [which] indicated that only twenty-two percent of the bomber crews got within five miles of their targets. When bombing heavily defended targets . . . the number even fell down to no more than seven percent."[18] In The Archers' film, of course, such problems are effaced; the crew of B. for Bertie delivers its payload and strikes its target with perfect accuracy.

One reason why strategic bombing campaigns persisted in spite of dismal success rates was their propaganda value. According to Wendy Webster,

---

[12]Ibid.
[13]See Michael Richard Daniell Foot, *Holland at War Against Hitler: Anglo-Dutch Relations, 1940–1945* (London: Frank Cass, 1990).
[14]James Chapman, *The British at War: Cinema, State and Propaganda, 1939–1945* (London and New York: I.B. Tauris), 225. Scott Salwolke concurs, though he overstates the matter when he argues that asserting "the rationalism of bombing an occupied country" is the "primary objective of the film" (*The Films of Michael Powell and the Archers* [Lanham, MD and London: Scarecrow, 1997], 88).
[15]"First and probably most controversial is the discussion on the ineffectiveness and inhumanity of Royal Air Force (RAF) Bomber Command's avowed policy of area bombing directed against German civilian morale" (van Esch, "Restrained Policy," 3).
[16]Ibid., 21.
[17]Ibid., 5.
[18]Ibid., 11.

Solidarity in resistance even extended to support for British bombing raids on occupied countries—at least in media images. In fact, there was a good deal of anxiety about the impact of such raids on public opinion in continental Europe. A BBC European Intelligence Paper, drawing on letters received by the BBC and others, interviews with travelers, reports from neutral observers, and admissions made by Paris and Vichy press and radio, charted reactions ranging from acceptance and even welcome, through the view that Britain should focus on bombing Germany, to sharply anti-British opinion. But in resistance narratives RAF raids cement British-European unity rather than disrupt it.[19]

Aircraft itself argues systematically for the inspiring propaganda value of precision bombing, as we shall see. Powell was especially adamant that Britain's ability to make a strong case for bombing operations to the public depended simply on making known to them how they worked; he went so far as to argue that, prior to his film, the public had never witnessed what bombers did or what bombing missions were like: "These things had never been seen on the screen."[20] While the claim ignores the important documentary precedent *Target for Tonight*, which we discuss later—not to mention Powell's own depiction of a bombing raid in *The Lion Has Wings*—it nonetheless offers a revealing glimpse into The Archers' reasons for lavishing the early air scenes with such meticulous care and attention.

Powell's boast also reveals an insider's awareness of the crucial ways in which scenes of precision bombing sustained the reassuring image of the technological and military supremacy of the RAF and, by extension, Britain. Indeed, a third relatively obvious, if also more general, propaganda objective of the film was simply to prop up the RAF.[21] It achieved this largely through its humanizing portraits of six heroic Britons from different backgrounds, each with a distinctive personality and an irrepressible fighting spirit. Powell is perhaps the figure in British cinema most directly responsible for glorifying the popular image of the British air force and airmen. The filmography is impressive: Powell was the director in charge of the air scenes in Alexander Korda's *The Lion Has Wings*; of the five-minute propaganda short, *An Airman's Letter to His Mother* (1941), in which John Gielgud narrates the final letter home of a flier killed in the war; of *One of Our Aircraft Is Missing*, the first and, at least until Anthony Asquith's *The Way to the Stars* (1945), best of the British air force-focused feature films; of the

---

[19]Webster, "Europe Against the Germans," 972.
[20]Powell, *A Life*, 393.
[21]S. P. Mackenzie claims that the RAF participated in filmmaking enterprises as part of its recruitment strategy (*British War Films 1939–1945: The Cinema and the Services* [London and New York: Hambledon and London, 2001], 23). See also Fox, *Film Propaganda*, 110.

documentary short *The Volunteer*, starring Ralph Richardson and focused on the Fleet Air Arm of the Royal Navy; and of *A Matter of Life and Death* (1946), the remarkable opening scene of which thrusts RAF squadron leader Peter Carter (David Niven) into the center of a mysterious and surreal fantasy drama after his Lancaster bomber is shot down following a mission to Germany. Always in Powell's films— including in his collaborations with Pressburger, of course—the dignity, bravery, and individuality of airmen are emphasized above all else.

Beyond the three objectives we have just outlined, *Aircraft* shares with many other propaganda films an overarching aim: to stress the unity of the nation[22] and of the allied cause more generally.[23] On the most basic level, the plot itself performs a reversal of the disunity themes explored in Powell and Pressburger's previous film, as Powell himself notes: "Unlike *49th Parallel*, in which the U-boat crew dropped out one by one, this story depended upon keeping the crew together."[24] The major point of the film, however, is to think about how the B. for Bertie crew could function like a microcosm of all civilized peoples united in the fight against Nazism. According to Webster, such themes of unity and solidarity defined contemporary media strategies at this particular moment during the war:

> Initially British leadership was a prominent feature of the idea of a united Continent, but in 1942–44, despite a strong tendency to domesticate continental European characters for the consumption of a British audience, imagery increasingly shifted to cooperation, mutuality, trust, and partnership. In these years the media came close to identifying Britons as part of a united Continent—Europe against the Germans.[25]

She goes on to discuss how often the propaganda of unity outpaced the reality of relations between Britons and the inhabitants of occupied countries, citing a BBC European Intelligence Paper in which European observers express unmitigated frustration about RAF raids. "But in resistance narratives,"

---

[22]Geoff Hurd correctly notes that "Wartime cinema played an active role in mobilising support for the war effort by successfully constructing an image of popular national unity, one which placed ordinary men and women at its centre" (*National Fictions: World War Two in British Films and Television*, ed. Geoff Hurd [London: BFI, 1984], 18). For a more detailed account on the MOI's perpetuation of unity propaganda, see especially David Welch, *Persuading the People: British Propaganda in World War II* (London: BFI, 2016), 121–57.
[23]Ian Christie claims that "Rather than imagin[ing] a corner of Britain under German rule, the film asks its audience to identify with a whole people who have much in common with the British" (*Arrows of Desire* [London and Boston: Faber and Faber, 1994], 40).
[24]Powell, *A Life*, 396.
[25]Webster, "Europe Against the Germans," 981.

none of this matters, for in these, "RAF raids cement British-European unity rather than disrupt it."²⁶

In their only resistance film, Powell and Pressburger contributed to the systematic construction of the image of European unity.²⁷ Perhaps no filmmakers were positioned better to do so in 1942. Having already collaborated together on three successful pictures, the duo formed The Archers Film Production unit with the release of *Aircraft,* introducing their now-famous credit "Written, Produced and Directed by Michael Powell and Emeric Pressburger." Though numerous explanations have been given for their decision to signal their collaboration in this way,²⁸ the move was no doubt inspired by the wartime atmosphere of cooperation and unity being so deliberately cultivated by the state, its Ministry of Information, and the propagandists under its influence. As Powell admitted later, "I suppose the reason we shared the credits was the wartime atmosphere. Team spirit and all that."²⁹ Such a desire to forge a show of unity in support of British military operations may also suggest why the target logo that Powell and Pressburger chose resembles so closely the roundel used to identify the three major air forces of the United Kingdom.³⁰ Throughout the war, The Archers' films would continue to epitomize this spirit of unity and collaboration, which applied not only to the scores of film industry professionals that showed up to work on those films each day, but also more broadly to Britain, its people, and its allies (Figure 4.1).³¹

---

²⁶Ibid., 972.
²⁷Andrew Moor reminds us that "The ideology of Britain at war, founded as it was upon terms such as unity, common direction, shared interest and the relegation of the private in favour of the public, achieved an astonishing centrality and strove to forge that sense of oneness. It was obviously not universal, as history records markers of dissent, yet the discourse nevertheless held together, and the *myth* of universality was kept aloft" (*Powell & Pressburger: A Cinema of Magic Spaces,* 2nd ed. [London and New York: IB Tauris, 2012], 16–17).
²⁸See especially Christie's chapter "Archers and Outsiders" in *Arrows of Desire* (1–8). Moor provocatively asserts that the credit "promotes the role of the writer" in Powell and Pressburger's many collaborations (*Powell & Pressburger,* 5).
²⁹Qtd. in *Michael Powell Interviews,* ed. David Lazar (Jackson, MS: University Press of Mississippi, 2003), 173.
³⁰Ian Christie was probably the first to note the resemblance (see *Arrows of Desire,* 1).
³¹That contemporary audience members could already detect the distinctiveness, and quality, of the Archer's product is captured well by a Portsmouth respondent (sex and employment unknown) to the MassObservation survey. They cite *Aircraft, Blimp,* and *The Silver Fleet* as their favorite films of the year, observing, "It has surprised me that the first three films which I remember with pleasure have all been produced by one company 'The Archers.' All these films I enjoyed for the same reason. They were absolutely true to life. I could believe everything about them" (*Mass-Observation at the Movies,* ed. Jeffrey Richards and Dorothy Sheridan [London and New York: Routledge and Kegan Paul, 1987], 231).

FIGURE 4.1 *The Archers' famous logo, with its undeniable likeness to the RAF roundel. From* A Canterbury Tale *(1944).*

A Qualified Commitment to the Documentary Form

Only two years after the war ended, journalist and critic Dilys Powell published her important book *Films Since 1939*, in which she described British cinema's "new movement towards concentration on the native subject, the movement towards documentary truth in the entertainment film. The war both encouraged a new seriousness of approach by British producers and directors, and drove them to look nearer home than before in their themes."[32] One interested in British cinema history might reasonably identify the war period's commitment to realism as the seed that eventually gave life to 1950s and 1960s "kitchen sink" realism, but—even if such a story were true—Powell and Pressburger's films have never fit easily into this narrative.[33] Andrew Moor has argued that "Powell and Pressburger's cinema betrays their oblique relationship to accepted, national models of 'British cinema,'" not least due to the fact that "Reality is banished" in the "sequestered territory of their artistic imagination."[34] He calls this territory a "Cinema of Magic Spaces."

---

[32] Dilys Powell, *Films Since 1939* (London: Longmans, Green & Co, 1947), 22.
[33] As the melodramas of Gainsborough Pictures or the Ealing Comedies demonstrate, Powell and Pressburger were, of course, not alone in complicating this story, which has always been reductive.
[34] Moor, *Powell & Pressburger*, 3.

But as we suggested in the Introduction, Moor overstates the case when it comes to the banishment of reality in The Archers' war films. What is striking about *Aircraft* is the extent to which it traffics in the conventions of film documentary; as Moor notes, the film stands out among Powell and Pressburger's features thanks to its "'qualified' commitment to the documentary form."[35] Powell tended to stop short of openly acknowledging such a commitment and voiced his anxiety about being viewed as a documentarian. Even while discussing *Aircraft*, with its obvious tie-ins to contemporary documentaries, his words betray a certain distrust of the form: "I had decided on complete naturalism. There would be no music. There would only be the natural sounds of a country at war. It was not a documentary; it was a detached narrative, told from the inside, of what it is like to be a pawn in the game of total war."[36] It was *not* a documentary. Powell keeps reminding us of this. Elsewhere in *A Life*, he complains that audiences sometimes refused to see *Aircraft* because the title misled them into believing it was a documentary[37]—a fact that might help explain his aversion to the term. We think the aversion is more general, however, part of the signature ethos that The Archers deliberately—and somewhat misleadingly—constructed to separate themselves from the majority of British filmmakers, for whom realism was a primary commitment:

> Our business was not realism, but surrealism. We were storytellers, fantasists. This is why we could never get on with the documentary film movement. Documentary films started with poetry and finished as prose. We storytellers started with naturalism and finished with fantasy.[38]

At least retrospectively, Powell denied documentary influence first and foremost in order to present an image (not entirely inaccurate, but most apt when applied to their postwar films) of The Archers as iconoclastic fantasists who pushed back against British mainstream cinema.

In fact, Powell understood and strategically embraced Britain's documentary tradition when he felt it could serve him, which was quite often. Given that *The Lion Has Wings* was the first British wartime propaganda film, Powell's role as a founding father of the wartime documentary movement seems undeniable. His final non-feature film, *The Volunteer*, is unabashed propaganda for the Fleet Air Arm and features a traditional male documentary voice-over (Richardson) as well as ample footage of military

---

[35]Ibid., 51. Nearly every Powell and Pressburger scholar has agreed (see, for example, James Howard, *Michael Powell* [London: BT Batsford, 1996], 39; Macdonald, *Emeric Pressburger*, 194; and Salwolke, *The Films*, 87).
[36]Powell *A Life*, 389.
[37]Ibid., 397.
[38]Ibid., 532.

sites, facilities, and so forth. Powell and Pressburger insisted on calling it a "semi-documentary."[39] In doing so, they were perhaps choosing to highlight the fictional storyline of the film created by Pressburger, which develops the character of Fred Davey (Pat McGrath) in order to show the positive impact of the military services on his confidence and skill set. However, even after the Griersonian documentary revolution, the presence of such fictional features in a documentary would hardly have been uncommon. "Semi-documentary" could be said to be synonymous with what we call "docufiction" today, a term that describes a hybrid cinematographic genre combining documentary and fiction. Furthermore, as film historians have often noted, such blendings of documentary and fiction were hardly new in the 1940s, being present in the earliest multi-reel films ever recognized as documentaries—including Robert Flaherty's *Nanook of the North* (1922) and *Moana* (1926)—and originating in the trick effects and restagings of the so-called "actualities" that preceded them. Even in the 1940s, gifted and influential documentarians such as Humphrey Jennings were especially keen on reenactments and other staged scenes; and as Brian Winston argues, "[F]or Jennings and his contemporaries, this [i.e., the reenactment of events] was simply not an issue. The use of non-actors, actual firemen, and the legitimations of various types of prior witness were enough to mark the project as a documentary, re-enactments notwithstanding."[40] Especially in light of the fact that such hybrid films were common, Powell's numerous disavowals of his own role as a documentarist stand out all the more sharply. Given the choice of how to discuss the hybrid characteristics of The Archers' films, Powell repeatedly sought to downplay, or at least qualify the importance of, documentary elements in favor of fictional ones. Doing so served well the self-constructed image of Powell the anti-realist.

We wish to rethink Powell's denials of his own participation in wartime documentary as having less to do with his rejection of the indexical relationship between the real and representational, and more as a key to The Archers' systematically *dialectical* approach to reality and fiction. Understanding this approach helps define both the power and originality of their wartime propaganda features, especially in the years following *Aircraft*. Though only partially worked out by 1942, the approach involved a constant interplay between documentary and fictional film conventions that helped Powell and Pressburger to ground their stories in plausible worlds; the stability and familiarity of those worlds would, in turn, make The Archers' propensity for flights of fancy all the more powerful and meaningful.

---

[39]Early in the film's planning, Powell admits to asking Pressburger, "Emeric, what is a semi-documentary? ... I have never made a documentary in my life. The thought of making a semi-documentary scares the shit out of me" (Ibid., 401). Powell is again exaggerating.
[40]Brian Winston, *Fires Were Started* (London: BFI, 1999), 58.

Both *The Lion Has Wings* and *The Volunteer* deliberately combine documentary and fictional film elements to make their respective cases for the RAF and Fleet Air Arm, thereby casting light on the similar, "semi-documentary" approach of *Aircraft*. As we discussed in the Introduction, *The Lion Has Wings* is a highly flawed piece of propaganda, one that in many ways stands in opposition to the propaganda program that would emerge out of The Archers' films. The Powell-directed sections of *Lion* are usefully illustrative, though, of an emerging style since they revolve around a reconstruction—though some of the footage is real—of an early Wellington raid on German warships in the Kiel Canal. For the purposes of helping Powell to render the scene as realistically and powerfully as possible, officials gave him tours of RAF aerodromes and supplied him with parts of bombers and fighters, as well as access to RAF officers and crewmen—though he was forbidden from accompanying the crew on an actual raid.[41] Like the opening of *Aircraft*, the raid sequence begins with a station officer giving orders to a specific bomber crew; they are relieved to learn that this will be the "real thing," that they won't just be dropping "propaganda leaflets this time." Once aboard their bomber, the men are individualized according to their professional roles (their faces are often shot in close-up), though their names are not given. Voice-over helps educate the audience as to the functions of each member: "At the tail, another gunner: a solitary sentinel protecting the ship from attack from the rear." The statements all are factual, but the fliers' involvement in a rapidly developing, high-stakes story gives the men's bravery and importance greater emphasis. Though the scene is composed of both combat footage and reconstruction, and though continuity problems and stylistic incongruities are noticeable, the raid is handled quite marvelously by Powell, who ratchets up the tension until the bomber has successfully delivered its payload and managed its safe return back to base.

One better understands Powell's achievement in *Lion* after viewing *Target for Tonight*, Harry Watt's heralded 1941 documentary about an actual Wellington nighttime raid on the Rhine River. In this film, as in *Aircraft*, the target is a major oil storage facility in Germany. The similarities between *Target* and *Lion* are remarkable enough to remind us how thoroughly Powell's rendering of the bombing sequence was based on the detailed information the RAF granted him, as well as the access he was given to real facilities and crew members. Director Watt may have learned from Powell's sections in *Lion* the value of individualizing the crewmen, and even the airplane, which is called "F. for Freddie" and seems to have been an inspiring predecessor to *Aircraft*'s "B. for Bertie"; in fact, *Target* goes further than *Lion* did in this regard. Each man is singled out

---

[41]See Mackenzie, *British War Films*, 28.

according to his professional role on the bomber, but he is also called by his name at different moments in the film. And as in both *Lion* and *Aircraft*, *Target* manages to build tension by crosscutting scenes of the bomber and operations back in the aerodrome—especially by showing the changes being made to the Fighter Command slate chalkboard as technical information of various sorts is sent back and forth. *Target* also pinpoints the crew's return to base as the natural conclusion of a narrativized raid, again reminding us of Powell's choices almost two years earlier in *Lion*. That earlier film's conclusion highlights Powell's attempt to balance the use of documentary footage and reconstructions in conveying as successfully as possible the drama of an actual raid: "And although you have been watching a reconstruction of that raid on the Kiel Canal, the men you now see stepping out of these bombers are the officers and men of the RAF who actually carried out that heroic raid. These are the men who flew the planes and dropped the bombs on Hitler's battleships." *Target for Tonight*, which would win an honorary Academy Award in 1942 for Best Documentary, appears to have learned many of its most important technical lessons from Michael Powell's earlier documentary work.

The Archers' "semi-documentary" *The Volunteer*, "A Ministry of Information Film," is narrated by Ralph Richardson, who plays himself. In the beginning, he is acting in a stage production of *Othello*, but we see him only behind the scenes, in his dressing rooms, where he is assisted by his friendly, well-meaning, but thoroughly incompetent dresser, Fred Davey. Already, the line between reality and fiction is thin. Then the war begins. Newspaper headlines announce the invasion of Poland. Richardson, understanding that his theater-playing days must be put on hold, mutters in an extraordinarily telling line that "it was the end of one world ... and the beginning of another"—from playing one part to playing one's part.

Fred struggles for a while to figure out which service he will join, deciding in the end on the Fleet Air Arm for one well-considered reason: "on a ship everybody has equal opportunities, everybody shares the same dangers." Some of the class- and hierarchy-based tensions evident in Fred's relationship with Richardson surface here, revealing the underling's desire for a fair shot at proving his worth and potential. Sure enough, many months later, Richardson is astonished to find Fred doing meticulous, important work as a mechanic on an aircraft carrier. While Fred appears in the world of the theater as an anxious, underskilled bumbler, he finds himself in the more practical world of the Navy. "Three years ago," Richardson exclaims as he looks on in wonder, "he couldn't drive a nail into a wall. No good for anything." In short, the film's main propaganda line is about more than simply the virtues and advantages of the Fleet Air Arm as a military branch of the Royal Navy; it also hammers home the point that the military is succeeding in training up a largely unskilled labor force. In this regard, *The Volunteer* already is looking beyond the war period.

The short film features a fascinating film-within-a-film sequence that both sustains its semi-documentary style and shows off Powell and Pressburger's characteristically self-reflexive approach to propaganda. With Richardson looking on, the carrier's crew is treated to a packed screening of recently developed films from the ship's various adventures, ranging from "goggle fishing" and girl-chasing in the Mediterranean to the men's defense of the ship against a partially successful German bombing. In a dark room lit only by the film projector, they laugh and hoot as the images move between scenes of R&R and actual military conflict—all narrated by a live guide and commentator. These are the sights and sounds of a Second World War aircraft carrier. Powell films life on the carrier as if it were the exotic subject of some documentary travelogue, though the scenes are as fictional in reality as is Fred's story.

Realism flirts ambitiously with metacinema here and in the film's close, Michael Powell plays the part of a photographer who snaps a picture of Richardson besides a newly medaled Fred just moments after his investiture ceremony at Buckingham Palace. Interestingly, Fred is the true subject of the photo, with Richardson just happening to be in the picture. In a sense, this snapshot tells the entire story of the film: Fred, who three years ago "couldn't drive a nail into a wall," has now not only displayed enough skill and courage to acquire a medal from the King, he has also earned enough respect and status to equal, and even outdo, Richardson. Whereas in the beginning of the film it had been the educated, upper-class actor who was signing autographs and posing for celebrity magazines, the three intervening years of war have given the lowly Fred an opportunity to become a hero. The fact that Powell, as the film's director, doubles as something like a paparazzo serves to underline the film's propaganda strategy of showing working men that, like Fred, they too can be the stars of the moment. At the same time, the presence of Powell reminds us of the fictional aspect of the story, of the fact that we are witnessing "reality" as it gets constructed on and by film.

Each of these MOI documentaries, *Lion* and *The Volunteer*, reveals a great deal about Powell's approach to subjects concerned with events in the real world, but the collaboration with Pressburger goes further than *Lion* does. In the earlier film, we witness the smudging of the "real" (actual footage) and the "fictional" (reconstruction) at the level of the production of the film—a smudging that, as we have seen, is typical of period documentaries. In *The Volunteer*, we witness the same, but we also encounter a degree of self-referentiality and self-reflexivity within the representation itself. Powell and Pressburger make the documentary their own as "semi-documentary," a term that satisfies their preference for storytelling over the documentation of reality—and one that also describes the appropriately dialectical relationship between the two.

Aircraft is the fullest expression of the "semi-documentary" impulse in Powell and Pressburger. The opening half hour of the film—from the announcement of B. for Bertie's mission until the abandonment of the plane by the parachuting crew members—is very much like a documentary film. In fact, it replicates quite directly numerous elements, even specific images, of the RAF raid presented in *Target for Tonight*. As we've noted, the film opens with several text cards that announce its authorization by official government entities. A moment later, one of the cards is replaced by a close-up on an actual Netherlands Government Information Bureau memo: "IN THE SUMMER OF 1941 FIVE DUTCHMEN WERE EXECUTED BY THE HERRENVOLK FOR ASSISTING IN THE ESCAPE OF A BRITISH AIR CREW. THESE ARE THEIR NAMES." Besides their listed names, additional identifying details reveal that all were "Farmers" or "Farmer's Help." "THEIR NAMES SHALL BE REMEMBERED," the memo concludes. Next, a slow panning shot of the airfield marks the beginning of the film proper, introduced by a superimposed caption that reads simply, "SUNDAY MORNING, 04.26, AT AN OPERATIONAL STATION SOMEWHERE IN ENGLAND." The first character we see is Michael Powell himself in the role of the station dispatching officer. He is filmed from below in a shot that is identical to the one of the real dispatching officer in the opening of *Target for Tonight* (Figures 4.2 and 4.3).

What a tremendous opening scene. The textual material introducing the film requires some analysis, as does this series of self-reflexive, intertextual shots. Both the opening card and the shot of the memo are nondiegetic

FIGURE 4.2 *Michael Powell himself as the dispatching officer in* One Of Our Aircraft Is Missing *(1942)*.

FIGURE 4.3 *The similarly framed dispatching officer of* Target for Tonight *(1941).*

texts designed to authorize the story that will follow and to announce its investment in the real-world, wartime context in which the film was made. However, the appearance of the memo also marks a shift to the fictional story the film will tell. Both the production facts and the story provide audiences with background information that together suggest the truthful spirit of what soon will follow.

The subsequent caption shifts our attention toward the diegetic world of the film, now establishing the time and place of the new, fictional story, whose basic qualities have nonetheless been linked indexically to those of similar stories that have played out, or will play out, in the real world. The fact that Powell is the first fictional being we see—that the real director of *Aircraft* plays a fictional director of flight operations at the station—punctuates The Archers' examination of reality's constructedness. The additional fact that Powell films himself in a direct homage to a memorable shot in the most successful RAF documentary made to that point, one released only months earlier, foregrounds parallels between fictional and nonfictional propaganda and cinematic storytelling. To return to Powell's own words, he and Pressburger have begun with prose in order to ease their way into the poetry—using naturalism to sanction their adventures into fantasy. In *Aircraft*, that adventure comes early in the film, as the audience must contend with the eerily competent flight of a ghost ship, for, until the unmanned Wellington collides with the electric-power pylon that clarifies it has been abandoned, the film gives no explanation as to what we are seeing. The inclusion of such (literal and figurative) flights of fancy does not signify, though, that the prose will simply disappear. Rather, naturalism coexists in a delicate balance with fantasy.

"You don't seem to think very much of women": From "We Can Take It" to "V for Victory"

The Volunteer employs its "semi-documentary" approach in order to show working-class men the advantages of joining the war effort. On the one hand, the film's propaganda message is simple, akin to the US Army's late-twentieth-century "Be all that you can be!" campaign. More complexly, though, the Second World War film attempts to communicate to its primary audience a vision of how radically different postwar life could be as a result of military participation: by joining us in this fight, the film implies, you level the playing field once you're back home by allowing yourself to compete against more advantaged, more educated men of a higher social standing. Interestingly, *Aircraft*'s similar "semi-documentary" approach advances almost identical practical and political messages: the film expresses its recruitment goals—which, this time, are focused on continental, occupied Europeans and Britons alike—by communicating how participation in the war effort helps level the playing field for all members of society. Powell and Pressburger appear to be directing much of this messaging to women specifically—not least those women on the British home front—by exhorting them to join the war effort. Immediate action is needed from every individual capable of fighting back against the Allies' would-be oppressors, and the resistance movement the film champions provides the ultimate opportunity for greater female agency and action.[42] There was nothing inevitable about their decision to focus so much attention on women in *Aircraft*, however. V for Victory was a relatively broad idea encompassing many ways of fighting against the German occupiers (including, for example, sabotage; work stoppages or slowdowns; or, as we emphasize, resistance movements). We find particularly striking, therefore, the film's attempt to support the V for Victory campaign by attending to the crucial role women play in winning the war.

Powell and Pressburger's only resistance film, *Aircraft* manages to advance its goals by highlighting shifting British propaganda strategies and their distinctive relationships to both British and occupied audiences. Late in *Aircraft*, a truck transporting the British airmen to Jo de Vries's location passes directly by a prominent graffito scrawled across an alleyway wall: "V." This is one of several direct references by The Archers to the V for

---

[42]It could also be reasonably argued that this unifying logic was merely an extension of "The People's War" concept that most historians would date to 1940. That concept urged men and women of all backgrounds to transcend their societal dissimilarities and join together in the national interest. Since it tended to be focused on home front activities, what it didn't do as forcibly as the V Campaign did was to urge taking it to the Germans.

Victory propaganda campaign,[43] which was launched in July 1941 as part of an attempt to unify the British and European causes as the war raged on: "The V sign," explained Churchill through a BBC proxy on the evening of the July 18, "is the symbol of the unconquerable will of the occupied territories and a portent of the fate awaiting Nazi tyranny. So long as the peoples continue to refuse all collaboration with the invader it is sure that his cause will perish and that Europe will be liberated."[44] In shifting away from the more passive, UK-focused "Britain can take it" campaign to the more active, resistance-oriented V campaign, Churchill was taking advice from the man who first proposed the idea, Victor de Laveleye. As a former Belgian parliament member forced to seek exile in England after the occupation of his country in 1940, Laveleye was well positioned to understand the type of symbolism that could instill hope in millions of occupied Europeans, as well as the importance of British leadership in the fight against Hitler. Massively successful, the V campaign gave Britons a sense of their country's primary importance in the war, and Europeans a sense of how they might do more than merely "take it" by joining in with the resistance movements that continued to gain steam across the continent.

The V campaign acknowledged the primary role played by Britain in the fight against Nazism but also presented occupied European peoples as equal and active partners in the war effort. *Aircraft*'s plot structure, according to which British airmen are saved by Dutch women, strikes the same balance in its focus on both the bravery and skillfulness of the downed RAF bombers, and the powerful heroism of the Dutch women who make possible their escape. The film contends that everyone must contribute to the fight against tyranny, not just the British and not just the men—a point which would have resonated loudly on the British home front, since women were being mobilized in massive numbers to assist the war effort. The film's explicit replacement of "we can take it" with "we will fight" is key to its success as propaganda that responds to contemporary popular and governmental needs.[45] The film registers how the MOI's original plan to use foreign allies

---

[43]In addition to the numerous *Aircraft* references discussed in this chapter, the campaign is also explicitly acknowledged in *The Silver Fleet*, which was produced by The Archers. Vernon Sewell and Gordon Wellesley's excellent film focuses on shipbuilder Jaap van Leyden's (Ralph Richardson) apparent collaboration with—but actual violent resistance to—Holland's Nazi occupiers. Early in the film before Dutch shipyard workers know that van Leyden is an ally, they try to kill him by dropping a crate from a massive crane positioned high above his head. It just misses him. In the close-up of the crane operator, one can see a prominent "V" painted on the crane cab.

[44]Radio speech on July 19, 1941. Qtd. in Henning Krabbe, *Voices from Britain: Broadcast History, 1939–45* (Bloomington, IN: Indiana University Press, 1947), 93.

[45]Webster says that "As early as 1943, the Ministry of Information reorganized the European section of its films division to plan for such propaganda, anticipating that, since 'the continent has been starved of everything except Nazi controlled films and very old French ones,' liberation

to ensure the future well-being of Britain shifts, at least symbolically and rhetorically, toward one designed to unify all of Europe.

Such a plan would have been comforting to the Dutch government in exile, which by 1942 was well aware of the asymmetric relationship between Britain and Holland. According to David Stafford, most British military operations in Holland, in the early days of the war, were carried out with the cooperation of that government.[46] The situation was already quite different, though, more than a year prior to *Aircraft*'s release. Albert E. Kersten and Marijke van Faassen explain:

> As the war was mainly a European affair the Netherlands could regard itself as an important ally, but by the end of 1941 it was apparent that the Dutch had become a minor ally, and that in Whitehall their views did not count for much. Being marginalised in the general direction of the war in Europe and Asia was difficult to swallow for the Dutch government. Increasingly the Big Four—the United States, Great Britain, the Soviet Union and China—made the important decisions amongst themselves.[47]

The reality may have been, then, that the UK regarded Holland as something like a little sister to the key allies—or perhaps Holland simply perceived that to be so. In any case, the somewhat inevitable dynamic of inequality between the non-occupied, fighting nation of Britain, and the occupied nation of Holland threatened to undermine any images of unity and partnership the two nations wished to perpetuate. In light of such a dynamic, *Aircraft*'s own leveling of various playing fields—between nations, between members of different classes, and between men and women—is particularly striking.

We should not miss how progressive the film's sweeping egalitarianism was in its context. According to Wendy Webster, many contemporary films represented the key relationships between nations and national representatives in predictable, stereotypically gendered ways while, at the same time, beginning to challenge traditional male-female relationships:

> Female resisters are often foregrounded in resistance narratives, while the British, like Germans, are male. Gender is thus important in the construction of British-European relations as it is in the construction of German-European relations, but with entirely different meanings. . . .

---

would mean 'a thirsty market for both entertainment and propaganda films.' By September 1945 it had produced a lengthy catalog of films for distribution in liberated European territories" ("Europe Against the Germans," 977).

[46]Stafford, *Britain and European Resistance*, 159–60.

[47]Kersten and van Faassen, "'Goodbye, Mr. Churchill': Anglo-Dutch Relations during the Second World War," *Unspoken Allies: Anglo-Dutch Relations Since 1780*, ed. Nigel Ashton and Duco Hellema (Amsterdam: Amsterdam University Press, 2001), 157.

Through ... romantic plots and their construction of national relations through gender relations, early resistance films had reinforced an image of British benevolent paternalism, but in films made in 1942-44 the image is frequently one of British men's strong admiration for the courage of female resisters as well as their dependence on them for safety and survival.[48]

Aircraft is, presumably, one of these later resistance films, but it is sophisticated in its approach to the Anglo-Dutch relationship in ways that have to do with more than gender alone (though gender will be our main focus moving forward); especially noteworthy is its desire to avoid the "strong tendency [of most resistance films] to domesticate continental European characters for the consumption of a British audience."[49] Certainly, the realism and believability of its Dutch settings, costumes, character accents (however weakly or strongly performed by the predominantly British cast), and other cultural markers cause us to think about the specific ways in which Britishness and Dutchness are differently represented but not hierarchized.

Any discerning viewer will immediately notice that all of the major British parts are played by male actors, whereas all of the significant Dutch parts are played by female ones. This correlation between nationality and gender also maps onto the film's structure. Speaking broadly, *Aircraft* can be perceived as consisting of two distinct sections: the bombing of Stuttgart that leads to B. for Bertie being shot down; and the shepherding of its crew out of Holland and back to England by two strong female Hollanders, Els Meertens and Jo de Vries. With only small exceptions, Britishness is marked in the film as masculine (and masculine prowess is associated with official military operations), and Dutchness is marked as feminine.[50] At first glance, the stage appears to be set somewhat disastrously for a knight-in-shining-armor narrative. Will this be a resistance film in which the resourceful (male) British fliers show the defenseless (female) Dutch how to fight back? Instead, from the film's beginning, audience expectations are dashed to pieces when it comes to the presentation of women and how men regard and depend upon them.

In the opening, documentary-style segments of the film, which show the crew flying over Holland into Germany, the men have a conversation about German girls they knew before the war. This threatens to devolve into little more than a dialogue about their sexual conquests. Scanning the skies nervously, Geoff remarks, "Nice girls in Stuttgart aren't there, skipper?" John

---

[48]Webster, "Europe Against the Germans," 972–3.
[49]Ibid., 981.
[50]As we shall see, Dutch children also occupy an important role in the story; however, the two major, Dutch male figures are a quisling and a Catholic priest.

replies, "Well, one anyway," a little pained, seemingly unwilling to talk about it. Geoff, ever oblivious, confesses to having known a nurse from Stuttgart, and this prompts John to join in because his girl happened to be a nurse also.

> John: What was your nurse like?
> Geoff: Oh, she was a big blonde job. . . . She worked for a doctor in Gerrards Cross. She used to sing that song, um, "I Kiss Your Little Hand, Madame." [Frank hums the tune]. That's right, and she used to sing it in German, you know. [Struggles to do so]. She was always singing it, but it was probably because she wasn't allowed to sing it in Germany. The composer was a Jew, wasn't he? What was your nurse like, Skipper? . . . Was she a good cook?
> John: Her name was Ilse. She was blonde too. . . . She was good at everything. I was very upset when she left me. My next nurse wasn't half as good.
> Geoff: You seem to specialize in nurses, skipper.
> John: Well, I did then. I was only two, you see.

The revelation that John's affection for his nurse was that of a small child for his caregiver brings home the degree to which English and German people's lives were often intertwined between the wars. The scene works in characteristic Archers' fashion to individualize Germans, all of whom happen to be women in this case, even as it appears at first to be offering mere generalizations about objectified blondes. The truth reinforces the idea that Stuttgart is, as Frank says, "just like all those continental towns," no different, that is, from similar ones in France and Holland and Belgium. The result of this exchange is to shrink the gap between Britain and Germany, the British people and German people. As important, the conversation highlights the crucial roles women have played in these men's lives; those roles may be somewhat romanticized, but they are rendered plausibly as deeply felt and fondly remembered ones.

The episodes in Holland work to challenge male expectations about women's roles and their impact on the lives of men and women alike. On the morning after the crew's abandonment of their plane, the first Hollanders they meet are a group of small children who recommend that the British airmen make their way to the nearest farm to meet the local schoolteacher.[51] The men reflexively assume certain things about this teacher, Ms. Meertens: "Well, apparently she's a schoolmarm. Sounds a useful old bird." Once they arrive in the schoolhouse, however, they are prevented from seeing her until the locals can decide, behind closed doors, what to do with the men.

---

[51]In the illustrated storybook published to promote the film, the narrator George Corbett proudly notes that "The R.A.F. seems to be tops in Holland" (*One of Our Aircraft Is Missing* [London: His Majesty's Stationery Office, 1942], 13).

Listening to sounds of impassioned argument coming from the next room, John shrugs and says, "Ms. Meertens," implying he's slightly afraid of this imposing figure, and Geoff jokes, saying, "I'll never put a ferret down a rabbit hole again, I know that." The implication is that the voices coming from the next room are threatening, that the men feel uneasy as to whether they will be protected or trapped like rabbits in their den by these potential predators. This disruption of the men's first assumption that Meertens would be "an old bird"—presumably a kindly, harmless figure—already works to raise expectations for what this school teacher might be like; but the reveal of the beautiful young Pamela Brown, as she opens the door a moment later, truly throws off everyone, the crew members and film audience alike. The reaction shot of John captures his surprise at Els's appearance. If the men think that they'll be dealing with a dove, however, simply because Els is a young, attractive girl, she quickly shatters that expectation while grilling them about their identities, thereby fully revealing her confidence, shrewdness, and intellect. The men are caught off guard throughout the scene, which, in the end, validates Els's perspective that, especially in a time of fear and unspeakable menace, relying on people's appearances to ascertain their motives or natures can be truly dangerous: "Can any one of you prove beyond any reasonable doubt that you are what you say you are?" Her concern, of course, is that the men are Germans disguising themselves as British airmen in order to test the loyalty of the Dutch community. In making the logic of her interrogation so explicit, she inadvertently comments on the dangers of generalizing about individuals based on their appearances or purported professions. The film has already shown how such expectations, and their resultant dangers, might be extended to problematic assumptions about gender. Most important in this regard is the film's shattering of traditional assumptions about women's roles in times of war—for *Aircraft* is crystal clear about the importance of women's participation in the war effort, not only in Holland but also in Britain. In championing the heroic efforts of Els Meertens or Jo de Vries, Powell and Pressburger invite audience members to consider how British women might make significant contributions on the "home front," a term intended to signal that the war was being fought not just militarily but through rationing, farming, and munitions work in factories. Importantly, needs on the home front were changing dramatically around the time of *Aircraft*'s production.

Perhaps the most significant change involved the recruitment of women for jobs that were relatively dangerous and/or traditionally reserved for men. This change followed the government's recognition in 1941 of an impending labor crisis. According to Ian Gazeley,

> The total number [of workers] in munitions and the forces was roughly 8 million, rather than the 9.5 million that had been forecast. In addition, it was thought that another 1.5 million people would be needed for the

armed forces in 1942, plus 775,000 for munitions and essential services. Thus, Britain was entering a period of acute "labour famine" even before the geographic scale of the conflict was drastically enlarged by the outbreak of war in the Pacific in December 1941.[52]

Therefore, for the first time in British history, the Ministry of Labour began the conscription of women into such wartime services as the WAAF (Women's Auxiliary Air Force), the ATS (Auxiliary Territorial Service), and the WRNS or "Wrens" (Women's Royal Naval Service), which together employed women as searchlight operators, radar controllers, engineers, telephonists, mechanics, and in other such professional capacities. Though women were not drafted into military operations, per se, they were allowed to volunteer for work in anti-aircraft (AA) operations; they managed barrage balloons, for example, or even located and targeted enemy aircraft (they were not allowed to pull any triggers, however). According to D'Ann Campbell,

> Britain had to balance public doubts and ingrained gender norms against pressing needs. When [Fredrick Alfred] Pile and Churchill first assigned women to AA jobs, they encountered resistance from public opinion. It was not so much that the women were in danger—every woman in every British city was in danger of death from German bombs, and tens of thousands did die. The public would not support a proposal to allow women to fire the AA guns. But the British were a practical people, especially when bombs were falling. They soon decided, "A successful air defence was an even stronger political imperative than the possible moral and physical dangers to the daughters of the nation." The government did concede some details to public opinion by not formally classifying these AA jobs as combat and by symbolically prohibiting the women from pulling the lanyard. The mixed AA crews were as much combat teams as were the airplane crews they shot down.[53]

We quote this passage at such length because it usefully captures the ambivalence of a nation struggling to balance, on the one hand, traditional, patriarchal expectations for women, with, on the other, the crisis-driven need to put women to work; this need, in turn, revealed that it was those patriarchal expectations which had restricted female behavior in the first place.

---

[52]Ian Gazeley, "Women's Pay in British Industry During the Second World War," *Economic History Review* 61 (2008): 651–71, 656.
[53]D'Ann Campbell, "Women in Combat: The World War II Experience in the United States, Great Britain, Germany, and the Soviet Union," *Journal of Military History* 57 (1993): 301–23, 313.

Aircraft's home front is, of course, a specifically Dutch one. But in the midst of the British "labour famine"—a period that saw a concerted national propaganda effort to recruit women into "men's jobs"—the film's (all-female) Dutch resistance would certainly have evoked the war-related efforts of women on the British home front. Furthermore, the film's unambivalent portrayal of these women as capable and strong laborers in the war effort went far enough to challenge the patriarchal assumptions of the nation. This point is highlighted by a sequence in which Els leads the disguised crew toward members of the Dutch resistance living near the North Sea. "We will dress you in Dutch clothes," she tells the men, but Frank, the actor, is given the additional camouflage of a new gender. The prose account from the storybook version of the film published shortly after its release captures yet another instance of thwarted expectations: George explains,

> I glanced at the line of Dutch ladies, their velvet skirts and multitudinous petticoats billowing in the breeze, their lace caps, and wide patterned collars and cuffs gleaming in the sun; the nearest one to me was a particularly stately dame, with a formidable bosom and a collaret of coral beads: her lace cap, her heavy clogs, her flowing gown were authentically Dutch, but her face was the face of Francis Shelley, Actor, late Navigator of one of H. M. Wellington Bombers.[54]

As in any Shakespearean comedy, the cross-dressing disguise works here for the purposes of humor, but it also carries an intrinsic political dimension in exposing gender as no more than a cultural construct dictating social behavior and expectations. In this particular, non-Shakespearean case, a male character is forced to disguise himself as a woman rather than the other way around, all while one heroic, charismatic female leader pushes him toward the protective custody of another heroic, charismatic female leader. Powell and Pressburger appear to be suggesting—in an argument mainly intended, of course, for British audiences— that all expectations about "proper" gender roles should be set aside or at least suspended for the duration of the war.

In the case of Jo de Vries, as in that of Els Meertens, gender expectations work like a trap for undiscriminating audiences—the most important of which is comprised of the German occupiers within the film. Jo is the organizer of the coastal underground, and, as such, she is the key to the British airmen escaping back into England. Before the men travel to the coast, Els explains who Jo is and how her own disguise enables her activity and protects her from German suspicion: "Jo de Vries, the wife of Hendrik de Vries. . . . Hendrik de Vries was killed by the British in the mass air

---

[54] *One of Our Aircraft* (illustrated storybook), 19.

attacks in Haarlem. Since then his wife hates the British more than anything in the world." Logically, Tom and the others question whether they should therefore be given over to Jo's custody. Then somebody notes that the British never bombed Haarlem.[55] "The Germans want us to believe it," says Els, "so Jo de Vries obliges them. They like her because they believe she hates the British. That is what she wants, so everyone is happy." From the German perspective, Jo is an ally won over by them through a deliberately manipulative propaganda campaign against the British; because she is a grieving widow, they assume, she is easy to dupe, easy to turn into a tool of the Third Reich.

Powell and Pressburger perform a clever maneuver in Jo's case, however, not just by showing us how she's always one step ahead of the Germans but also by gradually revealing that she's been one step ahead of all of us as well. Even Els is ignorant of the truth that Jo shares with the men once they are safely installed in her apartments: that she is in command of the resistance operation in her coastal town. Noting George's surprise at this fact, she criticizes his seemingly low estimate of women, announcing, "I was afraid when I first started, just as a pilot is afraid the first time he goes solo. Then after a few minutes, when he finds he's still alive, he begins to like it." Jo not only defends women for their courage but also equates RAF fighters and female Dutch resisters. She then asks, "Would you do something for me.... I want you to go and see my husband when you get back to England." The men are shocked by the request. "I'm not mad," she continues, "I spread that story [of his death] myself. Nobody knows the truth, not even my friends, but he's alive." The entire plan behind the resistance operation has been hers alone. In three separate cases, then, women are not what they appear or are expected to be. In all three cases, women are shown to be active, brave, and at least as shrewd as any of the men in the film. Nor is the power of any one episode diminished by objectifying a woman, stripping her of her agency, or relegating her to the role of a trophy for one of the airmen; stereotypes about women never resurface in *Aircraft* once they are raised and then systematically demolished.

As mentioned earlier, nearly every critic notes what Powell and Pressburger sometimes stated in interviews, that the B. for Bertie crew's display of solidarity runs in stark contrast to the Germans' backstabbing and disorganization in *49th Parallel*, but one key misperception needs to be corrected. While the men discuss electing a leader, they never single out one member of the crew to serve in this capacity—and this notable inconsistency between their words and actions serves to elevate the Dutch women yet further. After the men have collected their parachutes and counted their

---

[55] This detail may serve as its own form of counterpropaganda, implying that stories of British bombings of occupied countries are false.

number the morning after jumping from their plane, they immediately debate the merits of electing a leader. George, the most experienced, remarks, "John, you command in the air, [so] there's no reason why you shouldn't command on the ground." A reluctant John then asks, "Why should anyone command? Let's hear what we've *all* got to say." Frank then says he'll take "John's view." When George asks him what his plan is, he proves to be clueless, validating the idea that a leader is required in such situations. The others laugh at Frank, which prompts George to elaborate: "I've been lost, dozens of times, sometimes alone, sometimes with other men, several times with a whole regiment, so I know this much: either we separate now and it's each man for himself, or we stick together and somebody must command." Before they ever make a decision, however, the conversation shifts, and they are discovered by the Dutch children. It would be easy to think that George has emerged as the "commander," but he never moves into this role in the scenes that follow. Instead, the debate is followed by the emergence of Els, and then Jo, the only two "ground" commanders the film clearly presents.

Ian Christie has noted how striking is "the unusual importance of women in the story,"[56] but the significance of this has not been adequately accounted for, especially in light of the fact that Powell's one directive to Pressburger prior to sending him off to write the script was that he should focus on writing strong female characters.[57] In what remains of this chapter, we shall explain how this emphasis on strong female leaders meshes even more directly with the particular propaganda concerns of the year in which the film was produced.

Earlier we mentioned that the "V" graffito on the alleyway wall is merely one of several direct references to the Victory campaign in the film. *Aircraft* presents ample evidence of how effective propagandizing—within the diegetic world of the film and by the film itself—works equally well for Britain and its European allies by emphasizing themes of partnership, equality, mutuality, and, first and foremost, unity. In addition, the film makes the case to domestic audiences—especially women—about the importance of their participation in the war effort. In the scenes centering on Els's efforts to evacuate the airmen from central Holland, numerous events signal the Dutch villagers' organized resistance to Germany and support of Britain. The children who greet the downed airmen, for example, wear safety pins on their clothing as a "sign against the Germans and quislings; a safety pin means keep together, keep your mouth shut." Moments later, in the farmhouse where Els considers what to do with the men, they spot orange

---

[56]Christie, *Arrows of Desire*, 40.
[57]Powell claims that when "it was time to think about casting," he "begged Emeric to write some decent parts for women" (*A Life*, 391). The anecdote is curious since, throughout his career, Pressburger didn't require much urging to pen strong female characters.

blossoms draped over the furniture; this "shows they're loyal" to the House of Orange, specifically to Queen Wilhelmina, who is in exile in England. These covert symbols of defiance and independence from their German occupiers build morale and firm up communities that can act together when necessary, as when Els's group discovers a quisling (Robert Helpmann) in their midst and humiliates him and renders him utterly harmless. In these cases, as with the V for Victory campaign, symbols have teeth.

Jo de Vries's resistance movement uses symbols also but, as the graffiti in the alleyways outside her rooms suggest, the symbols become more *directly* responsive to the V campaign the closer the crew gets to Britain. When Jo locks the men in her room, for instance, she instructs them not to answer the door unless they hear the Morse telegraphic knock for V, which is three dots and a dash. More important to these scenes, however, is the central role played by the BBC, which joins the RAF as a British institution responsible for helping the Allies to win the war. Again, everyone plays their part so that radio announcers—whom some might call outright propagandists—prove as important as bombers. When the men discover a radio in Jo's bedroom tuned to the BBC, they huddle around it like they would around a fire in the most unforgiving wilderness.

Perhaps no twist in this propaganda film about propaganda is more satisfactory, however, than the reveal that Jo's husband is "one of the Dutch announcers of Radio Oranje—the Radio Orange." Jo reveals this when Tom asks whether she ever hears from her husband. "Five times a week," she says, referring to the Dutch-language program on the BBC European Service, which was broadcast into the Netherlands from 9:00 p.m. to 9:15 p.m. every evening. She then emphasizes that radio propaganda and/or news represent an important form of active resistance: "So you see we [my husband and I] are two, on both sides of the channel. We're still fighting." Jo's words serve to de-emphasize further the relevance of traditional gender roles since she is the one who is *literally* fighting against the Nazis. Whereas most British men were on the front and most women at home, Jo's marriage offers the reverse situation, suggesting again the basic idea of the V Campaign: that winning the war requires true unity, equality, and mutuality among *all* members of the Allied resistance. Just as physical fighting and espionage are productively dissociated from a purely masculine realm, so too are art, broadcasting, and other forms of democratic propaganda produced "at home" dissociated from the realm of the purely feminine. On the contrary, the film presents propaganda production as the serious weapon it was by this phase of the war.

Indeed, the Germans viewed programs such as Radio Oranje as enough of a problem by 1943 as to require a ban on radios in Holland; even in *Aircraft*, radios are kept hidden in secret places, especially ones such as Jo's that are kept tuned to the BBC. According to Dutch historian Harry Paape, hundreds of thousands of Hollanders listened regularly to these broadcasts:

For those in Holland who understand English, and even 50 years ago there were many who did, the names BBC, Home Service and European Service were not meaningless noises. . . . [T]he [BBC] news was reliable, and on every occasion it gave a clear picture of the resoluteness and the optimism of the British—however much they may have been out of place particularly in 1940. Of course, the propaganda element was recognized, but it was also accepted as part of the common struggle. Perhaps the latter was the most important: every day new *hope* came from the other side of the Channel.[58]

Paape's words resonate strongly with the dramatic speech Jo gives as the air raid sirens begin blaring and the Nazis scramble to take cover:

You see? That's what you're doing for us. Can you hear them running for shelter? Can you understand what that means to all the occupied countries? To enslaved people having it drummed into their ears that the Germans are masters of the earth, seeing those masters running for shelter, seeing them crouching under tables, and hearing that steady hum night after night [looks up to skies], that noise which is oil for the burning fire of our hearts.

The lines, which evoke the voice-over in pro-RAF propaganda, would hardly seem out of place in a documentary like *Target for Tonight*.[59] But in the context of *Aircraft*, the speech's emphasis on the hope that "enslaved people" can take away from the sounds—that steady hum—of the planes from Britain serves to equate the bomber pilots and the BBC radio broadcasters as active partners in the fight for freedom. Britain is doing her part in providing the Dutch the fuel they need to do theirs, whether those Dutch reside within Britain (like Jo's husband and Queen Wilhelmina), or are in Holland itself (like Jo and Els). The Dutch have shown that they can take it; but they also show throughout the film that they can give it too. All that's left to do now is for Jo to lead the airmen to their boats so that they can escape to England and get back to their planes, so that they may fly over Holland once more.

Of course, the ending of *Aircraft* stages this very scene of B. for Bertie's crew climbing aboard a brand-new bomber, but Powell and Pressburger's playful, self-reflexive finale meditates on their own role in the fight against

---

[58]Paape, "How Dutch Resistance was Organized," *Holland at War Against Hitler: Anglo-Dutch Relations 1940–1945*, ed. M. R. D. Foot (London: Frank Cass, 1990), 68–92, esp. 91.
[59]This speech about the RAF raids might undoubtedly be understood as a response to dissenting views regarding the RAF's bombing of Holland, as noted earlier. It is, among other things, a response to a darker view of things—an expression of unity that seeks to dispel the threat of disunity represented by British destruction.

Nazism. Just after the airmen are rescued, the film cuts away from the Royal Navy vessel to a caption that reads, "That was going to be the end of our story, BUT—first, the Actors—" [standard cast credits follow] "—and then the Technicians—" [again, standard credits]. But then a final caption informs us that the film's own cast and technicians have requested an alternate ending to better satisfy their curiosity about the future of the airmen we've come to care so much about: "all of them wanted to know what happened afterwards to the Crew of B. for Bertie. So—three months later. . . ." A dissolve returns us to the aerodrome and, more specifically, to the fighter command chalkboard onto which the names of our heroes are once again being written. We then see the men climbing aboard their new bomber and preparing themselves to fly to their new target, Berlin. There is no musical score, and we seem to have returned to the more self-conscious "semi-documentary" mode of the film's opening. A shot of the airborne plane then cuts to the Dutch Royal crest before the captions, first in Dutch, then in English, appear, promising us that "The Netherlands Will Rise Again," a line itself associated directly with the V campaign.[60]

Whereas the film's opening credit sequence portrays events occurring hours after the narrative proper begins, the final credit sequence projects months into the future—to a time when the steady hum of British bombers will deliver more than just hope to the Dutch people. In constructing the story's time scheme in this way—and presenting it in a self-reflexively realist mode—the filmmakers remind the audience of the ways in which *Aircraft* itself functions as morale-boosting propaganda. Had the film ended with the sight of the navy vessel towing away the "lobster pot," the audience would not have known for sure whether George had lived, or whether the crew stayed together in order to fight another day. The film's actors and technicians, surrogates for real audience members everywhere, are depicted as needing to know the answers to those questions and other, more important ones—answers that Powell and Pressburger choose to provide them, thereby making the point that hope is of the utmost importance at

---

[60]As Webster notes: "Reporting on the V campaign in 1941, a BBC European Intelligence Paper also deployed the language of 'them' and 'us,' suggesting that 'these people (of oppressed Europe) still need from us symbols, songs, slogans, jokes, rolls of honour, names of traitors.' The language of 'them' and 'us' is also apparent in different versions of a slogan that was used a good deal in 1942, expressing confidence that Europe would rise again. As 'We Shall Rise Again,' it appeared at the end of *Uncensored* printed on the bottom of *La Libre Belgique*, clutched by a Belgian who has just been shot by Germans. As 'The Netherlands Will Rise Again!' it was the final intertitle of *One of Our Aircraft Is Missing*, shown first in Dutch—'Nederland Zal Herrijzen!'—and then duly translated. But in the BBC series, broadcast in 1942, it became *They Shall Rise Again*—a title that identified the difference between British and continental European wartime experience. The 'we' of 'we shall rise again' is continental Europe only. Britain, having escaped invasion, occupation, and oppression by Germany, had no need to 'rise again'" ("Europe Against the Germans," 971).

this point in the war. Like the hum of the airplanes or the voices on the airwaves, films themselves play their part in the war effort—promoting a spirit of unity, partnership, and mutual cooperation between Britain and its allies. RAF fighters, BBC announcers, ordinary men and women, Dutch and English—and now The Archers' film unit—all are part of a growing alliance of forces unwilling to sit back and take it.

5

"England Isn't as Bad as All That"

Propaganda and Censorship in *The Life and Death of Colonel Blimp*

Blimpish ignorance in the face of the Nazi menace is perhaps best epitomized by the lessons the fictional Clive Candy fails to learn from Dunkirk. In *The Life and Death of Colonel Blimp* (1943), Clive (Roger Livesey) is scheduled to deliver the BBC's Sunday night "Postscript," the title of which is "Dunkirk—Before and After." The imagined date is June 16, 1940, some twelve days after Churchill's legendary "We shall fight on the beaches" speech to the House of Commons and, as important, eleven nights after J. B. Priestley's hopeful refashioning of that speech in the first of his monumentally popular "Postscripts" for the BBC: "What began as a miserable blunder, a catalogue of misfortunes," Priestley said of Dunkirk, "ended as an epic of gallantry."[1] Although the arch-conservative—some might even say Blimpish—Prime Minister Churchill and the left-wing author Priestley both immediately understood the propaganda opportunity that Dunkirk represented, Clive's intention is to explain how he'd rather "accept defeat than victory" if the latter means stooping to the un-sportsman-like methods of warfare used by the Nazis. Failing to understand that defeat to the Nazis is not the same as defeat on a cricket field, Clive shows up at the Blitz-proofed underground offices of the BBC prepared to embarrass himself before some thirty or forty percent of the nation (Figure 5.1).

In the first of three short scenes, the BBC director and his secretary nervously rehearse their excuses for why MOI officials have cancelled

---

[1] The speech from June 5, 1940, is quoted from J. B. Priestley, *Postscripts* (London, 1940), 2.

FIGURE 5.1 *Clive being given the bad news by the BBC director in* The Life and Death of Colonel Blimp *(1943).*

Clive's speech. A radio voice subsequently informs us that J. B. Priestley has been assigned to replace Clive. In one vastly underappreciated sequence, then, the British government substitutes the aging, increasingly irrelevant establishment conservative with the younger, Yorkshire-accented liberal realist who, for several months in 1940, would be among the most respected and influential voices in the United Kingdom. Outraged and deeply wounded by the cancellation, and especially chafed by the communication of it by a nonmilitary member of the media, Clive returns home to a War Office letter informing him that he's being officially retired. He is then further chastened by his best friend for failing to see the reality behind his outmoded principles; in what is perhaps the film's most explicit statement about the dangers of Blimpism, the German émigré Theo (Anton Walbrook) remarks:

> If you preach the rules of the game[2] while they use every foul and filthy trick against you, they'll laugh at you! They think you're weak, decadent! .... You forgot to learn the moral [of the First World War]. ... You've

---

[2] It is quite certain that Pressburger is deliberately alluding to Jean Renoir's 1939 critique of bourgeois myopia on the eve of the Second World War, *The Rules of the Game.*

been educated to be a gentleman and a sportsman, in peace and in war. But, Clive, dear old Clive, this is not a gentleman's war. This time you are fighting for your very existence against the most devilish idea ever created by a human brain—Nazism.

After Dunkirk, the film suggests, the MOI sees it. The BBC sees it. Right- and left-wing politicians and commentators see it. German refugees like Theo, driven from their homeland, see it most clearly. Only gradually is Clive also forced to see it. This extended sequence about Clive's censored radio broadcast is at least as much about the threat posed by Blimpish propaganda as it is about Nazism. In it, moreover, Powell and Pressburger zoom in on the complex machinery of wartime propaganda itself, depicting actions taken by the War Office, the MOI, and even the nation's lone radio broadcasting company. By doing so, they invite the audience to reflect upon the relationship of The Archers' films to the propaganda produced by these government-regulated offices and media.

The Life and Death of Colonel Blimp (hereafter referred to as *Blimp*) is perhaps most famous for its own tangled history as the subject of attempted government censorship—by Winston Churchill himself, no less. Far less attention has been paid to the film's examination of the relationship between propaganda and censorship. It might seem ironic that the Powell and Pressburger film most interested in censorship happened to endure so much harassment and obstruction by government officials, but we argue that the film's explicit interest in government censorship and its actual government reception are more organically linked than critics have noted. In a very real sense, Powell and Pressburger's Technicolor epic—released in the middle of the war, after several immensely successful, but undeniably simpler propaganda efforts—functions as a renegotiation of the filmmakers' relationship to the wartime state and British mainstream media. More specifically, the film constitutes a declaration of The Archers' artistic and political freedom that also poses crucial questions about the interrelations of freedom of expression and censorship, the individual and the state, and the auteur filmmaker and the propagandist. *Blimp* is at once Powell and Pressburger's most probing reflection on the insidiousness of propaganda, and their most self-assured reassertion of its importance as a tool against fascism.

What we'll henceforth refer to as the "BBC Sequence" culminates the film's sustained rumination on propaganda, counterpropaganda, and, most importantly, the machinery of state censorship. Much like *49th Parallel* (1941) and *Aircraft* (1942), *Blimp* both *is* propaganda and *is about* propaganda. Unlike those films, however, which cautiously celebrate the distinctiveness of British propaganda, especially in relation to its totalitarian counterpart, *Blimp* calls attention to the internal struggles among the national government, the military, and the media to define and represent the nation in wartime. Whereas a film like *Aircraft* meditates on the finished *forms* of British propaganda, *Blimp* explores the contested *formation* of such propaganda—especially as it involves the relationship between the ethics of propaganda and of warfare.

Furthermore, through Clive, *Blimp* seeks to inculcate in the viewer a more sophisticated apprehension of the relationship of media to propaganda than he himself evinces throughout most of the film. Direct and self-reflexive about the ethics of producing propaganda, the film is also preoccupied with questions about the *reception* of propaganda by an increasingly experienced British viewing audience that knows what it is encountering. By illustrating the costs of Clive's gullible consumption of fake news, *Blimp* insists on the importance of an educated audience capable of discerning the differences between truth and lies, and between democratic and totalitarian propaganda forms and methods. The faith that Powell and Pressburger have in their audience's ability to sort through their propaganda film's undeniable complexities—its ambiguities and even its seemingly irresolvable contradictions—reveals itself, in fact, as the surest sign of their commitment to practical democracy.

In what follows, we begin by introducing *Blimp*'s notably ambitious plot and the conundrum it poses for audiences by attempting to negotiate two related but separate matters: the ethics of warfare, on the one hand, and the ethics of wartime propaganda, on the other. As we shall see, questions about the ethics of *Blimp* have perplexed many of the film's viewers, from contemporary critics to modern scholars.[3] In the second section, we flesh out this conundrum in greater detail, partly through in-depth analysis of the film's numerous treatments and scripts, as well as government reactions to them. We also break down one of the film's most neglected central motifs, that of the prisoner of war, which serves as a major point of return for the filmmakers as they attempt to transition between the film's numerous historical periods and locations, and to contend with the various ethical questions posed by each one. The next two sections delve more deeply into *Blimp*'s exploration of the war of representation: whereas section three considers propaganda and counterpropaganda, section four focuses on

---

[3]In a thoughtful but rather quirky essay, Stephen G. Williams sets out to answer the question, "How can a film be a great work of art when it has been devised as a vehicle of propaganda?" ("Propaganda and Artistic Merit: The Case of *Colonel Blimp*," *Ethics at the Cinema*, ed. Ward E. Jones and Samantha Vice [Oxford: Oxford University Press, 2011], 43–65, 44). Though arguing that "a work of art . . . created as propaganda provides a *pro tanto* reason for supposing it to be flawed or diminished aesthetically" (44), Williams defends *Blimp* as an artistic masterpiece thanks to the fact that its propaganda material has "mutated" since the war—partly due to Powell and Pressburger's prescient sense of postwar realities, and partly due to luck—"into material that is not propaganda" (58). In contrast, our contention is that artistic achievement and propaganda are not necessarily antithetical, as we discuss most directly in the Coda.

censorship, taking up the British government's—and its prime minister's—infamous attempt to stop the film's production. In the final section, we reconsider the film's reception, then and now, and its role in renegotiating The Archers' position in relation to the British state and cinema.

But What Is It About?

Blimp is the decades-long story of an establishment military figure whose conservative views of the British character and state are revealed to be outmoded in a period of total warfare. While based on the immensely popular David Low cartoon that, beginning in 1934, ran off and on in the *Evening Standard*—a relentless satire of the pomposity and stupidity of a stereotypical British reactionary type—The Archers' Major-General Clive Wynne-Candy is more humanely and even sentimentally drawn.[4] Except for the first fifteen and the final five minutes of this nearly three-hour-long film, *Blimp* is an extended flashback of Clive's life between 1902 and 1940. In the film's World-War-Two-era opening, an aged Clive—currently a commander of the Home Guard—is lounging around in the Turkish baths of the Royal Bathers' Club hours before a scheduled training exercise. He is suddenly captured by a British Army battalion led by the young Lieutenant Spud Wilson (James McKechnie). Outraged that Spud has attacked before the designated starting time for the exercise, Clive assaults the Lieutenant, the two men fall into one of the baths, and a tour de force flashback transition takes us back to 1902, when a much younger Clive is seen exiting the same bath. He is a lieutenant on leave from fighting in the Boer War. Rather than enjoying his time off, the younger Clive chooses to defy his superiors' orders by going to meet Edith Hunter (Deborah Kerr), a young woman working in Berlin who has complained to the British Embassy about a German who has been spreading anti-British propaganda. Once abroad, the inevitable confrontation between Clive and this man, Kaunitz, culminates in Clive accidentally insulting the entire German Army officer corps. The British Embassy is quickly drawn in, and Clive is forced to participate in a duel against a randomly selected officer—and the film's "good German"—Theo Kretschmar-Schuldorff (Anton Walbrook). Both injured in

---

[4]Powell has noted that Blimp's air of sentimentality has much to do with Livesey's personality and performance. After losing Laurence Olivier, who would have played the character as more bitter, Powell says, "I told him [Rank] that I was going to take Roger Livesey, who I knew was another good actor; but being sentimental, the film became sentimental" (*Michael Powell Interviews*, ed. David Lazar [Jackson, MS: University Press of Mississippi, 2003], 37). This raises important questions, of course, about the evolution of the character across Pressburger's numerous scripts. Interestingly, Pressburger's grandson calls the film's sentimentality "its only shortcoming" (Kevin Macdonald, *Emeric Pressburger: The Life and Death of a Screenwriter* [London and Boston, MA: Faber and Faber, 1994], 220).

the duel and hospitalized together for several weeks, Clive and Theo become close friends. Visited regularly by Edith, both men fall secretly in love with her, but Theo makes the first move. Heartbroken and regretful, Clive is nonetheless happy when he learns that his friends will be married.

A second jump in time takes us to 1918 and the First World War, when Brigadier General Candy meets a young nurse, Barbara Wynne, while stationed in France. Also played by Kerr, Wynne, of course, reminds Clive of Edith, and the two are married soon after the war ends. He also sees Theo again, after he learns that his old German friend is being detained in a prisoner-of-war camp near Clive and Barbara's home. Their meeting is fraught, revealing both Theo's fears about how the British will treat Germany in the coming years, and Clive's naïve belief that all bad feelings between the enemy nations will soon be forgotten. After Barbara quite suddenly dies a few years later, the film makes its final leap ahead in time to 1939. Having lost Edith to illness and his sons to Nazi indoctrination, an aged and exhausted Theo seeks asylum through British immigration. Desperate, he appeals for assistance from his old friend, and the now-powerful Clive is able to help Theo gain his stay in Britain. During their time together, the two old men are often accompanied by Clive's driver, "Johnny" (Kerr), in what amounts to a platonic restaging of the triangulated relationship that developed in the Berlin hospital back in 1902. The final episodes of the film, which include the BBC scenes described earlier, meditate on Clive's failures to grasp the threat posed by Nazism, leading up to his retirement from the army and his joining of the Home Guard. Only gradually—with the patient help of Theo and Johnny, and as a result of the hard lesson he is taught by Spud about the necessity of prosecuting the current war in a properly modern way—does Clive begin to embrace the fact that, as the times are seriously changing, he will need to change too.

The relative sentimentality of Powell and Pressburger's portrait of Blimp is epitomized by the fact that the character's titular death refers not to the aged Clive's literal departure from this world but to his epiphany in the film's final scene. The old man is symbolically reborn once he acknowledges and then exorcises the Blimpish side of himself. According to Powell, the idea for this story originated during the editing of *Aircraft*: "The genesis of this new film was a scene between Godfrey Tearle and Hugh Burden in *One of Our Aircraft is Missing* which depicted the conflict between intolerant youth and experienced age. . . . They are two editions of the same man. Sir George was just like this young idealist when he was in his twenties, and John will be an old Blimp like him when he is in his fifties."[5] The scene was ultimately cut on David Lean's recommendation. Lean apparently remarked

---

[5]Michael Powell, *A Life in Movies* (1986; London: Faber and Faber, 2000), 399.

that "It's the sort of idea you could make a whole film about," and shortly thereafter Powell and Pressburger took up their editor's challenge.[6]

Pressburger often claimed that the screenplay for *Blimp* constituted his greatest screenwriting achievement,[7] and it's easy to understand why since the three-part flashback structure of the film so beautifully serves the narration of Clive's gradual awakening to the changing realities of war. Beginning with the 1902 episode focusing on the Boer War, proceeding to the final days of the First World War and the 1918 armistice, and concluding with the Blitz in the early days of the Second World War, Pressburger was able to show the ways in which wars and the world in which they were fought had changed while—at the same time—capturing Clive's own lack of understanding and growth. In all three episodes, Clive's stagnation is additionally exposed through his most important relationships: with Theo, and with the three most important women of his life, all played by Kerr: Edith, Clive's platonic ideal; Barbara, whom Clive marries because of her striking resemblance to Edith but winds up loving deeply (she dies tragically in 1926); and the much younger "Johnny," Clive's MTC driver and a sympathetic daughter-figure. Because the pragmatic Theo changes so much during the tumultuous period the film covers, and because Edith, Barbara, and Johnny represent three different generations of English women, these relationships all highlight a protagonist frozen in time.

This fact is poignantly captured in the Turkish bath sequence. In spite of the fact that the exercise attack on the Home Guard by the regular army is supposed to begin at midnight, Spud interprets literally his C.O.'s command to treat the war exercise "like the real thing." Because no formal rules would apply in a real modern military conflict, Spud decides to launch the invasion as a surprise "like Pearl Harbor." When Clive finds himself a prisoner of this impertinent, younger Lieutenant, he becomes belligerent, first tackling Spud into one of the baths and then interrogating him for his lack of respect: "How do you know what sort of man I was—when I was as young as you are—forty years ago?" As the grappling men sink beneath the steamy water, the words "forty years ago" echo through the bath house, and the camera pans up and away from their submerged bodies. Through a mesmerizingly slow tracking shot, we traverse the immense span of the bath only to see a 26-year-old Clive climb out on the side opposite to the one his older counterpart entered. That slow tracking shot measures nothing less than the space of forty years. It is 1902.

---

[6]Ibid.
[7]In a "Bundle of handwritten autobiographical notes" in the Pressburger papers (EPR/9/1/), Pressburger refers to the motorbike cavalcade opening of the film as one of his greatest writing achievements and to the closing lines of the film as perhaps his favorite self-authored dialogue. He was especially proud of the flashback structure the film employed.

Pressburger establishes several key binaries in this memorable opening sequence, and they are mapped onto the bodies of Spud and Clive, respectively: youth and old age; instinct and experience; innovation and tradition; "the real thing", war, and the mere facsimile of it. The setup works so effectively because it manages to fracture the audience's sympathies, forcing us both to accept the logic of Spud's position (since we meet him first, we are somewhat complicit in his sneaky actions) and to feel the full emotional weight of Clive's position as Spud's victim. As A. L. Kennedy notes, "Spud is happy to beat the Nazis by becoming one. He is not merely advocating a new efficiency, he is destroying morality."[8] Kennedy's final claim seems overstated, especially in its refusal to acknowledge Spud's pragmatic intelligence and realism, but she is correct that Spud is willing to sacrifice the moral high ground to beat the Nazis at their own game. Thus the film thrusts us into a dialectical conundrum whereby we are forced to reconcile our desires for fairness, for moral behavior, and for cooperation between human beings with our practical knowledge of what is required to address a new reality, which is Nazism. We generally agree, then, with Andrew Moor's argument that "Powell considers English conservatism and insularity to be *virtues*, and longs for them to remain fixed in the nation's character, alongside a rosy (and possibly naïve) commitment to fair play. He implicitly admits, though, that such virtues can become dangerous if they are divorced from *realpolitik*. . . . Simply put, this is what *Blimp* sets out to demonstrate."[9] Moor is right that *Blimp* is a warning cry for a more pragmatic response to the realities of total warfare. At the same time, as Kent Puckett notes, the film is also "[e]ssentially ambivalent" because it "both accepts and deplores the all-in tactics of modern total war."[10] This profound ambivalence, born out of the Archers' real grappling with complex issues of morality and wartime praxis, explains why the film provoked such confusion upon its release. Indeed, it explains why the well-known question posed by *The Observer*'s film reviewer C. A. Lejeune—"but what is it about?"[11]—has continued to resonate with so many critics and viewers.

---

[8] A. L. Kennedy, *The Life and Death of Colonel Blimp* (London: BFI, 1997), 25.
[9] Moor, *Powell and Pressburger: A Cinema of Magic Spaces*, 2nd ed. (London and New York: I.B. Tauris, 2012), 54–5. See also Maroula Joannou's argument that "Fair play is always linked to Englishness in the film but at the same time, the conviction that modern warfare cannot be conducted 'by the National Sporting Club rules' is a *leitmotif* which represents Powell and Pressburger's most explicitly propagandist contribution to the war effort" ("Powell, Pressburger, and Englishness," *European Journal of English Studies* 8 [2004]: 189–203, 195). While Joannou's final assertion about The Archers' "most explicitly propagandist contribution" is overstated, the central point is persuasive.
[10] Kent Puckett, *Cinema, History, and Violence in Britain 1939–1945* (New York: Fordham University Press, 2017), 2.
[11] Lejeune, "The Films," *Observer*, June 13, 1943.

From the beginning of *Blimp*, Powell and Pressburger distinguish between the ethics of warfare itself and the ethics of representing, or reporting on, warfare—whether through BBC radio, newspapers, magazines, posters, or even a film such as *Blimp* itself.

When it comes to actually fighting and winning the war against Nazism, they suggest, the rules of the game very well may need to be broken. In *that* realm, their ethical position might be described as a "means to an end" form of pragmatism. When it comes to representing the war, or governing how the war is represented, however, Powell and Pressburger insist that certain rules must be maintained—especially regarding the need for transparency and the right to report accurately. In this case, the ethical position is defined according to the basic belief that the right to know and represent the truth is the "end" in and of itself. We believe that the confusion that many critics (and viewers) have experienced with the film can be attributed to their failure to separate out the two topics—to see that the film comes perilously close to saying "whatever it takes" when it comes to winning the war, but advances a more moral and ethical conception of how wartime propaganda should work.

In suggesting that honest news reports and other forms of propaganda were not irreconcilable with a military commitment to *realpolitik*, Powell and Pressburger were sharing a position gradually embraced by the MOI by the middle years of the War. According to Ian McLaine,

> Through stern practical experience the Ministry came to realise the cardinal importance of full and honest news as a factor in civilian morale. The sheer doggedness with which the department fought the service ministries and even Churchill himself over news and censorship was a measure of the strength of this conviction and, indeed, of a determination that, in fighting totalitarianism, Britain should not borrow one of its chief weapons. . . . [T]he Ministry also came to regard the British people as sensible and tough, and therefore entitled to be taken into the government's confidence. Possessed of this belief, the erstwhile propagandists became the evangelists of a novel attitude towards the people, furnishing them and the government with the means for a more cohesive national war effort.[12]

Whereas in the first few years of the war, the British effort was hampered by a relatively condescending and cynical propaganda operation that made the people doubt the government and media alike, the more respectful and

---

[12]McLaine, *Ministry of Morale: Home Front Morale and the Ministry of Information in World War II* (London, Boston, and Sydney: Allen and Unwin, 1979), 11. We have taken up this quotation in the Introduction as well.

transparent propaganda of later years ironically enabled the solidarity that total war requires from all sectors of a nation. The crucial distinction Powell and Pressburger draw between the ethics of fighting a war and the ethics of representing one can undoubtedly be difficult to discern in *Blimp*, a fact that contributes to the confused responses to the film we alluded to earlier.[13] It *is* a logical distinction, however, and one that helps the filmmakers to further differentiate British and Nazi belief systems even as they cautiously urge the British military to embrace *realpolitik*. Before turning specifically to the film's thorough treatment of such matters, however, the specific ethical problem posed by *Blimp* requires additional analysis.

It Means that Right Is Might After All

Generally speaking, Pressburger's early drafts of the script go furthest in pointing out the moral dangers of *realpolitik*, though even the final cut continues to emphasize those dangers. Deletions across the many treatments and scripts are often telling. In the original script, for example, one of Spud's subordinates asks him what the C. O. means when he commands the men to "make it like the real thing," and he replies, "Obviously, [prisoners must be bayoneted to death, women must be raped,] our losses divided by ten and the enemy's multiplied by twenty!"[14]

We should see, first of all, that Spud is combining two potentially contradictory ideas of "the real thing" here: the true horrors of war, on the one hand, and false propaganda, on the other. Though the line about the inflation of enemy losses and deflation of British ones remains in the final cut, any mention of prisoner abuse or rape is eliminated.[15]

How are we to read Spud's tone here? Is he annoyed by the C. O.'s command and so sarcastically exposing the ridiculousness of it? Is he making an off-color joke whose sheer absurdity demonstrates the superior virtue of the British military? In either case, an actual soldier's recognition that war, real war, involves abused or murdered prisoners, raped women, and shameless propaganda designed to misrepresent the truth immediately establishes a dividing line between the brutal reality and its representation

---

[13]One reason for this confusion has to do with the fact that lies and dirty propaganda can easily be folded under the umbrella of the realities of war. It's as if Pressburger is suggesting that, while the lines we draw in the sand are, by necessity, somewhat arbitrary, they still need to be drawn.

[14]The bracketed material is from the original script and did not appear in the film (qtd. in Ian Christie, ed., *The Life and Death of Colonel Blimp* [London: Faber and Faber, 1994], 80).

[15]Considering the release date of Olivier's *Henry V* on November 22, 1944, a year after *Blimp*'s own, the composition and subsequent deletion of lines about rape and the murder of prisoners (which were written to be spoken by Olivier himself) seems a fascinating coincidence.

by government and media alike. It also establishes a cynical tone that Powell and Pressburger would work increasingly to mute. Though the cut is hardly surprising in light of the production challenges the film faced, it offers insight into Pressburger's thematic and structural approaches to the project, and exposes perhaps the most troubling moral questions the film takes up: What does it mean to *endorse* realistic methods of warfare while acknowledging the actual, specific atrocities such an endorsement seemingly sanctions? In championing Spud's approach over that of Blimp, are we coming close to championing Nazi methods? If so, are we claiming that moral concerns should be irrelevant in a time of total war?

Beginning with Spud's line about manipulating the numbers of wartime casualties, the finished film highlights the fault lines between the official British narrative and the realities of war that the government and media manage to suppress. In spite of his war experience, Clive is not a conscious liar or manipulator of the truth. He is rather the naïve embodiment and mouthpiece of a systemic, nationalist ideology that allows him to reconcile his rigidly conservative morality and the military career that gives his life meaning and purpose. In the beginning of the 1902 episode, Clive is in London on sick leave, having taken a bullet in the shoulder in South Africa, and he is determined to do more than merely rest or recreate. In a scene set in the War Office, Clive requests permission from a Colonel Betteridge (Roland Culver) to visit Berlin on a counterpropaganda mission designed to shut up the German Kaunitz who has been spreading stories about British crimes in the Boer War:

> They hate us in Germany. They are spreading propaganda all over Europe that we are killing women and children in South Africa, that we are starving them in concentration camps, shooting mothers, burning babies—you wouldn't believe the things they have invented!

Clive sincerely believes that the British have been slandered, and that such "things" have been fabricated by lying enemies. In reading the original treatments and script, one is struck by how much more profoundly these lines resonate—especially after encountering Spud's (eventually deleted) lines about prisoner abuses and the rape of women. Whereas Spud has already told us that such things are "real," Clive is indignant at the very suggestion. In a bold directorial decision, Powell cuts to a medium shot of Betteridge's back as he stares out of a window while Clive speaks the just-quoted lines. When Clive stops and Betteridge turns around to face him, he shows no emotion whatsoever, seemingly unfazed by Clive's revelations. Though Clive is horrified by the very suggestion of British war crimes in South Africa, the high official who is in the know says nothing and gives up nothing—and the camera highlights his *non*-response. His eventual advice to Clive, "Keep quiet for a bit, eh," registers dramatically as an additional sign that even the younger Clive is out of his depth in wartime (Figure 5.2).

FIGURE 5.2 *Betteridge's seeming disinterest in Clive's stories about German propaganda in* The Life and Death of Colonel Blimp *(1943).*

Of course, the truth is that during the Boer War the British were responsible for significant war crimes. Inspired by the discovery of diamonds and gold, the Empire fought the so-called Second Boer War (1899–1902) against two Boer states, the Orange Free State and the South African Republic (Republic of Transvaal), in an attempt to expand British territory in South Africa. Hindered by the early success of Boer guerilla tactics, the British eventually resorted to a devastating "scorched-earth" campaign, systematically burning the crops and homesteads of both Boers and black Africans; they also installed concentration camps in which tens of thousands of Boers and Africans died— many of them women and children. As Gregory Fremont-Barnes notes of the British camps, "Images of enfeebled, emaciated and dying children were not simply the product of anti-British propaganda, but a cruel reality for thousands of innocent victims."[16] Nor could the problems of the camps be

---

[16]Fremont-Barnes, *The Boer War: 1899–1902* (Wellingborough: Osprey, 2003), 8. He also notes that "almost 28,000 Boers had died in the 46 concentration camps. Women accounted for two-thirds of the adult deaths. Nearly 80 percent of the fatalities were children under 16 years old, most commonly dying from measles, pneumonia, dysentery and typhoid. Official figures record 14,000 deaths among the 115,000 black Africans interned, but the true figure is now thought to be closer to 20,000" (81).

deemed the inevitable result of wartime realities: "Though the camps did not represent a deliberate policy of genocide, they may rightly be condemned as the product of gross indifference by British government officials remote from the scene, together with culpable negligence on the part of many of the camp administrators actually present."[17] This indifference and negligence were already well reported by 1902, due in part to the successful activist work of women like Emily Hobhouse—who almost single-handedly brought to public attention the terrible conditions within the British concentration camps—and they were certainly widely known by 1943 when *Blimp* appeared in British theaters. While it would be easy enough for a modern viewer to mistake Clive's sincere indignation at Kaunitz's "propaganda" as a position the filmmakers shared, Betteridge's response to Clive's indignation serves to underline the protagonist's absurd naiveté.

Long before the scene was actually filmed and Powell's bold shot of Betteridge was seen by anyone, an MOI Films' Division script reviewer showed how well he understood the subversive implications of Pressburger's script. Under the subheading "PRO-BOER PROPAGANDA," the reviewer noted a potential gap between the presumably patriotic intentions of the filmmakers and the way the scene was likely to read to audiences:

> The authors undoubtedly want to impress on the public the fact that forty years ago the Germans believed these stories [about British atrocities in South Africa]. In the middle of the war and making a film which may be shown to world opinion I think this is a very dangerous thing to do. From the story point of view there is no need to describe in detail what we are supposed to have done to Boer women.[18]

The subtext is clear enough: "you and I both know those reports about British war atrocities are well founded, but we're living through a historical crisis that requires that British methods look completely distinct from German methods, so let's be careful not to confuse the two." Powell's eventual response to the report is equally remarkable, and decidedly confusing too: "We agree that the Boer atrocities need handling with care, but in view of present German propaganda in South Africa it would be foolish to ignore the stories altogether; and good counter-propaganda to show the reactions of a typical British officer who has been there."[19] Powell acknowledges the reality of "the Boer atrocities"; the value of counterpropaganda even when it is designed to address true, or partly true, enemy propaganda; and, finally, the importance of an eyewitness account from a man whose persuasiveness

---

[17] Ibid., 81.
[18] Qtd. in Christie, *Life and Death*, 34–5.
[19] Ibid., 39.

depends precisely on his successful indoctrination as an establishment hero. In calling Clive a "typical British officer," Powell is likely fudging slightly, attempting to downplay the scene's acknowledgment of war crimes by suggesting that any typical British officer witnessing atrocities surely would have attempted to stop them. Clive is hardly "typical," however, since he sincerely believes the atrocities could not have been committed. He is wrong, of course, but Powell knows that British audiences would prefer the profound ignorance of an officer to the outright lies of one. Powell is invested in preserving the scene's subversive ambiguity, again revealing much about The Archers' view of how democratic propaganda should activate audiences. We will have more to say about this point in what follows.

Pressburger's brilliant callbacks to Boer war crimes in the film's First World War section underscore his willingness to be critical of the pre–Second World War military campaigns and practices of the British. When Clive first meets up with Major Van Zijl (Reginald Tate) in Flanders, whom the script describes as a veteran of the Boer War, their dialogue highlights the simple realities that remain constant from war to war:

Van Zijl: Glad to see you, sir. I've got another umbrella for you.
Clive: You've a marvellous eye for loot, van Zijl.
Van Zijl: Learnt from the English in the Boer War, sir.

Van Zijl's joke about English wartime looting raises an issue that may seem trivial in comparison to concentration camp abuses or rape. However, it seems reasonable to assume that he is alluding to the British imperial theft of diamonds and gold. Whether or not Clive recognizes this, what are we to make of his ambiguous chuckle? Is he simply anticipating the fact that Van Zijl stole the umbrellas from Nazi soldiers, or is he tacitly acknowledging the fairness of the South African's jab at the English?

In any case, the challenge of walking the line between producing jingoistic pro-British propaganda and a potentially radical, and therefore unreleasable, cinematic act of national self-reflection is best captured by The Archers' exclusion from the finished film of much of the scripted Flanders material.[20] In the film, Clive and Van Zijl question a group of eleven Nazi prisoners about their plans for detonating dynamite found among their seized equipment stores. Clive's toothlessness is particularly pronounced here; because he plays by the international rules of the game, he manages to get nothing from the Germans—in spite of his declaration that "I assure you that we have means to get what we want." Only a moment earlier, he had taken the opportunity to ask whether any of the prisoners knew Theo or his whereabouts, revealing to the audience, at least, that he is preoccupied with

---

[20] Surviving stills suggest some of these were actually filmed.

personal matters rather than being focused appropriately on the matter at hand. The scene reveals how Clive's personal ideals and desires are rendering him an increasingly out-of-touch, even useless, military leader.

Only when Clive exits and Van Zijl takes over the interrogation do we have any confidence in British methods for acquiring information from prisoners of war:

> Now listen. I am in command here now and I know how to deal with you scum. I am not a simple English gentleman but a simple South African and I assure you that I have means to get what I want.

He then gives the German soldiers thirty seconds to respond. After filming Van Zijl in close-up and shadow, lighting carefully the facial scars that he surely acquired in the Boer War, Powell cuts away before the countdown commences, emphasizing the menacing nature of what cannot be shown. One might reasonably view the cutaway as offering an interesting echo of Betteridge's turned back or, perhaps more importantly, of the famous crane shot in which the camera pulls up and away as the duel between Theo and Clive commences. All such shots contribute to a pattern of withholding within the film, one that appears to thematize its and/or propaganda's relationship to martial violence—of which there is almost none on display in *Blimp*.

Ironically, this particular, ominous cutaway may actually darken a scene that was originally much longer and more explicit in showing British violations of international law. In Pressburger's original script, there is no cutaway. Van Zijl waits for the thirty seconds to go by, and then he orders the three prisoners "nearest the door" to be taken outside and shot. Nervous glances are exchanged by British and German soldiers alike. The prisoners are taken outside, "*A command rings out: 'Fire!' There is a volley, other ominous sounds.*" After Van Zijl begins the countdown for the next three prisoners, one German protests, "You cannot shoot us—there is an international convention about prisoners!" Van Zijl ignores the point, ordering the next three prisoners outside. Another volley. He then erupts in front of the remaining five prisoners: "International conventions! You think they are useful on this side of the line, don't you?"[21] He starts his watch again, and only at this point does Pressburger signal a cut.

In three brief scenes that follow, we learn that the prisoners are still alive and that the gunfire is part of a plan to make the remaining prisoners talk. Though no violence has been committed, one of the prisoners points out again that international laws are being broken. In the MOI's June 1942 report on this script, these scenes are referred to as part of The Archers' "over complication of ideas [which] is much more dangerous. . . .

---

[21]The eventually cut lines of script are quoted in Christie, *Life and Death*, 193.

[W]e must be very careful not to appear to stand behind and support a film which can be taken in the wrong way by a fair proportion of people."[22] This government official is particularly shrewd in articulating precisely the sort of moral confusion the film invites in its arguments for adherence to the logic of *realpolitik* in warfare. We quote his report at greater length because it captures so well what critics such as Lejeune have struggled with in trying to interpret the film:

> The authors attack the British outlook on life as expressed in the terms of sportsmanship and fair play. They show this in contrast to German (not Nazi) efficiency and ruthlessness. They suggest in the end that Germans can only be defeated with their own weapons. Powell's letter of June 3 reveals that he had not seriously analysed the full implications of the obviously dialectical position in which efficiency in waging war must be combined with the civilised qualities which are part of our tradition. The script exaggerates the fair play idea to the point of ridicule and does not show those ways in which it has a constructive value. For instance, in the 1917 [*sic*] sequence, Candy fails to get information from the German prisoners: the tougher personality is more successful . . . . This is one of the scenes which suggests confusion of mind on the part of the authors, unless they merely wished to say that we must become like Germans before we can win the war. If this is what they wished to say—and I don't think it is—then it is a film we can only deplore. It is more likely that their own minds are in conflict and they have rather wantonly played with ideas.[23]

It's an analysis that might make a film critic proud, and it isolates in many ways the questions that Powell and Pressburger must have found themselves wrestling with throughout the long production process: once you argue that Nazi methods are the ones that everyone needs to adopt in order to survive, how do you justify the superiority of your own value system or morality? The MOI reviewer insists on the importance of maintaining a clear vision of why British values ("civilised" qualities) are superior; in failing to maintain such a vision, the film's argument can only be regarded as "deplorable."

Powell clearly was chafed by this report, addressing it directly and systematically in a memo to the Films Division dated June 16, 1942. "We resent intensely any suggestion that we are sympathetic to the German way of life," he states, just before turning to the MOI reviewer's comments on

---

[22]It is slightly unclear what the "over complication of ideas" is *more dangerous than*, though the reviewer says a few sentences earlier that he sees no harm in the film's claim that "we have had our fair share of blimpism but that we are self-critical and . . . have already relegated it to the scrapheap" (qtd. Christie, *Life And Death*, 31–3).
[23]Ibid., 33–4.

the 1918 prisoner interrogation scene, and pointing out that the Germans, unlike Van Zihl, "would have shot the prisoners."[24] Powell is, of course, right in making the critical, and obvious, point that no one is actually killed in the sequence, and yet his comments ignore the problems that the reviewer seems intent on exposing. What would be the repercussions of ignoring the clear rules of international law even while attempting to draw some sort of line between the way "we" violate them and the way "they" do so? That being said, the eventual decision to cut the firing squad sequence and leave ambiguous the fate of the German prisoners at the hand of Van Zijl arguably produces an even more radical scene that surely would have worried this same reviewer. In the film's final cut, the clear, inescapable conclusion the viewer must draw, after all, is that the prisoners will be tortured and perhaps killed if they do not give up the information Van Zijl is seeking. British methods, indeed, wind up seeming indistinguishable from German ones.

In both the 1902 and 1918 episodes, then, *Blimp* ostensibly demonstrates how earlier wars were conducted differently than Spud suggests the current conflict should be, all the while complicating the notion of such difference. In the case of the so-called "last gentlemen's war," the Boer War, the film subtly acknowledges the atrocities committed by the British in South Africa. In the case of the Flanders First World War episode, Powell and Pressburger push yet further in suggesting the extent of British war crimes and violations of international law. Both episodes excuse Clive from moral culpability, but they also accuse him of an ignorance aggressive enough to constitute a type of gross negligence. Together these episodes raise a host of questions about the value and authenticity of British traditions and national ideals, as well as about their sustainability in the face of German methods.

A crucial, common denominator between these period episodes and the film's contemporary, Second World War scenes is an emphasis on the way prisoners of war are treated by their captors. In many ways, the prisoner of war is the central motif of the film, though, surprisingly, the topic has never really been discussed by reviewers or critics. As we shall see in a moment, the varied conditions experienced by different prisoners of war serve in *Blimp* to measure the distance that their captors have traveled from the baseline of ethical or fair treatment as set down by the 1929 Geneva Convention; thus, such conditions speak to the relative civility or barbarity, idealism or realism, Britishness or Nazism of the people responsible for maintaining them. This serves as a convenient through line in the film, conjoining its various episodes and subplots through their shared concerns about each period's, and each nation's, treatment of prisoners.

An alternative but directly related point of return that *has* been frequently discussed by the film's critics, especially A. L. Kennedy, is the

---

[24]Ibid., 38.

literal and figurative idea of *home*, which she lists among the film's major themes: "comprehension of self, personal truth, understanding of life and death, time and home."[25] This focus on home is acknowledged by Powell himself, in the letter to Wendy Hiller we took up in the Introduction. Powell discusses the theme's centrality for Pressburger, who once claimed that "if he was to write a play of 'Blimp', it would be in one set: the home to which he returns from his various campaigns."[26] We wish to suggest that home's antithesis in the film is the prisoner-of-war camp, within which the foreigner is restrained.

In addition to the Boer War prisoners (including Kaunitz, who was held captive within Clive's blockhouse for seven weeks) and the German prisoners in Flanders, our major characters also face imprisonment at different moments in their lives. Theo is, of course, depicted as a prisoner in Derbyshire just after the First World War ends. Situated on the beautiful, pastoral grounds of an old aristocratic country house, the British camp for "400 or 500" German prisoners offers Schubert and Mendelssohn concerts for the officers and seems organized to communicate a sense of English hospitality. Such hospitality is captured by Clive's visit to the camp and the written invitation he sends to Theo to join him. In one of the film's most moving scenes, Theo first rejects the invitation and then refuses to acknowledge Clive in person, acts of "dignity" and "honour" that absolutely befuddle Clive:

> What "Dignity," what "Honour"? Who has hurt his "Ehre"? They lost, we won. What of it. We've been defeated too sometimes. Fortune of war!

While Clive is still collapsing sport and war into one another, still proving himself naïve and childish, Barbara indulges his "Good old sporting spirit" while also articulating her own more realistic understanding of the entire scenario's awful hypocrisy:

> I was thinking how odd they [the Germans] are! How queer! For years and years they are writing and dreaming wonderful music and beautiful poetry and then all of a sudden they start a war, shoot innocent hostages, sink undefended ships, bomb and destroy whole streets in London, killing little children—and then, dressed in the same butcher's uniform, they sit down and listen to Mendelssohn and Schubert. There's something horrible about that, don't you think so, Clive?[27]

---

[25]Kennedy, *The Life and Death*, 10.
[26]Qtd. in Christie, *The Life and Death*, 18–19.
[27]This scene originally followed Clive's confused comments about Theo rejecting him. In the finished film, it comes before Clive is rejected.

Her speech defines what is "horrible" about the German sensibility, as she perceives it, but it also indirectly highlights what is grotesque about the current camp conditions and the assumptions made by certain British powers—including Clive—that an armistice will somehow settle the matter and allow enemies to start acting politely toward one another again.

That sort of grotesquerie certainly extends into the next scene in Cadogan Place, where Theo joins Clive's dinner party following their reconciliation over the phone. Just as Barbara finds the German ability to produce great artifacts of civilization at odds with their barbarism in war, Theo finds the British gentlemen's naïvete baffling and a symptom of both denial and decadence. The scene reads like a great interrogation of British Blimpishness from an outside "enemy's" perspective. At one point, a General Taylor-Grant says that he "Can't imagine anything more awful than to be a prisoner of war in England." Theo's rejoinder that "I don't think it can be much good anywhere" highlights the absurdity of the comment, reinforcing what we've just seen in Derbyshire. "It was not so bad," he points out, "we had books, concerts, lectures." The talk shifts momentarily to the cooking in the camps, whether the food was good enough and whether prisoners were fed too well considering the rationing so many British citizens were forced to endure. Everyone laughs, but Theo is honest in communicating his disbelief: "Your people . . . cannot be adjusted from war to peace as easily as you can, gentlemen."

The scene ends with a discussion of British reconstruction policy in which numerous English gentlemen—those ever-good sports—say that their wish is simply to befriend the Germans again as quickly as possible. Theo is disgusted, explaining to his fellow German officers back at the railway station that "They are *children*! *Boys*! Playing *cricket*! They win the shirts off our backs and now they want to give them back, because the game is over! . . . This child-like stupidity is a raft for us in a sea of despair!" In Theo's more realist view of what reconstruction should look like, a more pragmatic British nation would treat his country as the enemy nation it is, would build it back up much more cautiously. It would embrace the strategy of making a *real* prison camp out of Germany, in other words, rather than perpetuating the self-serving lie that the two countries can be friendly again by simply signing an agreement; the double indignation of military defeat and economic devastation suffered by Germany would ensure the failure of such a postwar agreement. In his final lines in the Cadogan place dinner party scene, Theo speculates that home in Germany will be just like a prison camp anyway, but one that the self-deluding British will refuse to recognize as such. Clive is baffled by the comment, so Theo explains, "Aren't we going to have foreign troops occupying our cities for years," and then—in a line cut from the final film—"You set us prisoners free but we shan't be free because our whole country is going to be a prison camp."

Together, these scenes at the Prisoners-of-War Camp and Cadogan Place recreate a debate, still being hashed out today, about the impact of British and Allied policies and attitudes toward Germany following the Great War. According to Michael S. Neiberg, even at the time, "Some saw the treaty [of Versailles] as too harsh toward Germany, others as too lenient."[28] One point is clear, however: whereas the war-devastated French were understood to have sought too draconian a postwar settlement with Germany—one closer to what Theo seems to think appropriate—the British were associated with too much leniency:

> Indeed, many Allied politicians, especially in Britain, wanted to see Germany quickly recover, both to restore a balance of power on the Continent and for German consumers to once more be in a position to buy British goods. Britain needed a treaty that kept Germany strong enough to serve as the engine of a postwar European economic recovery but not strong enough to pose a threat to the European political system. It is highly unlikely that any treaty could have negotiated that peculiarly deadly Scylla and Charybdis of the postwar years.[29]

With this in mind, we can see that the film believes the Blimps to be terribly naïve about the postwar settlement and—to the degree that Versailles and later postwar treaties could actually be equated with a logic of appeasement—even implies that Hitler's rise to power was one inevitable result of British "stupidity." At the same time, Theo's slightly masochistic call for harsher treatment is naïve in its own way. To the degree that Versailles and other treaties could be interpreted as being too harsh toward Germany, especially economically, Theo could be accused of failing to understand the real conditions that would lead to Hitler's rise. The crucial factor here is that the scenes expose the views of dangerous extremists: on one side, the "childlike" Blimps; on the other, the German boys whose masculine pride and patriotism have been injured by military defeat. (We should remind ourselves that it took Theo almost a year after Hitler's appointment as chancellor to understand how dangerous to humanity the would-be dictator really was[30]). Theo's awakening will happen long before Clive's but, at this point in their lives, they both are depicted as prisoners of severely flawed mindsets.

Finally, it's worth exploring the obvious point that Clive is declared to be a "prisoner of war" after Spud's army has broken the rules of the game

---

[28]Michael S. Neiberg, *The Treaty of Versailles: A Concise History* (Oxford: Oxford University Press, 2017), xii.
[29]Ibid., xvi.
[30]When Theo presents his case for asylum to the refugee committee, he admits, "I had nothing to fear from Hitler [in 1933]. At least I thought so. It took me eight months to find out I was wrong."

scheduled to begin at midnight. Whereas Theo had been imprisoned by an English army that worshipped those rules, Clive is outraged precisely because Spud's new army wins by breaking them. More interesting than the conditions of Clive's imprisonment, however, are Spud's rationalizations of his realist military strategy. If Deborah Kerr's Barbara was a voice of *realpolitik* in the Derbyshire sequences, Kerr's protective Johnny offers a more nuanced position regarding the choice between Nazi and Blimpish methods. When she learns from Spud that he plans to attack Clive before midnight, she protests on the grounds that he's playing dirty. This prompts Spud to reply:

> Capture him! War starts at midnight! We're going to bag him hours before that. Nazi methods. You know.
> JOHNNY: You're not a Nazi!
> SPUD: We're not training to fight Englishmen! . . . Don't be a sissy! In war anything goes!

On the one hand, Johnny rejects this notion by criticizing Spud's methods as Nazi-like and racing to protect Clive from the unfair assault. On the other hand, she shows herself willing to use any means necessary ("anything goes") to stop Spud and fight what she thinks to be a just war. In fact (just moments after Spud utters the eventually cut line, "You have to use the first weapon that comes to hand,")[31] Johnny brains him with an ashtray, knocking him unconscious, before racing off to the Royal Bathers' Club. In this relatively lighthearted sequence, then, Johnny suggests a third way between Nazi and Blimpish methods: doing whatever it takes in the service of what she believes is right.

Throughout the film, Powell and Pressburger struggle to criticize Blimpish stupidity and naiveté without openly endorsing Nazi methods. It can be argued that they fail at this task, that the MOI reviewer is correct when he wonders whether "their own minds are in conflict." When Clive learns late in the Flanders sequence that the Germans have accepted the terms of surrender, he explains to his batman Murdoch (John Laurie) what this victory means to him:

> It means that Right is Might after all. The Germans have shelled hospitals, bombed open towns, sunk neutral ships, used poison-gas—and *we won!* Clean fighting, honest soldiering have won!

It is unclear whether Murdoch, who simply utters "Sir," is moved or embarrassed by Clive's interpretation of events, but the film has trained us

---

[31] Qtd. in Christie, *Life and Death*, 279.

to recognize that the reality is much more complex than he understands.³² So how do we separate out the official, nationalist rhetoric from reality? And how can we solve the moral problem that Powell and Pressburger seem to have taken on so directly in *Blimp* by offering up the "deplorable" suggestion that Nazi methods need to be adopted until the Second World War has been won?

Propaganda and Counterpropaganda

We might reasonably argue that Pressburger's original script included just one clear description of "real" war, voiced by Spud, and that most of it was eventually cut from the film: "prisoners must be bayoneted to death, women must be raped, our losses divided by ten and the enemy's multiplied by twenty!" Importantly, and as we have seen, Pressburger defines real war in terms of both horrific actions and intentionally deceitful propaganda. By conjoining a certain form of propaganda with crimes against humanity such as murder and rape, Pressburger offers a clear enough statement about the insidious type of German propaganda he and Powell had already condemned in earlier films such as *49th Parallel*. At the same time, one is hardly surprised that Spud's line was cut; as discussed earlier, it revealed all too clearly the moral conundrum Pressburger's script was to lay bare. If Spud's methods are being endorsed, after all, then what are we supporting when we support the new ways?

That the film does support the new ways, within reason, is again clear from the script. A planned dedication that was also cut from the finished film confirms the point:

> THIS FILM IS DEDICATED
> to the New Army of Britain,
> to the new spirit in warfare,
> to the new toughness in battle,
> and to the men and women who
> know what they are fighting
> for and are fighting this war
> to win it.³³

In the end, after Clive has been retired by the Army, humiliated by Spud, and set straight by Theo, he decides he must embrace this new Army; he comes to

---

³²These lines originally followed dialogue that had to be deleted from the film due to the cutting of the Van Zijl firing squad sequence. In them, Clive learns about what has happened to the prisoners and explodes: "If we are fighting gangsters that is no reason why we should behave like gangsters" (Christie, *Life and Death*, 209).
³³Ibid., 76.

see a bit of his old self in Spud and understands finally that he must change with the times. In the film's final shot, Clive salutes the new Army with a smile on his face. He is saluting clever new methods and a certain amount of piss and vinegar. He is not supporting rape and Goebbels. Nonetheless, a critic as discerning as Lejeune could still feel confused by the film or, at least, feel that the film is confusing. How do we square—and how did The Archers square— its endorsements of a new model army and its condemnation of Nazi methods? The answer lies, we believe, in Powell and Pressburger's conviction that the propaganda war was as real, and as important, as any military operation, but that it needed to be conducted on different moral and ethical terms.

Like their earlier wartime films, *Blimp* places an extraordinary emphasis on propaganda's importance as both a wartime weapon and a distinguishing feature of both totalitarian and democratic societies. This film goes behind the scenes, showing audiences the governmental offices of propaganda as well as the media outlets with which they work, and it zooms in on internal debates about propaganda and censorship within those offices. As noted previously, almost as soon as we meet the young Clive, he is petitioning the War Office to be sent on a counterpropaganda mission to Berlin. Because he'd spoken of his military service in Jordaan Siding in a recent *Times* issue, Edith Hunter contacts him to report that Kaunitz has been spreading lies about the British operations there; as Clive explains the matter to Betteridge,

> Now this girl writes from Berlin that the worst stories of all are being put about by a fellow named Kaunitz who says he saw with his own eyes British soldiers kill two hundred and fifty women and children at Jordaan Siding in order to save feeding them!

Edith wants Clive to address the matter for partly selfish reasons, since all this German anti-British propaganda has led to her governess appointment in Berlin being canceled: "They hate us in Germany. They are spreading propaganda all over Europe that we are killing women and babies." The reader will recall that, as Clive speaks these lines, Powell chooses to film Betteridge's back, giving us a non-reaction that functions in much the same way that Murdoch's near-silence in the Flanders scene does, by indicting Clive. After Clive explains who Kaunitz is and what he's been saying, Betteridge simply asks, "Now what do you want me to do?" Much to Clive's surprise, the Colonel is unmoved by, and seemingly indifferent to, his astounding revelations.

Betteridge does attempt to draw a clear line, however, between the duties of military personnel and the professionals charged with handling political matters, especially foreign diplomacy. When Clive asks for permission to go to Berlin, Betteridge explains,

> This isn't Army business, it's Embassy. Leave politics to the politicians. You wouldn't like a diplomat to come charging into the front line with your company, would you?

Betteridge's additional advice to Clive, eventually cut from the film, is to keep his mouth shut and to play golf. Such advice renders explicit a strategy the Colonel enacted earlier in the scene when he steered Clive off-topic multiple times to discuss Conan Doyle's most recent Sherlock Holmes stories. Although Clive tries to explain that Conan Doyle himself is "collecting material about our campaign in South Africa to counter German propaganda," Betteridge keeps the conversation on *The Hound of the Baskervilles*.

The scene captures some of the confusion that surrounded British propaganda efforts prior to Dunkirk—and it leaves the audience feeling quite uncertain about the wisdom of Clive's decision to leave for Berlin against his superior's better advice. Is Betteridge a Blimp himself, incompetent and feckless and unaware how damaging this German propaganda can be? Or is he more knowing and cynical (as his turned back and silence would suggest), and is he responding to Clive in this way because he can discern the younger man's naiveté and impulsiveness? Regardless of how we answer these questions, it's hard not to feel that we're witnessing governmental incompetence. In spite of the Colonel's claim that the "politicians" are working on these issues, we as an audience feel little confidence that the War Office is being properly run. Betteridge is either passing the buck onto the Foreign Office (i.e., the "politicians" and diplomats in charge of handling propaganda and counterpropaganda during the Boer War period), or he's deliberately obfuscating in order to hide what he knows, either about British war crimes in South Africa or, less plausibly, about German lies about such crimes.

Once in Berlin together, Clive and Edith engage in a bit of dialogue that highlights, however inadvertently, the film's approach to the propaganda question. Acknowledging Edith's unfortunate joblessness, Clive asks,

> Clive: Well, what are you going to do now?
> Edith: Go back.
> Clive: To England?
> Edith: I'm afraid so.
> Clive: Cheer up! England isn't as bad as all that.
> Edith: That is what we both want to prove, isn't it, Mr. Candy?

It's precisely the sort of exchange that makes *Blimp* so wonderfully baffling (and so bafflingly wonderful). As in so many other moments of the film, counterpropaganda becomes indistinguishable from propaganda. On the surface, two young English people wish to defend their country. Look deeper, though, and the situation seems murkier. Edith, after all, is motivated almost entirely by personal necessity; she needs England's reputation to improve in order to re-secure employment in Germany. Clive is no doubt more straightforwardly patriotic, but are they speaking the same language when they admit their need to prove that England isn't all that bad? Either way, England's "goodness" must be demonstrated. An argument needs to be made. Evidence needs to be presented. Counterpropaganda emerges here not as the mere *revelation* that England actually is good but, instead, as a form of propaganda itself, one whose purpose is to construct England in a positive light. *Blimp*'s mere recognition of this fact would arguably disrupt the MOI's mandate regarding how filmmakers should approach their task, in part because it openly admits a disturbing gap between reality and representation. Powell and Pressburger pull back the curtain here and show us the wires, inviting us to interrogate even their own evidence for England's goodness. To delve deeply into *Blimp* is to delve deeply into the brain and guts of filmed propaganda.

In our Introduction, we discussed the common idea that ideology is to the propaganda film as critical thinking is to the non-propaganda film. According to such a view, the propaganda film imposes ideological positions onto an audience prefigured as passive and helpless, whereas the non-propaganda film caters to an audience prefigured as capable of sorting out complex, potentially contradictory ideas. Steve Neale characterizes "democratic cinema"—which he takes to be non-propagandistic by nature—as inscribing "spaces for reflection and discussion, for counter-proposition and counter-argument, even if, necessarily, it sets the terms for this."[34] We have seen how, even in Powell and Pressburger's earliest propaganda films, their insistence on producing filmic spaces for reflection, discussion, counterproposition, and counterargument is quite consistent and adamant. We have also seen how their characteristically explicit self-reflexivity regarding propaganda forms and processes renders such spaces quite capacious. In *Blimp* these specific tendencies are pushed to the edge of their acceptable limits, however, and in at least two specific ways: first, the questions Powell and Pressburger ask are more complex and therefore more threatening to the government agencies and officials tasked with maintaining public morale and support for the war; second, the duo seems more trusting than ever before of their audience's ability to wrestle with the contradictions and ambiguities the film presents. In this way, and especially in comparison with films such as *Contraband* (1940) or *49th Parallel*, *Blimp* presents itself less as a vehicle for ideas than as a model of a propaganda cinema that is also democratic cinema.

"Propaganda Detrimental to the Morale of the Army"

In one of Pressburger's earliest, handwritten treatments of *Blimp*, there are no scenes involving the BBC or Clive's canceled radio address. In their

---

[34]Neale, "Propaganda," *Screen* 18 (1977): 9–40, 33.

place is a scene in which Clive returns to the War Office previously occupied by Betteridge, but the year is now 1940, in the days just after Dunkirk. Crucially, Clive bears some responsibility for the British military's failure. According to Pressburger's dialogue commentary,

> [There] is an investigation of the campaign in France and Belgium. We hear the investigations. We hear Bl's ideas about the sporting war. He was outmaneuvered all right but he was happier being on the losing side than on the victorious. The victors have to shame themselves.[35]

In the following scene, Clive (still named Blimp [and abbreviated Bl] at this early stage of the film's development) is back with Theo, to whom he explains that the army has retired him. Note that the function of the original scene is quite similar to that of the ones that eventually replaced it, serving to highlight how out of touch Clive is with the realities of total war. The result is also the same: in both cases, he is fired and will join the Home Guard. The deliberate shift in the finished film from the War Office to the BBC massively impacts the story, however, especially when it comes to the nature of the audience's identification with Clive. In the scrapped treatment, he is at least partly responsible for the loss of France, for actual military blunders and the flawed philosophy underlying them. In presenting the Clive character as a direct cause of the disaster at Dunkirk, rather than a mere commentator on it, the treatment casts him in a much more critical light than does the actual film. Pressburger's decision to insert the BBC scenes—to foreground the role of the media, of propaganda, and of censorship in the war against Germany—suggests the crucial importance not just of fighting wars properly, but also of making certain that they are properly represented.

The choice to name J. B. Priestley as Clive's replacement brilliantly amplifies the stakes by lending the film a high degree of specificity in its handling of propaganda. Priestley's "Postscripts"—the Sunday night, 9:00 p.m. broadcasts second in popularity only to Churchill's own—were deliberately launched to diversify the BBC's offerings: "Among many other proposals, . . . [it was] suggested that the predominance of the 'cultured' voice of the BBC should be diminished, and working-class and left-wing speakers should be brought to microphone to counteract enemy propaganda proclaiming that imperialists and capitalists controlled Britain."[36] The first of these broadcasts, on June 5, 1940, focused on the rescue of the stranded men at Dunkirk, overlapping perfectly with the fictional time line of *Blimp* and suggesting the degree to which the conservative Clive should be contrasted

---

[35]EPR 1/22/1.
[36]Peter Buitenhuis, "J. B. Priestley: The BBC's Star Propagandist in World War II," *ESC: English Studies in Canada* 26 (2000): 445–72, 446.

with Priestley, who, according to Graham Greene, "gave us what our other leaders have always failed to give us—an ideology."[37] That left-wing, voice-of-the-people ideology refocused listeners on the potential of the war to bring about social change; it redirected Churchill's exclusive focus on the need to win the war toward the social change that winning could bring about.[38]

Siân Nicholas notes that Priestley's rise also coincided with that of the BBC after its problematic early months covering the war: "In the period between Dunkirk and D-Day BBC news reporting underwent some dramatic changes that turned the negative attitude to the BBC into a far more positive endorsement."[39] Much of the change was owing to the strategic decisions that put Priestley and other non-traditional voices on air, and more specifically to the concerted efforts of the BBC (including Priestley) and the state, which "created an instant myth [about Dunkirk], conveying some of the confusion of the real situation, but in general reporting the retreat in a florid and dramatic style."[40] Prior to Dunkirk, the BBC was not only irritating large numbers of listeners by underestimating their desire for honest reporting about the war; it was also failing to convince many of them that Germany was a threat. Both Nicholas and Ian McLaine have shown that up to one-sixth of adult radio listeners regularly tuned into German propaganda and refused to see Germans as enemies: "The most serious indictment of the quality of British broadcasting was the extent of British listening to German radio, and in particular the notorious Lord Haw-Haw."[41] Several of his broadcasts, it is estimated, were heard by about fifty percent of the British radio-listening population. The nickname of the British (American-born) broadcaster of German propaganda, William

---

[37]Qtd. in Paul Addison, *The Road to 1945: British Politics and the Second World War* (London: Quartet, 1977), 119.
[38]According to Buitenhuis, "Conservative MPs, and particularly Churchill himself, were reluctant to talk about war aims, and unwilling at this stage in the war to commit the government to particular post-war programs. Priestley considered that a clear statement of why Britain was fighting was essential to morale" ("J. B. Priestley," 456). This filmic shift of focus onto what will happen after the war is a popular subject of contemporary British cinema, as we show in our chapters on *IKWIG* and *AMOLAD*.
[39]Siân Nicholas, *The Echo of War: Home Front Propaganda and the Wartime BBC, 1939–45* (Manchester: Manchester University Press, 1996), 197.
[40]Ibid., 196. According to Anthony Aldgate and Jeffrey Richards, "Nothing perhaps encapsulates the difference of style between Churchill and Priestley so much as their response to Dunkirk. Where Churchill spoke in ringing heroic terms of the abstract qualities it demonstrated . . . Priestley eulogized the little seaside pleasure steamers pressed into service for the evacuation. . . . Even more significantly, a difference emerged about the ultimate aim of the war. For Churchill it was simple: 'We have to gain the victory.' . . . But for Priestley it was what came after the war that was vitally important" (*Britain Can Take It: British Cinema in the Second World War* [Oxford: Basil Blackwell, 1986], 50).
[41]Nicholas, *Echo of War*, 45. See also McLaine, *Ministry of Morale*, 55.

Joyce, Haw-Haw used medium wave radio and an upper-class British accent to offer distorted news of the war, such as inaccurate numbers of British and German casualties in military conflicts. Like Clive, Priestley was especially concerned about allowing German propaganda to go unaddressed abroad (Haw-Haw's broadcasts reached the United States on short wave radio); his persuasive defenses of "the democratic way of living" massively impacted the popularity of Haw-Haw's broadcasts, so that the latter's influence declined precipitously after Dunkirk.[42]

Powell and Pressburger's choice to supplant Clive with Priestley, along with their decision to replace a War Office scene with one set at the BBC, shifted attention from the battlefield to the arena of popular propaganda and counterpropaganda. This shift in focus is particularly appropriate insofar as the BBC "[o]ver the course of the war . . . developed from an instrument of official propaganda into a participant in its own right in the propaganda process."[43] Moreover, by the time of the film's release, Priestley's story had accrued additional layers of complexity due to his increasingly uncomfortable relationship with the state and the British right wing more generally. According to Peter Buitenhuis, "Priestley, revealing a class bias that became increasingly strident in his broadcasts, had a particular animus against the civil service and the wealthy and influential people whom he thought were profiting or left unaffected by the war,"[44] and these positions all contributed to the (temporary) cancellation of his broadcasts in late October 1940. Undoubtedly, reluctance on the part of Churchill and conservative MPs to discuss war aims or social reforms led to immense pressure being put on the BBC to tamp down Priestley's so-called radicalism. At one point, after the BBC appeared to cave in to government demands to end the series, Priestley even referred to the conservatives as "the political Gestapo."[45] We might say that just as Priestley's first ever broadcast, on the Dunkirk fiasco, was indirectly referenced in *Blimp*, so too were his final days as a broadcaster—and in the unlikely form of a Blimpish broadcaster being canceled by the government and the BBC. Through the BBC sequence, then, Pressburger represents the government's erasure of an establishment voice and its replacement with one that would become increasingly critical of the government itself. That *Blimp* professes the necessity of that replacement reads paradoxically as both a critique of the government and a defense of its right to censor "problematic" voices.

Ironically, the question of whose voices should be censored would come front and center for Powell and Pressburger in the months of development

---

[42]Ian Whittington, "*Out of the People*: J. B. Priestley's Broadbrow Radicalism," *Writing the Radio War: Literature, Politics and the BBC, 1939–1945* (Edinburgh: Edinburgh University Press, 2018), 30–64, 44.
[43]Nicholas, *Echo of War*, 6.
[44]Buitenhuis, "J. B. Priestley," 452.
[45]Ibid., 460.

leading up to the film's release. Since the history of the government's attempts to quash the production is well known—as is Churchill's own role in those efforts—we will summarize here only the most important details. As James Chapman notes in the most authoritative and comprehensive account of this history, Powell's numerous, contradictory explanations of what happened tend to confuse the roles of the MOI, the War Office, and the Cabinet in setting up obstacles to the film's production and release.[46] The discovery in the late 1970s—by Laurence Hayward and Ian Christie[47]—of documentary evidence of Churchill's direct intervention in this process has managed to shed only partial light on the matter. What we can say with certainty based on the Churchill Papers in the Public Record Office, the Powell Papers and Pressburger Papers available in the BFI, and the work of scholars such as Chapman is, first, that officials seem to have responded initially to the treatments in directly opposed ways. Whereas Minister Brendan Bracken, Films Division head Jack Beddington, and the MOI more generally seem not to have wavered in their initial support of The Archers, Sir James Grigg determined that the War Office could not give the film its blessing: "[A]t a time when public confidence in the Army and its leaders is justifiably increasing, it would be a pity to divert attention to a caricature."[48]

Second, by late June 1942, the MOI decided to mirror the position of Grigg and the War Office: "[W]e cannot bring ourselves to feel that the public interest would be served by the production of the film as it stands [they are referring to the shooting script written a few weeks earlier], nor do we see how it could be rendered of positive value from the point of view of national propaganda" (40). In addition, the MOI refused at this point to release Laurence Olivier from the Fleet Air Arm to play the part of Clive, or to authorize Powell and Pressburger's use of military facilities and equipment. In early July, Bracken informed Powell that the Ministry could not "properly support" the film, basically backing the MOI's decision to block Olivier's release and suggesting that, if the film were to be made at all, it would be made without government resources or even approval.

Third, in September, after shooting began, Grigg began his correspondence with Churchill, urging the prime minister to stop the film based on the following representation of its content: "The War Office have refused to give their support to the film in any way on the ground that it would give the Blimp conception of the Army officer a new lease of life at a time when it is already dying from inanition" (43). At this point, Churchill himself attempted to intervene in so direct a manner as to actually test the difference

---

[46]James Chapman, "*The Life and Death of Colonel Blimp* (1943) Reconsidered," *Historical Journal of Film, Radio and Television* 15 (1995): 19–54, 26.
[47]See Chapman, "*The Life and Death*," 27, on the question of who deserves credit for the discovery.
[48]Qtd. in Christie, *The Life and Death*, 27. This exchange is henceforth cited in the text.

between democratic and totalitarian institutions. First, he urged Bracken to "stop this foolish production" on the grounds that any "propaganda detrimental to the morale of the Army" could not be defended (44). When the MOI explained they had no power to suppress the film, Churchill sought to extend the minister's "special authority" to do so (45–6). To his credit, the minister refused to take such an extraordinary measure.

Perhaps more important, and to *their credit*, both The Archers and Arthur Rank stood by their film through this period of pressure. After Grigg and War Cabinet representatives finally saw a rough cut of the film in the spring, they expressed their belief that "it was unlikely to attract much attention or to have any undesirable consequences" (47). Churchill himself screened the film the night before its general release on June 10, 1943, at the Odeon, Leicester Square, and, shortly after, urged Bracken to "stop it going abroad as long as you possibly can" (49). Whereas Grigg seems to have given up his insistence on the film's dangerousness—though perhaps due to the MOI's recognition that nothing could be done to stop it—Churchill continued to thwart its distribution through the fall of 1943. Only in September, a year after shooting began and months after the film's release, did Churchill apparently withdraw his ban on the film's export.[49] Presumably, Churchill would have relished the fact that the film was not released in America until 1945, and then in a severely cut and repackaged version called *The Adventures of Colonel Blimp*, which—in a most bizarre case of misrepresentation—marketed Clive as a swashbuckling romantic in the Errol Flynn tradition.[50]

Reception and Renegotiation

This chapter has considered the corner that *Blimp* paints itself into, and whether it manages ever to escape from it: Is the film advocating the "Nazi methods" that Spud openly endorses? If so, how can the British differentiate themselves morally from their Nazi enemy? "What is it about?" That was Lejeune's nagging question. As we have attempted to make clear, we understand why viewers have disagreed so dramatically about *Blimp*'s politics and meaning, though we have also sought to explain what we see as perhaps the major source of their disagreements: the film's attempt to separate its related arguments about the ethics of warfare, on the one hand, and the ethics

---

[49]See Chapman, "*The Life and Death*," 30.
[50]As Geoffrey Macnab reports, "United Artists tried to sell the film as a ribald tale of a lusty old soldier, a sort of Colonel Bluebeard. On the posters the slogans read as follows: 'The lusty lifetime of a Gentleman who was sometimes Quite a Rogue! Duelling—hunting big game—and pretty girls—life's a grand adventure with Colonel Blimp!'" (*J. Arthur Rank and the British Film Industry* [London and New York: Routledge, 1993], 68).

of wartime propaganda, on the other. When it comes to warfare, Powell and Pressburger appear to be sympathetic to Spud's "anything goes" mentality, agreeing that the only way to beat dirty Nazis is to play dirty. In moral terms, this leads them down a potentially dangerous path. When it comes to propaganda, however, the filmmakers insist on a crucial ethical distinction, as always, between totalitarian and democratic forms of messaging. The film wants to have its cake and eat it too; it wants to say that whereas, in the arena of combat, we must be like the Nazis, in the arena of propaganda, we must be different from them. Considering the complexity, or perhaps the contradictoriness, of these two positions, viewers can hardly be blamed for feeling confused by *The Life and Death of Colonel Blimp*.

While we have seen period critics raise the question of what *Blimp* means, they also worried that its confusing nature might compromise its clarity or even appropriateness as propaganda. Lejeune called *Blimp* "possibly the most controversial film produced in this country during our entire screen history."[51] One of her contemporaries, a reviewer from *Kinematograph Weekly*, labeled the film the first truly "provocative" one of the war period in its "handling of the complex British character and its attitude towards war."[52] Another unattributed contemporary review in the *Tribune* admitted that the film was interesting but noted that "all that [ambiguity] is a grave fault in a propaganda picture, which is what 'Blimp' is, or is supposed to be."[53] Reviewers seem to have agreed that *Blimp* was a courageous film, though they were divided over the film's coherence and political intentions. As we've seen, government officials were also divided over *Blimp*'s potentially dangerous perspectives on British methods and militarism—as well as its ambiguities and possible contradictions. Jack Beddington, for example, signaled his agreement with one of the MOI reviewers, R. B., who had complained that "There is no serious distinction between Germanity and Nazidom and although the total tone of the picture is not anti-British nor Pro-German it is to a certain extent wantonly provocative."[54] Nor were such provocations missed by contemporary audience members. Though it fared well at the box office—finishing as the fourth most successful British film of the year—many seem to have agreed with the War Office official who remarked, "this is subversive. It's against the army."[55] The Robsons were, of course, among the first to pounce:

> "The Life and Death of Colonel Blimp" is one of the most wicked productions that has ever disgraced the British film industry and [been]

---

[51] Lejeune, "The Films."
[52] Qtd. in Chapman, "*The Life and Death*," 39.
[53] *Tribune*, June 18, 1943.
[54] Qtd. in Christie, *The Life and Death*, 36.
[55] This is Powell's paraphrase of Grigg's complaint to Churchill (in Lazar, *Michael Powell Interviews*, 124).

inflicted upon the long-suffering British people. We shall later have occasion to mention a few others from the same "Blimp" stable, but this one in particular offers a vivid example of how the living, crawling germs of World War Three are being carefully hatched.[56]

The Robsons are as incompetent and unnuanced as readers of complex texts can be, but if ever a film lent itself to proving their conspiracy theories about British cinema's secret hatred of Britain, it must have been *Colonel Blimp*.

So distant now from the concerns of 1943 and the imminent threat of annihilation, modern critics have found it easy to downplay *Blimp*'s troubling ambiguities. Perhaps in response to sometimes-hyperbolic mainstream advertising of *Blimp* as one of the most subversive British films ever made, scholars have felt a need to qualify its radicalism. Ian Christie, perhaps our greatest authority on the government response to the film, has referred to *Blimp* as "a fantasy . . . a million miles removed from most people's conception of a solid, serious, propaganda film."[57] Christie may be speaking here more to the film's appearance than to its content, but the description does offer insight into how moviegoers today can view it as relatively apolitical art. Andrew Moor usefully corroborates such a hunch, noting, "Despite its boldness in presenting a sympathetic German in 1943, it looks now like a film in which the dominant myths of the Home Front are expressed, and in many ways it conforms to some of the ideals of its time."[58] Like so many others, then, Moor is willing to characterize the film according to what he acknowledges is a *retrospective* view.

However, when in a 1989 interview Richard Jameson claimed that it was "astounding to see *Colonel Blimp* and to imagine why anybody was ever afraid of it because it can't be represented as an anti-war film or anti-establishment or anything," Powell cut him off before he could finish in what was, presumably, a slightly sarcastic tone that drew laughter from the live crowd. He reminded Jameson that historical contexts actually matter: "Yes but they were touchy about it *in the war*."[59] Perhaps the only modern scholar to truly confront the film's thwarting of contemporary propaganda norms is Kent Puckett, who rightly calls *Blimp* "a committed work of propaganda that nonetheless embraces a thematic and aesthetic complexity that would otherwise seem antithetical to propaganda."[60] We agree with Puckett that

---

[56]E. W. and M. M. Robson, *The Shame and Disgrace of Colonel Blimp: The True Story of the Film* (London: Sidneyan Society, 1944), 4.
[57]Qtd. in Lazar, *Michael Powell Interviews*, 108.
[58]Moor, *Powell and Pressburger*, 55.
[59]Italics ours. Qtd. in Lazar, *Michael Powell Interviews*, 163.
[60]Puckett, *Cinema, History, and Violence*, 1. Overall, Puckett is an unusually nuanced reader of the "quietly disturbing" questions *Blimp* raises about Britain's desires to differentiate itself from nondemocratic states (63).

it's all too easy to misread *Blimp*'s political dimensions due to Powell and Pressburger's significant redrawing of the rules for British propaganda films.

Within its early 1940s context, *Blimp*'s disturbing lack of clarity—its profound ambiguities—were perceived as potentially dangerous precisely because they violated the government's mandate for propaganda films with clear, relatively simple formal features and messaging.[61] As we've also discussed in earlier chapters, the government preferred films that could communicate simplified ideas about who the British were, who the Nazis were, and what they were each fighting for. Such calls for simplicity and clarity in the messaging also echoed the work of contemporary propaganda theorists and psychologists, who often went so far as to define effective propaganda as precisely that which *inhibits* critical thinking.[62] Not only did Powell and Pressburger regularly violate this norm; they went so far as to flaunt their scorn for both simplistic messaging and the massaging of government officials' talking points. In many ways, when looked at in this specific historical context, *Blimp* reveals itself to be both a propaganda film and, in its provocation of critical thought among audience members, a counterpropaganda film.

Powell and Pressburger's insistence on making *Blimp* in the face of serious government opposition speaks especially to their growing belief in their own importance as collaborators in the war effort—alongside the military branches, the BBC, the War Office, and other such institutions. It also demonstrates their conviction in their ability to determine exactly what sort of propaganda British audiences needed and were capable of comprehending. Though their earlier propaganda films certainly reveal an independent streak, a desire to do more than merely conform to prescriptive models, in *Blimp* The Archers brazenly push the boundaries more than ever before. Indeed, long before the auteur movement in international cinema, the formation of The Archers as an independent production unit that reveled in its own autonomy speaks to Powell and Pressburger's growing conception of themselves as artists. More specifically, they consistently present themselves as possessing a unique and identifiable temperament characterized by a level of integrity that transcended contemporary expectations for filmmakers.

---

[61]Nonetheless, it seems important to note that among cinemagoers responding to a Mass Observation survey about the best films they saw in 1943, a large number praised *Blimp* without expressing reservations about its content (*Mass-Observation at the Movies*, ed. Jeffrey Richards and Dorothy Sheridan [London and New York: Routledge and Kegan Paul, 1987], 220–91). Moreover, *Blimp* topped the list of most popular films among the women who were surveyed, and came in second among the men (220).

[62]As noted in the Introduction, Ian McLaine discusses contemporary psychologist E. H. Henderson's recognition that "the aim of the propagandist is to inculcate certain attitudes by means which prevent critical thinking." McLaine goes on to show the ways in which the MOI attempted to accomplish this very feat. See *Ministry of Morale*, 137–8.

Powell and Pressburger's fight to realize their own artistic vision—even in the face of government obstruction and prohibition—hinges on their own record of success as reliable, successful propagandists for Britain. In Powell's systematic response to the MOI's 1942 report on the script of "The Life and Death of Sugar Candy," he speaks for himself and Pressburger in saying that "our beliefs and our loyalty to our common cause cannot be questioned after the work we have already done."[63] *49th Parallel*, he points out, is "more timely now than at any other period" (37). In this way, Powell stresses that The Archers have proven not only their ability to make timely films, but also their ability to make timeless ones: "[I]t is . . . possible to make films for future audiences and for future occasions" (36). The War Office was not convinced, as we've seen, but Grigg's repeated attempts to stop production of the film were powerfully met by Powell's allusions to the service he and Pressburger had done the state as cinematic propagandists. In a letter from June 1942, he asks Grigg to withdraw his objections to the film, citing the "reputation" of The Archers and referring to the "procedure" they had adopted in making *Aircraft* as the best reason to allow "eminent" men to make the films they want to make (30–1).[64]

The Archers' undeniable success in contributing to the war effort made them more determined to assert their independence in the face of pushback from state officials. It is a case again of an embrace of propaganda that does not necessitate the surrender of autonomy. Their simultaneous commitment to the war effort and yearning for independence is best indicated at the very earliest stages of *Blimp*'s production, when Powell sought to convince Wendy Hiller, in the letter discussed earlier, to play the roles eventually performed by Kerr by insisting on the unique artistic integrity of The Archers. This argument was predicated especially on their commitment to their own "responsibility as independent film makers" (16). Of the five proofs of this commitment offered to Hiller by Powell, at least two stress independence: "we owe allegiance to nobody except the financial interests which provide our money"; "every single foot in our films is our own responsibility and nobody else's" (16). Interestingly, Powell's letter suggests he anticipates outside encroachments on The Archers' autonomy, a prospect he greets by

---

[63]Qtd. in Christie, *The Life and Death*, 39. Powell's response is henceforth cited in the text.
[64]None of this is to suggest that Powell and Pressburger's fight was simply about their own pride or artistic autonomy. Kevin Macdonald feels that his grandfather especially showed his willingness to push back against the government as a matter of ethical and political principle, as we saw in the *49th Parallel* chapter: "On one significant point Emeric disagreed with the Ministry of Information memo. What was needed, in his opinion, was not the nostalgia and cosiness of *Goodbye Mr Chips*, but a film which realistically portrayed the brutality, sadism and proto-religious zeal of the Nazis. Gagged and bound by appeasement, the British public still had very little idea what it was they were really fighting against. As someone who had experienced Nazism first-hand, Emeric thought it was his duty to tell it how it was" (Macdonald, *Emeric Pressburger*, 166).

insisting on the whole team's steadfastness and solidarity. Certainly, the colorful production history and contemporary reception of *Blimp* proved Powell an honest man in his letter to Hiller.

As we've seen, even in early government-backed films such as *49th Parallel*, Powell and Pressburger showed a willingness to move beyond the guidelines listed in Kenneth Clark's MOI memorandum on ideal film propaganda—especially when it came to the topic of the increasingly unpopular "good German" type. Their basic conformity to the spirit of Clark's language, however, meant that a majority of audience members and critics rightly saw such films as contributing unequivocally to a concerted propaganda push by British filmmaking units. Due largely to their success, Powell and Pressburger were able to consolidate their stylistic priorities and principles. The key here is that they were able to use their own important service to the state as evidence of their virtuosity and worthiness, as a foundation upon which they could build to reach ever higher. The case of *The Life and Death of Colonel Blimp* is especially fascinating because the entire brouhaha surrounding its production and release demonstrates Powell and Pressburger's independence from, and willingness to push back against, the most powerful governmental officials in their attempts to dictate what they communicate about the war. In a unique series of events, Powell and Pressburger created a film in *Blimp* whose very production circumstances epitomized the main differences between propaganda in democratic and totalitarian nation states. Just as the assumed opposition between critical thinking and propaganda breaks down in *Blimp*, so too does the one between artistic independence—or what we might regard as a type of proto-auteurism—and propaganda.

As we soon shall see, in *A Canterbury Tale* (1944), *I Know Where I'm Going!* (1945), and *A Matter of Life and Death* (1946), The Archers will refuse to step backward from the hard-earned position they won through their production of *Colonel Blimp*. They will stay committed both to their nation and to disrupting or stretching the boundaries of what constitutes appropriate cinematic propaganda—insisting always that the case for Britain need not rest on oversimplification or lies, and it need not assume an anesthetized audience. *Blimp* stands today as the apotheosis of a certain kind of propaganda film intent on thinking deeply about how the war should actually be fought. Its boldness in this regard continues to surprise and even confound audiences. The Archers' films that follow *Blimp*, however—increasingly confident as they are in an imminent, Allied victory—will shift their audiences' attention to what must happen *after* the war is won. And the propaganda of peace, it turns out, will prove no less challenging, or fruitful, a subject than the propaganda of war.

PART THREE

6

"The Values That We Are Fighting For"

Reconciling Tradition and Modernity in *A Canterbury Tale*

As we noted at the end of the previous chapter, Powell and Pressburger's final wartime films—*A Canterbury Tale* (1944), *I Know Where I'm Going!* (or *IKWIG*, 1945), and *A Matter of Life and Death* (or *AMOLAD*, 1946)—are marked by a significant shift in emphasis. *49th Parallel* (1941), *One of Our Aircraft Is Missing* (1942), and *The Life and Death of Colonel Blimp* (1943) all concern themselves with relations among allies and enemies, with particular attention paid to differentiating the British from the Nazis. With *A Canterbury Tale*, *IKWIG*, and *AMOLAD*, the films are centered on British values and history, and, in the first and third works, the Anglo-American alliance. Most significantly, each movie concerns itself with what comes after the war—specifically, with the values that must be preserved and the practices that must be reformed in order to create a better future.

Regarding *A Canterbury Tale* and *IKWIG*, Pressburger's biographer Kevin Macdonald observes:

> No longer were The Archers interested in how to win the war (by 1943 an American-aided victory seemed assured sooner or later), but in the moral health of the country. They were asking the population to remember the values they had fought for, and to think about what sort of brave new world they would like post-war Britain to be. The film-makers had turned from propagandists into preachers.[1]

---

[1] Kevin Macdonald, *Emeric Pressburger: The Life and Death of a Screenwriter* (London: Faber and Faber, 1994), 233; see also Ian Christie, *Arrows of Desire: The Films of Michael Powell and Emeric Pressburger* (London: Faber and Faber, 1994), 48.

While Macdonald is right to recognize that *A Canterbury Tale* and *IKWIG* demonstrate a change in focus for the filmmakers—as Powell states more than once in his autobiography, the two movies stress the theme of anti-materialism—that change is commensurate with rather than antithetical to their work as propagandists. In "asking the population to remember the values they had fought for," Powell and Pressburger are building upon that part of the original MOI "Programme for Film Propaganda" that is concerned with "What Britain is fighting for."[2]

The articulation of values is only one of *A Canterbury Tale*'s three primary objectives, each of which is propagandistic; the other two are, in the words of Paul Stevens, "to validate the role of women in the war" and to "improve Anglo-American relations."[3] What makes the film so fascinating, and at times confounding, is the way in which pursuing these often overlapping objectives can seem either to undermine them—Thomas Colpeper (played by Eric Portman) is both the admirable spokesperson for enduring cultural values and a mystically inclined crackpot—or to place them at cross-purposes—the rural village that the film holds up as exemplary is also marked by sexist, even misogynist, doubts about the capacities of women.[4] Relatedly, while the appeal to lasting values aligns Powell and Pressburger with the traditionalists—an alignment often emphasized in criticism of their work[5]—*A Canterbury Tale*'s treatment of women is in many ways progressive. If these contradictions are not entirely resolved, they are explicable in terms of the film's negotiation of the relationship between the past, present, and future. Rather than just championing the past, *A Canterbury Tale* shows that certain behaviors associated with it must be discarded in order for the nation to move forward; and rather than discrediting modernity, it concerns itself with infusing the modern with the virtues of tradition. In these ways, the film approaches what Powell terms "the spiritual values and the traditions we were fighting for" not as a stable historical inheritance but as one part of an invaluable but conflicted cultural legacy.[6] Moreover, The

---

[2]We have discussed this document in the Introduction. See James Chapman, *The British at War: Cinema, State and Propaganda, 1939–1945* (London: I.B. Tauris, 1998), 26.
[3]Paul Stevens, "The Unending Charity of Cultural Memory," *The New Elizabethan Age: Culture, Society and National Identity after World War II*, ed. Irene Morra and Rob Gossedge (London: I.B. Tauris, 2016), 119–33, 127.
[4]For more on The Archers, women, and the war effort, see Chapter 4.
[5]Graham Fuller states that "The movie is a High Tory lesson in cultural conservationism" ("A Canterbury Tale," *Film Comment* 31 [1995]: 33–6, 34), while Peter Conrad attributes to the film, and especially the opening sequence, a "pining conservatism" (*To Be Continued: Four Stories and Their Survival* [Oxford: Clarendon Press, 1995], 27). In his autobiography, Michael Powell intimates the film's more conflicted take on conservatism by suggesting that while the character of Thomas Colpeper is a traditionalist, he is also a "loony English squire" (*A Life in Movies* [1986; London: Faber and Faber, 2000], 437.)
[6]Powell, *A Life*, 437.

Archers believe that this legacy must be mined for what is worthwhile in it both to meet the wartime moment and to construct a better postwar future. Significantly, Powell and Pressburger see this construction project as being bound up in the Anglo-American dynamic at the heart of the film.

The first part of this chapter discusses how *A Canterbury Tale*'s opening scenes constitute the relationship between past and present. From there, we turn to Colpeper, paying particular attention to the way in which his actions intimate the close connection between sexism and tradition. These actions are at odds with a phenomenon that Powell and Pressburger celebrate, which is the increased participation of women in many facets of the war effort. In its final section, the chapter takes up both the question of the postwar future and the issue of Anglo-American relations. If, in articulating the need for social and economic reform, *A Canterbury Tale* looks forward, the emotional power of the film's concluding sequences derives from the way in which it imagines its British and American characters will remember the war and the relationships they formed during it.

Reforming the Past

Kevin Macdonald tells us that the impetus for *A Canterbury Tale* was a conversation that Powell and Pressburger had during the filming of *One of Our Aircraft Is Missing*. Emeric first observed that "There is so much talk about the country and the people, and about protecting the women and children," and then asked, "[B]ut who is going to think about the human values—the values that we are fighting for?" Michael replied, "That should be our next film."[7] At the same time, and as we mentioned, *A Canterbury Tale* was also designed to address deteriorating relations between Britons and Americans; it was through the film that Powell and Pressburger intended to articulate the values and traditions for which both nations were fighting.[8] Starting in August 1943, *A Canterbury Tale* was shot in Canterbury and surrounding villages, near where Powell grew up, and at Denham Studios.[9] Ironically, Pressburger was unable to stay in the area for the location shooting: "Although [Pressburger was] now technically exempt from the numerous regulations imposed on enemy aliens, the Chief Constable for

---

[7]Macdonald, *Emeric Pressburger*, 233.
[8]Powell, *A Life*, 437.
[9]"Shooting began on *A Canterbury Tale* in August 1943 and was trade shown in May 1944, then presumably held over on account of the D-Day landings of June, before being released in August" (Ian Christie, "'History Is Now and England': *A Canterbury Tale* and its Contexts," *The Cinema of Michael Powell: International Perspectives on an English Film-Maker*, ed. Ian Christie and Andrew Moor [London: British Film Institute, 2005], 75–93, 76).

Kent . . . saw fit to refuse him a temporary residency permit."[10] As it would happen, suspicion of the outsider is a minor theme in The Archers' film, although it is developed in gendered more than national terms.

A *Canterbury Tale* centers on the relationship of three strangers to the fictional town of Chillingbourne with Thomas Colpeper, the local magistrate. Not long after meeting for the first time at the village train station, Alison Smith (Sheila Sim), Peter Gibb (Dennis Price), and Bob Johnson (John Sweet) have a nighttime encounter with the Glue Man, whom the viewer comes to learn shortly thereafter is Colpeper. The Glue Man pours a sticky substance into women's hair; Alison is his eleventh victim. A member of the Women's Land Army who traveled to Chillingbourne to work on Colpeper's farm, Alison teams up with Bob, a US Army sergeant on leave, and Peter, a British Army sergeant stationed nearby, to discover the true identity of the Glue Man. Over the course of a few days, their investigations acquaint them with the village, its inhabitants, and the surrounding countryside, although Alison had previously been in the area; she traveled there summers before with her geologist fiancé, who was subsequently killed in action. As the three strangers accumulate proof of Colpeper's guilt, they also develop an admiration for his love of the region's history and his efforts to educate the visiting soldiers about it. (This, it turns out, is his stated reason for the glue pouring: without being distracted by women, he thinks, the soldiers will come to his nighttime lectures.) The final section of the film depicts the four central characters journeying together to Canterbury, where Peter intends to turn Colpeper in to the authorities. This does not happen. Instead, the three visitors to the area each receive a blessing: Alison learns her fiancé is, in fact, still alive; Bob discovers that his girlfriend, who he believed had abandoned him, still loves him, her long silence explained by her traveling to Australia with the Women's Army Corps; and Peter, a classically trained musician turned cinema organist, realizes in Canterbury Cathedral his thwarted ambition to play a big organ, and this on the eve of his deployment overseas for what might be the final push of the war. Only Colpeper remains unblessed, although he is changed by his experiences. Having previously excluded women from his lectures on sexist grounds, Colpeper, we learn during the film's closing credits, now welcomes both men and women to attend.

Left out of the preceding plot summary is the beginning of the film. In a manner suited to its title, *A Canterbury Tale* at first appears to be focused on, and centered in, the medieval past. After the credits roll over footage of cathedral bells ringing, the screen dissolves to the first page of the General Prologue of *The Canterbury Tales*; we hear the poem's opening lines read

---

[10]Macdonald, *Emeric Pressburger*, 239.

in voice-over.[11] From there, we turn to an antique map of England. As the narrator continues his recitation of Chaucer, the camera slowly zooms in on the pilgrimage route to Canterbury. We next see a book illustration of pilgrims, which dissolves into footage of their flesh-and-blood counterparts as they merrily process through the countryside. This sequence culminates in a famous match cut: a falcon that slices the sky is suddenly replaced by a fighter plane, and a close-up of the face of a falconer tracking his bird's progress is supplanted by one of a soldier (played by the same actor) who traces the passage of the aircraft. After a brief silence, the narrator states that "600 years have passed," and asks, "What would they see, Dan Chaucer and his goodly company, today?" The answer he provides emphasizes continuity—"the hills and valleys are the same"—but also acknowledges alterations: "But though so little has changed since Chaucer's day, another kind of pilgrim walks the way." This particular alteration occurs on-screen in startling fashion. A shot of the old pilgrim's way meandering through "wood and brake and many a fertile field" is troubled both by a quickening of the narrator's tone as he refers to "another kind of pilgrim" and by the sound of a rapidly approaching vehicle. Suddenly, a Bren carrier rises up into the extreme foreground. We see only a portion of it as first it ascends into the frame and then plummets quickly out of sight, to be promptly succeeded by other military vehicles in the middle distance. The carrier's eruption into this pastoral setting is disconcerting. And yet, the men manning such vehicles represent "another kind of pilgrim." This is a striking statement for two reasons. First, it links Chaucer's pilgrims to soldiers engaging in military exercises, and thus also frames their impending push overseas as a form of pilgrimage; second, it articulates historical continuity even though what is depicted jars with the landscape of wood and brake and fertile field (Figure 6.1).

With this incongruity in mind, it is worth returning to the match cut featuring the falcon and the fighter plane. As a formal device, a match cut works to bridge time and/or space by yoking superficially similar but substantively different things (a bone and a space ship, a lit match and the rising sun, a falcon and an airplane); it does so, moreover, in a manner that diverges from the protocols of continuity editing. As Andrew Moor points out, "*A Canterbury Tale*'s match-cut functions as a blatant underscoring of narrative/cinematic technique, a naked piece of authorial manipulation which unexpectedly disturbs the viewer's sense of unimpeded engagement with the smooth-flowing text." In this regard, the match cut (in contrast

---

[11]Powell and Pressburger toy with the conventions for film adaptation in this period, as it was common for Hollywood versions of literary works to begin with a shot of the first page of the adapted text. See Greg M. Colón Semenza and Bob Hasenfratz, *The History of British Literature on Film, 1895–2015* (New York: Bloomsbury, 2015), 212–14. For Semenza and Hasenfratz's discussion of *A Canterbury Tale*, see 215–19.

FIGURE 6.1 *Another kind of pilgrim walks the way* (A Canterbury Tale, 1944).

with, say, a slow dissolve) starkly juxtaposes historical moments rather than transporting the viewer seamlessly from one to the other. At the same time, the sequence as a whole emphasizes the connections between the present and past rather than the differences between them. In this regard, Moor notes, the match cut "suggests a continuity as well as a disjuncture, conservatively binding past to present in a deeply reactionary way."[12] Similarly, Jefferson Hunter sees the image of the "aggressively clanking Army vehicle" as offset by the fact that "[the past] is somehow persistent and accessible, while the camera gives shot after shot of the abiding landscape."[13]

We argue that the sequence works slightly differently. By juxtaposing continuity with the past (represented by the landscape) with discontinuity (telegraphed especially by the shot of the Bren carrier), the sequence forecasts in formal terms the issue that both Colpeper and the movie seek to address, which is the alienation of present-day Britons—as represented here by the

---

[12] Andrew Moor, *Powell & Pressburger: A Cinema of Magic Spaces* (London and New York: I.B. Tauris, 2005), 114, 115. The "deeply reactionary" element of the match cut comes from the way in which it "achieves a time-bending synthesis between medieval feudal society and the RAF" (115).
[13] Jefferson Hunter, *English Filming, English Writing* (Bloomington and Indianapolis: Indiana University Press, 2010), 52.

soldiers in their carrier—from certain enduring values associated with the rural past. This is different from positing that, as has been argued, the film is hostile toward modernity;[14] it is to suggest, instead, that the movie's ambition is to bring the modern into alignment with those values, which, according to the representational logic of both this sequence and the film as a whole, are there to be accessed in the timeless landscape.[15] Dispatched to a camp in Kent, the soldiers are, crucially, Colpeper's imagined audience, the ones in whom he seeks to instill a sense of history. From Colpeper's perspective, the blessing to be extended to them is a new awareness of the values they are fighting for. Moreover, it is Colpeper's role in inculcating that awareness that leads Hunter to assert that the film's opening sequence "introduce[s] the idea of continuity later to be associated with [him]."[16]

While we have seen Powell reference *A Canterbury Tale* as a film conceived to advocate for "human values," he does not specify what he and Pressburger take those values to be. Based on the finished film, what might we say they are? Certainly, "the idea of continuity," which is expressed in customary forms and behaviors that undergird social and political life in an English village, is a primary value, although we will argue that the film also supports breaking from the past in specific ways. Continuity's association with the landscape makes plain that the countryside itself is a value, even as, crucially, it has a broader symbolic significance. As Ian Christie and Andrew Moor have each stressed, *A Canterbury Tale* advances an agrarian conception of nationhood, emblematized by the South of England, that was culturally powerful during the war, a conception in which land, history, and memory are all interwoven.[17] (This conception of the nation is also a mystification, insofar as the majority of Britons lived in urban areas.) Linked to this idea of the nation is a communitarian ethos captured by the putatively organic society of rural villages and towns. And, of course, the film develops the anti-materialist ethos that we mentioned earlier, which also plays a significant role in *IKWIG*. We contend that, while The Archers are undoubtedly sincere in their advocacy of the values we have just identified, they are also aware of how elements of the past with which those values are associated do not align with the needs of the historical moment in which the filmmakers live. We can begin to see this by considering the unsettling fact that Thomas Colpeper is identified with much that the film endorses.

---

[14]Conrad, *To Be Continued*, 28.
[15]That being said, the timelessness of the landscape is undercut slightly by a reference in voice-over to the practice of enclosure, which transformed agricultural practice in the late medieval and early modern periods. Nevertheless, that reference does little to trouble the overall emphasis on geographic continuity ("the hills and valleys are the same").
[16]Hunter, *English Filming*, 52.
[17]Christie, "History," 82–9; Moor, *Powell & Pressburger*, 85–93.

"What Is This, an Old Chillingbourne Custom?": Colpeper, Tradition, and Misogyny

The most obvious problem with Colpeper being the spokesperson for abiding cultural values is his status as the Glue Man. How are we to reconcile the perverse behavior of "a deviant, crusading mystic" with the film's apparent championing of his worldview?[18] Critics have plausibly squared this circle by pointing to the character's personal growth. Ian Christie suggests that "The 'bad' Colpeper of misogyny and resentment has been exorcised, through contact with [Alison, Bob, and Peter], to become a 'good' Colpeper";[19] Paul Stevens asserts that "By the end of story, all three are blessed, but this happens only after Colpeper himself has changed and his ... prejudices have been exorcised";[20] and Chris Wicking contends that "[T]he film's view of [Colpeper] is slowly modified to allow for understanding and even a certain pity. This misogynist (a bachelor, living alone with his mother, entirely self-absorbed and didactic) has had his conceptions (misconceptions) entirely changed by knowing Alison."[21] There is truth in each of these claims. However, we believe the crucial point to be that Colpeper's failings, as well as his virtues, are all informed by his relationship to tradition. What is at issue, then, is not that Colpeper is a flawed spokesperson for a set of imperishable values and beliefs that the film unequivocally champions; it is that Colpeper's flaws are bound up in, and expressive of, those values and beliefs. One of the film's most significant objectives is to assess as well as champion the past, to extract from it those elements that are commensurate with a better future and to abandon the rest in favor of positive cultural developments, such as the refiguration of gender and class relations that has already been initiated by the war. The emergence of the "good" Colpeper is inseparable from the film's heralding of a better future that, it argues, can be attained only through the critical examination, and reformation, of the past.

Colpeper is first mentioned by Thomas Duckett, the Chillingbourne station master (Charles Hawtrey), who informs Alison that she will be escorted to the town hall by Peter and Bob. When she asks why, the conductor replies, "No young lady must go alone at night. Mr. Colpeper's orders." From the beginning, Colpeper is associated with prohibitions on female behavior, with nighttime mobility most likely connoting sexual license.[22] Colpeper is

---

[18]Macdonald, *Emeric Pressburger*, 236.
[19]Christie, "History," 88–9.
[20]Stevens, "Unending Charity," 126.
[21]Chris Wicking, "A Canterbury Tale," *Monthly Film Bulletin* 51 (January 1, 1984): 355–6, 356.
[22]See Antonia Lant, *Blackout: Reinventing Women for Wartime British Cinema* (Princeton, NJ: Princeton University Press, 1991), 197–219.

mentioned twice more in this same scene: when, in response to a question, Duckett tells Alison that Colpeper is the local magistrate and justice of the peace; and when he informs the three travelers that "All visitors arriving must report to Town Hall. Mr. Colpeper's orders." These three references to Colpeper, which occur within a minute of one another, establish both the character's importance to the narrative and his status as the representative of civic authority in Chillingbourne.[23] While one might associate the strictness of Colpeper's orders with wartime discipline, a possible reason for prohibitions on the nighttime mobility of women emerges shortly thereafter, when a shadowy figure pours a sticky substance into Alison's hair. The three strangers to Chillingbourne chase that figure into the Town Hall. That structure, then, is associated early on with both authority and its transgression: it is where visitors must report, at Mr. Colpeper's orders, and it is where a malefactor goes to hide. This apparent contradiction is resolved in retrospect, as we come to learn that Colpeper is both the authority figure and the transgressor.

Returning to the scene in the Town Hall, two policemen, having learned from Bob and Alison that the Glue Man has taken refuge in the building, spot a light on in the courtroom while searching the building. Expecting to surprise the perpetrator, they, instead, come upon their magistrate, by whom, it becomes clear from their manner, they are intimidated; it does not occur to them that he and the Glue Man might be one and the same person. After the police sergeant mentions that Alison had come to Chillingbourne to work on his farm, Colpeper replies, "There must be some mistake"; when shortly thereafter he and Alison meet, Colpeper refuses her employment on the putative grounds that she will not be able to do the work. However, we were introduced to his misogyny in the preceding scene, in which he identifies for Bob Johnson the ducking stool suspended from the ceiling of the court room as having been "very sensibly used for silencing talkative women." (It is telling, of course, that the courtroom contains a ducking stool, even amongst a number of other historical objects associated with judicial activity.) As for Colpeper's subsequent refusal of employment to Alison, his reasons extend beyond her potential capacity as a laborer. He alludes to the "camp near this village full of soldiers," implying that they could pose a sexual threat to her. If at this moment Alison is rhetorically cast by Colpeper in the role of a young virgin in need of protection, he next insinuates, when he learns that Alison is aware of the camp, that she might, instead, be a woman of dubious virtue capable of leading soldiers

---

[23]Interestingly, about seven minutes later, when Bob and Alison are in the Town Hall trying to remove glue from her hair, Bob asks the police sergeant, "Who's Mr. Colpeper?," even though that question was answered for the three strangers and us by Duckett. The issue of Colpeper's identity is repeatedly posed in the early portion of the film.

astray (and away from his lectures). This leads Alison to protest that she is "not interested in soldiers," to which Colpeper's victim-blaming rejoinder is, "Perhaps they're interested in you." He follows this up by suggesting that she should be afraid as a result of "what's happened to [her]"—which is to say, what he in the guise of the Glue Man has done to her. Over the course of the film, the ironies related to Colpeper continue to ramify: "a sexualized action—glue in hair—is . . . employed to prevent sexual activity in women";[24] Chillingbourne's nighttime scourge is also the person who, as magistrate and Justice of the Peace, should be concerned with curbing the Glue Man's actions; and, more generally, the spokesperson for higher values and for civic order is an agent of social disruption. (This final irony is enhanced by the fact that Colpeper takes on the role of Glue Man only when he is on Home Guard duty or serving as a fire watcher.) If Chillingbourne represents an exemplary English village, there is something—or someone—rotten at the heart of it.[25] That rottenness isn't complete, however. Instead, it is associated with some of the more retrograde, if not malign, aspects of tradition, especially when it comes to the treatment of women.

A crucial aspect of Colpeper's misogyny is that it is conceptually tethered to the past, as the reference to the ducking stool tells us. In support of this point, we see Bob Johnson ask of the glue pouring, "What is this, an old Chillingbourne custom?" While the literal answer is no—the Glue Man's attacks begin with the war, when the soldiers come to the village—the question invites us to associate the Glue Man's behavior with historical practices aimed at policing female behavior, such as the ducking of "talkative women."[26] Indeed, while critics have puzzled over the symbolic significance

---

[24]Lant, *Blackout*, 200.

[25]It is not an accident that the film's early nocturnal scenes echo the Universal horror movies of the 1930s. The film's screenplay makes clear that The Archers are exploiting a basic narrative premise of the horror film, which is that the sinister side of civilized society is revealed after dark: "But at night [the train station and village, which, the script says, appear 'prosaically' in daylight] loom, awful and mysterious, of dimensions unknown, of potentialities undescribable, full of strange shapes, stranger sounds, menacing shadows and hard corners" (Screenplay to *A Canterbury Tale*, BFI SCR-5072 [appears as S13976 on the first page], 11). Moreover, in developing this notion, *A Canterbury Tale* shares an affinity with another British wartime film that also owes a debt to the 30s horror movie, Cavalcanti's brilliant *Went the Day Well?* (1942). Also relevant here is Robin Wood's analysis of two other 1940s films—Frank Capra's *It's A Wonderful Life* (1946) and Alfred Hitchcock's *Shadow of a Doubt* (1943)—that feature "the disturbing influx of film noir into the world of small-town domestic comedy" ("Ideology, Genre, Auteur," *Film Genre Reader IV*, ed. Barry Keith Grant [Austin: University of Texas Press, 2012], 78–92, 82).

[26]The question also draws our attention to the fact that this is a practice that the villagers have not managed—or perhaps tried all that hard—to stamp out. It should be noted that the historical usage of the ducking (or cucking) stool for the purposes of social humiliation could also be physically dangerous to the women being punished. See Lynda E. Boose, "Scolding Brides and Bridling Scolds: Taming the Woman's Unruly Member," *Shakespeare Quarterly* 42 (1991): 179–213.

of the glue pouring, one thing they have not attended to is its status as a variant of traditional forms of policing and punishing female behavior. To put it simply, Colpeper's admiration for the ducking stool, coupled with Bob's reference to glue pouring as customary practice, prompts us to see the Glue Man's endeavors not only as an extension of Colpeper's misogyny but also as an expression of his historical sense, his admiring suggestion that, in the case of the ducking stool, they knew how to silence talkative women back then.

Significantly, Colpeper's historically inflected misogyny is at odds with, and undoubtedly fueled by, changes in female behavior engendered by the war. Antonia Lant has written powerfully of the ways in which wartime British cinema worked to negotiate those changes, most notably when it came to the figure of the "mobile woman." This classificatory category, derived from the Ministry of Labour, was used to describe those women whose life circumstances allowed them to travel to different parts of the country to work on behalf of the war effort. However, Lant takes up the mobile woman as a cultural figure (and especially a cinematic one) who represented two different possible models for female behavior: "the reliable, invaluable war-worker on whom victory depends, and the capricious, whimsical, flighty companion and potential collaborator who distracts male attention."[27] Whereas Alison reveals herself to be the former kind of mobile woman, Colpeper obviously treats her—and, indeed, all of the women whom the Glue Man assails—as the latter.[28] Indeed, Colpeper seems at the beginning of the film incapable of recognizing, or is perhaps hostile to, the manifold contributions millions of women had been making to the war effort.

As we noted in Chapter 4, female conscription was announced in December 1941. By mid-1943, shortly before shooting began on *A Canterbury Tale*, nearly three million married women and widows were employed: "It was calculated that, among those between eighteen and forty, nine single women out of ten and eight married women out of ten were in the forces or in industry."[29] As for The Women's Land Army, it came into existence in the First World War, although it was disbanded in the wake of that conflict. It was re-formed in 1939, and by 1943, "there were over 50,000 women filling jobs previously done by men around the country, and a third of these came

---

[27] Lant, *Blackout*, 89.
[28] As Lant has shown, when Alison first materializes from the shadows of the Chillingbourne train station waiting room, she evokes the *femme fatale* in a film noir (Lant, *Blackout*, 209). This witty bit of misdirection is typical of Powell and Pressburger, and, indeed, of this film, which, as we note earlier, resembles at first an adaptation of Chaucer's *The Canterbury Tales*. On the tricksiness of opening sequences in other films by The Archers, see Macdonald, *Emeric Pressburger*, 248–9.
[29] Angus Calder, *The People's War: Britain 1939–1945* (New York: Pantheon Books, 1969), 331.

from London and other large cities."[30] Many of these women were subjected to sexist treatment, in large part because they were taking on jobs that were perceived to be exclusive to men.[31] As Ian Christie notes, "In *A Canterbury Tale*, this [treatment] is transmuted into Colpeper's brisk refusal to employ any women, balanced by Alison then finding work at an all-female farm."[32] Colpeper's blinkered behavior notwithstanding, the broader reality was that, as we suggested earlier, conventional roles for women were undergoing a profound change as a result of the war. Moreover, while Colpeper might look askance at female labor, at least of the agricultural variety, Powell and Pressburger approach the topic with respect and sympathy, and in a manner that is, of course, commensurate with one of the film's three propaganda objectives. Stevens rightly observes that, "as Alison interviews other victims [of the Glue Man], we discover the central if hardly known role of women in running the community and by inference the nation at war. They [are] supply farm managers, agricultural labourers, publicans, bus conductors, mail carriers, and railway workers—they are strong, confident, disciplined and capable."[33] In the case of farm work, Colpeper's benightedness is rebutted by the scenes in which we see Alison at work with other women, including her boss Prudence Honeywood and a fellow victim of the Glue Man, Fee Baker. Not only are they all presented as industrious, as Stevens suggests, but their labors are depicted in a matter-of-fact fashion that underscores their capability. It's not that The Archers stage an argument for women in the workforce in these scenes; it is that they treat the matter as settled in a way that Colpeper fails to comprehend.

The failure is not Colpeper's alone, however. If sexism takes an acute form with the Glue Man, there is a more quotidian example of it on display within the film. Significantly, it occurs within one of the film's most lyrical depictions of village life, one that also foregrounds the special bond between the United States and Britain. The scene takes place at the local wheelwright's workshop and it concludes after Bob Johnson and Jim Horton (Edward Rigby) have recognized a kinship because of their shared vision of timbering practices. It begins, however, as Alison, having secured employment at an area farm, awaits the repair of a wheel on a horse cart. Much of the first part of the scene centers on Alison's conversation with Ned Horton (George Merritt), which occurs in front of an all-male audience ranging in age from

---

[30]Christie, "History," 78; see also Calder, *The People's War*, 428–30.
[31]Sonya O. Rose, *Which People's War?: National Identity and Citizenship in Wartime Britain 1939–1945* (Oxford: Oxford University Press, 2003), 110.
[32]Christie, "History," 78.
[33]Stevens, "Unending Charity," 128. For a snapshot of different women's experiences in the WLA, see Virginia Nicholson, *Millions Like Us: Women's Lives During the Second World War* (London: Penguin Books, 2012), 149–54.

very young to very old.³⁴ Ned asks Alison various questions about cart wheels: "Know what soling down means?" "You know what felly joints is?" When she admits not knowing the answer to the first question, Ned replies, unhelpfully, "soling down means soling down"; and after she also responds to the second query in the negative, he exclaims, "Ah, you ought to know that." The tone of this exchange is not hostile, but the stakes are nevertheless clear: Alison's credibility as a farm laborer is being tested in front of many of the men of the village.³⁵ Moreover, it's equally apparent that she recognizes this, as is made explicit in the film's screenplay. When Bob offers to help her to back the horse between the shafts of the cart, she politely refuses. "ALISON: (she knows she is on trial and is quite confident) [']Thanks, Bob, but I'd sooner do it alone.['] She backs the horse skilfully in and starts to harness up . . . The show is over. Alison has 'passed'."³⁶ If, as Christie says, Colpeper's refusal to employ Alison is the fictional transmutation of sexism experienced by Land Girls, one must say the same thing about this episode. Indeed, the scene's other outsider, Bob Johnson, is subjected to nothing like this kind of scrutiny, and when Jim Horton asks Bob to lunch, Alison, who is sitting right next to him in the cart, is excluded from the invitation.³⁷

There is another dimension of Alison's encounter with the Hortons that needs to be commented upon. Bob mentions that the Glue Man has struck again, which prompts Jim to ask, with a touch of amusement in his voice, "Who was he after this time?" After Alison announces that she is the latest victim, Jim, says "Oh, you," then looks at his hand in apparent embarrassment. Alison's revelation prompts Ned to observe, "I suppose that'll learn you not to run around at night." Notice the way in which Ned stigmatizes female mobility. The reason Alison has been attacked, he thinks, is that she has ventured out not only in a spatial sense, but also in a social one; she has behaved in ways he deems unsuited to a woman. When Alison, instead, voices her intention to "go out every night until I catch him," Ned shakes his head and says, "Aren't likely," defending the Glue Man's capacity

---

³⁴The scrutiny extended to Alison here stands in oblique relation to an earlier shot in which a small group of men, including Bob and the two policemen, gather around her to wash the glue out of her hair. (This action is preceded by the police sergeant asserting, "We know how to handle this"—more masculine confidence.) The camera slowly zooms in on the men's hands as they massage Alison's wet hair. In a witty and telling dissolve, the shot gives way to one of Bob and Colpeper, having just met, shaking hands, an act of common courtesy rendered significant by the latter character having poured over Alison's head the glue that the former one had just been working to wash away.
³⁵It should be noted that Alison's boss, Pru Honeywood, also questions her about her farming skills, but that scene lacks the performative dimension of this one as well as the sexism.
³⁶Screenplay to *A Canterbury Tale*, 46.
³⁷It should be noted that while the Hortons's skepticism toward Alison is primarily gendered in nature, it is also informed by regional difference—specifically, her prewar status as a London shop girl. The scene begins with Ned quizzing, and dismissing, Alison's previous WLA experience in Northumberland ("They don't know nothing about farming up there").

to evade detection. Ned evinces a degree of admiration for the Glue Man's nocturnal attacks; the problem is not his glue pouring, but the fact that women are "run[ning] around at night." It is, of course, this possibility of female culpability that Colpeper hints at when he interrogates Alison about the degree of her interest in the soldiers. Moreover, we learn that Ned is not alone in his sentiments. On the train to Canterbury, Colpeper mentions that the "older people" were unhappy with local women going out with soldiers, while Alison has learned from one of the other victims of the Glue Man that many in the village endorse his actions.[38]

As is also the case with Colpeper's misogyny, the wheelwrights' sexist treatment of Alison is interwoven with the deep history of the area. In response to Bob's comment about the Canterbury pilgrims, Jim Horton opines that "Them was the days for a wheelwright." Shortly before this, Ned observes, "I've been a blacksmith for 37 years. My father was a blacksmith, and his before him." If sexism takes a pathological form with the Glue Man, the Hortons's treatment of Alison shows that it is also a thread running through the fabric of traditional society as The Archers depict it. That being said, it would be a mistake to push this line of argument too far by suggesting that the aspects of life in Chillingbourne that the film critiques significantly erode the idyllic view of the area on offer in *A Canterbury Tale*.[39] (This view, we hasten to add, is shared by Alison, who also comes to develop a deep sympathy with Colpeper.) Instead, we would contend that The Archers' championing of the eternal values enshrined in the countryside does not entail the wholesale embrace of either the historical past or present-day forms of benightedness associated with it. Rather, in looking to the past with an eye to both the present and the future, Powell and Pressburger recognize that some of it needs to be jettisoned in the service of creating (in

---

[38] In *A Canterbury Tale*, it is British soldiers who are going out with local women, but we would wager that, in pursuing Anglo-American amity, the film is also displacing onto those soldiers cultural anxiety about the amatory efforts of Yank servicemen, who were often disparagingly referred to as "overpaid, over-sexed and over here." See James Chapman, "'The True Business of the British Movie'?: *A Matter of Life and Death* and British Film Culture," *Screen* 46 (2005): 33–49, 35; and also Chapter 8 of this book.

[39] The depiction of the so-called village idiot strikes a similarly discordant note to the one produced by the Glue Man's activities. Moor observes that the treatment of both the Glue Man and the village idiot "critique[s], through association, the totalitarianism of Chillingbourne's apparently ancient feudal structure" (*Powell & Pressburger*, 109). The figure of the village idiot has long been associated with traditional village life. In the late nineteenth century, William Sime contends that "villages remote from the pressure of the competitive spirit [which Sime associates with industrial labor] still like to have their idiot. He has come down to them, like the castle-walls on the cliff. The oldest inhabitant does not remember a time when an idiot was not wandering out and in. . . . The idiot best assorts with remote communities. Their industrial habits being as slow as the march of the seasons, the villagers find him an aid to local philosophy, an incident for local humour, and a convenient standard of comparison" (*To and Fro; Or, Views from Sea and Land* [London: Elliott Stock, 1884], 221–2).

Macdonald's words, quoted earlier) the "brave new world they would like post-war Britain to be."

That The Archers critique rather than merely depict the sexism that they associate with the past is made explicit in the final section of the film. After Alison, Peter, and Bob confront Colpeper in the train to Canterbury, he justifies his glue-pouring activity as part of an effort to draw soldiers to his lectures, in order to educate them about the region and its history. (There is a slightly unhinged dimension to Colpeper's undoubtedly sincere interest in educating the soldiers; he compares himself to a missionary who can't believe his luck when, thanks to the construction in Chillingbourne of an Army camp, "There's no need to travel into the jungle to find converts, because the savages are coming to him." One wonders if Powell and Pressburger are here cocking an eyebrow at the religious dimensions of British imperialism, a topic they will explore more fully in *AMOLAD* and *Black Narcissus* [1947].) Alison poses a question to the magistrate that is, in its own simple way, devastating: "Mr. Colpeper, didn't it ever occur to you to ask the girls to your lectures?" If this does not serve as Colpeper's blessing, it does function as his epiphany. As Wicking puts it, "there's an extraordinary sense captured in his silence [after acknowledging that he had not considered including women] that he knows she's right, and that he has indeed learned much."[40] This view is confirmed during the final credits, which feature a shot of women and men entering one of Colpeper's lectures. His efforts to inculcate the virtues of the past, we are led to assume, are no longer marred by the sexism informing his sense of history. In this regard, Colpeper's lectures are now understood to serve a more egalitarian future, in which both women and men will benefit from his knowledge.[41] More generally, we contend that Colpeper's narrative journey takes him from privileging the past to recognizing that certain aspects of modernity—most importantly, the wartime increase in opportunities for women, as emblematized by Alison—represent hope for the continued vitality of the values that he most cherishes.[42]

The change in Colpeper's worldview is not solely engendered by the question that Alison puts to him *en route* to Canterbury. As we have

---

[40]Wicking, "A Canterbury Tale," 356.
[41]Earlier in the film, Peter urges Alison to attend one of Colpeper's lectures with him, noting that, while the lectures are restricted to those in His Majesty's Forces, this includes Alison as a member of the Women's Land Army. Alison's attendance both anticipates and paves the way for Colpeper's change of policy.
[42]In the screenplay, a character named Susanna Foster says of Colpeper that he is "A raving maniac. The man has nothing in his head but old stones! Old stones, old books, old iron, old holes in the ground" (Screenplay, *A Canterbury Tale*, p. 34). However, as Ian Christie has observed, Colpeper is forward-looking in one way. Close scrutiny of the contents of his study suggests that he "is intended to be at least a progressive gentleman farmer, up to date with the latest thinking about ecology and fertility" ("History," 87).

mentioned, the two characters develop an affinity for one another over the course of the film, and, as critics have acknowledged, the film implies that the misogynist magistrate falls for the Land Girl.[43] This happens in part because of the interest they share in the history of this region—a history made manifest by Alison's possession of old Belgian coins, discovered on her earlier trip to Kent with her fiancé, that she plans to donate to the local museum. Moreover, this shared interest has an almost mystical dimension, as when Alison, on a grassy hilltop, hears "horse hooves, voices and a lute": the sounds of medieval pilgrims progressing down the old road.[44] In aurally hallucinating the presence of the pilgrims, Alison is following the train of argument articulated by Colpeper in his lantern slide lecture: "But there are more ways than one of getting close to your ancestors. Follow the Old Road and, as you walk, think of them and of the old England." Immediately after having her hilltop experience, she discovers that Colpeper is also there, reclining and hidden in the tall grass.[45] Alison tells Colpeper that her supposedly dead fiancé, the aptly named Geoffrey, loved this spot. In response to a question about their three-year engagement, Alison tells the magistrate, "His father was the trouble. . . . They were a very good family. He thought his son should marry someone better than a shopgirl." If at other points in the film The Archers train their gaze on antiquated notions of appropriate female behavior, here the emphasis is on class. Strikingly, it is Colpeper who points out the obsolescence of traditional social divisions: "Good family. Shop girl. Rather dilapidated phrases for wartime." When Alison replies that it "would have taken an earthquake" for Geoffrey's father to have countenanced her marriage to his son, Colpeper replies, "We're having one."

In its focus on class, this scene echoes one from Launder and Gilliat's *Millions Like Us* (1943) that we will discuss again in the next chapter. In that film, a character named Charlie, also played by Eric Portman, expresses uncertainty about whether the smudging of social divisions produced by the war effort will lead to a permanent alteration of the class system.[46] "Shall we go on like this or are we going to slide back? That's what I want to know." Colpeper expresses greater certainty about the transformation

---

[43] Fuller, "A Canterbury Tale," 36; Tim Cawkwell, "A Cathedral Tale," *Theology* 111.863 (September 2008): 370–6, 372.
[44] See Anita Jorge, "Liminal Soundscapes in Powell and Pressburger's Wartime Films," *Studies in European Cinema* 14 (2017): 22–32, 23–4.
[45] "Now he startles her by speaking while invisible in the long grass, before rising like a supernatural *genius loci*, his clothes crumpled and eyes bright with a strange intensity" (Christie, "History," 79). On Colpeper as *genius loci*, see also Douglas McVay, "Michael Powell: Three Neglected Films," *Films and Filming* 328 (1982): 18–25, 19.
[46] Robert Murphy also compares these two moments from *A Canterbury Tale* and *Millions Like Us* ("Strong Men: Three Forms of the Magus in the Films of Powell and Pressburger," *Screen* 46 [2005]: 63–71, 66).

that the war has engendered, and the film seems to endorse this view—ironically, at the expense of Colpeper himself. While in Canterbury visiting the caravan that she inherited from Geoffrey—the caravan in which they had stayed years before in her first visit to the area—she learns that her fiancé is, indeed, alive, and that his father had been waiting to tell her as much in a Canterbury hotel. In one of the final shots of the film, which takes place in the Cathedral, Alison and Geoffrey's father walk right by Colpeper without seeing him, and, as they do, Geoffrey's father, dressed in a double-breasted pinstripe suit that jars with Alison's farmer's attire, puts his arm around her. The earthquake Colpeper referenced earlier has leveled the wall that once separated Alison from her future father-in-law. This act of destruction is expressive of Powell and Pressburger's hope for a broader social transformation—the kind of transformation that, as we shall discuss in Chapter 8, Peter Carter is thinking of when he dubs himself "Conservative by nature, Labour by experience." In its depiction of both gender and class relations, then, *A Canterbury Tale* answers a question central to wartime propaganda—"What is Britain fighting for?"—by appealing both to the past and to a better future portended by developments in the present.

If Canterbury Cathedral emblematizes enduring cultural values, it is noteworthy that the final portion of the film presents us with not only that glorious structure, but also the extensive bomb damage that has been done to the town—damage that inevitably evokes the culturally pressing topic of postwar rebuilding. We take up this topic in some detail in the next chapter; for now, it is enough to recognize that, at the time of *A Canterbury Tale*'s conception and production, the question of reconstruction was an urgent one, with many concerned that the social inequities that marked the interwar period not be reproduced in the wake of the Second World War. From at least the time of the December 1942 release of the Beveridge Report (discussed in the next chapter), there was a widespread recognition that it was not going to be adequate to rebuild; it was necessary to improve upon what came before, to fashion a more equitable society that provided opportunities for everyone. Alison's walk to the garage in which her caravan is stored takes her past the exposed foundations of numerous bombed-out buildings, most of them posted with signs advertising the new or temporary locations of the businesses that had once been there. Excepting the high quality of Erwin Hillier's cinematography, these could be images from a run-of-the-mill newsreel or documentary focused on the need to reward British resilience by way of thoughtful postwar reconstruction. In coming to Canterbury, then, the characters have not only followed in the footsteps of Chaucer's pilgrims (though they've actually traveled by train), they have also journeyed to a town that is very much of their own historical moment, the bomb sites attesting not to the deep history of the film's opening sequence—"600 years have passed"—but to the fresh, traumatic May 1942 "Baedeker raid" on the town.⁴⁷ These scenes convey both the continuance of British identity and values in the form of the Cathedral's survival and the recognition that much work must be done, in reconstruction, to move beyond those aspects of the past that stand in the way of social progress.

"This Odd and Unexpected Excursion": Remembering the Anglo-American Alliance

Thus far, we have focused on two of the propaganda objectives that animate *A Canterbury Tale*: its championing of values and its advocacy of more equitable gender (and class) roles. The third objective concerns the alliance between Britain and the United States. More specifically, one of the film's reasons for being—which it shares with *AMOLAD*—is to address the wartime deterioration of the Anglo-American relationship. Ian Christie puts the matter this way:

> After America's entry into the war in 1941, growing numbers of service personnel were stationed in Britain. From fewer than 5,000 at the beginning of 1942, the total rose rapidly to just under a quarter of a million in October, and, after a slight dip in mid-1943, rose again to 1.5 million in Spring 1944. . . . The problem that had emerged early in 1942 was how to counteract poor relations between the incoming US service personnel and the British civilian population, which is certainly where *A Canterbury Tale* started from.⁴⁸

Powell and Pressburger's primary means for achieving this objective was by way of values: not only does *A Canterbury Tale* remind the British what they are fighting for, but it also attests to the strong cultural connections between the United States and Britain. This occurs most obviously in the wheelwright scene that we discussed earlier, during which Bob and Jim Horton learn how much they have in common ("We speak the same language. . . . He knows about wood and so do I"). Moreover, these commonalities depend upon a shared anti-materialist ethos: the two characters disdain "capitalists" (Jim's word, uttered pejoratively) who would try to rush the process by which trees are felled, seasoned, and turned into manufactured goods. As Andrew Moor has observed, "While the values which the film champions are allied with

---

⁴⁷The Baedeker Blitz or Baedeker raids were assaults by the Luftwaffe on sites of cultural significance in Britain, mostly conducted in May and June 1942. The name refers to the Baedeker travel guide.
⁴⁸Christie, "History," 76.

Englishness, through Bob they are internationalised, and naturalised."⁴⁹ The broader point is that, at the level of narrative, *A Canterbury Tale* operates to reinforce the Anglo-American connection through an appeal to all that the two countries and their inhabitants have in common; in this way, the film evinces The Archers' commitment to cosmopolitanism, which we discussed in the Introduction.

There is another way in which the film treats US-British relations, however, and that is by means of what Bob at one point refers to as "the Glue Man mystery." Hunter places the combined efforts of Alison, Peter, and Bob to discover the Glue Man's identity in dialogue with the war effort: "If an American soldier and two English people can work effectively together on the small scale of village crime-solving, then the Allies ought to be able to do the same on the large scale of a war; so the logic of the film runs."⁵⁰ It is significant, moreover, that the crime they set out to solve is one that, as we have seen, is informed by Colpeper's benighted ideas about women, ideas that the film associates with the least salubrious aspects of traditional society. If Bob, Peter, and Alison are all in need of the blessings that Colpeper in some mysterious way is instrumental in providing, as detectives they pit themselves against the retrograde customs and beliefs with which both he and the Glue Man are associated.⁵¹

But what of these blessings, as well as their impact on the miniature Anglo-American alliance established in the dark of night in the village of Chillingbourne? It is by way of the blessings, which Peter, Alison, and Bob receive near the end of the film, that they are able to realize long-thwarted ambitions or resuscitate seemingly moribund relationships. The film suggests that Peter's prewar existence as a cinema organist represented, at least to him, the failure to realize his musical promise; playing the organ at Canterbury Cathedral on the eve of his deployment overseas is the attainment of that promise. As for Bob and Alison, the former believes his girlfriend has left him while the latter understands her fiancé to be dead. Both of these characters learn otherwise, and as a result, they are at the film's ending on the cusp of reestablishing connections with loved ones whom they had believed to be lost to them. These are meaningful blessings, indeed (Figure 6.2).

Given this joyful outcome, it is striking how melancholy the final portion of the film is. Some of this is attributable to the manner in which Colpeper is shut out of the happy ending, when Alison and Geoffrey's father walk right past him.⁵² Also significant, of course, is the momentous nature of the occasion: Peter and hundreds of other British soldiers are about to be sent off

---

⁴⁹Moor, *Powell & Pressburger*, 101.
⁵⁰Hunter, *English Filming*, 30.
⁵¹On Colpeper's responsibility for the blessings, see Christie, "History," 88.
⁵²Tim Cawkwell is sensitive to the force of this moment: "[W]hen at the end, Alison and Geoffrey's father walk into the Cathedral, they go past Colpepper [sic] standing with a lost

FIGURE 6.2 *Colpeper shut out of the happy ending in* A Canterbury Tale *(1944)*.

to combat, a fact that lends a real pathos to his playing "Onward Christian Soldiers" to his fellows in the Cathedral. (The movie is also explicit about the fact that Bob and the American soldiers will be following Peter's lead in the near future.) We would suggest that there is also another, more elusive aspect to the wistfulness that runs through the film's ending. It is captured, if not fully explicated, in Ranbir Sidhu's insightful remarks on the film. Of its three pilgrims, Sidhu observes the following: "No doubt in the lives these people live from here on out, they will always look back to this odd and unexpected excursion as something special but will not quite know why. That's what's so moving about this picture. It takes a few unheralded lives, over a few seemingly insignificant days, and shows us what is really grand in them."[53] We agree, but what exactly about these lives is so grand? One obvious answer lies in the way in which, in an all too brief period of time, these characters are transformed not merely by the idyllic place in which they find themselves, and whose virtues they imbibe, but also through the connections they form with one another. *A Canterbury Tale* is the story

---

expression at the side. Alison does not notice him, as if to say, like Henry V to Falstaff, 'I know thee not, old man'" ("Cathedral Tale," 374).

[53]Ranbir Sidhu, July 2010. Accessed on December 19, 2022, at http://www.powell-pressburger.org/Reviews/44_ACT/. This website, hosted by Steve Crook, is an invaluable resource for those interested in Powell and Pressburger.

of three pilgrims, characters who establish a friendship *en route* to their destination. The film begins in earnest when they meet at the Chillingbourne train station, and it ends when they part in Canterbury. Having lived with them over the course of the movie's running time, we experience their separation from one another—and, indeed, from Colpeper—as a form of loss. This sense of loss is heightened in the final scene, which, while it places all three of them in the Cathedral, presents them as each unwitting of the others' presence; Bob even stands at the base of the stairway to the organ loft without recognizing that Peter is the one up there playing. They have already drifted apart from one another, as most of those brought together by the war are bound to do, and it is left to us to lament their separation. Moreover, as Sidhu suggests, the significance of what they shared, and what they are just now leaving behind, will only become fully apparent to them in retrospect, when they look back on their "odd and unexpected excursion." The crucial point, though, is that the audience already glimpses that significance, even if it doesn't entirely understand it.

So, what does this mean for the film's propaganda message regarding the Anglo-American relationship? Certainly, as Hunter suggests, *A Canterbury Tale* shows Yanks and Brits effectively working together; and, as Moor observes, it internationalizes British values by way of Bob. But it also does something more subtle and more moving, by making filmgoers feel the affective weight borne by this particular Anglo-American alliance at the very moment of its dissolution. To put it another way, and as Sidhu intimates, part of the emotional force of *A Canterbury Tale* lies in it making palpable to the viewer something that will become apparent to its characters only in the future, which is that they have lived through something special, something heightened, and something in which both nations played a crucial and shared role. In this regard, Powell and Pressburger's film harmonizes with Anthony Asquith's *The Way to the Stars* (1945), the opening sequence of which treats both the war and the Anglo-American alliance in a manner that is both mournful and nostalgic. As Anthony Aldgate and Jeffrey Richards observe, this sequence, which carries the viewer through a deserted airfield that formerly housed British and American crews, "evokes the feeling of the recent past, recollected with sadness and pride."[54] Sadness and pride, yes, but also longing. If the emotional force of this opening derives partly from its acknowledgment of those who have died during the war, it also emerges out of a sense that the war engendered interpersonal connections that will end

---

[54] Anthony Aldgate and Jeffrey Richards, *Britain Can Take It: British Cinema in the Second World War*, 2nd ed. (London and New York: I.B. Tauris, 2007), 283. Aldgate and Richards note that *The Way to the Stars* was made in cooperation with the MOI with the objective of promoting Anglo-American friendship (280), and that the opening sequence was designed late in the production process, when it became plain that the war would be over before the film received a general release (282).

or grow attenuated with the cessation of conflict. And yet, Sidhu notes of *A Canterbury Tale*, these connections will be remembered fondly as something mysterious and special; as such, they will play some part, however small, in starting to stitch back up the fabric of Anglo-American relations that had frayed during the war.

If *The Way to the Stars* looks back at the war with mixed emotions, especially in its opening sequence, the ending of *A Canterbury Tale* anticipates that retrospective gaze. In recognizing this about the original version of Powell and Pressburger's movie, the otherwise unsatisfying frame narrative produced for the film's 1949 American release is on the mark. After the opening credits, we witness a tongue-in-cheek presentation, peppered with dubious statistics, about Americans who served in Europe, and especially Britain, during the war. The presentation plays to various clichés about G.I.s, noting that most of those who managed to enjoy their time abroad did so because of the pubs or the women ("the natives"). Of the vanishingly small number of soldiers who relished the "old churches," we are told, "two-thirds want to revisit England, to see the places where they served during the war." After more pandering to stereotypes, including gender-based ones, the presentation gives way to a disagreement, conducted atop Rockefeller Center, between Bob Johnson and his brand-new bride (Kim Hunter) about whether to honeymoon in England or Sydney, Australia, where she was stationed as a WAC. When in making his case Bob asks his wife if she had read the book he gave her about the pilgrims, she replies, "That old stuff? Not me!" In a way that resonates with Alison's aural hallucination of the medieval pilgrims, he then asks, "Couldn't you see the Cathedral? Couldn't you hear the chimes of the bells?" We then dissolve to the footage of peeling bells that comes at the beginning of the British version of the film—although much else was cut from that version, including the opening sequence featuring Chaucer's pilgrims, discussed earlier in this chapter.[55] The point, though, is that as ill-conceived as this frame narrative is, it builds upon the feeling of longing expressed in the original film's concluding moments. At the same time, the American ending carries little of, and arguably seeks to neutralize, the emotional charge of the original. By having Bob return to Canterbury with his wife for their honeymoon—and, indeed, to the very tea room where he received his blessing in the form of her letters—the US version of the film tries to turn *A Canterbury Tale* from a tribute to the bond between Yanks and Brits into an American comedy of marriage.[56]

---

[55] The famous match cut remains, but absent its original reason for being, the yoking of the past and the wartime present.

[56] It should be noted that, insofar as the film repeatedly teases us with the possibility that Alison and Bob might become romantically involved, it also toys with the kind of Anglo-American romantic alliance that we later encounter in *A Matter of Life and Death*.

Timeless Verities and Timely Reconstruction

If in *A Canterbury Tale* Powell and Pressburger set out to show what the two great transatlantic allies have in common, the success of the film, in aesthetic terms at least, resides not only in the articulation of shared values but also in the lyrical representation of the characters' shared experience of a place and a landscape. The film goes even further, however, in offering much the same experience to the moviegoer. One of its primary artistic ambitions is to inspire the audience to see with fresh eyes. During their first meeting, Bob explains his love of moviegoing to Colpeper in this way: "It's a great thing to sit back in an armchair and watch the world go by in front of you." The magistrate's reply, while explicitly anti-cinematic, actually hints at one of Powell and Pressburger's main objectives for *A Canterbury Tale*: "The drawback is, Sgt. Johnson, that people may get used to looking at the world from a sitting position. . . . And when they really do pass through it, they don't see anything." The Archers seek to produce a cinema that does not blind us to the world we pass through but, instead, heightens our sensitivity to it. Peter Conrad says of Powell that he "wants to change film from a fickly mobile, inattentive substitute for seeing . . . to an entranced meditation on images. . . . For him, film is not a convenience for documentation but a means of engineering transcendence."[57] While we disagree with aspects of Conrad's analysis, including his marginalization of Pressburger, he gets at something central to this film: it wants to change the way the moviegoer perceives the world. This, too, is a key element of its aesthetic success, and also an indicator of the way in which Powell and Pressburger's works of cinematic propaganda grow ever more artistically ambitious in the second half of the war.

Unfortunately, *A Canterbury Tale*'s ambition was not rewarded at the box office; it was The Archers' first wartime flop. Writing decades later, Powell explains the failure by noting that, at the time of the film's release, the war had entered a different phase—the Americans were by then fighting on the continent—and that "[t]he values that we tried to discuss in the film were already 'old hat', and if you weren't interested in the theme of the film, there was something unnecessary and even unpleasant about the activities of Mr. Culpepper [sic]."[58] Powell's intimation that Colpeper's actions would not seem unnecessary or unpleasant if one were "interested in the theme of the film" is somewhat bizarre, and it does not do justice to the strangeness of a movie that binds value, as well as a lyrical mysticism grounded in "wood and brake and . . . fertile field," to the behavior of the Glue Man. It is perhaps relevant to take note here of two related points: first, that Powell and Pressburger each understood *A Canterbury Tale* to be a personal

---

[57] Conrad, *To Be Continued*, 30.
[58] Powell, *A Life*, 451.

film for its screenwriter, far more Emeric's movie than Michael's despite the latter's Kentish roots;[59] and second, that *A Canterbury Tale* has been persuasively seen as channeling through Bob Johnson the exile's experience of his adopted homeland.[60] As Tobias Hochscherf argues, "exile cinema self-consciously interrogates concepts such as Englishness and national identities rather than taking on unquestioned images of the new host country. This at least partially explains the discontinuities and ruptures of an otherwise 'perfect' filmic England in *A Canterbury Tale*."[61] We would add that another reason for the film's "discontinuities and ruptures" is supplied by the cultural and political forces shaping the final years of the war. Traditionalists in many ways, Powell and Pressburger were not immune to the effects of the earthquake that was transforming their society—an earthquake that was both scrambling traditional political impulses and rendering the question of the future ever more pressing.

We have emphasized in this study the remarkable self-reflexivity of Powell and Pressburger's films—the way in which the two meditate upon both their cinematic practice and their status as propagandists. With this in mind, and in conclusion, it is worth noticing that Thomas Colpeper is, among other things, a stand-in for the filmmakers. Many critics have noticed that his magic lantern-enabled lecture evokes the movies. As Jefferson Hunter puts it, "What [we see in this scene] is nothing less than a little allegory of the cinema, in which lecturer corresponds to director, darkened lecture hall to theatre, magic lantern to projector, the mesmerized Alison to the real audience of *A Canterbury Tale*, held in its seats—so The Archers would wish—by the power of moving images and of language recorded on a soundtrack."[62] Additionally, Colpeper gives voice to the filmmakers' desire to change the moviegoer's perception of the world; and, like Colpeper, Powell and Pressburger seek to clarify for their audience the abiding values for which Britain has been fighting.

And yet, as we have shown, Thomas Colpeper is a highly problematic character. If Powell and Pressburger locate themselves in Colpeper (insofar as he is a spokesperson for values they cherish), they simultaneously distance themselves from him (insofar as they decry retrograde elements of those same values). Through their self-reflexive identification with the Chillingbourne magistrate, Powell and Pressburger both articulate their commitment to enduring cultural values and demonstrate their recognition of the past's equivocal legacy. The closing credits suggest that Colpeper

---

[59]Macdonald, *Emeric Pressburger*, 234.
[60]Kevin Gough-Yates, "Exiles and British Cinema," *The British Cinema Book*, 3rd ed., ed. Robert Murphy (London: BFI, 2009), 125–32, 129.
[61]Tobias Hochscherf, *The Continental Connection: German-speaking Émigrés and British Cinema, 1927–1945* (Manchester: Manchester University Press, 2011), 193.
[62]Hunter, *English Filming*, 49.

FIGURE 6.3 *Canterbury Cathedral among the ruins in* A Canterbury Tale *(1944)*.

has reformed his own worst impulses; they additionally telegraph that The Archers recognize the necessity of sloughing off moribund views and practices in order to create a better Britain. The way forward, their film suggests, is through the marriage of tradition and modernity, timeless verities and timely reconstruction. If the survival of Canterbury Cathedral avers to the enduring national spirit, the bomb-scarred empty lots in its vicinity cry out not merely for rebuilding but also for the broader reimagining of society (Figure 6.3).

7

Building Up a New Britain

Scotland and Postwar Reconstruction in *I Know Where I'm Going!*

In *I Know Where I'm Going!* (or *IKWIG*, 1945), Powell and Pressburger's approach to the postwar future is animated by two widely shared convictions that were voiced in late-war propaganda: that the British people must hang on to the collectivist values that were understood to have shaped many of their wartime experiences; and that society must be rebuilt so as to create greater economic equity and opportunity.[1] What makes *IKWIG* a complex and even conflicted work, though, is the way in which Scotland is represented within the film. On the one hand, Scotland functions in a *symbolic* (or even mythic) register to express the collectivist values that need to be maintained; on the other hand, in a *realistic* register, the film's portrayal of the country as lacking economic opportunity identifies it as one of those parts of Britain that most requires rebuilding. In this regard, the film's depiction of Scotland, which operates in both registers simultaneously, is at representational and ideological cross-purposes. Assuredly, *IKWIG* offers a symbolic solution to the problem of anti-collectivist materialism that also gestures toward the problem of the Scottish economy; it does so, however, only elliptically and perhaps unconvincingly. The resolution offered by *IKWIG* is the most

---

[1] On the significance of these topics for propaganda, see Siân Nicholas, *The Echo of War: Home Front Propaganda and the Wartime BBC, 1939–45* (Manchester: Manchester University Press, 1996), 228–68.

tenuous and uncertain of any of those on offer in Powell and Pressburger's wartime propaganda films.

If The Archers' earliest war films inevitably take up Anglo-German ideological and military conflict, *IKWIG*'s focus, like that of *A Canterbury Tale* (1944), is on the British home front, with no foreign enemy in sight. *I Know Where I'm Going!* centers on Joan Webster (Wendy Hiller), who informs her father (George Carney) over dinner at an expensive restaurant in Manchester that she is journeying that night to the (fictional) island of Kiloran, where she will marry Sir Robert Bellenger, one of the wealthiest men in England.[2] (Bellenger is present in the film only as a voice over the radio.) After traveling by train, boat, and car, she arrives on the Isle of Mull only to discover that the final leg of her voyage will have to be postponed because of dense fog. On her first night on Mull, Joan meets Torquil (Roger Livesey), who is later revealed to be the Laird of Kiloran and thus the owner of the property Sir Robert has been renting. Like Joan, Torquil is going to Kiloran, in his case to hunt and fish during his brief leave from the Navy. Torquil's childhood friend Catriona Potts (Pamela Brown) takes in the two stranded travelers, and although the fog dissipates by the next morning, gale-force winds make the journey to the island equally impossible. Joan and Torquil move into a hotel in Tobermory. Alarmed by her growing feelings for Torquil, Joan seeks to evade him by visiting Sir Robert's English friends, the Robinsons (Valentine Dyall and Catherine Lacey, with a young Petula Clark as their precocious daughter), who are renting a castle for the duration of the war. When Joan accompanies the Robinsons on a visit to a neighbor, she again meets Torquil. The two attend a ceilidh, at which Torquil makes his feelings for Joan plain. Desperate to get to Kiloran despite the dangerous weather, the next day Joan bribes a young man named Kenny (Murdo Morrison) to take her there. An angry Torquil first tries to prevent her from making the treacherous journey, but after Catriona convinces him that Joan is fleeing her feelings for him, he joins Kenny and Joan on the boat. When the storm hits, the engine malfunctions and the boat is drawn ever closer to Corryvreckan, a deadly whirlpool. At the last moment, Torquil is able to restart the engine and the three return safely to Tobermory. The next day, the weather clears. After Joan and Torquil part—the former sets out on the final leg of her projected journey—Torquil sets foot in Moy Castle for the first time, in defiance of an ancient curse on any Laird of Kiloran who dares to enter. Hearing the sound of bagpipes, he sees from within the castle Joan striding toward him, with the three pipers originally hired for her wedding to Sir Robert providing a musical accompaniment. The two

---

[2]Sir Robert's surname is often spelled Bellinger in criticism, but it is written as Bellenger in the itinerary provided to Joan on the train.

lovers embrace, and the film concludes with a shot of them walking together toward an uncertain destination.

After briefly situating *IKWIG* in relation to cinematic propaganda focused on postwar British society, we will discuss the film and its making, with a particular emphasis on research that Powell and especially Pressburger conducted on Scotland and its economy. While acknowledging the elements of fantasy in *IKWIG*'s depiction of the Highlands (and, indeed, of Manchester), our primary focus will be, first, on the film's realistic depiction of its economy; and, second, on the implications of that depiction for our understanding of the film's romantic ending. We will next consider how Pressburger's treatment for *IKWIG* expresses concern about the form that postwar reconstruction might take—a concern that, we argue, is both latent in the finished film and symbolically addressed in its conclusion. We will conclude this chapter with a brief discussion of the different visions of the postwar future that we encounter in *A Canterbury Tale* and *IKWIG*.

Cinema and Postwar Reconstruction

The question of what the postwar world would look like was not only a pressing one for everyone in Britain, it was by the time of *IKWIG*'s production a familiar propaganda subject. A case in point is Humphrey Jennings's *A Diary for Timothy* (1945), which was created for the MOI's Crown Film Unit (CFU) and centrally concerns this question.[3] However, while some in the MOI recognized as early as 1941 that they could help maintain civilian morale by focusing on a brighter postwar future, they ran into resistance from a prime minister and government that desired to keep the focus on the war itself and were opposed to many of the reform efforts mooted at the time.[4] This resistance was at odds with the tenets of the Atlantic Charter of August 1941, in which Churchill and Roosevelt laid out some peace aims, with Churchill even reluctantly agreeing to take up the issue of social security.[5] This tension between embracing the topic of postwar reconstruction and

---

[3] Roy Boulting's short *The Dawn Guard* (1941) muses on this question much earlier in the war. For more on wartime cinema's attention to what comes next in British society, see Robert Murphy, *Realism and Tinsel: Cinema and Society in Britain 1939–1948* (London and New York: Routledge, 1989), 76–98; and Anthony Aldgate and Jeffrey Richards, *Britain Can Take It: British Cinema in the Second World War*, 2nd edition (London and New York: I.B. Tauris, 2007), 12–15.

[4] Ian McLaine, *Ministry of Morale: Home Front Morale and the Ministry of Information in World War II* (London: George Allen & Unwin, 1979), 171–85; see also Paul Addison, *The Road to 1945: British Politics and the Second World War*, rev. ed. (London: Pimlico, 1994), 164–89.

[5] Addison, *The Road to 1945*, 168.

holding it at arm's length is on display in the history of the CFU: its director, Ian Dalrymple, resigned in 1943 partly because the MOI did not want to take up the topic, which Dalrymple believed should be a significant focus of the CFU's efforts.[6] And yet, as Siân Nicholas puts it, "the MOI recognised that the continued endurance of war conditions would necessitate looking forward to something that would justify the sacrifices; the Britain of the post-war world must be *better* than that which had preceded it."[7] The need to look forward was also recognized by feature filmmakers: witness not only *A Canterbury Tale* (the future-oriented dimensions of which we discussed in the previous chapter) and *IKWIG*, but also Launder and Gilliat's *Millions Like Us* (1943) and Basil Dearden's *They Came to a City* (1944). For our purposes, the key point is that Powell and Pressburger, in articulating their hopes for the future, were developing a propaganda topic which was felt to be of urgent importance in the final years of the war.

If many filmmakers shared the conviction that, in Nicholas's formulation, "the Britain of the post-war world must be *better* than that which had preceded it," they also expressed trepidation that things might not turn out that way. In *Diary*, the voice-over is suffused with melancholy apprehension that the world that Timothy grows up in will not mark a significant improvement on its prewar counterpart;[8] and in *They Came to a City*, the socially variegated visitors to the unnamed city react extremely differently to it—some see a utopia while others think it a nightmare. Their varied reactions attest to the political, cultural, and economic barriers that would need to be overcome in order for dramatic change to occur. (Of course, dramatic change in the form of the welfare state was ushered in by the Labour government after the 1945 election.)

It is an episode in *Millions Like Us*, though, that offers the clearest counterpoint to *IKWIG*'s romance plot. In the final minutes of *Millions*, the upper-middle-class Jenny (Anne Crawford) and the working-class Charlie (Eric Portman), who is the foreman of the factory in which Jenny works, discuss their future. Charlie suggests that he is "turning [her] down [for marriage] without ever asking [her]." His reasoning is as follows:

> The world's roughly made up of two kinds of people. You're one sort and I'm the other. Oh, we're together now there's a war on—we need to be. What's going to happen when it's over? Shall we go on like this or are we

---

[6] James Chapman, *The British at War: Cinema, State and Propaganda, 1939–1945* (London: I.B. Tauris, 1998), 135.
[7] Nicholas, *The Echo of War*, 241.
[8] The film concludes with this question, posed by the narrator Michael Redgrave to the infant Timothy: "Are you going to have greed for money or power ousting decency from the world as they have in the past? Or are you going to make the world a different place—you and the other babies?"

going to slide back? That's what I want to know. I'm not marrying you, Jenny, until I'm sure.

Millions gestures toward the cultural and economic gulf that has separated the classes and threatens to do so again if wartime unity melts away with the coming of peace.[9] In the case of *IKWIG*, there is the added fact of national difference; moreover, whereas The Archers' film presents us with a romantic conclusion that intimates a brighter future, that upbeat ending is complicated by the filmmakers' concern, bred of their cultural conservatism, that the values the movie champions might be incommensurate with economic and social reform.

Fantasy, Materialism, and Anti-Materialism

Ironically, the original conceit for *IKWIG* echoes the circumstances behind the making of the film. Pressburger had long wanted to create a movie about a woman who embarks on a journey to an island but never gets there. The Archers planned to make *A Matter of Life and Death* (or *AMOLAD*, 1946), but the production was stalled by the unavailability of Technicolor stock. Because of the delay, the filmmakers turned to Pressburger's idea, with Powell suggesting the story should be set in the Western Isles of Scotland. (Powell had a deep love for the Scottish Highlands. His breakthrough work, the lyrical *The Edge of the World* [1937], was filmed on location on the island of Foula in the Shetland archipelago; and, as we have seen, *The Spy in Black* takes place in the Orkneys.) While Powell scouted locations, Pressburger wrote an initial version of the script. During the weeks he spent in Scotland, Powell "read everything I could lay my hands on about the Western Isles. I was determined to make the film as authentic as possible in every detail."[10] Upon returning to England, Powell was pleased to discover his partner's initial script built upon the themes explored in *A Canterbury Tale*; it was then that he realized the new film "would fit into the logical pattern of our war work."[11] The two then embarked upon what Powell describes as an example of their typical revision process:

[M]y job was to add to and change the location sequences, bringing in all I had learnt of the authentic dialogue, atmosphere and names of the

---

[9]As Chapman notes, however, the relationship between Charley and Jenny is also informed by regional difference: he is a Yorkshireman and she is a Londoner (*The British at War*, 214).
[10]Michael Powell, *A Life in Movies* (1986; London: Faber and Faber, 2000), 477.
[11]Ibid., 468.

Western Isles. . . . As soon as I had completed the first few sequences, and numbered them with regular script numbers, I turned them over to Emeric for him to agree or disagree . . . By the end of the three weeks, we had the first complete draft of the script for our collaborators to work on and for us to discuss with prospective actors and actresses.[12]

To develop the film's message, Powell asserts, The Archers would need to represent "a whole new world, full of people with their own standards and judgments, dependent upon one another, feudal, democratic and totally devoid of materialism."[13]

If we grant that the Western Isles of *IKWIG* are depicted so as to serve the film's anti-materialist agenda, then we should also recognize that the early Manchester scenes present a vision of materialism that is to be contested once the film moves to Scotland. This vision is tightly tethered to Joan Webster's story, which is elliptically represented in the film's witty opening credit sequence. That sequence offers us a view of Joan that centers upon her knowledge from a young age of three things: of where she is going, of what she wants (and often gets), and, by extension, of who she is.[14] The links that the credit sequence forges between desire (what she wants), subjectivity (who she is), and directed movement through space (where she is going) are also on display in the first scene, which begins with a shot of the adult Joan's legs as she strides purposefully into an upscale nightclub and restaurant to meet her father. The entire scene upends convention in a way that both gestures toward wartime changes in gender roles and bespeaks Joan's self-assurance.[15] In a cheekily audacious manner, she not only informs her father that she is engaged, she tells him the wedding is to happen in a few days—he is obviously not invited—and convinces him to see her off at the train station. If there are echoes of incest in Joan planning to marry a man almost as old as her father, it is also clear that her biological father has little sway over her or where she is going—just as, in the end, her older fiancée will not be able to determine her future.[16]

The restaurant scene deploys a representational shorthand to capture succinctly Joan's worldly emphases. An obvious example of this is the close-up of her engagement ring. Lit and shot through filters so as to give it a

---

[12]Ibid.
[13]Ibid., 465.
[14]Tom Gunning, "On Knowing and Not Knowing, Going and Not Going, Loving and Not Loving: *I Know Where I'm Going!* and Falling in Love Again," *The Cinema of Michael Powell: International Perspectives on an English Film-Maker*, ed. Ian Christie and Andrew Moor (London: BFI Publishing, 2005), 94–116, 98–100.
[15]On Joan Webster as a "mobile woman," see Pam Cook, *I Know Where I'm Going!* BFI Film Classics (London: BFI, 2002), 25–9.
[16]Ibid., 21; Andrew Moor, *Powell and Pressburger: A Cinema of Magic Spaces* (London: I.B. Tauris, 2005), 124.

strikingly luminous look, the opulent ring, which we later learn comes from Cartier, captures for Joan the allure of becoming the wealthy Lady Robert Bellenger. The prospect of soon adopting that identity is accompanied by an attitude toward consumption that is strikingly at odds with the wartime ethos of austerity and sacrifice. Joan has the maître d' take the soup away because it has gone cold. In doing so, she casually acknowledges that the fault lies not with the kitchen, but with the fact that she and her father have been talking. Shortly thereafter, when her entrée comes, she takes a couple of bites before, in an attempt to deflect concerned paternal comments about her fiancé's age, she insists that her father dance with her. We can only imagine that the entrée, too, will be returned from whence it came. Joan's cavalier and wasteful attitude toward food not only attests to the resources she has at her disposal, it also jars with the experience of an audience grown accustomed to rationing, which, indeed, extended well into the postwar period.

Another significant example of the filmmakers' representational shorthand for materialism is more subtle. After moving with her father from the bar to the dining area, Joan expertly tips the waiter who carried their drinks. Without looking, she reaches across the front of her body to put a coin on the drinks tray. There is an air of studied casualness about the action; her way of dispensing gratuities bespeaks her familiarity with the social protocols of affluence. Joan does not directly engage the waiter, as if it would be unseemly to give her full attention to either the transaction or the person at the other end of it. This brief incident might not compel our attention were it not for the fact that, a few minutes later on the train, Joan's action is echoed by Sir Robert Bellenger's factor, Hunter (Walter Hudd). Just before Joan tells Hunter that it was clever of him to get her a sleeping car for her journey north, Hunter removes a folded bill from his overcoat and, while looking straight ahead, surreptitiously hands it to the railway porter standing beside him. In this instance, Hunter seems to be offering a bribe rather than a tip (we see him hand a coin to a different porter in a less secretive fashion).[17] In the restaurant episode, Joan notes that everything has been arranged, and Hunter says the same thing on the train; the small gesture of money changing hands serves as a visual synecdoche for that notion. Moreover, because Joan and Hunter share this gesture, we assume that it emblematizes life as it is lived by, and within the orbit of, Sir Robert Bellenger. It is in itself a demonstration of *how* everything is arranged. And yet, while events are orchestrated by way of money, the baldness of the transactional logic is masked or disavowed through Joan and Hunter's surreptitious actions, as if to suggest that it is Sir Robert's merit rather than his bank account that greases the wheels. The crucial point, though, is that

---

[17]Moor, *Powell and Pressburger*, 121.

these two episodes provide us a view of social relations as defined by and organized around the transfer of money. They concretize the materialist worldview to which the scenes in Scotland will provide an alternative.

There is another dimension to the scenes in Manchester that needs to be explored before we turn to Joan's journey to Scotland. Tom Gunning shrewdly observes that, for all her materialism, Joan is a very likable character in these opening scenes. Part of this can be chalked up to Wendy Hiller's exuberant performance, but Gunning also suggests that "Powell and Pressburger's understanding that deep desires underlie Joan's materialist longings allows us to sympathise deeply with a woman we might otherwise dismiss as a gold-digger and nothing more."[18] Those desires are on display at a moment when she rhapsodizes to her father about the beauty of Kiloran, which she has at this point traveled to only "in [her] dreams." The restaurant scene suggests in another way that Joan is not quite the mercenary figure she might be confused with. In response to her ongoing performance of entitled certitude, Joan's father says, "Now, here, Joan. Stop acting. You're not Lady Bellenger yet." After a long pause, Joan offers a wry smile that confirms her father's sense that she is not really as she appears; there is more to Joan than the role that she has taken on as the future Lady Bellenger. Needless to say, the film's comic resolution depends upon the divergence, only glimpsed here, between Joan's subjectivity and that of the thoroughgoing materialist she thinks she is.

For all that, Joan's famous dream sequence on the train to Glasgow seems to confirm her materialism. On the edge of sleep, Joan recalls her father saying, "You can't marry Consolidated Chemical Industries," to which she replies, "Can't I?" (This exchange hearkens back to the restaurant scene, in which Joan has introduced her father to the identity of her fiancé by handing him her works pass. While the pass bears on it the names of both the firm that employs her, CCI, and its owner, Sir Robert Bellenger, her father initially spots only the firm's name.) Joan then dreams of a wedding ceremony, officiated by her father in ministerial garb, between herself and CCI, with the industrial concern signaling its assent to the marriage by way of an unseen factory whistle that, by way of an audio bridge, merges with the whistle of her speeding train. As Joan sleeps contentedly, dreaming of being Lady Bellenger, the sound of the rapidly turning wheels is mimicked in voice-over by the repeated phrase, "Everything's arranged." The sleeping Joan appears in a blond hairpiece—is this a dream in which her slumbering self is bewigged!?—with bank notes floating in the air around her, while various unseen tradespeople voice their delight at capitulating to Lady Bellenger's purchasing power. Her dream then shifts dramatically to a fantasy version of Scotland featuring tartan-covered hills and the recognizable voice of

---

[18]Gunning, "On Knowing," 99.

FIGURE 7.1 *Joan's dream of Scotland in* I Know Where I'm Going! *(1945).*

John Laurie intoning "You'll Take the High Road." Just after Laurie states, "You're over the border now," Joan is abruptly awakened by a voice over a loudspeaker identifying the train station as Glasgow Central (Figure 7.1).

If the leitmotif of Joan's dream of her future is "everything's arranged," The Archers signal the fallacy of this view shortly after she arrives in Mull. Despite the bad weather, Joan commits to staying on the pier in Port Erraig, stating "It's been arranged for the boat to meet me here and I better be here to meet it." While she is sitting there, her itinerary is blown out of her hands and into the water. In a witty touch, the projected stages of Joan's journey are intoned in voice-over just until the document sinks beneath the waves, signaling both visually and aurally the submersion of her plans. This moment, which occurs very shortly after Joan arrives on Mull, is reprised in the storm scene, when the wind plucks her wedding dress from out of the boat. As critics have noticed, these two episodes offer intimations of supernatural intervention,[19] and as such they exemplify how The Archers' version of the Western Isles evokes fantasy, myth, and legend.[20] Pam Cook goes so far as to argue that *IKWIG* "generates a fantasy world, from the moment its heroine falls into a dream state on the train taking her to Scotland to meet her future husband to the primeval nightmare of the Corryvreckan

---

[19]Ibid., 103.
[20]See Moor, *Powell and Pressburger*, 120; Ian Christie, *Arrows of Desire: The Films of Michael Powell and Emeric Pressburger* (1985; London: Faber and Faber, 1994), 54–5; and Stella Hockenhull, *Neo-Romantic Landscapes: An Aesthetic Approach to the Films of Powell and Pressburger* (Newcastle upon Tyne: Cambridge Scholars Publishing, 2008), 115–46.

whirlpool that almost swallows her up."²¹ We do not contest that *IKWIG*'s Scotland evokes myths and fables: the ancient curse of Moy Castle and the legend of Corryvreckan are only the two most obvious illustrations of this. However, in identifying Scotland with fantasy, critics have tacitly associated England with realism.²² To the contrary, we would argue that the scenes in Manchester traffic in a different kind of fantasy. From the perspective of an average (or, indeed, almost any) British filmgoer in 1945, the world of affluence and excessive expenditure associated with Sir Robert Bellenger is as remote and otherworldly as are the Western Isles. As superficially realistic as the film's version of Manchester might appear to be, it is nonetheless crafted to articulate an extreme version of the value system that Powell and Pressburger are critiquing. The scenes there express the materialist fantasy that, through the marvelous efficacy of money, everything in life can be arranged, and that you can know with certainty who you are, what you want, and where you are going. It is this certainty that, in Joan's case, is to be so effectively dismantled by her experience on Mull.

Pressburger, James A. Bowie, and *The Future of Scotland*

In emphasizing Scotland's status as a fantasy world, critics have missed the extent to which the country's representation is grounded in realism. As we have seen, Powell has asserted that they sought "to make the film as authentic as possible in every detail."²³ Before taking up the portion of the film set in Scotland, we want to discuss the research Pressburger conducted in the service of such authenticity. The British Film Institute's Emeric Pressburger Collection houses what it identifies as a "handwritten treatment [in pencil]" for the film.²⁴ This "treatment" is more various than that term might suggest. It includes, among other things, different iterations of an opening scene for the film; background sketches of "The girl" and "The man"; and extended passages of dialogue. While aspects of the finished film can be glimpsed in

---

²¹See Cook, *I Know*, 17.
²²Discussing the ways in which Scotland has typically been represented on film, Duncan J. Petrie argues that "Viewed from the centre, Scotland is a distant periphery far removed from the modern, urban and cosmopolitan social world. . . . Consequently, Scotland tends to be represented as a picturesque, wild and often empty landscape, a topography that in turn suggests certain themes, narrative situations and character trajectories. Central to this is the idea of remoteness—physical, social, moral—from metropolitan rules, conventions and certainties" (*Screening Scotland* [London: British Film Institute, 2000], 32).
²³Moor argues that "'Real Scotland' is just within the film's reach, but it is its re-creation which makes the viewer long for its distant reality" (*Powell and Pressburger*, 120).
²⁴Emeric Pressburger, Treatment for *I Know Where I'm Going!*, BFI EPR/1/24/1.

these pages, there are a number of striking differences between it and the treatment, some of which we will take up later in this chapter. For now, the most important thing to observe is that, almost midway through this sheaf of handwritten pages, we encounter Pressburger's notes on Scotland and its people. Toward the end of these notes, Pressburger identifies the source from which they are derived: James Alexander Bowie's *The Future of Scotland: A Survey of the Present Position with Some Proposals for Future Policy*. Bowie's book was published in 1939, and, as he writes in its preface, it was "written while war threatened and completed after war had broken out."[25] Bowie was at that time the Director of the Dundee School of Economics, and the Keynesian proposals that he lays out in *The Future of Scotland* chime with the sorts of initiatives put forth by many postwar planners a few years later. Christopher Harvie puts it this way: "Recognising that the resources of Scotland lay primarily in its people, and the importance of retaining them in their communities, [Bowie] wanted a state-financed Scottish Development Commission to plan the economy, control the heavy industries, and assist the growth of light industries."[26] More generally, Bowie had long advocated for increased economic planning by the state. Additionally, he was, according to his entry in the *Oxford Dictionary of National Biography*,

> much concerned with the antagonism between capital and labour, and called for schemes that would result in co-partnership in industry, where labour had equity stake and shared organizational responsibility. His views were radical and progressive, but he was against violent change, much as he recognized the rights of labour for a greater degree of control.[27]

The ideas Bowie had been developing in the 1920s and 1930s anticipated the progressive, reform-based cultural turn of the war years. Crucially, Bowie was worried about the nature and size of the role that Scotland would play in the broader economic rebuilding of Britain. Unfortunately, Bowie's worries were realized, as Scotland's failure to achieve industrial diversity meant that after the war it remained vulnerable to economic downturns to a degree that England was not.[28]

---

[25] James A. Bowie, *The Future of Scotland: A Survey of the Present Position with Some Proposals for Future Policy* (London and Edinburgh: W. & R. Chambers, 1939), 5.
[26] Christopher Harvie, *Scotland and Nationalism: Scottish Society and Politics, 1707 to the Present*, 3rd. ed. (London and New York: Routledge, 1998), 77.
[27] J. M. Alec Gee, "James Alexander Bowie (1888–1949)," *Oxford Dictionary of National Biography*. Published September 23, 2004. Accessed online December 19, 2022.
[28] Richard Finlay, "The Turbulent Century: Scotland since 1900," *Scotland: A History*, ed. Jenny Wormald (Oxford: Oxford University Press, 2005), 241–71, 261. While the war provided Scotland's economy with a boost, Bowie recognized that the benefits were to be short-term ones: "[I]f Scotland falls asleep on the seductive bed of rearmament she must some day suffer a rude awakening" (*The Future*, 105).

One of the major focal points of Bowie's analysis is Scotland's declining population, which was caused in part by the redistribution of its inhabitants within Britain.[29] Bowie presents estimates suggesting that between 10,000 and 12,000 Scots a year migrated to England.[30] He argues that "This southern drift of Scots, mainly young, may ultimately be a more serious matter for Scotland than the alleged southern drift of her industries. For it is one thing to redistribute an expanding population and quite another to redistribute a static or shrinking population."[31] A significant reason for any "southern drift," of course, was the availability of opportunities in both England and the British colonies that could not be found in Scotland itself. Moreover, Bowie observes that Scotland has long developed in its people what he dubs an "emigration ideology":

> [L]arge groups in Scotland have, for a variety of reasons, had to move, or been moved, and the roving instinct is now in the blood. Add to that the love of adventure, the lure of opportunity, the narrow and unremunerative market in Scotland for a professional competency which she creates but cannot employ, and we see how the syphon of emigration once started tends to continue its flow.[32]

In addition to various economic problems, it is the emigration ideology that Bowie feels needs to be addressed. In his notes on Bowie's book, Pressburger paraphrases the matter this way: "The time has come when Scotland needs the best of her sons within her own borders, men who will break with the tradition of going forth and succeeding and instead remain at home to tackle the social and industrial problems which have grown acute [sic]."[33]

The population problems faced by Scotland were particularly severe in the Highlands. Summing up the relevant data on the region, Bowie offers this grim diagnosis: "[T]he Highlands are fast becoming, from the point of view of numbers, a more and more insignificant part of Scotland's national life.... [T]he population of the Highlands is ageing, the number of married

---

[29]Decennial census data adduced by Bowie suggests that the population decreased in 1931 for the first time since 1801. While Bowie describes evidence that would suggest that a small increase in population would occur by the 1941 census, the general trend he finds is toward a shrinking population, with emigration being an abiding concern (*The Future*, 14–18).
[30]Ibid., 21.
[31]Ibid., 22.
[32]Ibid., 23–4. For a discussion of the "abiding reputation of the Scots for mobility and ubiquity [abroad]," see David Armitage, "The Scottish Diaspora," in Wormald, ed., *Scotland*, 272–303, 272.
[33]Pressburger, Treatment, page 11v. On the same page, see also: "Sc[otland] turns out hundreds and thousands of well trained young folk to whom it seldom occurs that their own country is desperately in need of their knowledge. Their eyes are turned to England, the dominions and Colonial Service."

women aged 15–45 is falling, and families are becoming smaller. Unless heroic measures are taken, there is every indication that the Highlands will become the Sahara of Scotland."[34] Pressburger's notes include only one comment specific to the Highlands: "Rough country and bad transport isolate the crofting population. Primitive standards."[35] However, in responding to Bowie's discussion of the folly of continuing to rely on past economic practices, Pressburger makes a statement that stands in fascinating counterpoint to the mythical aspects of the Western Isles that *IKWIG* depicts: "Romantic nostalgia must give way to the reality and urgency of present and future."[36]

We have mentioned that Bowie's book anticipates the calls for state planning and economic reform that became more urgent over the course of the war. Such calls also reverberate with something we described at the beginning of this chapter, which is a propaganda emphasis on the new Britain for which its inhabitants were fighting. Moreover, with the publication of the Beveridge Report in December 1942, which "came to be seen as the main blueprint for the [postwar] welfare state,"[37] public opinion moved definitively in the direction of state planning; according to one survey, 86 percent of those surveyed believed the report's recommendations should be adopted.[38] However, the cultural appetite for examining the issue of how to reconstruct Britain—of how to plan for peace—can be traced back at least to the Blitz and its aftermath. To put it another way, one of the most pressing questions of the period is captured in the title of a radio discussion series planned by the MOI and BBC but never inaugurated: *Where Are We Going?*[39]

In reviewing the research that Powell and Pressburger conducted on Scotland and the Highlands, our objective is obviously not to suggest that *IKWIG* offers a documentary-style account of life on Mull.[40] Nor is it

---

[34] Bowie, *The Future*, 30.
[35] Pressburger, Treatment, page 12r. Crofting is a form of small-scale agricultural production that is specific to the Scottish Highlands and islands.
[36] Ibid. Pressburger is referring here to this passage or one like it: "Most Scotsmen have farming blood in their veins, idealise the farming life through their only present contacts with it during holiday periods, and let their sounder judgment be warped by sentimentalism. . . . The returned emigrant particularly and quite naturally deplores the changes, and there is as a consequence much wasted effort to restore the old that would be much better spent in moving forward to a new equilibrium" (Bowie, *The Future*, 120).
[37] Peter Malpass, "Wartime Planning for Post-War Housing in Britain: The Whitehall Debate, 1941–5," *Planning Perspectives* 18 (2003): 177–96, 180.
[38] Nicholas, *The Echo of War*, 251.
[39] Ibid., 246–7.
[40] It is worth noting that *Edge of the World* comes closer to offering such an account, its focus being on the depopulation of the island of Foula. On Powell's rejection of critical comparisons between *Edge* and documentaries like Robert Flaherty's *Man of Aran* (1934), see Petrie, *Screening Scotland*, 37–8.

to deny the role that myth and fantasy play in the film. It is, instead, to point out that *IKWIG*'s folkloric or fantastic elements have taken critical precedence over the film's engagement with crucial aspects of present-day life in wartime Scotland, with the result being that scholars have failed to grapple adequately with the contradictions within a work that Ian Christie dubs a "fable of post-war optimism."[41] These contradictions complicate the film, tempering its optimism with questions about the sustainability of the society whose anti-materialist value system *IKWIG* champions.

Highland Economics

For a movie steeped in myth and fantasy, *I Know Where I Am Going!* provides a surprisingly full depiction of the parlous economic condition of the Western Isles. The first and arguably most significant example of this concerns Erraig House, the home of Catriona Potts, née Maclean. Of the Maclean clan, Joan's driver tells her that, with the exception of Catriona, "They'll all be dead now, or in New Zealand." A childhood friend of Torquil, Catriona married an Englishman named Potts; her husband is in the Middle East, presumably on military service, and the couple have a child in boarding school. Catriona's survival, we learn, depends upon what she can shoot: "We live off the country. Rabbits, deer, a stray hiker or two." As for Erraig House, Catriona acknowledges that it has been "knocked about a bit," a statement supported on our first viewing of the place by the paint peeling off the walls, the leaves that have collected inside the doorway, and the chickens that wander across a long hallway. The reason for the building's sorry state? For two years, the RAF housed eighty servicemen in and around Erraig House. The conversation then turns to compensation. Catriona attests to the fairness of the RAF on this point, "apart from their trying to sell me their concrete foundations." She suggests that "They'll pay a lump sum or do the place up as it was. After the war, of course." When Torquil asks which option she will choose, Catriona replies, "That's the question, Torquil my boy. Maclean vs. Potts." While Torquil registers his opinion on the matter—"Up the Maclean!" he vigorously asserts—we do not learn who will win the case of Maclean versus Potts (Figure 7.2).

In a very literal sense, this conversation concerns postwar reconstruction. Moreover, it intimates a divergence in the Scottish and English views on how such reconstruction should take place ("Maclean vs. Potts"). But what precisely is at issue in this elliptical exchange? We can't know for sure, but it seems highly likely that the Maclean view would be to restore Erraig

---

[41]Christie, *Arrows of Desire*, 55.

FIGURE 7.2 *Joan enters Erraig House in* I Know Where I'm Going! *(1945).*

House with an eye to continuing to live there. As for the Potts option, the "lump sum" might be used to build a more modern structure, or it might serve as the prelude to selling the house and its land and clearing out of the Highlands. With the latter possibility in focus, it is worth keeping in mind, first, that all of the Macleans but Catriona have died or emigrated from Scotland; second, that her hand-to-mouth existence, while obviously made more extreme by the war, conveys the tenuous economic situation of those who live in the Western Isles; and third, given that situation, the cost of maintaining a rebuilt Erraig House would undoubtedly place a significant burden on the Potts family. If the case of Maclean versus Potts is neither fully argued nor settled, we do get a significant gloss on it later in the film. After Catriona tells Joan that she'd swim to Oban for £10, the latter asks why she doesn't sell, to which a puzzled-looking Catriona replies that "money isn't everything." In his autobiography, Powell writes about the banality of this line, as well as the difficulty Pamela Brown had in delivering it in a way that pleased him.[42] For our purposes, what matters is Catriona's resistance to the notion of selling her property. If in Manchester everything can be arranged by way of money, in the Western Isles there are limits to what it can accomplish and, excepting Joan's bribe of Kenny, to what one will do for it.

Significantly, the question of Erraig House's future is echoed in a scene at the home of Rebecca Crozier (Nancy Price). When the Robinsons and Joan

---

[42]Powell, *A Life*, 491–2.

visit Rebecca, Mrs. Robinson, in a characteristically insensitive manner, asks her hostess, "How on earth can you manage with [a small staff of] three people in a house like Achnacroish?" Mrs. Robinson conveys by this comment her impression that Rebecca lacks the resources necessary to maintain her large, presumably ancestral home. Later in this scene, after Mrs. Robinson chides Torquil for asking too much in rent for Kiloran, Torquil offers an illustrative example of "Highland economics": "For three years rent, I can live there myself for six." Rebecca adds that "If I were to let my house, I should never live to enjoy the money I would get for it." Whereas Torquil absents himself from his home for long periods in order to earn an income that allows him to live there intermittently, Rebecca, like Catriona, stays put, even if the financial feasibility of doing so is in question.

In addition to enabling Torquil to live on his own island, Sir Robert Bellenger's tenancy has an impact on the livelihoods of the Highland natives. As Torquil and Joan take a bus ride to Tobermory, some of the islanders, not knowing Joan's status as Bellenger's fiancée, marvel to Torquil about the strange actions of the "rich man of Kiloran." For instance, he builds a swimming pool when the ocean is practically at his doorstep. When Torquil observes that such a construction project at least benefits those who labor on the pool—"Money spent is money earned"—his interlocutor agrees. However, he then points out the pernicious effects of Bellenger "bring[ing] salmon here from the mainland": "But who would be fishing when there's no one to be buying?" On the one hand, some of Bellenger's money bolsters the island economy by providing jobs; on the other hand, some of it bypasses that economy altogether, supplanting local salmon with its mainland equivalent. Moreover, Sir Robert's disdain for the inhabitants of Mull—the only people worth knowing, he says, are his fellow affluent émigrés from war-beset England—attests to his indifference to their social and economic plight.

That plight is most vividly conveyed by Kenny's acceptance of payment from Joan in order to get her to Kiloran, weather be damned. Joan offers Kenny £20 to make the crossing in the boat of Ruairidh Mhór (Finlay Currie), his employer. The precise figure is a significant one: it is the amount that it would take for Kenny to buy a half interest in the boat and thereby be in a position to marry Ruairidh's daughter, Bridie (Margot Fitzsimons); upon their marriage, Bridie says, Ruairidh would provide the other half to Kenny as a gift. It is clear that £20 is a huge sum within the world of the film: Kenny states that it would take him three or four years to earn that much. The bribe, then, represents for Kenny the financial means to establish a household with Bridie. However, it also poses an existential threat to both him and his hopes, given the real possibility that he might perish, along with the boat, in the gale. In other words, what Joan offers Kenny is a kind of poisoned gift that promises to realize his hopes but jeopardizes both them and him.

Perhaps the most important aspect of the £20 payment, though, is the way in which it scrambles both expectations and interpersonal relationships. In first describing the prerequisites for his marrying Bridie, Kenny is matter of fact about the time it will take to underwrite a new household, with Ruairidh playing no small part in the process by agreeing to sell him half of the boat. By accepting Joan's payment, Kenny not only seeks a shortcut, he knowingly (if uneasily) goes against Ruairidh's wishes. By taking the money, then, he sows discord among Bridie, Ruairidh, and himself. Simply put, while the Englishwoman's money holds out for Kenny the promise of establishing a new household, in which Kenny would serve as both husband and provider, it also threatens not only his life and his employer's boat but also his relationship with his would-be father-in-law.

Running through all of the episodes we have been discussing is the fundamental question of whether or not life as it has been lived in the Scottish Highlands can be maintained in the face of economic precarity. In this regard, *IKWIG* confronts us with a conundrum. The materialist English are pitted against the non-materialist Scots, with the latter clearly getting the better of the ideological contest. And yet, the Scottish economy is depicted as dangerously fragile, which in turn raises the question of just how viable the value system on display can remain. Indeed, *IKWIG* represents that system as being under considerable pressure. The future winner of Maclean versus Potts is uncertain, and it is not hard to imagine Kenny having to leave the Highlands to seek his fortune. This returns us to the "emigration ideology" of which Bowie writes (not to mention his prognosis regarding the "Sahara of Scotland"). Torquil's four-year absence from the area is clearly attributable to the war, but we also learn that revenue from Kiloran constitutes his only meaningful source of peacetime income. This means that he cannot live on the island for long stretches of time, or, at least, that, even as laird, he is denied full access to it. This raises the question of what Scotland has to offer the "best of her sons within her own borders." Whereas Torquil both identifies with and seems committed to the Western Isles, the lack of economic opportunity available to him makes one wonder if he will re-settle there. Interestingly, Eric Britton's 1946 novelization of *IKWIG*, which unsurprisingly sticks closely to the film even as it fleshes out certain events as well as the characters' motives, features a Torquil who, on the car ride back to the hotel from the ceilidh, tells Joan that he intends to migrate to Canada after the war. This leads Joan to share Sir Robert's observation that "Scotland will need clever Scotsmen after the war. And at *home!*" Torquil's reply is an approving one: "He's got something this Robert of yours."[43] As far as we know, Britton's dialogic embellishment doesn't

---

[43]Eric Britton, *"I Know Where I'm Going!": The Book of the Film* (London: World Film Publications, 1946), 51.

record The Archers' vision for Torquil's future. What it does do, though, is suggest the pervasiveness of the migrating Scot trope as well as demonstrate that at least some period viewers would identify Torquil as an example of that type. Moreover, it reverberates with the film's conclusion in ways we will discuss shortly.

In sum, the Western Isles of Scotland function in two different registers in *I Know Where I'm Going!* In a symbolic register, the region stands for anti-materialist values, with the elements of myth and fantasy in the film working to grant those values an aura of timelessness. In a realist register, however, the Western Isles stand in for a Scotland in desperate need of the kind of economic reforms touted not only by Bowie but also by advocates of postwar planning. The film's ending has a primarily symbolic force: in pairing off with Torquil, the Englishwoman Joan abandons her materialist certainties in favor of both romance and the anti-materialist allure of the Western Isles. And yet, as Cook has noted, although the ending "confirms the triumph of love over mercenary motives, one cannot help feeling that the lovers face a stormy future, and that their journey is not yet over."[44] Why is this? For one thing, Torquil's leave is up and he will need to return to his unit; for another, both Joan's life and her employment are back in Manchester. Most significantly of all, though, the film has taken great pains to depict the Western Isles as a site not only of considerable romance but also of great economic uncertainty. The question that the film poses of the region—is life viable there?—is suddenly a pressing one for the happy couple.

Now, it would not be fair to *IKWIG* to push this line of argument too far. While the concluding scene has its oddities and ironies—the curse of the Macleans resembles a Borscht Belt joke about marriage as a form of captivity—it also provides a satisfying romantic resolution to the film. Indeed, it is likely that most viewers of *IKWIG* do not linger long over the question of how the lovers will make a living in the "Sahara of Scotland" once the war is over. (Of course, those lovers could relocate, but, given that the film offers a celluloid tribute to Highland culture, such an outcome seems untenable.) And yet, *IKWIG*'s close attention to the economic harshness of life in the Western Isles undoubtedly contributes to our sense that the couple's future is uncertain. How, then, do we reconcile the film's happy ending, marked by the victory of anti-material collectivism, with this uncertainty? Can we square the film's status as a "fable of post-war optimism" with its clear-eyed view of the moribund Scottish economy?

One solution to the problem of the film's ending is suggested by its novelization. "Scotland will need clever Scotsmen after the war": this statement, which is in line with Bowie's diagnosis of the nation's economy,

---

[44] Cook, *I Know*, 71.

holds out the promise of economic revitalization by way of the reversal of Scottish migration ideology. The prospect of Torquil's permanent return to Scotland, then, can be read as a source of hope for the nation. This view also helps explain the oddity of the Maclean curse. That curse stipulates that the Laird of Kiloran who enters into Moy Castle will be "chained to a woman to the end of his days and shall die in his chains." Apprehension about this curse, then, reads as a fear of matrimony. By film's end, not only has Joan abandoned her materialist ambitions, so has Torquil overcome an aversion to marriage and, presumably, to establishing a household in Scotland. The alliance between Torquil and Joan can be seen, then, as more than the triumph of anti-materialism. Insofar as it entails the clever Scotsman—and his equally able English bride—staying put, it can represent the first step in the reformation of the national economy. To put it another way, *IKWIG*'s final scene addresses the real economic problems the film has identified in a symbolic register. In the manner of a Shakespearean comedy, *IKWIG* aligns marriage with cultural regeneration, seeing in the pairing off of the happy lovers a brighter future for the society in which they live. And yet, the film's romantic resolution offers not even a glimpse of a concrete way forward for that society; the idea of progress remains tacit, or even notional. This is not surprising, of course, given *IKWIG*'s status as a romantic comedy, but, given the movie's close attention to the reality of Highland economics, it is significant. The Archers' commitment to realism means that Scotland cannot be written off merely as a backdrop for romance. Consequently, there is a faint but detectable note of disquiet in the film's conclusion. As Cook suggests, this manifests as a palpable uneasiness about the future. However, the object of concern, we would argue, is not the lovers' relationship as much as it is the society that is to be putatively revitalized through their alliance.

Modernism and Postwar Planning in Pressburger's Treatment

In tethering hopes for reform to the fate of the two lovers, then, *IKWIG* develops its emphasis on the postwar future indirectly and by means of the film's romance plot. By doing so, it leaves largely unresolved the economic problems that it itemizes; we are to understand that the alliance between the Scottish and English lovers, as well as the tacit expectation that they will make the Highlands their home, is the harbinger of better times to come. Given this, it is important to note that, as the treatment discussed earlier in this chapter tells us, Pressburger at one time considered making the propaganda theme of rebuilding Britain—not just Scotland—much more explicit. As we have mentioned, the treatment includes background information on the lovers and provides some alternative ideas for opening the film; perhaps most notably, Pressburger wrote several variations of a scene in which an English character who has traveled to the Highlands for a wedding gets lost in a fog. (There is an amusing echo here of the "real pea souper" in which *AMOLAD*'s Peter Carter unwittingly evades the detection of Conductor 71.) For our purposes, what is most instructive is Pressburger's early conception of Joan's character, although in these pages she is either unnamed or identified only as "the girl." The daughter of a bank manager in "a fashionable London district," she is "a young architect, in love with one of the greatest architects of the country." As for the treatment's early iteration of Sir Robert Bellenger, we learn that he is "about 55, very rich, very influential, very refined, [and] she hopes to work with him to build up a new Britain." Additionally, we are told that "He built a very modern house for some rich people. These are the people she will visit. She knows the house from plans. She is very upset because they have changed things."[45]

These details from Pressburger's treatment require explication. First, and most obviously, we should note that the issue of rebuilding Britain—which, as we have seen, is the subject of much late-war propaganda—is front and center. Indeed, we might speculate that Pressburger abandoned the idea of Joan being an architect because he realized it was too on the nose; as we have seen, the film version of *IKWIG* engages the topic of postwar planning in a much less direct fashion. Second, the fact that the project of "build[ing] up a new Britain" is associated with the precursors to Joan and Sir Robert is worth lingering over. It is clear that from very early on in the writing process Pressburger intended to align his female protagonist with a value system that she would eventually abandon in favor of a better one. Had Pressburger stuck with his original conception, then, the vision for a new Britain with which the two architects are associated would, over the course of the film, come to be discredited. This is made clear by the reference to a "very modern house for some rich people." The "new Britain" symbolized by this house is quite literally built for the rich, and deviations from the architectural plans are presented as a source of dismay to the younger of the pair. Third, we must assume that Pressburger understands the construction of the "very modern house" as emblematizing an idea for the new Britain that is to be forced upon Scotland; it is not an architectural style per se that is at issue but the imposition of modernism onto the Scottish Highlands. Whereas in *IKWIG*'s final form materialism loses out to communitarian values, in Pressburger's treatment it is a particular blueprint for a new

---

[45]Pressburger, Treatment, pages 8r-v. It is worth noting that in the film, after Torquil suggests Joan count the beams in her room as a prelude to making a wish, Joan observes that "People in modern houses don't know what they're missing."

Britain that is, through its association with the young woman and her older fiancé, to be pitted against anti-materialist values.

It is important to recognize how closely aligned modernism and postwar planning were. Architectural historians such as Andrew Higgott and Elizabeth Darling have demonstrated how, in the words of the latter, "architectural modernism emerged as part of a wider project to modernize Britain" that was ascendant by the end of the war.[46] This project was clearly expressed in documents such as the County of London Plan of 1943.[47] The subject of considerable cultural fascination, not to mention of wartime exhibitions that drew over 75,000 visitors, this plan neatly demonstrates the extent to which modernism and postwar planning were conceptually tethered to one another.[48] As Higgott argues, the Plan

> proposed an ambitious reordering of most of the city, with new roads, parks and reconstructed neighbourhoods, and brought with it the more abstract qualities of efficiency and order. It is also clearly the product of ... the project of modernisation which shaped other aspects of British life. It reflected the assumptions of the emerging welfare state, not least that of strong centralised government, and embodied assumptions of social control, seen largely uncritically in the years of wartime and immediately after.[49]

It is not hard to imagine The Archers having mixed feelings about the broader project of social engineering expressed in plans such as this one; nor is it difficult to conceive of their dismay at the thought of any "ambitious reordering" of Highland culture. The key point, though, is that the *IKWIG* treatment's young architect and older fiancée should be seen as proponents of sweeping modernization projects such as the County of London Plan.

In developing a very brief sketch of a new Britain associated with wealth and modernity, Pressburger articulates the cultural conservatism that is a feature—though not necessarily the defining one—of many of The Archers'

---

[46] Andrew Higgott, *Mediating Modernism: Architectural Cultures in Britain* (London and New York: Routledge, 2007); Elizabeth Darling, *Re-forming Britain: Narratives of Modernity Before Reconstruction* (London and New York: Routledge, 2007), 4.
[47] On this, see Higgott, *Mediating Modernism*, 57–84.
[48] Ibid., 60. The connection between British modernist architecture and planning preceded the war. For example, F. R. S. Yorke writes in 1934 that "We need new types of buildings, new plans for them and new plans for our towns. Every development in life, and consequent adjustment in the mode of living, has a direct influence on these plans, because the plan of the building, or of the town, is the plan of the mode of living, the pattern of our daily lives" (*The Modern House* [London: The Architectural Press, 1934], 7–8). On how modernist architecture came "to exert a dominance over architectural and planning education and practice," see Darling, *Re-forming Britain*; quote from page 1.
[49] Higgott, *Mediating Modernism*, 58.

films. More specifically, he betrays the worry that Scottish culture might be a casualty of the rebuilding of Britain. Of course, as he revised his conception of *IKWIG*, Pressburger backed away from making a film that so explicitly engages the topic of postwar rebuilding; The Archers shifted their primary focus from reforming Britain to critiquing materialism. (It is worth noticing, however, how the Bellengerian mantra "Everything's arranged" could be ungenerously applied to social planning initiatives; and also how the case of Maclean versus Potts literally concerns postwar reconstruction.) And yet, some of Pressburger's initial worries are present in the finished movie. On the one hand, the Scottish Highlands emblematize the value system endorsed by The Archers; on the other, those values are tethered to a way of life that is recognizably in jeopardy. If the Scottish economy is reformed, will those values survive the process?

Insofar as Ian Christie is correct in identifying the film as a "fable of postwar optimism," *IKWIG* takes its place among a number of other works identified in this chapter as key cinematic expressions of the hope for a brighter, reformed future—a hope that animated propaganda production from at least mid-war on. And yet, we have seen how those very films are as anxious as they are hopeful. *IKWIG*, which was released months after the war ended in December 1945, similarly expresses trepidation about that future. Will the values that Powell and Pressburger identify with the Scottish Highlands—values for which Britain fought and which Britons are, The Archers fear, in danger of forgetting—survive the dawning of the brave new postwar world? To "build up a new Britain" is, in the filmmakers' view, to run the risk of destroying much of what is best in the old one. In this regard, *IKWIG* worries about where the nation as a whole is going.

A Canterbury Tale and *IKWIG* are united by an anti-materialist sentiment as well as a shared appreciation for traditional values; at the same time, they both articulate the need for economic and social reform. In this latter regard, these films explore issues often taken up in late-war propaganda. And yet, the differences between the films are noteworthy. *A Canterbury Tale* explores the equivocal legacy of the values and traditions that it nonetheless champions, whereas *IKWIG* worries over the potential fragility of those values and traditions without much attending to their limitations. Both works recognize the necessity for the postwar rebuilding of British society, but *IKWIG* betrays the filmmakers' concern about the possible cultural costs of that rebuilding—a concern even more fully articulated in Pressburger's treatment. These are differences less of kind than of emphasis; they are the product not of ideological contradiction, but of The Archers' ongoing interrogation of their own beliefs and convictions. This impulse toward self-interrogation suggests something significant not only about Powell and Pressburger, but also about the political and ideological reorientation many underwent during the war. As we observed in the Introduction, The Archers have often been characterized as High Tory traditionalists, but, as

A Canterbury Tale and *IKWIG* demonstrate, they were too reflective, and too sensitive to their cultural moment, to cling in hidebound fashion to a fetishized past. What we witness in these two films, then, is evidence of the filmmakers' ongoing process of political and ideological recalibration—a process that, as we shall suggest in the next chapter, is gestured toward in Peter Carter's self-description as "Conservative by nature, Labour by experience."

8

"Conservative by Nature, Labour by Experience"

The Propaganda of Futurity in *A Matter of Life and Death*

A Matter of Life and Death (1946) might reasonably be called The Archers' final wartime film because its conception, writing, and pre-production occurred long before the war's official end—and yet, what a meaningful coincidence that shooting officially began on September 2, 1945. Not only was it V-J day (the Japanese government had surrendered two weeks earlier and signed the surrender papers in an official ceremony that morning); it was also the date on which the US president Harry Truman abruptly terminated the Lend-Lease policy (1941–5), which had served as the greatest emblem of Anglo-American friendship and strategic diplomacy during the war years. Now that the war and the contract had ended, Britain and the United States would need to redefine the terms of their relationship. Even the players would be new, for Roosevelt had died back in April, and Churchill was crushed by Labour Party leader Clement Attlee on July 5, in a landslide general election victory. Soon, hundreds of thousands of G.I.s would be exiting Britain to return home, meaning that contact between Britons and Americans would, once again, be more cinematic than real. Indeed, when MOI Director Jack Beddington provoked Powell and Pressburger in the spring of 1944 "to think up a good idea to improve Anglo-American relations," no one could possibly have imagined just how timely their good idea, *AMOLAD*, would wind up being.[1]

---

[1] The story of Powell's fateful lunch with Beddington has been told again and again, but see especially Michael Powell, *A Life in Movies* (1986; London: Faber and Faber, 2000), 455–7,

The film presents the surreal adventures of a Royal Air Force squadron leader and poet named Peter Carter (David Niven), who, in the film's opening scene, jumps from a doomed Lancaster without a parachute and somehow lives. While still in his plane, Peter spends what he believes are his dying moments speaking with an American air traffic controller named June (Kim Hunter), with whom he falls immediately in love. The two meet shortly after, when Peter washes up on a Devon beach near where June is stationed. Meanwhile, in an Other World presented entirely in Black and White,[2] Peter's failure to arrive on schedule is discovered, and Conductor 71 (Marius Goring) is dispatched to Earth to retrieve the would-be dead man. However, Peter refuses to go with him since he and June are madly in love with each other. He successfully seeks permission to try his case before an otherworldly tribunal. Alarmed by Peter's headaches and hallucinations of a celestial conductor, June enlists Dr. Frank Reeves (Roger Livesey) who diagnoses Peter's brain injury and plans the surgery that could save his life. After Frank is killed in a motorcycle accident, he becomes Peter's legal defense in the Other World. The details of the trial, which pits Reeves against Abraham Farlan (cheekily played by Canadian actor Raymond Massey), an American Revolutionary War soldier with a hatred for the British, focus primarily on the nature of Anglo-American relations. After a grueling trial, June and Peter prove to an all-American jury that "nothing is stronger than love," and so Peter is granted his reprieve from death; his victory is mirrored in the success of his brain surgery on Earth. In the film's final scene, the British and American lovers are reunited in the world of color, symbolizing the successful triumph of Anglo-American amity in a decidedly more hopeful postwar world.

As the trial scene unfolds, however, serious tensions rise to the surface—tensions that the film's romantic-comedic ending cannot entirely relieve. The bitter American prosecutor questions not only whether a British man is worthy of an American girl of good "stock," but also whether Britain is worthy of America *in any sense*. The debate reflects upon America's emergence as a superpower and Britain's declining position in world politics. "I've been watching you English from upstairs," Farlan says. "Your wars, your politics, your business." England's past is then reduced by its American accuser to a history of military aggression and imperialism in France, South Africa, Russia, China, India, and Ireland, among other nations—as part of

---

and 497, in which the specific quotation appears; Kevin Macdonald, *Emeric Pressburger: The Life and Death of a Screenwriter* (London and Boston, MA: Faber and Faber, 1994), 240; and Ian Christie, *A Matter of Life and Death* (London: BFI, 2000), 12.

[2]Technically speaking, the "pearly" monochrome look of the Other World sequences was achieved by not adding color at the printing stage to the three-strip Technicolor film. The credits refer to this process as "Colour and Dye-Monochrome Processed in Technicolor." For more on the production of the sequences, see Christie, *A Matter*, 32–43.

a not-so-subtle critique of a government which had failed to end imperial rule in India and other British colonies. Reeves constantly chooses to shift the topic, and in doing so he emphasizes British classic literature, culture, and history. Farlan's begrudging acknowledgment of this legacy winds up being a first step toward reconciliation, and the film works to marry an old-world ideal characterized by past cultural achievements and a maturity born of experience (Britain), and a new world order characterized by industrial might and a naïve, though contagious, idealism (America).

While Britain comes in for some criticism in the film, America does not get off scot-free. Though the fact has been sorely neglected by critics, *AMOLAD* does more than harmlessly poke fun at America's wide-eyed, Coca-Cola-guzzling, aw-shucks, knee-slapping G.I.s. Within the context of actual mid-1940s Anglo-American politics, and especially given numerous local crises regarding the behavior of US soldiers in Great Britain, the film's rather sharp critiques of American bigotry, isolationism, and provincialism parallel—and demonstrate moral and ideological consistency with—its criticisms of British imperialism. In thinking up a good idea to improve Anglo-American relations, in other words, Powell and Pressburger in no way settled on merely flattering America and scolding England.

Sue Harper has convincingly described "the priority which Powell and Pressburger gave to the issue of history" in their final propaganda film, an idea this chapter will explore at some length.[3] Its main purpose, though, will be to interrogate the conclusion she draws that *AMOLAD*'s "propaganda aim was to suggest that what bound the British and the Americans together was their common history and their shared definition of culture."[4] While contemporary Allied propaganda did, indeed, seek to highlight cultural similarities between Britain and America, providing a useful template for The Archers, the film is striking for its willingness to engage, however cautiously, extraordinarily volatile issues troubling the two nations.[5] The most important of these issues involves conflicting cultural attitudes about, and governmental responses to, the haunting legacies of racism, classism, and colonialism. Though the presentation of Peter and June's love affair

---

[3]Sue Harper, *Picturing the Past: The Rise and Fall of the British Costume Film* (London: BFI, 1994), 107.
[4]Ibid., 108. Harper is not alone in highlighting the film's emphasis on Britain's glorious cultural and literary heritage: see also Christie, *A Matter*, 14–28; Greg M. Colón Semenza and Bob Hasenfratz, *The History of British Literature on Film: 1895–2015* (New York and London: Bloomsbury, 2015), 1–3; and Garrett A. Sullivan, Jr., "'More Than Cool Reason Ever Comprehends': Shakespeare, Imagination and Distributed Auteurism in *A Matter of Life and Death*," *Shakespeare Bulletin* 34 (2016): 373–89.
[5]It engages them, but in the Other World—and it seems reasonable to ask whether this matters. The political discussion is displaced onto the fantasy world, whereas the "real" world—which is actually a Technicolor world—can be perceived as being untroubled by these direct political discussions.

might reasonably be said to function as a metonym for the fantasy-union of two great nations, the human lovers come together only after the purging of an *actual* ailment; and the film recommends a similar trajectory for the two nations, which through the experience of having survived the Second World War are encouraged to reject their conservatism and embrace their more progressive, more thoroughly democratic principles. In this, the film rhetorically echoes William Beveridge's "first principle" as stated in the immensely popular Beveridge Report of December 1, 1942, which we briefly took up in each of the previous two chapters. That principle holds that "any proposals for the future, while they should use to the full the experience gathered in the past, should not be restricted by consideration of sectional interests established in the obtaining of that experience. . . . A Revolutionary moment in the world's history is time for revolutions, not for patching." Beveridge goes on to say, famously, that "The purpose of victory is to live into a better world than the old world."[6] In *AMOLAD*'s opening scene, Peter introduces himself to June as "Conservative by nature, Labour by experience"—highlighting, we wish to argue, the clearest philosophical path forward for the two wartime allies by indirectly endorsing the liberal idealism proposed in the Report.[7] Were the film merely suggesting the romantic idea that love conquers all, its propaganda message would hardly be worthy of a chapter in this book. By shifting our focus, however, from *AMOLAD*'s articulation of vague past and present similarities between Britain and America to its argument for the necessity of a *progressive* future trajectory for *both* nations, we position ourselves to see more clearly that the film's "true love" message is no mere hokum; instead, "true love" functions in *AMOLAD* as a symbol for a practicable and progressive strategic state policy predicated on ideals of tolerance, inclusion, and social justice.

As we shall also see, the slightly dreamlike or surreal impression given by *AMOLAD* has often been noted by viewers. This impression is due, of course, to the film's interest in mysterious, even seemingly supernatural phenomena, but it is heightened, we would argue, by its slightly awkward, though undeniably brilliant, negotiation of the romance plot, on the one hand, and its propaganda objectives, on the other. Though Powell and Pressburger have juggled these same elements before—in *Contraband*

---

[6]Qtd. in Angus Calder, *The People's War: Britain 1939–1945* (London: Pimlico, 1969), 528, 530. According to a Gallup Poll from later that month, nine out of ten Britons believed that the Report's immensely popular proposals should be adopted (Ibid., 528).
[7]Although the Report's hopeful, future-looking vision of Britain and the world was described even by the Conservative-leaning *Yorkshire Post* as "a most heartening affirmation of faith in the future of Britain" (qtd. in Calder, *The People's War*, 527), by the end of the war, it was associated with the agenda of the Labour Party specifically. Whereas early on Labour had endorsed the Report, Churchill had repeatedly attempted to stifle it, leading directly to Labour's landslide victory in 1945. As Calder notes, "the Beveridge debate came to symbolize in the mind of the public the difference between Labour and Conservatives" (Ibid., 532).

(1940), *The Life and Death of Colonel Blimp* (1943), and *I Know Where I'm Going!* (1945) for example—the earlier films tend to feel more cohesive for one particular reason: although the romantic relationships in them may have symbolic import, they are not explicitly presented *as* symbols. While watching *AMOLAD*, however, because the relationship between Peter and June is so obviously symbolic of the relationship between the United Kingdom and the United States, audiences can feel a bit disoriented when the focus shifts decidedly toward one of these relationships and away from the other. At points *AMOLAD* can feel like two separate films, one about Peter and June's love affair, and another about each nation's political grievances against the other. At the same time, the film's political focus raises dramatically the stakes of the love affair's success, and its romantic focus permits The Archers to safely explore the complexities of the Anglo-American relationship. The very quality that threatens to distract audiences from the film's more radical and sophisticated politics, therefore, is the same quality that allows the film's politics to be more radical and sophisticated.

In what follows, we begin by detailing the general crisis looming over Anglo-American affairs in the mid-1940s: the question of how to maintain the so-called "special relationship" after the war. We then turn to the specific problems of racism and classism in America and Britain, focusing especially on how they were thought to epitomize an old world order that threatened international relations and set up insurmountable obstacles to long-term alliances and future progress. To a surprisingly large degree, we'll see, the success of postwar Anglo-American relations was thought to hinge on the reform of racist and classist cultural systems and power structures. Another brief section then identifies, and seeks to correct, a certain critical tendency to read *AMOLAD* according to a priori assumptions about Powell and Pressburger's conservatism—ignoring in the process the film's rather explicit call for a more progressive postwar politics. That call is the focus of the chapter's final section, which is an extended close reading of the film's interrogation of systemic intolerance in both the United States and Britain. Only by confronting and eradicating the particular forms of intolerance plaguing its past and present will each nation, individually and in concert with one another, show itself capable of moving forward into an "other world" of stability, prosperity, and peace.

A Good Idea to Improve Anglo-American Relations

Anglo-American relations didn't suddenly find themselves strained in 1944; the problems that *AMOLAD* needed to address toward the end of the war weren't entirely different than those *49th Parallel* had taken up in 1941. From the British perspective, American isolationism remained a primary irritant, but American crassness, provincialism, racial insensitivity, and hypocrisy followed closely behind. From an American perspective, British snobbery might be said to have been the primary issue—a superiority complex capable of rationalizing imperial power and colonialism as cosmopolitanism—but British class insensitivity and hypocrisy were also important issues. More than an ocean seemed to divide two historically linked, English-speaking "friends" badly in need of a cultural translator. As David Reynolds summarizes the matter, "Just as the condescending British view of the U.S., as an immature but fundamentally British society, was still that of a mother country to her former colony, so American feelings towards Britain reflected the experiences of the Revolutionary era. Indeed, British visitors to the U.S.A. sometimes remarked that American perceptions had not evolved since 1776."[8] This final claim is particularly interesting in light of *AMOLAD*'s metonymic representation of Americanness in the character of Abraham Farlan. What makes the film's focus on the strained Anglo-American relationship so distinctive for the time, however— and also what makes it different from, say, *49th Parallel*'s similar concerns—is its emphasis on a postwar world. How could the relationship be appropriately sustained once the wartime bond was dissolved?

This was no merely academic question. In fact, it was being asked—obsessed over even—at the highest levels of government. No major figure is more associated with the fantasy of a perfectly unified Anglo-America than Prime Minister Winston Churchill, who posited the "special relationship" as key to Britain's continuing relevance after the war. According to Henry Butterfield Ryan,

> Churchill set out early in the war to form the tie, believing that what Great Britain could not be, Anglo-America could. As in any marriage, at least any modern one, each partner surrenders part of his and her sovereignty, but the couple, at least potentially, can have greater influence than either individual, and the weaker of the two, if older, cleverer and more experienced, can have great sway in the union.[9]

At one point, Churchill seriously considered the benefits of dual citizenship for citizens of both nations. Ryan goes on to remind us that the quasi-marital union Churchill envisioned never took place—a particularly resonant fact,

---

[8] David Reynolds, *The Creation of the Anglo-American Alliance, 1937–41: A Study in Competitive Cooperation* (London: Europa Publications Limited, 1981), 24.
[9] Henry Butterfield Ryan, *The Vision of Anglo-America: The US-UK Alliance and the Emerging Cold War, 1943–1946* (Cambridge: Cambridge University Press, 1987), 2.

we might point out, in light of *AMOLAD*'s romantic-comedy structure. In spite of Churchill's urgings, British and American attitudes toward the postwar relationship continued to diverge, with Roosevelt sidestepping the topic as politely as he could, largely in an effort to avoid alienating Russia. The strain caused by the two nations' conflicting visions of the future exacerbated those fissures which already existed between them. Indeed, historian Terry H. Anderson confidently states that "By the beginning of 1945, the eve of the Big Three conference in the Crimea, Anglo-American relations had deteriorated to their wartime nadir."[10]

We are in danger at this point, though, of downplaying the sophistication of Powell and Pressburger's art—and of insulting the intelligence of most contemporary film audiences—if we argue simply that The Archers answered Jack Beddington's challenge to "improve Anglo-American relations" with a "love conquers all" fantasy of romantic union. What's most remarkable about *AMOLAD*, in fact, is the film's direct engagement of so many specific, so many truly complex, points of disagreement and tension between the nations. As Powell himself notes, "almost every issue between the two nations, important or trivial, is brought up and examined."[11] Nor is the film's examination of these issues limited to simple confutations of popular stereotypes of each nation's peoples or cultural idiosyncrasies. Often, *AMOLAD* demonstrates a surprising willingness to confront profound and, again, highly specific, political quandaries.

The best case in point involves what is perhaps the film's most famous crux which, partly because it has never before been adequately explained, is worth considering at some length here. In a particularly pointed exchange in the film's Other World trial, Farlan says to Reeves that he's been "watching you English from upstairs. Your wars, your politics, your busyness. From the tax on tea in 1766 to a certain report on England by five members of the United States Senate in 1944." The bigoted prosecutor refers here to a report that would have been obscure to most Americans even at the time of the film's release; the same report was, however, the source of anger and resentment in Britain—a fact which clarifies greatly how the film's seemingly scathing criticism of England should be read. The *Report on the War: Observations by Five Members of the United States Senate on a 45,000-Mile Trip to the War Areas* was submitted to Congress following the reconnaissance and oversight tour of three Democratic and two Republican senators charged in 1943 by the Special Senate Committee Investigating the National Defense Program with "the duty of checking on all phases of war production."[12]

---

[10]Terry H. Anderson, *The United States, Great Britain, and the Cold War, 1944–1947* (Columbia, Missouri and London: University of Missouri Press, 1981), 1.
[11]Powell, *A Life*, 497.
[12]*Report on the War: Observations by Five Members of the United States Senate on a 45,000-Mile Trip to the War Areas* (Washington, DC: The United States News, n.d.), 2.

Over the course of many weeks, the senators traversed a 37,000-mile course (the additional mileage noted in the report's title factored in numerous side-trips taken by individual senators) starting from Maine and connecting such far-flung places as Newfoundland, southwest England, Marrakech, Cairo, Basrah, Calcutta, and Chungking, before returning via Australia and Hawaii to Los Angeles and then Washington, D.C. During the tour, "several days" were spent in the United Kingdom, especially in visits with the 8th Air Force. As one senator notes, "Wherever we went we were most courteously received by the officials of the British Empire" (7).

That senator was Democrat Richard B. Russell of Georgia, and his own criticism of "our British allies" wound up causing controversy in Britain when a member of the Committee leaked his observations to *The New York Times*' London correspondent. Russell's subsection of the Report complains about the leak, criticizes the press for focusing on his negative rather than his "commendatory" comments about Britain (3), and defends his critical position thus:

> I would be the last to do or say anything which would cause any breach between our country and our British allies. I believe that the future peace of the world largely depends upon a complete understanding between us. However, matters of this kind can surely be adjusted without disturbing good relations. No people are perfect, including our own, and I feel that there will be a better understanding and more mutual respect between us and less possibility of feeling which might prevent or postpone a complete accord after the war if such matters are worked out as we go along. (8)

Acknowledging that "what was said here has caused a great deal of bitterness and resentment in the United Kingdom" (11), Russell blames the problem on both an exaggerative press and an overly sensitive British public, all the while managing to absolve himself of any culpability:

> I would not have this statement construed anywhere as an apology for my position. If offense be found, I must say in all candor that our British allies have become unduly sensitive if an American citizen and Senator cannot discuss the operations and policies of his own Government, of which I am a part, without raising a storm of furor and resentment throughout the United Kingdom and the Empire. (11–12)

The undated report was certainly written near the end of 1943 but may have been published early in 1944. Henceforth cited in the text.

The remainder of Russell's somewhat tone-deaf subsection of the report offers further evidence of the way the senator offsets compliments of America's most important ally with his own resentful assertions about the state of the Anglo-American relationship.

So what does Russell assert that provoked such bitter resentment in Britain? The report is thorough and the causes of possible concern are many, but the single overriding refrain is that, once the war has ended, the British will not be able to pay back American material contributions to the war effort made through the so-called Lend-Lease Act. The "Act to Promote the Defense of the United States" was enacted in March of 1941, thereby ending, months before Pearl Harbor and the official US declarations of War against Germany and Japan, the US policy of neutrality. According to the language of the Act, the United States was to provide the United Kingdom, and other countries such as China and the Soviet Union, with food, oil, weaponry, et cetera, all free of cost. In exchange, the United States would receive no-cost leases on allied military bases and local supplies. Lend-Lease was a crucial component of the eventual Allied victory, a simultaneously generous and self-serving US policy, and a cause of much controversy in the States—especially among isolationist Republicans and conservative Democrats. In his report, Russell reveals one reason why many Americans loathed the policy so much: the lack of American oversight and control of the materials and resources that the nation was lending out. Russell repeatedly complains about the British giving away American-made tools and weapons to countries such as Turkey, for example, and he laments America's inability to supervise the ways in which the British are putting to use items "paid for by the people of the United States" (8). So how fair to America and how offensive to Britain is Russell's position? In his defense, Russell's major point may simply be that a clearer policy is needed when it comes to defining the terms of the Lend-Lease agreement once the war ends: "If our nation has a definite policy which extends longer than six months after the conclusion of the war in any of the far-flung lands in which American troops are fighting and American dollars are being spent, I was unable to find anyone among our officers abroad who could define it.... We cannot afford to rely even on so splendid an ally as the United Kingdom to protect all our interests or there will be inevitable conflicts and confusion after the war" (8). Fair enough. It seems amazing in retrospect that the terms of the agreement were not hashed out in greater detail, and one can easily see how that problem would become a central element of the postwar Anglo-American relationship.

In Britain's defense, however, the lack of clearly defined parameters on the use of American-made resources seemingly authorized its own decisions about how best to use those resources. Perhaps more important, Russell's somewhat barbed discussion of American and British differences (he contrasted America's more realistic or "modern" methods of diplomacy with Britain's more idealist or old-fashioned ones) came across as condescending at best.[13] At one point, Russell argues that "In my opinion, all of our civilian agencies operating outside of the United States should be co-ordinated in the hands of some two-fisted American who has an understanding of American interests in all international matters," as opposed to the "old type of kid-glove diplomacy" he sees defining the current situation (8). Worse, his casual characterizations of British oversensitivity, his complaints about British "lethargy" in dealing with "the Indian problem," and his criticism of the British press's misrepresentation of the American contribution to the war effort, all detracted from what he claims was his central, practical concern, and these insults dug unnecessarily at raw wounds (9). To a nation that had made manifold sacrifices while fighting the war for democracy almost entirely by itself for nearly three years, Russell's words must have seemed remarkably ungrateful.

That Powell and Pressburger choose to reference this specific controversy in *AMOLAD* is extraordinary and telling. In positing the faults outlined in the report as merely the latest crimes committed by a trans-historically tyrannical nation, Farlan directly parallels the British monarchy's eighteenth-century imposition of an unreasonable tax on colonial-American tea with the British misuse of American resources in the Second World War. To draw such parallels, though, Farlan has to ignore the obvious differences between the two historical scenarios—especially the fundamentally altered nature of the relationship between Britain and the now-free *United States of America*. That Farlan is a shortsighted bigot seems obvious, and his absurd conflation of the Tea Act and the Lend-Lease Act speaks to British anger about modern American misrepresentations of each country's role in the war effort. That the film lays bare such absurdity illustrates merely one of the ways in which it manages to critique the faults of both nations rather than take sides in an oversimplistic manner.

Moreover, what defines Farlan's jingoism throughout the trial is an isolationist streak (somewhat understandably) born out of his Revolutionary War experience. For Britain, such isolationism (somewhat understandably) defines the US position in international politics—and it certainly colors the way in which Britons read the words of Americans such as Senator Russell. It might be usefully pointed out here that Farlan is not, of course, a *real* American—even within the film's diegesis—but is, rather, precisely the American that Peter anxiously dreams up in a state of severe mental illness. This fact reveals the degree to which each nation's stereotypes of the other emerge in *AMOLAD* as problems in need of correction. American

---

[13]This condescension extended, though less overtly, into other sections of the report. Senator Albert B. Chandler (Democrat, Kentucky) mentions that "Mr. Churchill suggested to the Committee, during our visit at 10 Downing Street, the possibilities of dual citizenship between our two countries." He concludes that "American statesmen and officials of the Government should deal realistically with Mr. Churchill. He is a realistic man" (27).

isolationism, and the implications of it for both Britain and the free world, however, would continue to define what the British saw as the American "problem" even well after December 8, 1941—and it would continue too to threaten the Anglo-American relationship after the war.

One of the most widely read contemporary observers of this relationship was Denis William Brogan, a celebrated Scottish author and historian. Brogan wrote several books during the war geared toward helping American and British citizens to understand one another better, a most important practical aim in light of the thousands of G.I.s stationed in Britain. In *The American Character* (1944), for example, he sought "to make more intelligible to the British public certain American principles and attitudes,"[14] especially the young country's isolationism, its slow "awakening" to the realities of life outside the United States (xii–xv):

> The American problem remains. It is a double problem. It is the problem of making intelligible to the American people the nature of the changes in the modern world which they can lead, or which they can resist, but which they can't ignore. (xix–xx)

Brogan paints a picture—some might say a caricature—of an American society of consumers of nearly exclusively homemade products, of Midwesterners especially, hemmed in by thousands of miles on either side of them, ignorant of and reluctant to become more informed about the world beyond their little hometowns—let alone their vast country. Although to his credit Brogan deepens his analysis considerably, as we shall see in the next section of this chapter, his characterization of the isolationist "principle" as *the* American problem suggests precisely why it was also the British problem: for if isolationism was not a mere phase of the early twentieth century but, rather, a principle intrinsic to American history, sociology, and geography, then what could Britain expect from its ally after the war other than a return to its old ways—a return to what Brogan calls "natural isolationism" (167)? Where would this leave Britain as well as the entire postwar free world? "The American problem," explains Brogan, "is the British problem, the French problem, the Polish problem: the reconciliation of real national autonomy, of real national tradition, with the needs of a new world society" (169). Whether it was because of widely read academic commentaries by men such as Brogan or news accounts of the government's own diplomatic strategies regarding the Anglo-American relationship, Powell and Pressburger's cinematic treatments of the "Special Relationship" regularly addressed this so-called "American problem": whereas *49th Parallel* had sounded a

---

[14]D. W. Brogan, *The American Character* (New York: Knopf, 1944), ix. Henceforth cited in the text.

desperate and, as it turned out, prescient warning to the United States about the costs of isolationism prior to Pearl Harbor, *AMOLAD* expresses deep concerns about America retreating back into itself after the war.

Toward a "New World Society"

Brogan's study of the "American problem" features a provocative implicit link between isolationist and racist attitudes and laws. Just as America has generally managed to limit foreign influence, Brogan reasons, it has also managed to exclude from the American dream those foreign elements, or "others," living inside its own borders. Brogan describes the sensibility of all those shut-in Midwesterners as an "American frontier intolerance" deeply rooted in the national experience (100). Lamenting Alexander Hamilton's failure to unite the original thirteen colonies as the crucial missed opportunity for truly "a more perfect union," Brogan pulls no punches:

> Not all Americans are at home in America or are accepted as first-class citizens. For America has not, any more than other countries have, found a means of uniting all its people on the basis of freedom. . . . American unity has, in a sense, decreased as the original religious homogeneity of the thirteen states has been diluted by non-Protestant, non-Christian elements. America is now the capital of world Jewry, and anti-Semitism is one of the problems that perplex the wise American. . . . The Poles in Detroit who treated the Negroes of Sojourner Truth as the Germans in Poland treat Poles; the soldiers in Los Angeles who beat up the Mexican "zoot-suit" wearers; the woman who wanted the speaking of Spanish forbidden in Los Angeles; the Ku Klux Klan who came in to profit by the pathological situation largely created by Catholics in some Midwestern states; the Protestants who, for whatever innocent motives, are ready with facile charges against Catholics—all are enemies of American union. They are also friends with Hitler—and some of them know it. (99–100)

Brogan's scathing portrait of American hypocrisy—of the gap between the country's inclusive ideals and reality—catalogs reasons why the United States is just like "other countries"; it is only exceptional in its denial, even unawareness, of the major contradictions that its isolationist propaganda manages to conceal.

Further discussion of American antisemitism and anti-Catholic prejudice, especially aimed at the Irish immigrant, merely sets the stage for Brogan's most obvious example of exclusion and intolerance, the case of African American disenfranchisement. Brogan asserts that the American South "is analogous to the poor, feud-ridden, historically unfortunate border countries between Germany and Russia. . . . The main southern problem is the color problem. It is unhealthy for the South that over a third of its inhabitants are debarred, with more or less legality, from full legal rights. . . . It is a problem, too, affecting the whole nation, that the general 'Anglo-Saxon' color prejudice, so great a political handicap in a world overwhelmingly 'colored' and no longer in awe of the white man's murderous magic, should be reinforced by what is often an obviously pathological Southern version of it. And wartime tensions, the contrast between American promises and American performance, the justifiable Negro conviction that talk about race mixture and the like is a cover for economic exploitation, by American labor at least as much as by American capital—all make the situation more dangerous even than it was before" (112–13). While Brogan's focus here is on the American South, his description of the "general 'Anglo-Saxon' color prejudice" reinforces the analogousness of British and US cultural crises in the late-wartime era. He also subsumes racial intolerance under the general umbrella of "economic exploitation" and class conflict more generally.

In his 1943 book *The English People*, Brogan argues that the American view of England as a nation which embraces inequality is more than justified, for "In all fields of progress the Englishman has much to be proud of, in all fields but one. For the class-divisions in England, exaggerating and overlaying the great economic differences that are common to all Western society, are a great price to pay for national unity. . . . England will not be a full or anything like a full democracy as long as one of the kindliest and most united peoples in the world are internally divided in a fashion that so impoverishes the national life."[15] In both the United States and Britain, full citizenry, and democracy itself, are thwarted by what Brogan presents as the comparable plagues of race and class division. One might argue, however, that in spite of his attention to the problem of an unfree India, Brogan tends to ignore the overlap between British colonialism, English classism, and American racism—the ways in which class and racial hierarchies function in strikingly similar and mutually reinforcing ways.

This is a strange blind spot, though it seems to have been common enough at the time, and on both sides of the Atlantic. Terry H. Anderson reminds us that as late into the war as 1942, "almost six out of ten Americans regarded the British as oppressors who took advantage of their imperial possessions."[16] Just as numerous British observers saw no contradiction, then, in critiquing American racism while rationalizing an unfree India, similar numbers of Americans were hypocritical enough to label the English as "oppressors" while simultaneously championing and defending Jim Crow laws in the Southern United States, not to mention those systematic forms

---

[15] Brogan, *The English People: Impressions and Observations* (New York: Knopf, 1945), 155–6.
[16] Anderson, *The United States*, 4.

of segregation practiced in the North. As for the British, such hypocrisy was becoming increasingly clear during the war years, though state policy was taking a long time to address it.[17] Sonya O. Rose persuasively argues:

> In popular discourse as well as officially, the British understood their colonial relationships as fostering democracy and their nation as a benevolent, paternalistic imperial power. . . . But threatening Great Britain's reputation as a beneficent colonial power was the issue of race, and the persistent indications of a "colour bar" in the metropole in spite of the self-described "tolerance" that was supposed to characterize the British people as a nation.[18]

One obvious reason why Britain may have been awakening to its own blindness was Hitler's brutal use of racism to advance his fascist regime: "Nazi policy on the issue of race made British racial tolerance a particularly salient aspect of national identity during the war."[19] We might fairly ask why Nazi policy didn't have a similar effect on American national identity.

No particular wartime phenomenon better illuminated American hypocrisy—or the difference between it and the British variety—than the official segregation of African American soldiers. As Linda Hervieux points out, "the U.S. military was segregated in World War Two. It was a Jim Crow system of extraordinary breadth underpinned by virulent racism that mirrored life" at home.[20] As we discussed in relation to *A Canterbury Tale* (1944), much of the tension between the British and Americans was a direct result of the massive G.I. presence in Britain during the war years. Scholars have observed that *AMOLAD* winks repeatedly at the troubling, and often noted, romantic relationships between British women and American G.I.s, even reversing the gender dynamic through Peter and June's own relationship

---

[17]This awakening was largely due to the fact that Britain, long able to rationalize its policies according to a specifically imperial logic, suddenly needed to distance itself from the German Empire—and not least the fact that Hitler looked to the British Empire as a model for what he wanted Germany to become. See especially Gerwin Strobl, *The Germanic Isle: Nazi Perceptions of Britain* (Cambridge: Cambridge University Press, 2000): "The idea of Britain as a cold and calculating nation, always with an eye for the main chance, and preference for fighting dirty, produced in [Hitler] a profound sense of kinship. . . . [H]e looked forward to the day when Germany and Britain would be allies. . . . Fraternal feeling between Britain and the Third Reich would thus grow out of a shared lack of moral scruples. The British Empire, after all, had not been acquired—or maintained—by being nice to other races" (44–5).
[18]Sonya O. Rose, *Which People's War?: National Identity and Citizenship in Britain, 1939–1945* (Oxford: Oxford University Press, 2003), 239, 245.
[19]Ibid, 245.
[20]Linda Hervieux, *Forgotten: The Untold Story of D-Day's Black Heroes, at Home and at War* (New York: Harper Collins, 2015), xi.

as part of its project to repair Anglo-American relations.[21] More central to the film's project, we would argue, was the increasing tension between a British population that was appalled by the American military's treatment of Black soldiers, and an American government intent on making the British mind their own business.

The causes of this tension were multiple. Time and again, though, we learn two basic facts from British citizens; from British and American government officials; from American soldiers abroad (both Black and White); and even from contemporary government-issued literature and propaganda: first, that Black Americans could expect to be treated far better in Britain than they were in America; second, that White Americans abroad were perceived as treating all Black individuals—whether their American military brethren or British citizens and immigrants—in a racially abusive manner. A Black soldier stationed in London in 1943 might very reasonably have feared stumbling into a group of White American G.I.s on the very streets where British men and women had welcomed him with open arms. He would then be expected to risk his life in Germany to defend the very Jim Crow system that the US government saw fit to transport with the military across the Atlantic.

In *A Welcome to Britain*, the remarkable 1943 short film directed by Anthony Asquith under the supervision of the MOI and the US Office of War Information, the narrator (Burgess Meredith) directly confronts the controversial topic of race relations. The film is one of many similar propaganda documents designed to orient American soldiers to British life and culture. In a most extraordinary sequence, Meredith and a Black G.I. are seen departing a train car, on which remains an elderly British woman who wishes them goodbye and, while shaking the hand of the Black man, invites them both to her house in Birmingham. When the Black man moves off-screen to buy some cigarettes, a winking Meredith practically whispers:

> Now look men, you heard that conversation. That's not unusual here, it's the sort of thing that happens quite a lot. Now let's be frank about it. There are colored soldiers as well as White here, and there are less social restrictions in this country. Just what you heard, an English woman asking a colored boy to tea, she was polite about it, and he was polite about it. Now, look that might not happen at home, but the . . . the point

---

[21] Antonia Lant considers how contemporary British films showed Anglo-American romantic entanglements: "Ideologically speaking, the 'capture' of an American female by a British male was a narrative 'victory,' while an American male's 'capture' of a British woman was a loss. . . . A foreign woman could be absorbed into the British nation, but a native man could not be lost from it" (*Blackout: Reinventing Women for Wartime British Cinema* [Princeton, NJ: Princeton University Press, 1991], 213).

is, we're not at home, and the point is too, if we bring a lot of prejudices here, what are we gonna do about em?

At this point, Meredith is distracted by the arrival at the train station of General John C. H. Lee, who has "a lot of colored troops under him, and they're doing a big job over here." After telling us that Lee's family comes from Kansas and that his family fought for the Confederacy, Meredith says, "Let's go see what he says." At this point both Meredith and the Black soldier salute Lee and explain that they are wondering how Lee himself feels about "him and me." Lee then reads from cue cards the following lines:

> America has promised the Negro real citizenship, and a fair chance to make the best of himself. When the army needs Americans to fight for the country, it takes Negroes along with Whites. Everyone is treated the same when it comes to dying. And so the army wouldn't be true to America if it didn't try to live up to the promises about an equal chance.

"You mean we have to get over our prejudices," a bewildered Meredith asks. The smiling General then responds:

> You don't get over a prejudice that easily. There's no use pretending we're different from what we are. But we can try to live up to our American promises. I'd go further in saying, we can't do less and still feel ourselves patriots. We have promised to respect each other, all of us. That's one of the reasons that makes our world worth fighting for.

When the General salutes and departs, an impressed Meredith stays behind with his fellow American soldier, and the two men help to light each other's cigarettes.

The sequence constitutes a well-meaning attempt both to forge solidarity and to coach White soldiers into behaving properly while in Britain. Striking is the degree to which the film seems intended for White American soldiers only; the "men" that Meredith whispers to throughout are encouraged to think about their own relationships with African Americans. And in his discourse on the equality with which Black and White soldiers are treated abroad, Lee, as the spokesperson for the US Army, conveniently ignores both the fact of segregation and the ongoing abuses of Black soldiers that the sequence is intended to address.

Moreover, the MOI's central role in the production of the film raises the question of why the sequence on Black G.I.s abroad was included in the first place. Was the American Army invested of its own accord in protecting Black soldiers and enforcing appropriate behavior? Or was the Army, in promoting the message of this sequence, responding to the many British complaints about the Army's treatment of these men? One reason that the latter explanation is more likely is that none of the published books issued to arriving G.I.s, such as *Instructions for American Servicemen in Britain* (1942) and *A Short Guide to Great Britain* (1942), bothered to bring up the topic of race at all. It's true that these guides focus in more general ways on the importance of solidarity in the face of Hitler's murderous regime, and ethnic differences sometimes come up as a volatile issue, but the color line never does. For example, Americans are warned not to think of the British as "Redcoats who fought against us in the American Revolution,"[22] and Irish-Americans are instructed to avoid thinking of the British as their persecutors.[23] "It is by causing misunderstanding over these minor differences that Hitler hopes to make his propaganda effective," the soldiers are told.[24] Here the logic is clear enough, but it fails as usual to extend to the Black soldier, making the Asquith film even more of an exception to a general rule. If the Americans were willing to permit the MOI's engagement of the issue in 1943, the reason was a growing consensus among British observers that the situation was becoming intolerable, even dangerous. As historian Graham Smith points out, "Few in power realized how the Black presence in Britain would affect almost every government department, almost every facet of British life and almost every aspect of Anglo-American relations."[25]

Although Black soldiers constituted only about ten percent of the total number of G.I.s in Britain, their presence was something of a lightning rod for Anglo-American relations.[26] In addition, Black Britons faced an increase in racially motivated hostilities as a result of American troop arrivals. One member of the Colonial Office even recommended that "our Colonial coloured people" wear a badge to signal to US soldiers that they are Britons, not Black Americans,[27] an idea quickly dismissed by colleagues upon whom the irony of his suggestion was not lost. The Office's general conclusion was that any attempt to "educate" the Americans on the issue of race would cause enormous resentment.[28] So while American Whites continued to find

---

[22]*A Short Guide to Great Britain* (Washington, DC: War and Navy Departments, 1942), 1–2.
[23]*Instructions for American Servicemen in Britain, 1942* (Oxford: Bodleian Library, 1942), 3–4.
[24]Ibid.
[25]Smith qtd. in Hervieux, *Forgotten*, 164.
[26]In *Which People's War?*, Rose quotes the sociologist Kenneth Lindsay Little's admission that "I have . . . become somewhat depressed at the poor state of what I may call Anglo-Colonial relations. . . . I have never had any doubt that a very great improvement could be brought about if the Government and others concerned would adopt a more imaginative and even a more constructive attitude towards the implications which arise simply out of the question of 'colour'" (263).
[27]Rose, *Which People's War?*, 248.
[28]We would be remiss in failing to acknowledge that British racism was, of course, its own real problem. Even if the Brits implemented the "colour bar" in dance halls and restaurants because of the Yanks, they nevertheless implemented a color bar (see Rose, *Which People's War?*, 245). And there was a certain amount of predictable hysteria in Britain about racial mixing especially involving Black G.I.'s and White British women (Ibid., 258). While the specific problem we're

"the lack of 'proper' racial awareness in Britain appalling,"[29] and Black American soldiers continued to understand during their time in Britain how relatively awful their position back home really was,[30] George Orwell could declare confidently that "The general consensus of opinion seems to be that the only American soldiers with decent manners are the Negroes."[31] Whereas the Americans would continue to criticize the immorality of British colonial policy while sanctioning ever more racism toward Blacks, the British would continue to identify "racist practices with the United States, Germany, and South Africa" while somehow downplaying the centrality of race in both their own home country and their colonies.[32] In the end, even as the problems and the hypocrisies became more glaring, little was done by either government to curb them; according to Rose:

> The Foreign Office . . . was concerned that long-term diplomatic ties between the United States and Britain would be damaged if situations resulted that rankled the Americans. The Foreign Office, in fact, hoped to use the American presence as a way to strengthen these ties, and to instil in the Americans a positive opinion and appreciation for the British, just as the Colonial Office hoped to do with the colonials in the United Kingdom. The reluctance by members of the Government to directly confront the Americans about their treatment of Black Britons was even greater when it came to how White Americans treated their Black countrymen. The War Office was not just reluctant to call the Americans to task, it hoped that the government might issue instructions to encourage the British to accommodate American segregationist attitudes and practices.[33]

In short, lots of concern, much gnashing of teeth, and no real action. Contemporary progressives could see the problem, but few of those in power could identify a solution for it, especially while the two nations remained so entangled in the war effort. This state of affairs would lead many contemporary thinkers to place greater emphasis on the future, on the dream of real change in the arena of social justice once the war had ended—and it would culminate in an explosion, arguably the greatest period of progressive change in British or American history. At least theoretically, such an investment in social justice would have to extend beyond each nation's own peoples to include those impacted for so long by their own foreign

---

tracing here was largely defined by the racist behavior of White G.I.s, in other words, the larger problem of racism very much remained an "Anglo-Saxon" one.
[29]Hervieux, *Forgotten*, 171.
[30]Ibid., 172.
[31]Qtd. in ibid., 155.
[32]Rose, *Which People's War?*, 258.
[33]Ibid., 252.

and colonial policies. Brogan's idea that the American problem had become the problem "of all free peoples in the modern world" seemed suddenly persuasive not just to a progressive minority but to huge swaths of voting citizens throughout the free world (55). Suddenly, it had become "possible to believe that the kind of devotion and energy which the nation-state had evoked could be transferred, without serious loss in transit, to a new world community, whether that community was interpreted in terms of class, race, religion, or the whole mass of men of good will" (166). It was precisely within this environment of possibility that *AMOLAD* was commissioned, produced, and eventually released into the world.

"A Deliberate Bridge from War into Peace"

Scholarly commentaries on the politics of *AMOLAD* have tended to follow one of two general directions. A first group—taking its cue from certain contemporary film reviewers[34]—questions whether the film's embrace of fantasy or surrealism constitutes an eschewal of politics. Philip Horne, for example, believes it valid to regard "the propaganda commission more as a pretext for Powell and Pressburger, as artists, to construct an elaborate world of fantasy and romance, perhaps a model of the relations between the living and the dead 'in the mind of a young airman.'"[35] Whereas Horne praises The Archers for their choice of art over politics, some contemporary reviewers lambasted them for rejecting the realist filmmaking mode.[36] As we take up in relation to *One of Our Aircraft Is Missing* (1942), Powell had always bragged about The Archers' freedom from the strictures of realist cinema. In this regard, he viewed *AMOLAD* as the true turning point for The Archers in the 1940s, the moment when the scales tipped from a more realist style interrupted by flashes of surrealism to a style that could be called even anti-realist: "Film was what I had always thought it was—wonderful fantasies superimposed upon life. For me from then on, there was no more realism in films, only surrealism."[37] Although Powell is characteristically exaggerating the degree to which The Archers would leave behind realism (as we discuss in the *Aircraft* chapter), he does describe fairly accurately *AMOLAD*'s relatively greater commitment to fantasy in comparison with The Archers' other wartime films. Because realist cinematic modes were so

---

[34]See Macdonald for an example of such reviews (*Emeric Pressburger*, 257).
[35]Philip Horne, "Life and Death in *A Matter of Life and Death*," *The Cinema of Michael Powell: International Perspectives on an English Film-Maker*, ed. Ian Christie and Andrew Moor (London: BFI, 2005), 117–31, 118.
[36]Christie discusses these mainly leftist reviews on 61–2 of *A Matter*.
[37]Powell, *A Life*, 592.

closely tied to the documentary film movement, and increasingly tethered to Labour politics and ideals (especially regarding the topic of the postwar settlement), it's easy to see why critics have mistaken Powell's surrealist turn as an outright rejection of politics, an escapist fantasy. As we shall see, even the romantic-comedy ending of *AMOLAD*, which such critics viewed as the major proof of the film's rejection of politics, was, in fact, the logical culmination of a political film.

A second group of critics—responding directly to the harsh assessment of The Archers' right-wing nemeses, E. W. and M. M. Robson—works to characterize the Other World in relation to contemporary models of state governance, or even to certain specific states such as Nazi Germany. According to the Robsons' characteristically inscrutable logic, *AMOLAD*'s "naked German-Nazi-Fascist philosophy" is most evident in the Other World, which they assume represents The Archers' version of the Christian concept of Heaven: "Is this how Powell-Pressburger would like Heaven to be, a Heaven presided over by a Brunhilda type godess straight from Wagner's *Nibelungen Saga*, who rules over and commands a dead slave population in exactly the same way as Hitler ruled his slaves?"[38] Taking their cue in part from the American re-titling *Stairway to Heaven*, which Powell lambasted openly and regularly,[39] and also ignoring entirely the fact that the Other World is merely the fantastic conjuration of a brain-injured soldier, the Robsons argue that Powell and Pressburger's heaven is a "Perfect Nazi Paradise."[40] That this so-called Paradise is filmed in a drab monochrome film stock; that it exists as a consequence of trauma, both mental and physical; that it is rejected by Peter and the film alike in favor of life in England: all of this is ignored to serve the Robsons' arguments about the existence of a covertly fascist British film industry.[41] Their hysteria about *AMOLAD* grows out of the film's willingness to criticize outdated British attitudes, practices, and institutions, and their own unwillingness to hear any such criticism—regardless of how it is intended or how accurate it may be—leads them into an interpretive quagmire.

Better critics have followed the Robsons in analyzing the Other World as a representation of contemporary models of governance—but they have drawn nearly opposite conclusions. Nicholas Pronay, for example, makes a brilliant case for the Other World as the representation of the radical "planned

---

[38] E. W. and M. M. Robson, *The World is My Cinema* (London: Sidneyan Society, 1947), 68.
[39] Powell says not only that "heaven" is the wrong word for the Other World; he also spends two pages of the autobiography mocking the sort of "American salesmanship" that would try to suppress "the realities of life and death" less than a year after the end of the most devastating war in human history (*A Life*, 487).
[40] Robson and Robson, *The World*, 70.
[41] Especially relevant here is the thoroughly international nature of the film industry and especially of The Archers' crew. See our Introduction and Chapter 2.

societies" that so many wartime leftist documentary films were advocating; he argues that Powell and Pressburger rejected the documentarists' vision of the future, an idea that follows Raymond Durgnat's more famous claim that *AMOLAD* is actually an "anti-Socialist" film.[42] Both Durgnat and Pronay fall prey to something like confirmation bias here, assuming that because Powell and Pressburger have identified with High Tory positions in the past, *AMOLAD* must necessarily be more conservative than it is. Durgnat says, for example, that "The myth of Powell as a 'mindless eye' overlooks explicit ideological positions like the High Tory moral of *A Matter of Life and Death*."[43] But what arguments like Durgnat's miss, as really only Andrew Moor has acknowledged before us,[44] is that the film's Toryism has been badly overstated. Quite openly, the film tells us that Peter's wartime experience has changed his politics, for although he is "Conservative by nature," he is "Labour by experience," having undergone a personal trajectory that Pronay admits was exceedingly common during the war years: "by the close of World War II, significant sections of the British people had been treated to visions of a grandiose post-war Utopia which exceeded anything promised during World War I. . . . Moreover, it had been given a clear and specific party-political identification: if you want this wonderful future, you can only have it if you vote Labour."[45] Far from representing a future society built on the foundation of Labour Party promises, *AMOLAD*'s deliberately drab and fiercely hierarchical Other World epitomizes quite traditional values and stereotypes. That Powell and Pressburger so emphatically reject the Other World in favor of Technicolor splendor, and all the chaos and unpredictability of the living world, suggests the degree to which the wartime experience has, at least momentarily, checked their natural instincts toward conservatism.

"We're Living in the Twentieth Century, Not in the Eighteenth"

AMOLAD's opening credit sequence is followed immediately by scrolling captions which read as follows: "This is a story of / two Worlds / the one

---

[42]See Nicholas Pronay, "'The Land of Promise': The Projection of Peace Aims in Britain," *Film and Radio Propaganda in World War II*, ed. K. R. M. Short (Knoxville, TN: University of Tennessee Press, 1983), 51–77; and Durgnat, "Durgnat on Powell and Pressburger," *Powell Pressburger and Others*, ed. Ian Christie (London: BFI 1978), 65–74, 66.
[43]Ibid., 66.
[44]Andrew Moor, *Powell & Pressburger: A Cinema of Magic Spaces*, 2nd ed. (London and New York): I.B. Tauris, 2012), 144.
[45]Pronay, "'The Land of Promise,'" 54.

we know / and another / which exists only / in the mind / of a young airman / whose life & imagination / have been / violently shaped by war. / *Any resemblance / to any other world / known or unknown / is purely coincidental.*" A slow pan left and a male voice-over (John Longden) then lead the viewer through a disembodied tour of the universe—stars, solar systems, galaxies, and all. A nova, which the voice describes as an entire solar system that has exploded, is the first object that really captures our speaker's interest: "somebody must have been messing about with the uranium atom." The voice is almost whimsical. How are we to regard this joke about the American atomic bombs that killed several hundred thousand people in Hiroshima and Nagasaki a year before the film's release and just a month before shooting began? The speaker breathes a sigh of relief, noting that it's fortunately not "our" solar system we're looking at. The pan continues, and the voice sounds yet more relieved when "the moon, our moon" and "the earth, our earth" both come solidly into view. They are "part of the pattern," he tells us, stressing how "reassuring" this fact should be to us, just as this reassurance is undermined by the nondiegetic sounds of chords and cymbals complementing diegetic explosions as we are forced into a "night over Europe" on May 2, 1945. This is the very night that Peter Carter will be forced to jump from his bomber without a parachute.

In the space of this roughly two-and-a-half-minute sequence, and no less than three times during it, the film establishes a clear pattern of harmony disrupted by violence. First, in the captions, where the life and imagination of a young man are "violently shaped by war"; second, in the shift from solar system to nova, and the admission that humanity now possesses the ability to destroy entire worlds; and finally, in the disruption of a reassuring, universal orderliness by the sounds, and eventually the sight, of war over Europe. Violence, more specifically human warfare, is repeatedly depicted as destroying a peaceful, foundational natural harmony. The utopian potentiality of this elusive harmony is punctuated multiple times by the speaker's emphasis on the plural possessive adjective: *our* universe, *our* moon, *our* Earth. War is thereby constructed in specifically negative terms, as unnatural and disorderly, as anti-imaginative as well as destructive, and most important, as an existential threat to every single person on the planet. What might the world look like, the sequence asks somewhat more optimistically, albeit indirectly, if war were someday to end?

AMOLAD's focus on the postwar future has been largely neglected by scholars, who have preferred to meditate on the film's complex investment in the historical and literary achievements of a glorious British past.[46] Peter's rapid-fire quotations of English poetry in the bomber scene establish a foundation for the film's systematic embrace of high-culture references and

---

[46]See Note 4.

allusions, which, indeed, seem designed to establish British and American union as "a marriage of past and future greatness."[47] A shallow reading of the film, though, might easily overlook the fact that future greatness in no way depends exclusively on overvaluing traditional values and achievements—however important these may be. (In this way, *AMOLAD* resembles *A Canterbury Tale* in both celebrating tradition and recognizing the need to reform aspects of it.) Rather, the film constantly uses the past as proof of Britain and America's ability to lead the way forward, to embrace the cutting edge of historical change and progress.

In their first scene together, Peter reveals to June his fantasy of an Other World after death: "What do you think the next world's like? I've got my own ideas. I think it starts where this one leaves off, or where this one could leave off if we listened to Plato and Aristotle and Jesus, with all our little earthly problems solved, but with greater ones worth the solving." On the one hand, Peter holds up three of the great thinkers of the past in positing a dream vision of the future; on the other hand, he acknowledges that their philosophies have not yet been successfully understood or implemented. *AMOLAD* may suggest that the past holds the keys to progress, but it is careful not to bog itself down in a misleading or downright dangerous nostalgia; in spite of its deep reverence for true historical triumphs, there's no "make Britain and/or America great again" message to be found within its 104-minute running time.

When we actually see the Other World, it contains some traces of Peter's fantasy (it *is* a hallucination, after all),[48] but with all the limitations and distortions we would expect from a brain-injured patient who, because of June, suddenly wishes to live. The Other World is neither the fascist

---

[47]Semenza and Hasenfratz, *The History of British Literature*, 3.
[48]In respecting the film's own claim that "This is a story of . . . another [World] which exists *only in the mind* of a young airman" (our italics), we mean in no way to ignore *AMOLAD*'s deliberate smudging of the lines between Peter's imagined world and the real world he actually inhabits. As John Ellis has noted, "reviewers do not accord an absolute subjective status to the Other World sequences" because of the ways in which the film manipulates realist cinematic language and conventions ("Watching Death at Work: An Analysis of *A Matter of Life and Death*," *Powell Pressburger and Others*, ed. Ian Christie [London: BFI 1978], 79–104, 97). Indeed, certain elements of the film cannot be easily explained by that opening caption. For example, how should we understand the disembodied, God-like voice-over narration that opens the film, establishes the relative triviality of earthly issues, and presents the possibility of truths and even of conscious intelligences that greatly surpass anything known on Earth? How are we to read the many surreal images and events that occur in the so-called real world, such as the presence of the naked, flute-playing boy on the beach; Peter and June's convenient meeting and immediate, passionate love for one another; or Peter's miraculous survival of a jump from a burning plane? It's not that we cannot rationalize these contradictory or confusing elements if we work hard enough to do so; it's more that Powell and Pressburger remain so committed to making us work at all. Nonetheless, the film clearly defines the Other World's status as a project of Peter's imagination.

FIGURE 8.1 *The majestic—and also bureaucratic—Other World of* A Matter of Life and Death *(1946).*

concentration camp preposterously theorized by the Robsons, nor the quasi-socialist bureaucracy proposed by Durgnat and Pronay. The Other World is monochrome and sleek, clean and highly organized, but it's hardly totalitarian. The dead pilots who enter the Air Crew Section respond as individuals will do. They seem to be doing what they want to do, saying what they want to say, and many of them feel that they are finally where they have always wanted to be. After a division of American Air Force pilots comes skipping into the space, to the precise rhythms of the film's suddenly upbeat score, they eagerly grab Cokes from a machine; one excited young man remarks, "Boy, oh boy, home was nothing like this," prompting another to note, "Mine was." In both cases, the sight of the Other World seems to be welcome, albeit for completely different reasons[49] (Figure 8.1).

We also see immediate signs of a world that, in some ways, seems more progressive than the one the boys have left behind. The person in charge

---

[49]The second man's "Mine was" could perhaps be read in opposing ways—as either sentimental longing for home or a half-admission of some past familial trauma. Furthermore, the fact that Peter himself chooses to shun the very Other World he has created suggests that world's limitations. A usefully relevant contemporary intertext is Basil Dearden's *They Came to a City* (1944), based on the play by J. B. Priestley, in which the mysterious city discovered by nine different Britons is regarded by each of them as either a heaven or a hell.

of admitting new airmen is a young woman (Kathleen Byron), setting us up for the eventual reveal of another, older woman (Joan Maude) who is the "Chief Recorder" of all admissions into the Other World. When one energetic American airman (Bonar Colleano) asks the former woman about the location of the Officers' Quarters, she explains that "We're all the same up here, Captain." And, moments later, she explains to Peter's concerned crewmember Bob Trubshaw (Robert Coote), who has already become infatuated with her, that "Everyone on earth has a file: Russian, Chinese, Black or White, rich or poor, Republican or Democrat." Rather than being a clear analogue for any earthly political model, the Other World is the violently interrupted, and so woefully incomplete, projection of Peter's optimistic faith in a superior afterlife of harmony, peace, and reassuring orderliness.

The Other World, Peter's fantasy world, is imperfect precisely because Peter has fallen in love with June's voice. Prior to doing so, he is not only prepared to die; he is eager to do so. Powell and Pressburger deliberately insert into the burning cockpit of the bomber a protagonist who is driven above all else by something akin to the classic Freudian death drive.[50] Having flown nearly seventy missions, and knowing of many men in his position who have died—including his own father in the First World War, and now his own crew members and close friends—Peter's rhapsodic, adrenaline-infused quotations of carpe diem poetry and his uninhibited embrace of visceral emotions, especially toward June, suggest the degree to which he is already leaving this world behind him. But nature won't cooperate. Somehow he lives. One of the most common of the earthly problems Peter refers to earlier is love, of course, and we might surmise that now that Peter is experiencing it, he's less keen on leaving those problems behind. His death drive is replaced by a desire not only to live but also to shape the earth into a more ideal realm. At the same time, in the character of Frank Reeves, Powell and Pressburger present another man—in this case, an older one whose survivor's guilt is most likely due to the fact that he stayed home during the war—whose death drive is at least as pronounced as Peter's initially is. We see this each time Reeves hops onto his motorcycle, speeding maniacally and

---

[50]Sullivan builds the case that "Peter's love for June introduces a powerful counterpressure to his desire for death" ("More Than Cool Reason," 378). Interestingly, one of the film's earliest audience members, Eric Warman—charged with adapting the film to novel form for the Royal Command Film Performance—could also see Peter's conviction that he should be dead: "A strange exhilaration swept over the airman as his gaze took in the scene. To be alone in this rocking inferno, and with the inevitable end in sight, fired his senses. There was even a strange beauty in it, and the hopelessness of his position relieved him of any necessity for action" (Warman, *A Matter of Life and Death* [London: World Film Publications, 1946], 8).

unflinchingly across ditches and around bending, narrow roads.[51] Eventually his rides will kill him, thereby giving his character a new sense of purpose in an afterlife where his service to Britain and, indirectly, to the United States will take the form of his role as Peter's defense counsel. Whereas the Other World is, for Peter, who has suppressed his death drive, an incomplete one, it will be for Frank, Peter imagines, a place to thrive and triumph.

No longer wishing to leave the world behind him, Peter constructs an afterlife that still conforms in ways to his romantic beliefs, but numerous cracks and defects reveal themselves. They begin to do so with the absence of color, of course—the first and most obvious sign that all is not right in this "heaven"—and they are most humorously revealed in Conductor 71's error of losing Peter in the English fog, but there is much more. Alongside the magisterial stairway to heaven, for example, perfectly spaced statues of great historical figures capture precisely the sort of celebration of cultural traditions that Peter envisions for his afterlife. The Other World, indeed, begins where our world ends, with Plato and Jesus and Muhammad; at the same time, these are men of stone, and Peter knows instinctively that although he could choose Aristotle or Richelieu as his defense counsel, they would not be capable of serving him. This is not only because his "little earthly problems" have not yet been solved, but also because, as Frank will later note, "We're living in the twentieth century, not in the eighteenth." As Peter says to Conductor 71, "Look, it sounds a grand idea to have all these great men to choose from, but what do they know of our problems today?" Peter suggests here that present-day problems can be solved only by men such as Reeves, a man who epitomizes present-day wisdom.

The trial scene also does much to reinforce the point that this world is not Peter's vision of a perfect utopia: although we're all apparently "the same up here," the crowd at the trial is shown to be starkly divided, *segregated* really, into large, separate groups of British Revolutionary War soldiers, American pilgrims, Red Cross nurses, Napoleonic soldiers, Second World War Indian soldiers, (White) US air force pilots, Boers, USO girls, and Black American soldiers, to name just a few.[52] On the one hand, Peter's projection is thoroughly progressive and international (Muhammad stands beside Plato, and Black soldiers enjoy seats as close to the action as do the White soldiers); on the other hand, large fissures still exist, and they continue to drive wedges between souls. To reiterate the key point about Peter's hallucinatory invention: although he voices in the bomber scene a hope for an ideal Other World, in his sickness, after falling in love with June

---

[51]John Ellis may miss this point when he argues that "There is no real need to show Reeves' journey" other than to point out his recklessness ("Watching Death," 89).
[52]The film goes so far as to explain that "Front rows have been preserved for those who have a special interest in the case."

and somehow surviving his jump, he conjures into existence an Other World that falls short of, even as it realizes some aspects of, that same ideal.

No individual figure represents the incompleteness of the Other World better than Abraham Farlan, whose deep but provincial historical nostalgia, isolationism, nationalism, and bigotry ("America, sir, is the only place where man is full grown"), not only hilariously emblematize British stereotypes of White Americans, but also illustrate the ways in which this afterlife fails to match Peter's standard of a world that begins where our earthly problems leave off. On the contrary, Farlan is the embodiment of those conservative values Peter has learned through experience to distrust. He is also the embodiment of a man too stuck in the past. In addition to Farlan's inadvertently progressive critique of British imperialism, he bases most of his disdain for Britain on trivial cultural differences between it and the United States—precisely the sort of differences the government-issued manuals for US soldiers addressed. In his inability to forgive the British for their love of cricket, their warm beer, and their faulty plumbing, he shows himself to be the uneducated American rather than the new, more worldly one the propaganda was attempting to cultivate. He is open to criticism of American culture only when subjected to the R&B song popularized by the Andrews Sisters, "Shoo Shoo Baby," presented here in the voice of a male singer, and specifically coded as African American; as the song plays and Farlan expresses his disgust, a couple of the seated Black soldiers are shown nodding along in approval.[53] Conversely, the only time Farlan proves willing to acknowledge British cultural achievements is when he concedes that Shakespeare and Milton are among the world's greatest poets.

These exchanges become more politically barbed as Peter's brain operation becomes more complicated and potentially deadly. Recognizing the logic underlying Farlan's rhetorical method of criticizing British imperialism, Reeves calls him out: "You are trying to prejudice the jury, sir. I see that they have been selected from many races, creeds, and nationalities. I cannot believe them interested in ancient grudges against Peter Carter's ancestors, nor in present grumblings about drafty windows." Like all those government-issued propaganda manuals for foreigners, Reeves attempts here to redirect the diverse jury away from the political crises and cultural stereotypes staining Britain's past by focusing them squarely on a future that modern Britain is making possible by leading the international fight against fascism and Nazism. Reeves will eventually win Peter's case by investing in that jury's ability to see how a future predicated on faith in love can trump one unnecessarily tied to the past, with all its wars, divisions, and enmity.

---

[53] "Shoo Shoo Baby" was a 1944 song written by Phil Moore about a man leaving his family to join the Navy.

Farlan fails to anticipate Reeves's counterargument until it is too late. To Reeves's accusations, he snaps back:

> I don't need to prejudice the jury, sir. They're already prejudiced against your country, and with good reason. You can't pick a jury that isn't. Look closely at the distinguished members of the jury, sir. [*These members include a Frenchman, a Boer, a Russian (Crimean War), a Chinese man (the British attack on Peking in 1857), an Indian, and an Irishman.*] Choose a new jury anywhere, Dr. Reeves. It will always be prejudiced against your country.

Farlan here offers the stereotypical American complaint against British imperialism and, as Reeves's answer will reveal, he does so with no self-awareness regarding American hypocrisy about its own crimes against numerous national, ethnic, and racial groups. Reeves baits Farlan by asking where, other than in Britain, "the rights of the individual [have] been held so high?" When Farlan shouts, "In America, sir, where these rights are held to be inalienable," Reeves knowingly replies, "I doubt that you have more practical freedom in America than in England." The line seems especially poignant in light of the numerous Black US soldiers in attendance at the trial; they are segregated in their own rows like the other groups but, in this case, that fact serves as a constant reminder of the legacy of Jim Crow. Tellingly, Reeves then requests that he be permitted to replace the assigned jury with a new one composed entirely of Americans. The jingoist Farlan, of course, excitedly welcomes the swap[54] (Figure 8.2).

In doing so, Farlan almost certainly envisions the new jury in precisely the same way most of Powell and Pressburger's contemporary audiences must have done: as an all-White group of men ready to protect their women from the machinations of a British serviceman (and, indirectly, to protect America from Britain). But in selecting a jury of "Americans, sir, selected from every walk of American life," Reeves exploits the remarkable diversity of America: "If there is one who has fought in the wars of independence, I want one who has fought shoulder to shoulder with us against our common enemies in this century. If the third has a mind that can only think 170 years back, I want the fourth to be thinking 170 years ahead." Stressing through Reeves the importance of diverse experiences, as well as the need to balance historical appreciation and a focus on the future, the film employs a series of dissolve shots that transform the original international jury into a new one of similarly diverse but all-American members. Each individual then

---

[54]It seems worth highlighting the point that the fictional Abraham Farlan can be viewed as replacing the first man actually killed in the American revolution, the Black former slave, Crispus Attucks.

FIGURE 8.2 *The diverse American jury of* A Matter of Life and Death *(1946)*.

introduces himself and shares a name and national identity: a Chinese American introduces himself as "George Wong, American citizen." An African American man introduces himself as "Jefferson Lincoln Brown, American citizen" (at this point, Powell inserts a shot of the Black soldiers seated in the audience).[55] "Patrick Aloysius Mahoney, American citizen" introduces himself to close out the sequence. By explicitly paralleling the crimes of British (international) imperialism and American (national) racism and prejudice, the film draws together two issues crucial to British and US tensions at the time of the film. Here, in turning old divisions into new strengths, in celebrating rather than lamenting human diversity, the film suggests a way forward for the special relationship.[56]

While the opening of the film dramatizes the constant threat to order and harmony posed by numerous forms of violence, the ending seeks to sustain a new utopian vision by confirming that love is real and positing it as the ground zero of earthly harmony. To return to a point made in this chapter's opening, the genre of romantic comedy is absolutely crucial to the success

---

[55] The man's name alludes, of course, to both the principal author of the US Declaration of Independence (Jefferson) and the so-called "Great Emancipator" (Lincoln). A bitter irony almost certainly lost on Powell and Pressburger would have been Jefferson's ownership of hundreds of Black slaves.

[56] The film's representation of American diversity, it is important to note, does not include women jurors. American women were already regularly serving on juries in many states by the 1930s.

of this particular maneuver as the film's progressive propaganda claims are advanced within a familiar and entirely predictable (not to mention lighthearted) narrative pattern whose trajectory is predetermined. Romantic comedy also happens to be a cinematic genre whose basic structure and themes are perfectly in sync with those claims. As scholars have established, the rom-com grows out of an ancient literary tradition, though one reshaped largely by Shakespeare's dramatic comedies, in which the passions and promise of youth are allowed primacy over the reason-bound strictures of age and tradition: "When the Shakespearian couple unites," Sarah Kozloff argues, "their union serves as a birth of a new, better society, the triumph of spring over winter."[57] The same is true, of course, of Peter and June's victory over death at the end of *AMOLAD*. The film's final emphasis on true love also reconfigures human passions as a potential solution to the world's problems rather than the threat they represent in the film's opening voice-over tour of the universe. In the opening, the narrator emphasizes the laws of the universe that humanity constantly disrupts, even thwarts. In the trial scenes, Farlan lectures Reeves that "In the whole universe, nothing is stronger than the law"; after successfully proving that Peter and June love each other truly, though, Reeves can confidently reply, "Yes, Mr. Farlan, nothing is stronger than the law in the universe, but on earth, nothing is stronger than love." The exchange returns us to the same issues of scale introduced by the opening: whereas that scene guides us across the universe, into our own solar system, to our own planet, and then into Peter's bomber, before finally allowing us into his head, the ending insists on the power of both Peter's (i.e., the individual's) imagination and his interpersonal relationships to impact the very laws of the universe.[58] In any case, buoyed by the strength of their love, June and Peter passionately embrace before the inhabitants of the Other World who suddenly appear before us in vibrant Technicolor—as if illustrating that falling in love has led Peter to revise his fantasy of the ideal afterlife. This ideal now doesn't involve leaving the so-called small problems such as love behind but, instead, makes room for them because they are bound up in, and inseparable from, the bigger

---

[57]Sarah Kozloff, "Romantic Comedy," *Introduction to Film Genres*, ed. Lester Friedman, et al. (New York and London: Norton, 2013), 121–59, 121. In advancing this argument about the seasonal pattern of comedy, Kozloff is, of course, following Northrop Frye's famous discussion of the four major mythoi in *Anatomy of Criticism: Four Essays* (Princeton, NJ: Princeton University Press, 1957).
[58]This callback to the opening might also partly explain the functionality of the film's deliberate smudging of the line between the real and the imagined (see Note 48), precisely by illustrating the ways in which the individual is posed as the minute inhabitant and the god-like creator—as well as the potential destroyer—of worlds. For more on issues of scale in *AMOLAD*, see Garrett A. Sullivan, Jr., "'Bottom's Not A Gangster!': *A Matter of Life and Death* (1946), *A Midsummer Night's Dream* and Postwar Anglo-American Relations," *Shakespeare and British World War Two Film* (Cambridge: Cambridge University Press, 2022), 136–70.

problems such as war and, specifically, postwar Anglo-American relations. In the film's final moments, as Peter embraces June in the hospital bed where he is recovering from his successful surgery, his last words, "We won," have multiple meanings. They refer to the trial victory, to the union of British and American lovers, and to the victory of the Allied forces against their enemies. As the sun shines through the window onto Peter and June in the film's final shots, the audience can rest assured that spring has triumphed over winter.

In their final wartime film, then, Powell and Pressburger demonstrate their commitment to the propaganda imperative issued by Beddington to tell a story that might "improve Anglo-American relations." As was typically the case with The Archers' wartime films, though, *AMOLAD* manages to explore a subject important to British national interests without allowing that imperative to dictate the terms of their argument or the contours of their artistry. While making the case for the value of an Anglo-American alliance well beyond the end of the war, *AMOLAD* also is bold enough— and realistic enough— to suggest an ideological way forward for both countries, refusing to settle for shallow reassurances about America and Britain's historical friendship.[59] Focused squarely on the future, Powell and Pressburger advocate in *AMOLAD* a progressive policy position, preparing Britain—and perhaps its US ally—for the postwar consensus which would launch one of the great expansions of social welfare policy in world history, and gradually advance the decolonization of the British Empire. While Sue Harper is, of course, correct that *AMOLAD* is committed to the idea of Britain and America's "common history and their shared definition of culture," the film's true emphasis is on a *future* alliance rooted in progressive policies of equality and the rights of *every* individual.

---

[59]Another British film of the previous year, Anthony Asquith's *The Way to the Stars* (1945), had negotiated the Anglo-American relationship in a similarly honest and sophisticated way. It seems worth noting here, though, the almost certain influence of another 1940s supernatural/ fantasy war film on The Archers' future-focused thinking in *AMOLAD*; in Victor Fleming's Hollywood hit of 1943, *A Guy Named Joe*, a dead bomber pilot played by Spencer Tracy becomes the guardian angel of a younger pilot and romantic rival for his grieving girlfriend's affections. In the film's crucial speech, designed to focus Tracy's character on the necessity of looking forward, not lingering in the past, The General (Lionel Barrymore) expostulates that "That's what we're fighting for. . . . The freedom of mankind rushing to greet the future on wings. . . . No man is really dead unless he breaks faith with the future, and no man is really alive unless he accepts his responsibility to it. That's the chance we're giving you here—the opportunity to pay off to the future what you owe for having been part of the past. . . . You thought you were choosing between life and death when you flew in over that carrier, but you weren't. You're choosing between 'em now. It's up to you, Pete." Both films echo the sentiment of Brogan's conclusion that for Britain and America to move successfully into the future, "Understanding each other is not enough, but it is an indispensable beginning" (*The American Character*, 169).

Coda

The careers of Michael Powell and Emeric Pressburger flourished during the war.[1] In addition to developing a strong working relationship with the MOI, The Archers had a string of box office successes that earned them the trust of J. Arthur Rank, the film production, distribution, and exhibition magnate with whom they worked for much of the period. Thanks to Rank's hands-off approach, The Archers operated with a great deal of artistic freedom, and, as we have shown throughout this book, they found propaganda imperatives to be conducive to their filmmaking. Things changed, however, after the war ended. For one thing, Pressburger "stopped writing original stories." Kevin Macdonald explains the change this way: "[T]he great spur to Emeric's work was removed. What sort of films should he be now making? The certainties of propaganda had long gone. . . . The foundations upon which he had built his life for so long had collapsed. There was no longer a Nazi state to be fleeing from or fighting against."[2]

The Archers were also to lose the trust of Rank and his powerful associate John Davis. This occurred during the production of *The Red Shoes* (1948). "It was a curious situation," wrote Powell. "During the war, and subject to the Ministry of Information, we had total artistic freedom. Now that peace was here, we were to be reined in, bridled and curbed."[3] Powell overstates the case, as some of The Archers' boldest films—*The Red Shoes*, *Black Narcissus* (1947), and *Tales of Hoffmann* (1951)—came after the war. However, it is clear that peacetime brought new challenges and anxieties for the filmmakers. Moreover, in the duo's own estimation, the best films they produced during their partnership were made during the war.[4] For Pressburger, *The Life and Death of Colonel Blimp* (1943) was their greatest achievement; for Powell, *A Matter of Life and Death* (1946).

---

[1] Material from the first two paragraphs of this coda is adapted from Garrett A. Sullivan, Jr., *Shakespeare and British World War Two Film* (Cambridge: Cambridge University Press, 2022), 144.
[2] Kevin Macdonald, *Emeric Pressburger: The Life and Death of a Screenwriter* (London: Faber and Faber, 1994), 261, 258.
[3] Michael Powell, *A Life in Movies* (1986; London: Faber and Faber, 2000), 664.
[4] That partnership came to an end in 1957, although Pressburger would later write screenplays for a pair of movies directed by Powell.

Conditioned as we are by the view of The Archers as "rogue outsiders," it can be easy to forget how closely they worked with governmental authorities during the war, and how successful their films were at the box office.[5] Even more important, but just as easy to overlook, is the fact that their artistic achievements were fueled by, in Macdonald's phrase, "the certainties of propaganda." And yet, Powell and Pressburger did not approach propaganda as a vehicle for producing certainty. In *The Spy in Black* (1939), the drawing of a clear-cut distinction between national enemies is a byproduct of interpersonal betrayal; *49th Parallel* (1941), with its emphasis on Nazis on the run, was taken by some viewers to be pro-German; and *AMOLAD* contains within it a trenchant critique of British imperialism. This last example gets at something significant about Powell and Pressburger's propaganda films, which is that they are far from complacent about their own society's virtues. Even in championing British values and traditions, as in *A Canterbury Tale* (1944), The Archers demonstrate a keen awareness of where those values and traditions fall short, and where reforms are needed. For the two filmmakers, the "certainties of propaganda" leave ample space for British audiences to reflect upon their own society; their films constitute a form of democratic propaganda that both assumes and enables critical thinking.

As we have repeatedly observed, Powell and Pressburger did not find propaganda to be incommensurate with their art. In a June 1942 memo to the MOI Films Division, The Archers make this point in striking fashion. (The memo was composed in response to an MOI document articulating concerns about the script for *The Life and Death of Colonel Blimp*, at that point titled "The Life and Death of Sugar Candy." We took up both documents in Chapter 5.) The filmmakers contend that most British and American films are "self-admiring" and "easy to make. Their purpose can be seen and their effect can be judged. But it is also possible to make films for future audiences and future occasions."[6] There are three main points to draw from these assertions. First, in referring to "self-admiring" British and American films, The Archers have in mind works of cinematic propaganda that, in their view, are devoid of the complexity and nuance that characterize their own work.[7] Second, in disparaging films the purpose and effect of

---

[5]Andrew Moor, "No Place Like Home: Powell, Pressburger Utopia," *The British Cinema Book*, 3rd. ed., ed. Robert Murphy (Basingstoke: Palgrave Macmillan for the BFI, 2009), 240–6, esp. 240. On this way of characterizing The Archers, see the final section to the Introduction.

[6]Michael Powell and Emeric Pressburger, *The Life and Death of Colonel Blimp*, ed. Ian Christie (London: Faber and Faber, 1994), 36.

[7]It was likely praise for *Target for Tonight* (1941), which we discuss in Chapter 4, that prompted this irritated characterization of other films. As the MOI document puts it, "[I]t is very difficult to imagine an audience which could take 'Target for Tonight' in any other way but that intended" (Ibid., 32).

which can be easily ascertained, they put their faith in the discernment of their audience to interpret their own more sophisticated works. Finally, in "mak[ing] films for future audiences and future occasions," The Archers imagine a postwar afterlife for their work—which is to say, they are thinking about their movies as art as well as propaganda.[8] War is short, art is long. At the same time, both the war and the need for cinematic propaganda served as spurs to The Archers' filmmaking.

In concluding this study, we want to say just a few more words about The Archers, art, and propaganda. As we have noted, art and propaganda are often taken to be antithetical to one another; or, conversely, when a lack of separation between the two is posited, this is sometimes treated as counterintuitive, if not scandalous. The point is not to adjudicate between these views, but to observe that the relationship between art and propaganda is the subject of constant cultural renegotiation. In a famous essay on Charles Dickens written in 1939, George Orwell observes that "every writer, especially every novelist, *has* a 'message', whether he admits it or not, and the minutest details of his work are influenced by it. All art is propaganda.... On the other hand, not all propaganda is art."[9] Contrarily, in a 1975 review of Leni Riefenstahl's *The Last of the Nuba*, a book of photographs of an indigenous Sudanese people, Susan Sontag offers a compelling takedown of Riefenstahl's efforts to rehabilitate herself as a film artist who "resist[ed] 'Goebbels' attempt to subject her visualisation to his strictly propagandistic requirements.'"[10] In other words, as Sontag shows, the director of *Triumph of the Will* (1935) appeals to her status as an artist to whitewash her complicity in Nazi atrocities. Riefenstahl's specious gambit is predicated upon the premise that, *pace* Orwell, no art is propaganda.

In briefly considering these different ways of configuring the art-propaganda relationship, we mean to bring into sharper relief two things that we have touched upon throughout this book. First, there is the historical and cultural specificity of the situation in which Powell and Pressburger found themselves during the war, one in which they collaborated fruitfully with the MOI in producing a democratic propaganda of which they could be proud. Second, there is the masterful way in which they made the most of that situation as both artists and propagandists. However accurate The Archers' characterization of most other British and American films as

---

[8]It should be noted, however, that they support this claim by referring to the wartime reception of *49th Parallel*: released in America two years after it was first screened in Britain, it "is even more timely now than at any other period" (Ibid., 37).
[9]George Orwell, "Charles Dickens," *Collected Essays* (London: Secker and Warburg, 1961), 31–87, esp. 73.
[10]Susan Sontag, "Fascinating Fascism," *The New York Review of Books*, February 6, 1975. https://www.nybooks.com/articles/1975/02/06/fascinating-fascism/ (accessed December 19, 2022). The interpolated material is from jacket copy for *The Last of the Nuba*.

"self-admiring" exercises whose "purpose[s] can be seen and . . . effect[s] can be judged"—as, that is, unsophisticated pieces of propaganda devoid of aesthetic merit—there is no doubt that their war work sustained their artistry. Moreover, one of the objectives of this book has been to show that that artistry, while manifest in the films' formal and narrative brilliance, is also defined by the filmmakers' political and ethical commitments, which we articulate in their Program for film propaganda (see the Introduction). Powell and Pressburger produced a cosmopolitan, democratic propaganda that gained legitimacy not merely by championing British values but also by demanding more of the nation when it fell short of its own ideals. And, in the service of producing such a propaganda, they also created art "for future audiences and future occasions." Once disparaged as outsiders to their nation's cinematic tradition, Powell and Pressburger now carry the flag for it, with a number of their works widely regarded as among the best British films ever made. Their status as major artists is secure. What this study has sought to demonstrate is the invaluable role propaganda played in making that happen.

INDEX

39 Steps, The (1935)   25, 41–2, 65
49th Parallel (1941)   12, 16 n.54, 17,
  23–30 *passim*, 56, 78–9, 112–14,
  118, 136, 144, 163, 166, 175,
  175 n.64, 176, 179, 232, 237–8,
  259, 260 n.8
  American neutrality   86–7, 89–90,
    95, 97, 106–7, 109
  collaboration with MOI   85, 87–8,
    88 n.14
  depiction of Canada   89, 97–9,
    101–2, 108, 109
  ethics of propaganda   85, 86,
    94–7, 101–3, 108, 110
  German individualism   83–4,
    90–4, 99, 102–6, 110
  reception upon release   20 n.67,
    83–4, 92–4
  synopsis   86–7

accented films   61, 76–7, 79
Addison, Paul   168 n.37, 206 nn.4–5
Air Raid Precautions
  (ARP)   73 n.51, 75–6
Airman's Letter to His Mother, An
  (1941)   1, 117
Aldgate, Anthony   6, 85, 88,
  168 n.40, 199, 206 n.3
Allen, Jerry C.   40 n.26
Anderson, Terry H.   233, 239
Anglo-American relationship   25–6,
  29, 179–81, 190, 192 n.38,
  196–200, 227–39, 241 n.21,
  248–9, 254–5, 256 n.58, 256–7,
  257 n.59
  American audiences   16, 33–4,
    36 n.13, 39 n.24, 55, 87, 89–90,
  90 n.15, 95, 98 n.39, 111 n.1,
    112, 169, 171, 231, 233, 260 n.8
  American isolationism and
    neutrality   16, 28, 36 n.13, 55,
    86–7, 89–90, 95–8, 101–2, 109,
    112, 229, 231–2, 235–8, 253
    (*see also 49th Parallel*, American
    neutrality)
  the "American problem"   237–45
Anglo-Dutch relationship   111,
  114–17, 126, 128–31, 133, 136,
  138–41
Anthony, Scott   15 n.48
Archers, The, *see* Powell and
  Pressburger's Program for Film
  Propaganda
anti-realism   27–9, 122, 245–6
artistic independence   2, 7,
  16–17, 30, 94, 144, 174–6, 257,
  258, 261
  collaboration   5–7, 16, 23–4, 53,
    60, 118–19, 128, 137, 140–1,
    174, 197, 199, 208–9
  conservatism   19, 22, 149, 152,
    169, 180 n.5, 184, 208, 224–6,
    229–31, 246–7
  credo   2, 30, 175
  MOI, relationship with   6–7, 14,
    18, 19, 23, 26, 29, 36 n.13,
    58–9, 62–3, 85, 87–91, 97, 114,
    143–4, 154–8, 162, 166, 170–1,
    174–6, 227, 258–60
  postwar reconstruction   160–1,
    195–6, 202–3 (*see also IKWIG*,
    reconstructionist vision)
  realism   27–9, 55, 92–3, 98, 99,
    113, 114, 120–1, 123–7, 131,

135, 140, 151, 166, 175 n.64,
  206, 208–9, 213, 221–2, 245–6,
  249 n.48, 256 n.58
 surrealism   118, 121, 228,
  229 n.5, 230–1, 245–6,
  249 n.48, 256 n.58
 traditionalism   22, 26, 149, 157–8,
  180–1, 186–94, 197, 202–3,
  225–6, 247–9, 252, 259
Armitage, David   215 n.32
Asquith, Anthony   117, 199, 241,
  243, 257 n.59
Attlee, Clement   227
auteurism   5, 7, 144, 174, 176
 distributed auteurism   6

Badder, David   26 n.78
Baedeker Raids, The   195–6
Baird, Jay   12 n.43
Balcon, Michael   41 n.32
Barr, Charles   43, 45, 59 n.9
Bartlett, F. C.   97, 97 nn.35–7
Battle, Pat Wilks   40 n.29
Battle of the River Plate, The
  (1956)   1 n.2
BBC   17, 44 n.41, 74, 112 n.4, 117,
  118, 129, 138–9, 140 n.60,
  142–4, 147, 150, 167–9, 216
Beddington, Jack   114, 170, 172, 227,
  233, 257
Bell, Amy   73 n.51
Bernays, Edward   9
Beveridge Report, The   192, 216, 230
Black Narcissus (1947)   5, 28,
  193, 258
blackout   58, 73–6, 79
Blitz, The   87, 112, 142, 148,
  196, 216
Boer War, The   22, 148, 152–6,
  158, 165
Boose, Lynda E.   188 n.26
Bordwell, David   25, 42 n.37
Borzage, Frank   34
Boulting, Roy   35, 206 n.3
Bowie, James Alexander   213–14,
  214 n.28, 215, 216,
  220–1
Bracken, Brendan   7, 170–1

Briggs, Asa   21 n.70
"Britain Can Take It"
  (campaign)   112, 129
British film industry
 Alexander Korda Film
  Productions   18
 British National Films   62, 114
 continental émigrés   4–5, 24 n.75,
  53–4, 53 n.57, 58–61, 72–3,
  77, 79
 Crown Film Unit   56, 112, 206
 Denham Studios   39, 62 n.20,
  181
 Elstree Studios   62 n.20
 Gainsborough Pictures   27,
  120 n.33
 Hollywood, relationship with   3–4,
  25, 34–6, 38–9, 42 n.37,
  183 n.11
 London Films   4, 38–40
 national cinema   5, 27, 60–1, 77,
  79, 120
 Quota Act   3–4
 quota quickies   3, 4 n.11, 39
Britton, Eric   220
Brogan, Denis William   237–9, 245,
  257 n.59
Brown, Pamela   114, 133, 205, 218
Brunel, Adrian   18
Buitenhuis, Peter   167 n.36, 168 n.38,
  169 n.44
Burden, Hugh   113, 147
Byron, Kathleen   251

Cabinet of Dr. Caligari, The
  (1920)   39, 70
Calder, Angus   74 n.55, 189 n.29,
  190 n.30, 230 nn.6–7
Campbell, D'Ann   134
Canterbury Tale, A (1944)   5, 17,
  22–30 *passim*, 59, 74, 120, 176,
  205–8 *passim*, 225, 226, 240,
  249, 259
 American version (1949)   200
 Anglo-American alliance   179,
  181, 190, 192 n.38, 196–7,
  199–200
 anti-materialism   180, 185

expression of values   181, 184–6,
    192–3, 195–6, 201–3
  portrayal of women   180, 186–94
  representations of class   194–5
  synopsis   182–3
Capra, Frank   75, 188 n.25
Cardiff, Jack   5
Carney, George   205
Cawkwell, Tim   194 n.43, 197 n.52
Chamberlain, Neville   17, 64, 77–8,
    78 n.67, 87, 90
Chandler, Albert B.   236 n.13
Chandos, John   102
Chapman, James   6 n.23, 7 n.26,
    18 n.58, 19, 26 n.79, 87 nn.7–8,
    88 n.14, 116, 170, 171 n.49,
    172 n.52, 180 n.2, 192 n.38,
    207 n.6, 208 n.9
Chevassu, Francois   20 n.65
Chibnall, Steve   3
Christie, Ian   5 n.19, 21 n.71, 67,
    118 n.23, 119 n.28, 119 n.30,
    137, 151 n.14, 154 nn.18–19,
    156 n.21, 157 nn.22–3, 159 n.26,
    162 n.31, 163 nn.32–3, 170, 173,
    175 n.63, 179 n.1, 181 n.9, 185,
    186, 190–1, 193 n.42, 194, 196,
    197, 212, 217, 225, 228 nn.1–2,
    229 n.4, 245 n.36
Churchill, Winston   8, 87, 90, 112,
    115, 129, 134, 142, 144, 150,
    167–8, 168 n.38, 168 n.40,
    169–71, 206, 227, 230, 232–3,
    236 n.13
Clark, Bennett Champ   33–6, 55
Clark, Kenneth   15, 16 n.55, 17 n.56,
    19, 85 n.4, 87, 88 n.11, 176
Clark, Petula   205
Clouston, J. Storer   38, 40, 46,
    49 n.49
Cole, Hubert   40 n.30, 41 n.31
Colleano, Bonar   251
Confessions of a Nazi Spy (1939)   34
Conrad, Peter   180 n.5, 185 n.14,
    201, 201 n.57
Contraband (1940)   6, 15, 17, 24–9
  passim, 36 n.14, 40, 41, 94, 96,
    113, 166, 230–1

  as an "accented film"   58, 59, 61,
    72–3, 76–7, 79
  documentary functions   56, 58,
    62, 65
  generic conventions   56, 58, 65–7,
    70–2, 75
  synopsis   57–8
Cook, Pam   209 n.15, 212–13,
    221, 222
Cooper, Duff   7 n.27, 92
Coote, Robert   251
Corfield, John   62
Coultass, Clive   19
County of London Plan of
    1943   224–5
Crawford, Anne   207
Crook, Steve   198 n.53
Currie, Finlay   101, 219

Dalrymple, Ian   207
Dalton, Hugh   115
Darling, Elizabeth   224
Dawn Guard, The (1941)   206 n.3
Dearden, Basil   207, 250 n.49
Dewey, John   10, 107
Diary for Timothy, A
    (1945)   206, 207
Dochartaigh, Pól Ó   24 n.75
documentary   19, 27, 87, 117–18,
    120–5, 127, 246–7
  Griersonian documentary   14, 27,
    29, 122
  semi-documentary
    (docufiction)   26, 28–9, 56,
    58, 65–6, 98–9, 112–13, 121–5,
    128, 131, 139–40, 195–6,
    216 n.40, 245–6
Doherty, Thomas   4 n.12, 12
Doob, Leonard W.   12 n.43
Drazin, Charles   39
Drew, Philip   63 n.25
Dunkirk   28, 87, 90–1, 99, 142, 144,
    165, 167–9
Durgnat, Raymond   22, 28 n.84,
    247, 250
Dutch government-in-exile   114–15,
    126, 129–30, 140
Dyall, Valentine   205

Edge of the World, The (1937)   4, 208, 216 n.40
Ellis, John   27, 28 n.85, 249 n.48, 252 n.51
Esch, Joris A. C. van   115, 116

Faassen, Marijke van   130
Finlay, Richard   214 n.28
Fitzsimons, Margot   219
Flaherty, Robert   122, 216 n.40
Fleet Air Arm (Navy)   1 n.3, 118, 121, 123–4, 170
Fleming, Victor   257 n.59
Flynn, John T.   34–6
Foot, Michael Richard Daniell   116 n.13, 139 n.58
Fox, Jo   13, 36 n.15, 53 n.55, 88 n.14, 91, 112, 117 n.21
Fremont-Barnes, Gregory   153
Frye, Northrop   256
Fuller, Graham   180 n.5, 194 n.43

Gary, Brett   9, 10 n.34
Gazeley, Ian   133–4
Gee, J. M. Alec   214 n.27
Gemünden, Gerd   53–4 n.57
George, Richard   99
Gielgud, John   1 n.3, 117
Glancy, H. Mark   4 n.10
Godden, Maryse   101 n.40
Goebbels, Joseph   11–12, 12 n.43, 40, 96, 98, 104, 107–8, 164, 260
Goodbye Mr. Chips (1939)   92, 175 n.64
Goring, Marius   43, 228
Gough-Yates, Kevin   59 n.7, 61 n.17, 202 n.60
Grant, Mariel   10 n.37, 11
Greene, Graham   60, 61, 76, 79, 168
Grierson, John   14, 27, 29, 122
Grigg, (Sir) James   170–1, 172 n.55, 175
Gunning, Tom   209 n.14, 211
Guy Named Joe, A (1943)   257 n.59

Hargrave, John   12 n.42
Harper, Sue   40 n.27, 40 n.29, 53–4 n.57, 229, 257

Harris, Mark   33 n.1
Harrisson, Tom   74, 76
Harvie, Christopher   214
Hasenfratz, Bob   29 n.86, 183 n.11, 229 n.4, 249 n.47
Hayward, Laurence   170
Heckroth, Hein   5, 59
Heijden, Chris Van der   115
Helpmann, Robert   138
Henderson, E. H.   174 n.62
Hervieux, Linda   240, 243 n.25, 244 n.29
Higgott, Andrew   224
Higson, Andrew   5 n.15, 27 nn.81–2, 61
Hiller, Wendy   2, 2 n.4, 159, 175, 205, 211
Hillier, Erwin   1 n.3, 195
Hitchcock, Alfred   25, 42 nn.36–7, 77 n.64, 188 n.25
  Hitchcockian espionage narratives   26, 41–2, 56, 66, 67, 67 n.40
Hitler, Adolf   12 n.43, 62, 78, 89, 91 n.18, 96, 97, 101, 101 n.40, 103, 161, 238, 240, 240 n.17, 246
Hobhouse, Emily   154
Hobson, Valerie   36, 38, 41, 48 n.45, 51 n.52, 57, 61, 62
Hochscherf, Tobias   4, 5 n.14, 24 n.75, 53 n.57, 59, 202
Hockenhull, Stella   25 n.77, 212 n.20
Horne, Philip   245
Howard, James   4 n.11, 121 n.35
Howard, Leslie   106, 107 n.43
Hudd, Walter   210
Hunter, Jefferson   184, 185, 197, 199, 202
Hunter, Kim   200, 228
Hurd, Geoff   118 n.22
Hurst, Brian Desmond   18

I Know Where I'm Going! (IKWIG) (1945)   5, 23, 25, 26, 29, 168, 176, 179, 180, 185
  fantasy and mythology   211–13, 217, 221

reconstructionist vision 206–7,
214, 216, 217, 221–3, 225
representations of Scotland 204,
213, 216–17, 220–2, 225, 231
southern drift 215–16, 220–1
synopsis 205–6
treatment and production 208–9,
213–14, 222–3, 225
Ill Met by Moonlight (1957) 1 n.2
It Happened One Night (1934) 75

Jameson, Richard 173
Jennings, Humphrey 111–12,
122, 206
Joannou, Maroula 5 n.16, 149 n.9
Johns, Glynis 105–6
Jones, Emrys 113
Jorge, Anita 194 n.44
Joyce, William 168–9
Junge, Alfred 1 n.3, 5, 59, 59 n.6, 79

Kennedy, A. L. 149, 158, 159 n.25
Kerr, Deborah 146–8, 162, 175
Kersten, Albert E. 130
Knight, Esmond 57
Korda, Alexander 4, 18, 38–40, 59,
62, 117
Kozloff, Sarah 256
Krabbe, Henning 129 n.44
Kulik, Karol 39 nn.20–1

Lacey, Catherine 205
Lang, Fritz 67
Lant, Antonia 74, 75 n.59, 186 n.22,
188 n.24, 189, 241 n.21
Lasswell, Harold D. 9–10, 10 n.34
Last of the Nuba, The 260
Laveleye, Victor de 17, 112 n.4, 129
Lazar, David 23 n.73, 60 n.13,
119 n.29, 146 n.4, 172 n.55,
173 n.57, 173 n.59
Lean, David 28 n.84, 99, 108, 147–8
Lejeune, C. A. 149, 157, 164, 171–2
Lend-Lease policy 29, 227, 235–6
*Life and Death of Colonel Blimp,
The* (1943) 2, 5, 16, 17, 21–6
passim, 28, 30, 54, 85, 119 n.31,
179, 231, 258, 259

attempted government
censorship 144, 154, 156–7,
169–71, 175–6
Churchill's response to the
film 170–1
ethics of propaganda 144–5,
150–2, 163–7, 169, 174–6
ethics of warfare 148–52, 154–6,
158, 161–3, 172
legacy 145 n.3, 173
prisoners of war 158–62
reception upon release 149,
172–3, 174 n.61
synopsis 146–7
Lindbergh, Charles 34
Lion Has Wings, The (1939) 1,
15, 18–19, 29, 35, 96, 113,
117, 121–5
Lippmann, Walter 10, 107
Little, Kenneth Lindsay 243 n.26
Livesey, Roger 142, 146 n.4,
205, 228
London Can Take It! (1940) 111–12
Longden, John 248
Lovell, Raymond 57, 101
Low, David 146
Low, Rachael 3 n.6, 3 nn.8–9, 38, 60

M (1931) 67
Mabuse (1922) 67
Macdonald, Kevin 1 n.1, 4 nn.12–
13, 6 n.22, 38 n.17, 39 n.23,
51 n.52, 55, 56 n.1, 58, 62,
67 n.40, 87 n.9, 92, 98 n.38,
113 n.5, 114 n.6, 121 n.35,
146 n.4, 175 n.64, 179–81,
182 n.10, 186 n.18, 189 n.28,
192–3, 202 n.59, 227–8 n.1,
245 n.34, 258, 259
McGrath, Pat 122
Mackenzie, John 13 n.46
Mackenzie, S. P. 18 n.57, 117 n.21,
123 n.41
McLaine, Ian 7 n.27, 8, 11 n.39,
20 n.67, 21, 90, 150, 168,
174 n.62, 206
Macmillan, Hugh 15
Macnab, Geoffrey 62 n.20, 171 n.50

INDEX

McVay, Douglas   194 n.45
Madge, Charles   63 n.24, 74, 76
Malpass, Peter   216 n.37
Marriage of Corbal, The (1936)   60
Mason, Herbert   115
Mass Observation   18 n.57, 55 n.59, 63 n.24, 73 n.50, 74, 119 n.31, 174 n.61
Massey, Raymond   86, 228
Massey, Vincent   99
Matter of Life and Death, A (AMOLAD) (1946)   5, 17, 22–6 *passim*, 29, 30, 168 n.38, 179, 193, 196, 200 n.56, 208, 223, 258, 259
   Anglo-American "special relationship"   227–9, 231–6, 249, 255–7
   contemporary reception   245 n.34, 246
   fantasy   245–8, 249 n.48, 251–3, 256
   progressivism   230–1, 247, 251–3, 255–7
   race relations   229, 237–45, 253–5
   romantic comedy elements   228, 233, 246, 256–7
   synopsis   228
Maude, Joan   251
Medlicott, W. N.   63 nn.27–8, 65 nn.34–5
Mein Kampf   17, 89, 102–3
Meredith, Burgess   241–2
Merritt, George   190
Miles, Bernard   75–6, 111
Miller, Mark Crispin   8, 9 n.30
Millions Like Us (1943)   194, 207–8
Ministry of Information (MOI)   1, 7, 12 n.42, 13, 15, 20–1, 90–1, 97 n.34, 97–8, 112, 114, 129–30, 170–2, 206–7, 216, 227, 241–3, 259
   "Anger Campaign"   91
   Films Division   6, 29, 56, 87, 154, 156–63, 199 n.54
   Films Division's "Programme"   15–16, 17 n.56, 19, 23–6, 56 n.2, 85, 87–8, 90, 176, 180
   public perception of   7, 7 n.27
   "shadow" MOI   11, 14
   transparency   7, 7 n.27, 8, 21, 150
Moor, Andrew   27–8, 40 n.28, 41, 42, 43 n.39, 51, 52, 67 n.40, 69, 77, 119 nn.27–8, 120–1, 149, 173, 183–5, 192 n.39, 196, 197 n.49, 199, 209 n.14, 209 n.16, 210 n.17, 212 n.20, 213 n.23, 247, 259 n.5
Moreton, Percival   83–4, 88 n.13, 91, 110
Morrison, Murdo   205
Mortal Storm, The (1940)   34
Murphy, Robert   98 n.39, 115, 194 n.46, 206 n.3

Naficy, Hamid   61
Neale, Steve   20, 166
Neiberg, Michael S.   161
Newman, Kim   88 n.10
Nicholas, Siân   11 n.41, 13, 14 n.47, 90 n.16, 168, 169 n.43, 204 n.1, 207, 216 nn.38–9
Nichols, Bill   98
Nicholson, Virginia   190 n.33
Night Invader, The (1943)   115
Night Mail (1936)   15
Night Train to Munich (1940)   35
Niven, David   22, 118, 228
Nussbaum, Martha   23
Nye, Gerald P.   33–6 n.13, 55

Olivier, Laurence   91, 101, 146 n.4, 151 n.15, 170
Olympia (1938)   12 n.43
One of Our Aircraft is Missing (1942)   17, 25, 26, 28–9, 56, 119 n.31, 144, 145, 147, 175, 179, 181, 245
   depiction of Dutch resistance   114–15, 128, 135, 137–40
   depiction of gender roles   128, 130–3, 135–6, 138
   qualified commitment to documentary form   113, 117, 120–7, 131, 140
   synopsis   113–14

unity between Britain and occupied countries   111, 112, 116–19, 129–30, 136–41
Orwell, George   21, 244, 260

Paape, Harry   138–9
Pastor Hall (1940)   35
Pearl Harbor   35, 87, 148, 235, 238
"People's War," The (concept)   128 n.42
Pertwee, Roland   38
Petley, Julian   5 n.17, 27 n.82
Petrie, Duncan J.   213 n.22, 216 n.40
Petrie, Hay   57
"Phoney War," The   15, 58, 62–3, 66 n.37, 68, 74, 76, 87, 90–1 n.16
Ponsonby, Arthur   9, 9 n.33, 12 n.42
Portman, Eric   86, 93, 113, 180, 194, 207
Powell, Dilys   98 n.39, 120
Powell, Michael
  background   2–4
  Life in Movies, A   4 n.11, 6 n.21, 6 n.25, 7 n.26, 16 n.54, 19 n.62, 30 n.87, 38–9, 55 n.59, 59 n.5, 61, 62 nn.20–1, 73 n.49, 86 n.6, 87 n.9, 92 n.19, 109 n.44, 114 n.6, 117 n.20, 118 n.24, 121, 137 n.57, 147 n.5, 180 nn.5–6, 181 n.8, 201 n.58, 208–9 nn.10–13, 218 n.42, 227–8 n.1, 233 n.11, 245 n.37, 246 n.39, 258 n.3
  quota quickies   3, 4 n.11, 39
  and the Royal Air Force   18, 19, 116–18, 120, 123–4, 126–7, 129, 139–41
Powell and Pressburger's Program for Film Propaganda   16–17, 85, 110, 261
  cosmopolitanism   23–4, 58, 76, 85, 89–91, 118–19, 129–30, 137–8, 196–7, 201, 232–3, 245, 253
  Germanic individualism   24–5, 37, 83–6, 88–94, 106, 176
  ideological ambiguity   19, 20 n.67, 21–3, 84–6, 92, 95, 110, 154–5,
  157, 166, 172, 173, 176, 204–5, 225–6, 247, 259–60
  pluralism   23–5, 58, 76–7, 79, 85–6, 89–90, 98, 101–3, 117, 130–1, 137–8, 207–8, 222, 245, 253–7
  romantic sensibility   25, 41–2, 44, 48–51, 53, 56, 69–72, 131–2, 200 n.56, 207–8, 221–2, 230–1, 233, 245–6, 255–6
  self-reflexivity   17–22, 26, 30, 76–9, 84–6, 94–7, 99–100, 110, 112, 125–6, 139–41, 144–5, 155–6, 166, 174, 202–3, 259
Pressburger, Emeric
  background   2, 4, 54
  émigré experience   4–5, 54, 58–61, 72–3, 181–2, 201–2
Price, Dennis   182
Price, Nancy   218
Priestley, J. B.   28, 142–3, 167–9, 250 n.49
Private Life of Henry VIII, The (1933)   4, 38
Pronay, Nicholas   246–7, 250
propaganda
  and art   1–2, 7, 14, 16–19, 21–2, 25, 30, 56–7, 63, 79, 94–5, 113, 129–30 n.45, 144, 145 n.3, 174–5, 201, 245–6, 257–61
  conceptions of British   8, 10–15, 19, 42–3, 44 n.41, 53, 85, 88, 90–1, 97 n.34, 116–18, 151, 154–5, 157–8, 165–7, 171–2, 173 n.60, 240 n.17, 243–5 (*see also* propaganda, democratic)
  counterpropaganda   136 n.55, 152–8, 163–9, 174–5
  critical thinking   8, 9 n.33, 17–23, 34–6, 94–5, 145, 150, 166, 174–6, 259 (*see also* Powell and Pressburger's Program for Film Propaganda, ideological ambiguity; Powell and Pressburger's Program for Film Propaganda, self-reflexivity)
  democratic   7–14, 17–18, 20, 88 n.14, 89–90, 94–6, 99,

107–10, 138–9, 144–5, 154–5, 164–72, 176, 229, 236, 259
First World War 8–9, 11 n.40, 12 n.42, 53 n.55, 54, 90–1 n.16, 98 n.39
German 11–14, 19, 26, 43–5, 84–5, 88–9, 91 n.18, 95–9, 101–4, 106–8, 138–9, 154–5, 163–5, 168–9
"good German," the 24, 25, 37, 86, 91, 106, 146–7, 176
of peace 160, 176, 193, 203, 206–8, 216–17, 224–7, 230, 231, 248–9, 257
repetition 12–13, 96–7, 107
totalitarian 8, 11, 12 n.43, 14, 20, 85–6, 95–7, 99, 107–10, 144–5, 150–1, 164, 170–2, 176
Puckett, Kent 149, 173

Rank, J. Arthur 62, 87, 146 n.4, 171, 258
realpolitik 149–51, 157, 162
Red Shoes, The (1948) 5, 28, 28 n.85, 258
Reed, Carol 35
Reynolds, David 232
Reynolds, Quentin 112
Richards, Jeffrey 3 n.8, 6, 85, 88, 168 n.40, 199, 206 n.3
Richardson, Ralph 18, 18 n.57, 118, 121, 124–5, 129 n.43
Riefenstahl, Leni 12 n.43, 18, 19, 94 n.28, 102, 260
Robson, E. W. 22, 22 n.72, 93–4, 172–3, 246, 250
Robson, M. M. 22, 22 n.72, 93–4, 172–3, 246, 250
Roosevelt, Franklin 11 n.40, 206, 227, 233
Rose, Sonya O. 190 n.31, 240, 243 nn.26–8, 244
Royal Air Force (RAF) 15, 18, 19, 111, 114–19 *passim*, 120, 123–4, 127, 132 n.51, 136, 138, 139, 217
Royal Canadian Air Force (RCAF) 98, 101

Russell, Richard B. 234–6
Ryall, Tom 42 n.37
Ryan, Henry Butterfield 232

Sabotage (1936) 77
Salwolke, Scott 41 n.35, 116 n.14, 121 n.35
Schönfeld, Christiane 24 n.75
Schunzel, Reinhold 92
Sedgwick, John 20 n.27
Semenza, Greg M. Colón 29 n.86, 183 n.11, 229 n.4, 249 n.47
Sewell, Vernon 1 n.3, 115, 129 n.43
Shachtman, Tom 63 n.26
Shadow of a Doubt (1943) 188
Sidhu, Ranbir 198–200
Silver Fleet, The (1943) 1, 115, 119 n.31, 129 n.43
Sim, Sheila 76
Sime, William 192 n.39
Slater, Jay 88 n.10
Small Back Room, The (1949) 1 n.2
Smith, Graham 243
Sondern, Frederic, Jr. 64–5, 67
Sontag, Susan 260
Spies (1928) 67
Spy in Black, The (1939) 1, 2, 25, 56, 61–2, 90, 95 n.31, 104 n.41, 208, 259
Conrad Veidt's significance 36, 39–41, 53
portrayal of national difference 37, 40, 43–5, 48, 52–4
portrayal of propaganda in the film 37, 43–4, 53–4
production 38–9, 41
synopsis 37–8
Stafford, David 115, 130
Staiger, Janet 25, 42 n.37
Stevens, Paul 180, 186, 190
Strauss, Theodore 40 n.28
Street, Sarah 5, 59 n.6, 61 n.14
Strobl, Gerwin 91 n.18, 240 n.17
Student of Prague, The (1926) 39
Sullivan, Garrett A., Jr. 2 n.5, 6 n.20, 229 n.4, 251 n.50, 256 n.58, 258 n.1

Sweet, John   182
Swett, Pamela E.   104 n.42

Tales of Hoffmann, The (1951)   28, 258
Tallents, Stephen   14–15
Target for Tonight (1941)   113, 117, 123–4, 126–7, 139, 259 n.7
Taylor, John Russell   94 n.28
Taylor, Philip   13
Tearle, Godfrey   114, 147
That Hamilton Woman (1941)   4
They Came to A City (1944)   207, 250 n.49
Thief of Bagdad, The (1940)   4
Third Man, The (1949)   4
Thompson, Kristin   25
Thomson, David   28 n.84
Triumph of the Will (1935)   12 n.43, 18, 102, 260
Truman, Harry   227

"V for Victory" (campaign)   17, 26, 29, 112–13, 128–9, 137–8, 140
Veidt, Conrad   36, 38–42, 42 n.38, 45–7, 48 n.45, 50, 51, 53–4, 55, 57, 59, 61–2, 70, 79, 104 n.41
Vials, Christopher   11 n.40
Volunteer, The (1944)   1, 17, 29, 113, 118, 121–5, 128

Walbrook, Anton   59, 89, 143, 146
Wallas, Graham   10
Warman, Eric   250 n.49, 251 n.50
Watt, Harry   15, 123
Waugh, Evelyn   76
Waxworks (1924)   39
Way to the Stars, The (1945)   117, 119, 200, 257 n.59

Webster, Wendy   24 n.75, 112 n.4, 116–18, 129 n.45, 130–1, 140 n.60
Welch, David   97 n.34, 118 n.22
Welcome to Britain, A (1943)   241
Wellesley, Gordon   1 n.3, 115, 129 n.43
Whittington, Ian   169 n.42
Wicking, Chris   186, 193
Wilkie, Wendell   34, 36
Williams, Hugh   113
Williams, Ralph Vaughan   99
Williams, Stephen G.   145 n.3
Winnington, Richard   28 n.85
Winston, Brian   122
Withers, Googie   111
Wollaeger, Mark   90–1 n.16
women and the war effort   128–9, 133–4, 180–1
   the "mobile woman"   187, 189–90, 209 n.15, 193 (*see also A Canterbury Tale*, portrayal of women)
   the resistance   113, 128, 130–3, 135–8 (*see also One of Our Aircraft is Missing*, depiction of gender roles)
Women's Auxiliary Air Force (WAAF)   134
Women's Land Army (WLA)   182, 189, 190 n.33, 191 n.37, 193 n.41
Wood, Robin   41–2, 188 n.25
World War One   189, *see also* propaganda, First World War
   Flanders   155–8, 162–3
   "Once a Hun, always a Hun"   90–1 n.16
   Treaty of Versailles   161

Yorke, F. R. S.   224 n.48
Yule, (Lady) Annie Henrietta   62

www.ingramcontent.com/pod-product-compliance
Lightning Source LLC
Chambersburg PA
CBHW050627300426
44112CB00012B/1688